NATURAL MORALITIES

A Defense of Pluralistic Relativism

David B. Wong

OXFORD
UNIVERSITY PRESS
2006

OXFORD
UNIVERSITY PRESS

Oxford University Press, Inc., publishes works that further
Oxford University's objective of excellence
in research, scholarship, and education.

Oxford   New York
Auckland   Cape Town   Dar es Salaam   Hong Kong   Karachi
Kuala Lumpur   Madrid   Melbourne   Mexico City   Nairobi
New Delhi   Shanghai   Taipei   Toronto

With offices in
Argentina   Austria   Brazil   Chile   Czech Republic   France   Greece
Guatemala   Hungary   Italy   Japan   Poland   Portugal   Singapore
South Korea   Switzerland   Thailand   Turkey   Ukraine   Vietnam

Copyright © 2006 by Oxford University Press, Inc.

Published by Oxford University Press, Inc.
198 Madison Avenue, New York, New York 10016

www.oup.com

Oxford is a registered trademark of Oxford University Press

Library of Congress Cataloging-in-Publication Data
Wong, David B.
Natural moralities : a defense of pluralistic relativism / David B. Wong.
    p.   cm.
Includes bibliographical references (p.) and index.
ISBN-13 978-0-19-530539-5   1005076991
ISBN 0-19-530539-6
1. Ethical relativism.   I. Title.
BJ37.W66 2006
171'.7—dc22   2005056286

9 8 7 6 5 4 3 2 1

Printed in the United States of America
on acid-free paper

NATURAL MORALITIES

For Laura

Acknowledgments

I am fortunate to have Lawrence Blum and Owen Flanagan as good friends and philosophical interlocutors. They have shown me how philosophers can grapple with what is most important, not necessarily with what is most easily regimented or managed by one's favored philosophical method. They have shown me that striving to understand what is most important should take us across methodological and subject boundaries that divide philosophers from each other (has it struck anyone else how much the meeting rooms at the American Philosophical Association are like little islands?) and also across boundaries that separate philosophers from other humanistic and scientific disciplines. I have been stimulated and sustained by philosophical discussion groups that over the years have included Blum and Flanagan, Judith DeCew, Janet Farrell Smith, Sally Haslanger, Thomas Hill, Jr., Martha Minow, Steven Nathanson, Jennifer Radin, Margaret Rhodes, Amélie Rorty, Geoffrey Sayre McCord, David Wilkins, Kenneth Winkler, Kenneth Winston, and Michael Zimmerman. I have been able to weave into this book themes from Chinese philosophy and comparative ethics, and in this part of my work I have received a great deal of encouragement, stimulation, and challenge from Kwong-loi Shun, Joseph Chan, Antonio Cua, Chad Hansen, P. J. Ivanhoe, Xinyan Jiang, Henry Rosemont, Jr., Bryan Van Norden, and Jiyuan Yu. My colleagues at Duke—especially Flanagan, Martin Golding, and Alexander Rosenberg—have been generous with their time and talents in providing me with feedback and suggestions. Boris Kukso and Marion Hourdequin provided helpful comments on drafts of this book. Work on this book was supported by fellowships from the American Council of Learned Societies and the National Endowment for the Humanities. My thanks go to Peter Ohlin for his stewardship of this book.

Contents

Introduction

"Moral relativism" is overwhelmingly a term of condemnation, frequently of scorn or derision, a term for putting one's opponent immediately on the defensive: "You sound like a relativist—explain yourself!" or "You are a relativist—shame on you!" The prosecutor usually takes on the persona of the lone voice of reason beating back the howling dogs of spineless, trendy relativists. The rounds of accusation remind me of the children's game "Tag, you're it." If you get touched by the "it" kid, you are condemned to run after the others until you manage to touch the next unlucky "it" kid. Social conservatives accuse liberals of moral relativism for defending reproductive and gay and lesbian rights. Some liberals in turn accuse multiculturalists of moral relativism for not defending the universality of such rights. The rhetoric portrays these crimes as falling but a few slippery steps short of collaboration with the Nazis. The only ones who don't get to play this game are the ones who accept the label of moral relativists, but curiously enough, there are very few people willing to do so. If they are a howling pack, they do not come when their name is called!

Anglo-American philosophy (I suspect this is true in at least some other philosophical communities) engages in the same sort of game, except in a more genteel fashion. The aim of most philosophical discussions of relativism is to establish its manifest falsity. The standard characterizations of relativism make it an easy target and seldom reveal what really motivates people who are attracted to it. Introductory textbooks in ethics frequently portray the view as an extreme variety of subjectivism (or conventionalism)—a person's (or group's) accepting that something is right makes it right for that person (or group). Such a discussion usually comes early in the standard textbook—to get it out of the way so that the "serious" philosophy can start. The argumentative strategy is almost always negative in attacking the arguments on behalf of the view or purports to show some incoherence in it. Rarely does someone try to formulate some version of relativism that is nuanced and plausibly motivated. The role of the howling pack of relativists is often awarded to confused students in introduction to philosophy classes, or more recently, to postmodern literary theorists.

In other words, people typically use the term 'relativism' as a substitute for confronting hard questions. Here is how it works. The rhetorical use of the term imposes on the audience a dichotomy: either accept relativism, defined in the most extreme way possible, or accept absolutism or universalism. I use the terms 'absolutism' and 'universalism' for two different kinds of views about moral truth. Moral universalism is the view that there is a single true morality for all societies and times. Moral absolutism is universalism plus the view that the core of the single true morality is a set of general principles or rules, all of which hold true without exception. Often the further claim is made that these rules hold *no matter what the consequences*. For example, some assert that individuals have rights that can never be set aside for the sake of avoiding bad consequences—never, even if the heavens should fall. The more popular denunciations of moral relativism often do not distinguish these different possibilities and sometimes end up criticizing "situational" ethics that judge what is right by the context or circumstances. This is the criticism of relativism as the rejection of absolutism, but note that one could be a universalist and a "situational" ethicist at the same time. One could hold, that is, that right varies with the context in such a way that anyone reasoning correctly and with all the relevant facts would judge in the same way, regardless of one's society or culture.

I am among the handful of philosophers who are willing to be associated with relativism. The version I defend constitutes an alternative to universalism and to relativism as these views are usually defined. My alternative agrees with one implication of relativism as it is usually defined: that there is no single true morality. However, it recognizes significant limits on what can count as a true morality. There is a plurality of true moralities, but that plurality does not include all moralities. This theory occupies the territory between universalism—the view that there is a single true morality—and the easy target typically defined as relativism: the view that any morality is as good as any other.

This book further develops lines of thought initiated in *Moral Relativity*.[1] I argued there for a version of moral relativism that accounted for many aspects of the objectivity we attribute to morality. Morality, I argued, comprises an idealized set of norms in imperatival form ("A is to do X under conditions C") abstracted from the practices and institutions of a society that serves to regulate conflicts of interest, both between persons and within the psychological economy of a single person. A particular morality is distinguished from others not merely by its norms and by which norms have priority in case of conflict but also by its criteria for determining what counts as an adequate morality. Some of these criteria may be universally valid across all kinds of societies because of the very purpose of morality to regulate conflicts of interest. No adequate morality, for example, could allow torture of another person on one's whim.

---

1. David B. Wong, *Moral Relativity* (Berkeley: University of California Press, 1984).

Nevertheless, I argued, such universally valid criteria do not begin to determine a morality with content sufficiently robust and determinate to guide action. As a consequence, some criteria for adequate moralities will be local to a given society. They neither follow from nor are ruled out by the universally valid criteria. They are the source of moral relativity. One of the main sources of relativity I identified in *Moral Relativity* was the difference between rights-centered moralities and virtue-centered moralities. The latter are concerned with a good common to all members of a community, a good partially constituted by a shared life and structured by a set of norms specifying the contribution of each member to the sustenance of that life. Notions of a common good and shared life are not central to the former. Instead there is an emphasis on what each member of a community is entitled to claim from the others. Though not all moralities exemplifying these types are adequate moralities, some from each type are. That is, the rules from some of each type satisfy all universally valid criteria for adequate moral systems, and they satisfy the local criteria that flesh out a society's ideal for moralities.

I argued that moral statements about what agents ought to do have truth conditions deriving from these universal and local criteria, and since the local criteria differ, so will the truth conditions. Moral statements are a kind of second-order normative language indicating what actions are required by the norms of an adequate moral system, where adequacy is spelled out by the universal and local criteria. Two speakers may mean something different on the level of truth conditions by "adequate moral system," and therefore each may be saying something true even when one is prescribing that an action X be done and the other is prescribing that it not be done. Their judgments conflict on the practical level because one cannot conform to both judgments at the same time. I include within my conception of a morality not only its norms in imperatival form and the relations of priority between them that constitute a moral system of norms but statements with explicitly normative terms such as "A ought to do X" and "A's doing X is right" statements. Such statements specify what actions and attitudes are required by an adequate moral system of norms. It follows from my view that there is more than one single true morality. Let me emphasize that speaking of moral truth in my sense is compatible with radically different general theories of what truth is: minimalist theories and correspondence theories alike. I do not hold that truth is relative. I hold that the meaning and truth conditions of moral language can vary in such a way that moral statements conflicting on the prescriptive and pragmatic level can be consistent on the level of truth.

I remain committed to the main outlines of the relativism with limits defended in the first book, though I have changed my mind on some matters. For example, I now analyze moral "A ought to do X" statements in terms of A's doing X being required by the balance of reasons. In assessing the truth of such statements, moral language users bring to bear moral norms, which specify salient kinds of moral reasons, for example, the suffering of sentient beings as a reason not to harm them. They bring to bear what they believe to be the correct moral norms, but different users can mean somewhat different things when they conceive of the correct moral norms. The other significant change of mind concerns the question of whether reasons can apply to agents even if they have no preexisting determinate motivations that would be served by doing what they have putative reasons to do. In *Moral Relativity* I took an unambiguously internalist position, meaning that reasons cannot apply in the absence of preexisting motivations. In this book I take a more complex position that is externalist in one respect (individuals can not have moral reasons to do what does not serve their pre-existing motivations) but internalist in another (the kinds of moral reasons that exist must have a basis in what human beings generally can be motivated to do, even though some individual human beings might lack these motivations).

In this new book I primarily seek to further develop the relativistic themes defended in *Moral Relativity*. In that first book I primarily focused on the task of refuting universalism while defending a good measure of moral objectivity. My conception of the universally valid criteria for the adequacy of moralities was rather sketchy. In this book I offer a robust conception of such criteria, such that they rule out a significant range of moralities as inadequate. Whereas the first book focused on the relativity in my theory of relativism with limits, this book focuses to a much greater extent on the limits.

A second new development in this book is based on my keener appreciation for the ways in which different types of moralities share important values and are typically distinguished by their differing priorities and emphases on these shared values. This appreciation plays a much larger role in my argument, and it goes into my explanation of the widespread phenomenon of "moral ambivalence." Such ambivalence consists in recognition of severe conflicts between important values and of the possibility that reasonable people could take different paths in the face of these conflicts. I argue that moral ambivalence, in conjunction with a naturalistic conception of morality, supports the conclusion that there is no single true morality. I also argue, however, that the most plausible explanation for the overlap of values between different moralities implies that there are limits on the range of true moralities.

Third, there is here a new emphasis on taking a naturalistic approach to understanding morality, an approach marked not by a commitment to a purely physicalistic ontology (as naturalistic approaches are sometimes conceived) but rather by a commitment to integrate the understanding of morality with the most relevant empirical theories about human beings and society, such as evolutionary theory and developmental psychology. A naturalistic approach to morality, when applied to moral ambivalence, will support both the denial of a single true morality and the existence of significant limits on the plurality of true moralities. Hence the title of this book, *Natural Moralities: A Defense of Pluralistic Relativism.*

A fourth new development in this book is a greater focus on the problems posed by moral relativity for commitment to a particular configuration of values. Here too, my treatment of these problems was sketchy in the first book. I lacked then but think I have now a theory of reasons to be moral. This theory provides an answer to the worry that admitting the relativity of our present moral commitments undermines our confidence in them. It is not an answer that will satisfy in the way that many might desire or expect. The theory undermines the terms in which the problem of confidence is usually framed. Nevertheless, it is a major theme in this book that admitting moral relativity must affect the way we must act toward those with whom we are in serious moral disagreement. It must also affect the way we must seek confidence in our moral commitments.

Finally, my recognition of the ways in which different moralities can overlap and yet constitute different approaches to human problems has been fed by my work in comparative ethics and in Chinese and Western ethics in particular. While the Chinese tradition in some important cases simply poses different questions from those dominant in the Western tradition, in other cases the two traditions have a lot to say that is useful to the other on common problems—what it takes to foster effective moral agency, whether moral commitments are compatible with individual flourishing, and whether the acceptance of relativism undermines confidence in one's moral commitments.

The aim of part I is to sketch the outlines of a version of relativism that I call "pluralistic relativism." The theory is relativistic because it holds there is no single true morality. It is pluralistic because it recognizes limits on what can count as a true morality. Gilbert Harman once suggested that naturalistic conceptions of morality tended (though not in every case) to lead to relativist positions, while nonnaturalist conceptions tended (though again not in every case) to lead to universalist positions.[2] Whether one gets to a relativist or universalist position when starting from a naturalist approach depends both on the specific version of that approach and on other views one holds about morality. In chapter 1, I argue for a certain understanding of moral conflict that I call moral ambivalence, which stems from the plural sources of value and duty. In chapter 2, I argue that moral ambivalence is best explained using a naturalistic approach to morality. The result is the theory of pluralistic relativism, which can accommodate many intuitions we have about the potential objectivity of moral judgments. In chapter 3, I address the main objections to pluralistic relativism, and discuss the ways in which the theory has significant consequences for the ways in which we judge and act toward others who are in serious disagreement with us.

Part II supplies a closer look at a theme that is introduced in chapter 2: that the naturalistic functions of morality, human nature, the human condition, and the more particular circumstances of a group at a given time all work together to impose constraints of varying levels of generality on what constitutes an adequate morality for that group. In chapter 4, I discuss the general shape a morality must take if it is to promote effective moral agency in human beings. Such a constraint helps to explain the

---

2. Gilbert Harman, "Is There a Single True Morality?" in *Morality, Reason and Truth*, ed. David Copp and David Zimmerman (Totowa, N.J.: Rowman and Littlefield, 1985), 27–48. Reprinted in Harman, *Explaining Value and Other Essays in Moral Philosophy* (Oxford: Clarendon Press, 2000), 77–102.

universality of certain types of special duties toward particular others, such as duties to family members. I also use my conclusions about what is required for effective agency to argue that a life of relationships governed by special moral duties is a necessary part of flourishing. Chapter 4, therefore, partially confirms certain themes developed by the recent communitarian and neo-Aristotelian movements.

Communitarianism is usually opposed (by its defenders and critics) to liberalism. I question this opposition in chapter 5, arguing that certain themes central to communitarianism must and can be incorporated by liberalism. I go on to argue that a satisfactory moral ideal of family life can incorporate mutually supporting communitarian and liberal themes.

In Chapter 6, I discuss some contemporary attempts to derive constraints on morality from considerations about what is realistic to expect of human beings. I argue for a more nuanced view of how such considerations yield adequacy constraints. In particular, I suggest that we need to distinguish the constraints stemming from human nature from constraints stemming from more local factors such as our particular cultural circumstances and the way they have shaped us. The discussion of realistic possibility in chapter 6 also illustrates the way that we often make unfounded assumptions about what it is realistic to expect of human beings in order (perhaps unconsciously) to justify our falling short of our own values. It therefore illustrates a way in which pluralistic relativism can allow for fundamental criticism of one's own morality.

Part III brings into closer focus the issues raised in chapter 1: the difficulties for moral commitment stemming from recognizing a plurality of true moralities. Chapter 7 presents a theory of the reasons to be moral that enables us to partially resolve these difficulties. The theory I defend undermines the usual sense in which we mean the question "Why be moral?" I argue that there is no real answer to that question, because it presupposes that a commitment to moral values can be validated by a premoral rationality, and such a presupposition is false.

There is no answer to the question "Why be moral?" in the sense in which moral philosophers usually take it, but I argue that we should never have expected an answer. Nevertheless, we must answer a serious challenge to the reasonableness of moral commitment. We cannot show that it is irrational to be amoral or immoral, but we can ask whether it fulfills human needs to be moral. Chapter 8 addresses this question and the challenge raised to this sort of answer by Foucault's insight into the pervasiveness of power relationships. I argue that it is possible to turn back that challenge to some degree, but that defenders of modern liberal moralities have not fully answered some of its main points.

Even if the foregoing challenges could be met, we still may wonder whether the pluralism of alternative adequate moralities undermines our confidence in the commitments we have made to particular moralities. I address this problem in chapter 9, bringing to bear the philosophy of Zhuangzi (Chuang Tzu), who teaches us that recognizing the worth of other ways of life is not a threat to be avoided but an opportunity for enrichment.[3] Finally, we must deal with our moral conflicts with others even if we have nurtured a confidence in our own moral commitments. Chapter 9 supplies a detailed picture of the role of the value of accommodation in our attempts to cope with serious moral disagreement. I give examples of the way in which this value might be applied to moral conflicts such as the ones over abortion and over distributive justice. Finally I propose a role for a certain kind of ritual, as derived from reflection on the Chinese tradition, in strengthening the dispositions of citizens to act on the value of accommodation.

3. In this book I generally use the Pinyin system of romanizing Chinese words. However, much of the scholarship in Chinese philosophy employs the older Wade-Giles system of romanization. For example, Zhuangzi's name is rendered as "Chuang Tzu" under Wade-Giles. Wherever I refer to a Chinese philosopher to whom references are often made both in Pinyin and Wade-Giles, I will use Pinyin and place the Wade-Giles version in parentheses at my first use of the name.

NATURAL MORALITIES

How Pluralism and Naturalism Make for Natural Moralities

Pluralism and Ambivalence

Difference and disagreement over moral values is perennially thought to pose a problem for moral universalism. Yet universalists correctly point out that the mere fact of disagreement, even apparently irresolvable disagreement over important or fundamental matters, does not differentiate morality from other bodies of belief concerning, say, history and the sciences, that typically are thought to be true or false in a nonrelative manner. The fact that we might find it hard or even impossible to resolve some disagreement as to whether some historical event occurred in the far distant past, for example, does prevent us from thinking that the event really did occur or that it did not independently of what any group believes about that event. There is, however, a kind of moral disagreement that poses special difficulties for universalism. This kind of disagreement evokes a complex reaction I call "moral ambivalence." We see that reasonable and knowledgeable people could have made different judgments than we are inclined in make about these conflicts, and any prior convictions we might have had about the superiority of our own judgments get shaken. Moral ambivalence is the phenomenon of coming to understand and appreciate the other side's viewpoint to the extent that our sense of the unique rightness of our own judgments gets destabilized. In other words, the most discomforting kind of moral disagreement is not simply one in which both sides run out of reasons that are persuasive to the other but is also a disagreement in which coming to the other side brings along an appreciation of *its* reasons. The three chapters of part I constitute an argument that a naturalistic and pluralistic conception of morality best accounts for the nature of moral ambivalence.

Many of the ideas for the first three chapters of this book were originally expressed in less developed form in "Pluralistic Relativism," *Midwest Studies in Philosophy* 20 (1996): 378–400; "Three Kinds of Incommensurability," in *Relativism: Interpretation and Confrontation*, ed. Michael Krausz (Notre Dame, Ind.: University of Notre Dame Press, 1989), 140–58; and "Comparative Philosophy: Chinese and Western," in *Stanford Encyclopedia of Philosophy*. Rev. August 22, 2005, available at http://plato. stanford.edu/entries/comparphil-chiwes/.

In this chapter I introduce moral ambivalence by way of moral value pluralism: conflicts between basic moral values make especially hard cases for moral judgment. I then explain how moral ambivalence is compatible with plausible approaches to the interpretation of others' beliefs, and in particular with the most plausible construals of the principle of charity. On the principle of charity, we render others intelligible by analogizing from the body of beliefs, desires, and values we ourselves have adopted. On the most plausible construals of charity, we allow that the body of our own beliefs, desires, and values is internally diverse and contains elements existing in various relations of tension with one another. These tensions can be resolved in different ways. Coming to understand others is coming to understand that one shares in common important beliefs, desires, and values, but that they can resolve the tensions among these elements in ways different from the ways we have resolved them. We can understand how others could make different choices in the face of conflicts between shared moral values. The kind of moral disagreement that poses the steepest challenge for universalism is the kind in which others share values with us but in which they have made different choices in the face of conflicts among these values. Moral ambivalence comes from an understanding and appreciation of the others' perspectives. Once we grant the reality of moral ambivalence, however, it calls for a deeper explanation than universalist theories of moralities can provide.

1.1 MORAL VALUE PLURALISM: BASIC MORAL VALUES IN TENSION WITH ONE ANOTHER

A primary source of value conflict is the fact of plural and basic moral values. "Moral value pluralism" is the doctrine that there exists a plurality of basic moral values, where such values are not derivable from or reducible to other moral values. I use 'value' here in a very broad sense to include types of obligations and duties, as well as morally desirable ends. To some, it is pretty obvious that there exists such a plurality of moral values, but the history of modern Western moral philosophy is dominated by theoretical commitments to the supremacy of one or another value. It is impossible to conclusively refute moral value monism, but there are good reasons to find the various versions of monism unpersuasive.

To begin with, the nature and source of moral claims and obligations appear to be diverse and resistant to reduction. Consider Thomas Nagel's classification of five different sources of value:[1] first, specific obligations to other people or institutions that depend on some special relation to the person or institution in question; second, constraints on action deriving from general rights that everyone has, such as rights to liberty of certain kinds or freedom from assault or coercion;[2] third, utility, the effects

---

1. Thomas Nagel, "The Fragmentation of Value," in *Mortal Questions* (Cambridge: Cambridge University Press, 1979), 128–31.
2. Rights as a nonbasic source of value can be justified instrumentally as promoting utility or relationship and community, as shall be discussed in chapter 3.

of what one does on everyone's welfare; fourth, perfectionist ends or values, such as the intrinsic value of scientific or artistic achievements and creations; and fifth, commitment to one's own projects and undertakings.

One reason why each kind of value appears to be irreducibly basic is that it is easy to see deep tensions between the projects of realizing all of them. To take a well-known pluralist theme from Isaiah Berlin, we can envision no utopia in which the maximal realizations of these different sorts of value are made compatible with each other.[3] Therefore, if a morality prescribes a set of values to be realized or observed in human life, it must specify priorities to govern cases of conflict between these values, for example, when honoring individual rights conflicts with promotion of social utility, when an obligation based on friendship or kinship or another kind of special relation conflicts with honoring a right based on someone's humanity or with the promotion of social utility. A Chinese Confucian morality, for example, is partly distinguished by the way it places comparatively greater importance on duties arising from kinship when these come into conflict with duties to nonkin or considerations of public justice.[4]

In recognition of this fact, the anthropologist Ruth Benedict found virtues to appreciate in radically different ways of life and concluded: "It is most unlikely that even the best society will be able to stress in one social order all the virtues we prize in human life."[5] Note the "we" in Benedict's phrase "the virtues we prize." This suggests a common universe of values from which cultures must select a few to emphasize. If Benedict is right, and no one culture could possibly avoid sacrificing some things that human beings prize while it gives emphasis to other things, then a plurality of different cultures could provide legitimate satisfaction and sustenance to human beings, and in that sense be worthy of respect.

There are other fundamental conflicts that should be taken into account but are not mentioned by Nagel. He leaves off the list those values having to do with different stances that human beings might take toward the natural world, for example, the stance of striving for attunement to it versus the stance of mastering it. Consider the controversy in anthropology as to how to interpret magical rites as practiced by some tribal peoples such as the Azande. These divination rites, which in one form involved poisoning a chicken and seeing whether it lived or died after a certain question was asked, were used to get guidance on crucial matters, such as whether to build a house

3. Isaiah Berlin, "Two Concepts of Liberty," in *Liberty: Incorporating Four Essays on Liberty*, ed. Henry Hardy (Oxford: Oxford University Press, 2002), 212–7.

4. *Analects* 13.18 presents Confucius responding to the story of Upright Gong, who turned his father in for stealing a sheep. Among his people, Confucius says, upright fathers and sons cover up for one another. I do not take this passage as justifying the concealment of all kinds of crime committed by one's father or son, but it certainly represents the great importance placed on filial loyalty with Confucian morality and within the traditional Chinese culture as a whole.

5. Ruth Benedict, *Patterns of Culture* (New York: Penguin, 1934), 229.

or clear a plot of ground for seed, when there was the possibility that a witch might wreak some mischief.

The earliest interpretations construed these rites as rivals to science, misguided attempts to predict and control nature.[6] Later interpretations construed them as having another purpose altogether—that of expressing or symbolizing certain social values.[7] On the later interpretations we should be prepared to impute to the Azande a conception of rational acceptability for beliefs that is different from one aimed toward prediction and control—a conception that is intelligible in relation to a symbolic or expressive purpose. Peter Winch argued that the Zande rites constitute a "form of expression" that provides the individual the opportunity to reflect on how "the life he lives, his relations with his fellows, his chances for acting decently or doing evil, all spring from his relation to his crops." More specifically, Zande rites express the recognition that "one's life is subject to contingencies" and constitute a drama in which there are ways of dealing symbolically "with misfortunes and their disruptive effect on man's relations with his fellows."[8]

Charles Taylor presents a plausible assessment of the conflict between the older and later interpretations. It is a mistake, he claims, to assume that one or the other interpretation is correct. It is even mistaken, he further argues, to point out that the Zande rites can have both practical and expressive purposes, as if there were two separable purposes for them. The distinction between the two purposes may be an artifact of *our* conception of rationality and not theirs. Their conception of rationality is one that makes no distinction between understanding the universe and coming into attunement with it. Speaking from within the perspective of this conception, Taylor writes:

> We don't understand the order of things without understanding our place in it, because we are part of this order. And we cannot understand the order and our place in it without loving it, without seeing its goodness, which is what I want to call being in attunement with it. Not being in attunement with it is a sufficient condition of not understanding it, for anyone who genuinely understands must love it; and not understanding it is incompatible with being in attunement with it, since this presupposes understanding.[9]

Taylor believes Plato articulated a striving for attunement and that the European cultural tradition embodied it until the advent of modern science. The beliefs of the

---

6. See for example, Sir James Frazer, *The Golden Bough*, 3rd ed. (London: MacMillan, 1936).

7. J. M. Beattie, for example, asserts that Trobriand canoe magic expresses the importance of canoe building for Trobrianders and that the blood pact ritual emphasizes the need for mutual support between parties. See his *Other Cultures* (New York: Free Press of Glencoe, 1964).

8. Peter Winch, "Understanding a Primitive Society," in *Rationality*, ed. Bryan Wilson (New York: Harper, 1970), 100, 104–5.

9. Charles Taylor, "Rationality," in *Rationality and Relativism*, ed. Martin Hollis and Steven Lukes (Cambridge: MIT Press, 1982), 95–6.

Mbuti of Central Africa provide a vivid contemporary example of this striving. These hunter-gatherers regard the forest as sacred, the source of their existence, of all goodness. They talk, shout, whisper, and sing to the forest, addressing it as mother or father or both, referring to its goodness and its ability to cure or "make good."[10]

Modern science has prompted many to reject this view of the world as the possible object of attunement. Only then was it possible to make a clear-cut distinction between practical and expressive purposes. Taylor himself believes that the severance of understanding and attunement resulted in superior understanding at least of physical nature. But as he is careful to point out, it is difficult to demonstrate the absolute superiority of the modern scientific conception. Our alienation from nature grows along with our technological control of it.

Taylor seems right about the intimate connection between understanding and attunement for the Azande and for the premodern European tradition. He further seems right to point out the possibility of a "cruel dilemma" should our superior understanding be achieved at the cost of attunement. If we can understand the ideal of inhabiting a world one can love and find goodness in, it no longer appears irrational for the Azande to retain beliefs that in our own epistemology require extensive and ad hoc defense in the face of empirical disconfirmation.

While we believe that our own methods are more reliable modes of access to the world, we can recognize that the kind of access we favor is just one among the many things we value. The fact is that attunement is one of the other things still valued by many of us in societies dominated by modern science. Some of us, including significant numbers of scientists, retain a belief in the world's goodness in such a way that its basis is placed beyond empirical disconfirmation, or so some of us hope. This requires a nonliteral interpretation of older beliefs such as those about Creation that traditionally have accompanied the value of attunement in Western cultures. Others retain a literal interpretation and dispute the idea that such beliefs have ever been threatened by empirical disconfirmation. On the other side, the Azande or the Mbuti do get around in their worlds and accomplish their ends. They have a very sure grasp of causal relations on the level of daily life.

The Azande, therefore, value reliable access to the world in ways we can perfectly comprehend, and we can also understand their magical rites in analogy to premodern modes of thought that are at the roots of current Western cultures. We can understand the difference between the Azande and us as concerning the relative dominance of the values in question—attunement versus the mastery found in prediction and control. However, we must understand that in articulating a difference over the relative dominance of two values, we are conceiving them to be distinct and separable, and our way of understanding the difference between them and us is itself another difference.

10. See Colin Turnbull, *The Human Cycle* (New York: Simon and Schuster, 1983), 30.

There is another kind of value difference that Nagel's typology allows for but does not highlight. It is very much a salient conflict as we survey human cultures in the twenty-first century. My earlier work on relativism exemplified a contrast between two types of moralities, one of them having at its center the duties arising from the value of community (which I mean to cover relationships to particular others as well as to groups of varying sizes), and the other having at its center the rights persons have purely as individuals.[11] In the former type, for example, under Confucian morality, family relationships form a central portion of the good of individuals, and many of their most urgent duties are directed toward sustaining such relationships. In the latter type, individuals are seen as having interests (i.e., the interest in privacy) that need to be defended against others, even those who stand in important relationships to them (a parent's concern for the well-being of an adult child might lead him to invade her privacy). One might contrast these moralities by saying that in one kind relationship is the dominant focus, while autonomy is the dominant focus in the other kind.

This contrast, however, is meant to be consistent with the fact that the value of relationship and community is a part of Western moral traditions. Indeed, much communitarian criticism of liberal political philosophy would not have the force it does unless these themes were part of Western traditions. These traditions are distinct in the centrality they accord to notions of autonomy and individual rights, not by the absence of these other values. When values of relationship and autonomy conflict in the West, there is a comparatively greater tendency to give priority to autonomy.

1.2 How Moral Value Pluralism Can Provide an Alternative to "Radical Difference" Arguments for Relativism

The typical differences between actual moralities lie in the way they respond to such common conflicts of basic values. Note that this characterization of the differences between moralities allows them to share at least some values even if not all of them. Differences between moralities do not typically consist in radical difference: one set of values confronting another totally different set. It is often thought, in contrast to the view defended here, that relativism depends on the assertion of radical difference between moralities. The relativist reasoning, supposedly, is that judging other moralities on the basis of one's own is inappropriate. There is no point in comparing moralities that are radically different.

Such an account raises awkward questions. If the differences between moralities are so stark and complete, it is unclear why we should call the other code a *moral* code. To think of a system of norms as a morality, even when it is completely different from one's own morality, one would have to adopt a purely formal notion of what a morality

---

11. See *Moral Relativity* (Berkeley: University of California Press, 1984), chap. 9.

is. On such an account, a morality is simply the system of norms to which its members subscribe (e.g., is the system acknowledged to be the appropriate basis for evaluation of their conduct and attitudes, or is the system they are motivated to try to satisfy). There are no restrictions on the content of the norms. One problem with this formal account of morality, however, is that more than one kind of normative system fulfills such a description. Legal systems, rules of etiquette, and norms of prudential rationality, as well as systems more comfortably labeled 'moral', fit the bill. Another move that could be made in light of this problem is to further specify that a moral system of norms is the one taken by those who subscribe to it as the system that overrides all others in case of conflict. However, this move is subject to the objection that not all people in a group for whom there is a morality would acknowledge that system as the overriding normative system for them.

A more fundamental objection to formal accounts required by radical difference relativism, however, is that such accounts merely delay performance of a necessary explanatory task. Even if we were to suppose that all or most members of a group did subscribe in the requisite sense to a system of norms and that all or most acknowledged it to be the overriding system, we still have to make sense of why they have subscribed to those norms, with whatever particular substantial content these norms have. If we find that the acknowledged, overriding system for another group bears very little resemblance with respect to substantial content to our own acknowledged, overriding system, we have a problem. If we see the adherents of that other code to be striving after things so different from what we understand ourselves to be pursuing, we might well suspect that we have not understood these people. When we seek to make sense of others, we must invoke what *we* think makes sense, and this includes what it makes sense to pursue and to value in the world. This point, in fact, illustrates something fundamental about the nature of interpreting and understanding others. Inevitably, we must use ourselves as models in this task, even as we extend our imaginations and analogize from our own experience to understand people who live and are shaped by very different circumstances.[12] We do on occasion fail to understand other people. The question is whether such failures of understanding can constitute a forceful case for relativism. The problem is that the less we understand others, the less their way of life appears to be a *rival* to our own. If we don't understand how their way of life could be attractive to human beings, it is difficult to conceive of it as *competing* with our own.

The difficulties with using incomprehension as a basis for relativism are illustrated by an argument given by Samuel Fleischacker. He argues that we can understand others just well enough to know that we don't understand them.[13] His "moderate"

12. See chap. 8 of *Moral Relativity* and my "Three Kinds of Incommensurability," in *Relativism: Interpretation and Confrontation*, ed. Michael Krausz (Notre Dame, Ind.: University of Notre Dame Press, 1989), 140–58.

13. Samuel Fleischacker, *Integrity and Moral Relativism* (Leiden: Brill, 1992).

version of "cultural relativism" has roots in Wittgenstein's view that knowledge depends on a background of shared assumptions and standards of evidence. "World pictures" are embedded within cultures. Our world picture involves not only a distinctive set of beliefs about the world but also an ordering of interests that determines how we go about trying to have reliable beliefs. This ordering differs from those dominant in other cultures. We in the West have given precedence to our interests in "egalitarian knowledge" (wanting and believing that people have roughly equal access to the truth) and in prediction and control of this-worldly objects, while others have given precedence to an interest in eternal life and in both wanting and believing that certain people have special access to knowledge. Such differences may render us unable to prove to others that they are wrong, and indeed, unable to fully understand why they value the interests they do. Nevertheless, we understand that they do value these interests highly, and we think they are wrong to do so. We make such judgments despite our merely partial understanding because "we tend to see a certain set of interests as the proper guide for a minimally decent and/or sensible human life."[14]

While I think it is entirely possible for us to understand others just enough to realize that we do not fully understand them, it remains puzzling why we should blithely pass the judgment that they have made a mistake *precisely with respect to the matter we do not fully understand*. Consider Fleischacker's example about a Western-educated woman who has converted to fundamentalist Islam. To the charge that she has forsaken her own reflectiveness in order to convert, Fleischacker has her ask what we have gained from our reflectiveness and the institutions that uphold it:

> Despair of having any purpose in life, a science unrestrained by moral considerations, and in consequence a violent youth culture, broken marriages, and nuclear weapons. With such a record, who are you to complain of the violence in my tradition? And what with your televisions, and your mind-deadening jobs on assembly lines and at computer terminals, you have dubious claim even to intellectual advantages over us, at least as far as the bulk of your society is concerned.[15]

If we accept Fleischacker's assumption that we do not fully understand why the woman would value the benefits of not being reflective in the way Westerners value, it seems presumptuous to judge her *mistaken*. Perhaps she understands something that we don't. Indeed, it is not clear why the woman is any less reflective in *our* way of being reflective, given the retort that Fleischacker attributes to her.[16]

Fleischacker's example fails to illustrate the merely partial understanding he has in mind. The Islamic woman's retort to Western criticism has force for us (presents a

---

14. Fleischacker, *Integrity*, 71.
15. Fleischacker, *Integrity*, 18–9.
16. Thanks to Owen Flanagan for this point.

genuinely rival way of life) precisely to the extent that we *understand* it and *share* some of the values underlying it.[17] Even if we prefer our way of life, with all its costs and failings, we may think that the woman has a substantial reason for choosing another way of life. The same holds true for cultures emphasizing the value of attunement as discussed earlier.

1.3 THE JUDICIOUS APPLICATION OF CHARITY

Such an understanding of the two examples supports Donald Davidson's principle of charity. This principle, under his influential construal, says that we must interpret others on the assumption that they are rational beings, talking about and navigating "the same world" as we are. Otherwise, we shall not be able to interpret them at all as holding beliefs or making intelligible utterances. Charity directs us to "optimize" agreement between them and ourselves where ever it is plausible to do so. The idea is to make them "right, as far we can tell, as often as possible."[18]

Charity, Davidson explains, does not enjoin us from attributing intelligible error. As our interpretation of others takes shape, we might find that it makes better sense to attribute mistakes to them, given our emerging conception of how they are interacting with the objects of their beliefs. However, there is a limit to such attribution. To attribute massive error to them is to undermine a crucial assumption of interpretation: that they are forming beliefs about the same world we are. If we were to attribute to ancients the belief that the earth is flat and, what is more, virtually none of the other beliefs we have about the earth, we would undermine the assumption that they have beliefs at all about the earth.[19]

17. Consider that Seyyid (or Sayyid) Qutb, perhaps most influential Islamist fundamentalist of the twentieth century and a staple of the Islamic education of generations of jihadists, both moderate and extreme, peaceful and violent, was preparing to take his place among the liberal, Western-oriented Egyptian elite when he visited the United States for two and a half years. He was repulsed by its racism toward Arabs, its preoccupation with pleasure and material interest, and the cultural encouragement it gave to women to leave what he saw as their proper roles of bringing up children "merely to be attractive, sexy and flirtatious," to use "their ability for material productivity rather than the training of human beings, because material production is considered to be more important, more valuable and more honourable than the development of human character." See Seyyid Qutb, *Milestones* (Damascus, Syria: Kazi, 1993), 97–8. Egalitarians on the left in the West can find much to agree with in Qutb's criticism of the consumerist materialism and glaring inequalities in Western societies, while Christian fundamentalists may find much to agree with in his criticism of sexual permissiveness and gender equality ideals. Consider the Christian evangelist Jerry Falwell's statement that the September 11, 2001, attacks on New York City and Washington D.C., were God's judgment on America: "I really believe that the pagans and the abortionists and the feminists and the gays and the lesbians who are actively trying to make that an alternative lifestyle, the ACLU, People for the American Way, all of them who try to secularize America . . . I point the thing in their face and say you helped this happen." A transcript of his remarks on the "700 Club" telecast on Sept 13, 2001, is available at www.truthorfiction.com/rumors/f/falwell-robertson-wtc.htm.

18. Donald Davidson, "Radical Interpretation," in *Inquiries into Truth and Interpretation*, 2nd ed. (Oxford: Clarendon Press, 2001), 136.

19. Donald Davidson, "Thought and Talk," in *Inquiries*, 168.

Davidson notes that in his earlier work on interpretation, he tended to construe charity in terms of "maximizing" agreement in belief and that a more perspicuous statement of what he had in mind all along is that agreement in beliefs should be "optimized."[20] Rather than the "most" agreement, we need the "right sort" of agreement that enables understanding of others. We should try to reach agreement "as far as possible, subject to considerations of simplicity, hunches about the effects of social conditioning, and of course our common-sense, or scientific, knowledge of explicable error."[21] Explicable error, as Davidson recognized, might not be best explained by making most of others' beliefs true. Social conditioning might also have the effect of ramifying rather than minimizing the ways that others believe differently from us.

Matters become further complicated with the recognition that it is agreement not just in belief that must be optimized but also in the desires, values, and intentions we attribute to others, since we must understand their behaviors not only in relation to what they believe about the world but also in relation to what they want of it, value in it, and intend to do in it.[22] To make sense of the actions of others, we construe these actions as stemming from intentions, which in turn stem from certain patterns of beliefs, desires, and values. Some patterns make others intelligible to us, and others don't. However, such ways of making sense of others do not prevent us from attributing to them some desires, values, and intentions that are different from ours. For example, I accept that others want and value the having of power over people, even though the idea does not hold much appeal to me. For such reasons, Davidson was right to put some distance between "optimizing" and "maximizing" agreement as a necessary condition for making sense of others.

The earlier and less plausible "maximizing" version of charity shows up in an argument of David Cooper's against moral relativism. David Cooper holds that "We can only identify another's beliefs as moral beliefs about X if there is a massive degree of agreement between his and our beliefs." His conclusion is that the principle of charity refutes any significant form of moral relativism. It is difficult to disagree with Cooper's point that a moral belief must have for its subject matter something connected with "welfare, happiness, suffering, security, and the good life."[23] We *would* have strong reason to suspect our interpretation of another beliefs as moral beliefs if we were to construe them as having *nothing to do* with welfare, happiness, suffering, security, and the good life. This is not the same as refuting the possibility of significant differences over what is believed about these subjects. Quite a lot depends on how one

20. Donald Davidson, introduction to *Inquiries*, xix; "Radical Interpretation," 136.

21. Donald Davidson, "On the Very Idea of a Conceptual Scheme," in *Inquiries*, 196.

22. I am going to remain neutral, for the purposes of this chapter, on the question of how to understand a person's values in relation to her beliefs and desires, whether they are beliefs, desires, or some combination thereof.

23. David E. Cooper, "Moral Relativism," *Midwest Studies in Philosophy* 3 (1978): 101, 104. I discuss this kind of argument in my *Moral Relativity*, 114–6.

applies Cooper's requirement that there be a "massive degree of agreement" between our moral beliefs and those of another person. It seems arbitrary to say that among competing interpretations of another person's beliefs, the best interpretation is the one that simply produces the greatest *number* of overlapping beliefs, even if one had confidence in one's ability to count beliefs, which I do not. This is one of the correct reasons, I believe, why Davidson corrected his earlier statements of the principle of charity, from maximization to optimization.

Michele Moody-Adams gives a more recent formulation of Cooper's argument, starting with the premise that understanding others requires that there be "quite substantial agreement about many of the basic concepts that are relevant to moral reflection."[24] She then leaps to the conclusion that "ultimate" or "fundamental" moral disagreement is not possible.[25] To validate this conclusion, she must hold that disagreement over concepts relevant to moral reflection is limited to "nonultimate" or "nonfundamental" concepts. This seems a coherent stance to take, but cannot be derived in a priori fashion from a principle of charitable interpretation of others, as Moody-Adams attempts to do. Why must groups have moral beliefs only if they have precisely the same stock of "basic" moral concepts as we do? It would seem sufficient to have agreement on some critical mass, would it not, however the threshold is defined? And with respect to any one basic concept relevant to moral reflection, such as justice,[26] what counts as having the same concept? It seems that two groups might have sufficiently different conceptions of justice that it would be truer to say that they have two overlapping but different concepts of justice. Furthermore, when the values of justice and compassion conflict, making sense of others does not require us to interpret them as setting precisely the same value priorities as we do. This kind of disagreement can qualify as a fundamental disagreement even as it presupposes a sharing of values.

A Davidsonian principle of charity, properly interpreted as calling for optimization rather than maximization, cannot possibly resolve these questions by itself because the requirement of optimization itself requires interpretation. In illustrating this point, Henry Richardson has pointed out that interpreting a philosophical text requires taking account of the cognitive aims the authors had in writing what they did. Is it more charitable, Richardson asks, for a translator of Machiavelli's *The Prince* to resolve ambiguities and seek to maximize agreement between Machiavelli and the relevant audience? Or is it more charitable to set him out as intentionally provocative and deliberately cryptic?[27]

---

24. Michele M. Moody-Adams, *Fieldwork in Familiar Places: Morality, Culture, and Philosophy* (Cambridge, Mass.: Harvard University Press, 1997), 55.

25. Moody-Adams, *Fieldwork*, 56.

26. Justice and compassion were examples of some basic concepts given by Moody-Adams in "The Idea of Moral Progress," *Metaphilosophy* 30 (1999): 168–85.

27. Henry S. Richardson, *Practical Reasoning about Final Ends* (Cambridge: Cambridge University Press, 1997), 268–9.

The answer to such questions can only be supplied within a larger context of inquiry: the attempt to explain that person and her actions. In such a larger context, attribution of beliefs different from ours may be more or less reasonable depending on how it fits into a reasonable explanation of that person. And what counts as a reasonable explanation of a particular person will be set within the context of one's larger theories about persons and societies, among other things. One's explanation of a person can reasonably attribute error and false belief on an indefinite number of important matters that might even deserve to be called "fundamental," as long as it seems plausible to attribute error to him in his epistemic situation as we construe it.

Similarly, it might be reasonable to allow a large degree of overlap between the moral concepts of different cultures without insisting on an identity in the stock of moral concepts available to different cultures. Two moral concepts can overlap in meaning yet not be identical. Another common cause of what reasonably could be called "fundamental" moral disagreement is that different priorities are set between important values when they come into conflict. We can understand that the moral codes of others confront familiar tensions between values that we ourselves recognize as important, but we do not have to understand these others as setting the same priorities in the face of these tensions. This is consistent with optimizing agreement between them and us, where the evidence dictates that they are not exactly like us.

1.4 Confucian Examples of the Familiar yet Different

The way we understand others by modeling them after ourselves is more like the way we use analogies to understand others. I stress analogies because they highlight similarities between others and us while allowing for significant differences. To see some illustrations of understanding through analogy, consider three significant and distinctive features of the Confucian ethic as it is represented in classical works of Chinese philosophy, primarily the *Analects*.[28] We understand these features through noting their similarity with themes we find to be familiar and present in our own culture, but as with all analogies, the similarities coexist with significant differences. In all three cases, I shall claim, we have little reluctance to accept the differences.

The first feature is the centrality of *xiao*, usually translated as "filial piety." It is a common feature of many cultures that one should honor thy father and mother, of course, and it is not difficult to find analogies within American society to Confucian filial piety. At the same time, the Confucian tradition is unusual in the stringency of its duties to parents. *Analects* 2.7 identifies the requirements of *xiao* as going beyond

---

28. A discussion of these examples is contained in my "Where Charity Begins," in *Davidson's Philosophy and Chinese Philosophy: Constructive Engagement,* ed. Bo Mou (Leiden: Brill Academic, forthcoming).

providing parents material support when they are elderly but more fundamentally showing that it's not just about giving them food (supporting them when elderly) but *jing*—originally conceived as an attitude one should have when sacrificing to ancestors, an attitude of devotion to carrying out great responsibilities to one's ancestral spirits. *Analects* 2.8 amplifies the nature of *jing* in saying that the young should take on the burden when there's work to be done and let the old enjoy the wine and food, but that hardly deserves to be called filial. It's the expression on one's face or demeanor that is difficult to manage.

The scope of duties to parents includes taking care of what they alone could have given one—one's body. Cengzi, one of Confucius's students, is portrayed in *Analects* 8.3 as gravely ill and near death. He bids his students to look at his hands and feet, and quotes lines from the *Book of Poetry* to convey the idea that all his life he has been keeping his body intact as part of his duty to his parents. It is only now near death, he says, that he can be sure of having been spared and thus fulfilling this duty to parents. This very idea, that one must keep one's body intact as a duty of gratitude to one's parents, has remained a central idea in Chinese culture.

Why is *xiao* so central a virtue in the Confucian ethic? Part of the reason seems to be a view about its centrality to the development of ethical character. In *Analects* 1.2, one of Confucius's most prominent students, Youzi, says that being good as a son and obedient as a young man (meaning that one is obedient to one's elder brothers) is perhaps the root of character, the basis of respect for authority outside the family. One learns respect for others first by learning it for those within the family. Another part of the reason for the centrality given to filial piety is the need to express gratitude to those who have given one life and nurture. In *Analects* 17.21, Zaiwo objects to the traditional length of mourning for one's deceased parents. One year is enough to disrupt one's normal life in those ways, but the traditional period of three years is too long, he says. Confucius comments on Zaiwo's lack of feeling in this regard. All children are completely dependent on their parents for the first three years of life, he observes. Did not Zaiwo receive three years' worth of love from his parents?

The virtue and its rationale have analogues in American culture. We can certainly recognize the themes of gratitude, the need to reciprocate in some fashion for great gifts received, and the conception of family relationships as pivotal in the development of character. Such similarities of theme, however, seem to underdetermine the centrality of filial piety and the stringency of its duties in Confucianism and in the larger traditional culture. While we recognize such rationales for filial piety, we generally do not accord it nearly as central a place in the catalogue of moral virtues, nor do we conceive its duties to be so stringent. And the theme that one owes one's body to one's parents and that it is deep ingratitude not to take care of such a great gift is something that can be understood from an American perspective, but is not generally accepted.

Do such differences suggest that we have not correctly understood Confucianism or traditional Chinese culture? I submit that we accept such differences as part of the normal range of human possibility, perhaps because we can imagine ourselves having taken a path we have not taken. The themes of gratitude, reciprocity, and the importance of the family in moral development are familiar to Americans and at the same time have the potential for justifying a value of respecting parents that is far more stringent than the one many Americans accept. And indeed, taking the Confucian perspective, an American might come to have the strange feeling that that perspective makes more sense.

Consider another significant feature of Confucian ethics: its inclusion of an aesthetic dimension in its conception of a good and worthwhile life. Right action in Confucian is fitting action. It expresses appropriate care and respect for others in a manner that befits the nature of one's social relationship to them and to other, more particular features of their situation and one's own. There are often conventional forms for the expression of these ethical attitudes, ritual forms called *li*. To fashion oneself into a better person is to become practiced in the performance of such *li* such that they become second nature, but they must always express the appropriate attitudes. To attain the proper balance between form and feeling is to ennoble and beautify human nature. Antonio Cua's translation of a passage from Xunzi puts the point nicely: "human nature provides raw material, and constructive human effort is responsible for the glorification and flourishing of elegant form and orderly expression. Without constructive human effort, human nature cannot beautify itself."[29]

It is instructive that Cua draws analogies to the perception of qualities in works of art, likening the grace or joy that can be seen in accomplished ritual activity to the grace of a curve in a painting or joy in a piece of music.[30] David Hall and Roger Ames observe that the Confucian notion of the 'right' action has much in common with the artist's choice of the 'right' brush or the 'right' color in the execution of a painting.[31] For the Confucian, doing the right thing not only means doing one's duty—and not just for the right reason, and not just with the right feeling, but also with the proper grace and elegance that is both an aesthetic end in itself and bespeaks the ease and contentment of one who has attained the virtues and realized her humanity. These uses of analogy help to make intelligible the aesthetic dimension of Confucian ethics, but they also illustrate how analogy can help. They take what is familiar to us in one context (in this case, painting or music) and point to its occurrence in a different context. The analogy illuminates if we can conceive of the familiar taking place in that different context.

The third feature of Confucian virtue ethics is its emphasis on harmonious relationships as a central part of the ethical life, as illustrated by the *Analects* on an adult's

---

29. Antonio S. Cua, "The Ethical and Religious Dimensions of *Li*," *Review of Metaphysics* 55 (2002): 481, translating from Dishen Li, *Xunzi jishi* (Taipei: Zueshong, 1979), 439.

30. Cua, "Ethical and Religious Dimensions," 483.

31. David L. Hall and Roger T. Ames, "Chinese Philosophy," in *Routledge Encyclopedia of Philosophy*, ed. E. Craig. Rev. 1998. Available at www.rep.routledge.com/article/G001SECT4.

relation to her parents. Notice that in *Analects* 1.2, the crucial dimension of moral development that is started in the family is respect for authority. The strong Chinese preference for harmony emerges in 2.6, where the Master says one should give parents no cause for anxiety except for illness. Consider 4.18, where Confucius considers occasions on which one's own opinions as to what is right or best can conflict with one's parents' wishes. One should remonstrate with one's parents gently, he says. The value placed on harmony, as indicated by 4.18, does not require silence in the face of real disagreement with one's superiors. Indeed, the Confucian tradition celebrates the scholar-intellectual who says what he thinks about the ruler's methods and ends, often to the ruler's face. However, the ends served by such moral courage include the end of harmony. Rulers who fail to govern for the good of the community, the state, and the nation must be called to account precisely for the good of all.

Someone must have the authority to settle conflicts, if only in the sense of saying whose view prevails this time. Human beings have yet to invent a society without having to designate such authority and to inculcate some degree of respect for it. The reasons for preferring harmony are quite intelligible, but here again, the reasons underdetermine the degree of preference for it manifested in the culture: for example, informal negotiation involving interaction and reconciliation between the contending parties is still the traditional way of resolving business disputes in China; informal mediation committees operate to resolve disputes at the grassroots rural village and urban neighborhood levels; and Chinese courts encourage mediation between contending parties even after litigation proceedings have begun.

That Chinese culture should show this high degree of preference for harmony does not seem to threaten its intelligibility to those on the outside. Why? Some preference for harmony exists on the American side of the comparison, to which analogy can be made, however major the differences the analogy leaves in place. The American side, after all, embraces a significantly diverse range of subcultures in which a high degree of preference for harmony is shown. These subcultures include, of course, Chinese American and other Asian American subcultures, as well as Latino and Mexican American subcultures. Moreover, the various European-descended subcultures of American society have in the past demonstrated a stronger preference for family harmony and cooperation within various levels of community than they do now. It is in part this internal diversity that helps to make Confucian values intelligible as a path we ourselves could and in some cases have taken.

So far, I have been assuming that the relevant reference point for understanding Confucianism is the contemporary American perspective, and up until the previous paragraph I have assumed that this perspective is more or less unified. Of course, that is false. In reality, we treat such perspectives as unified only for the sake of certain comparisons, for the sake of certain comparative purposes. In other contexts, and for other purposes, we make much ado about the differences. The unification is at best relative to the purpose of understanding a presumably distant culture that is more difficult to comprehend. The 'us' in the comparison between them and us is diverse, and such diversity provides some of the analogies we use to make sense of 'them'. This raises the question of how this diverse group became 'us' in the first place.

If we are limited to beginning from our individual selves as models for understanding others, it seems quite unlikely that we could get the range of beliefs, desires, and values that we take for granted even within relatively small circles. I accept that some people are attracted to holding power and exercising it over others, even though my own psychology does not bear much resemblance to theirs in this respect. I accept that some of my students believe in the extreme libertarianism of Ayn Rand, even though there is an inevitable point where I fail to follow their thought processes when they explain them to me. I accept that some people believe that they have been abducted by alien beings, even though there is very little from my own experience that I could use to illuminate whatever experience and thought processes could have led to such a belief. I suggest that our self-understandings comprehend significant diversity because the very concepts we use to interpret both ourselves and others embody diversity in what we value and in how much we value it relative to other values.

1.5 MORAL AMBIVALENCE

Understanding others is therefore compatible with understanding them to be different from us in significant ways. Understanding other moral codes and the ways of life in which they are embedded is not to see them as alien and incomprehensible but in some respects familiar and in other respects constituting a challenge to our own codes and ways of life. Since we ourselves are complex and ambivalent moral beings, we are able to see that at least some other codes and ways of life may just as reasonably be adopted by decent and informed human beings as our own. We can recognize significant overlaps of value between cultures, contrary to Fleischacker's argument, and yet not collapse them all into one, contrary to Moody-Adams's argument. Neither sameness nor difference should obscure the other from view.

This complexity and ambivalence over the priorities to be given in case of conflict among plural values is reflected in our own moral traditions. For example, the source of disagreement in the United States over the moral permissibility of abortion seems not so much to be a difference in the ultimate moral principles held by opposing sides as partly a difference over the applicability of a commonly held principle requiring the protection of human life and partly a difference over the relative weight to be given in the circumstances to another widely held principle requiring the protection of individual autonomy. Philippa Foot has also suggested that there is no one universally acceptable moral principle concerning what to do when the interests of the individual and those of the community clash. Consider, for example, the decision between treating a cancer patient so that she will have the best chances of survival versus the course of action that, through knowledge gained, will enable doctors to save the most patients in the end. Foot believes that "we ourselves" would strongly object to using a patient for the benefit of others, but that it is unclear how one could rule out of court a strict utilitarian view that would allow such things.[32] This seems to be a conflict between the values of individual rights and utility, although I am not sure whether there is as much unanimity among "ourselves" as Foot seems to presume. As the recent debate over health care has emphasized, doctors face the prospect of having to "ration" care because of the increasing cost of medical technology. Many of us are reluctantly endorsing such a move, and it is not clear to me how we could rationalize such a move except on the utilitarian grounds that more people, or more people with more of their lives ahead of them, are helped. Therefore, serious value conflict occurs within a moral tradition not just in the sense that different strands of that tradition conflict but also in the sense that individuals can and do subscribe to both strands and feel within themselves the conflict.

Another example involves tensions between what Nagel calls impersonal values, such as rights and utility on the one hand and the duties arising from special relations with particular people and communities and from personal commitments and projects on the other. We do face serious conflicts between the need to address the severe deprivation and violations of rights in our own country or across the world on the one hand and tending to our special obligations to particular others and to our own projects and commitments on the other.

These sorts of conflict pose special difficulties because we can understand both sides. Even if we are firm in taking a side, we can understand that something of moral value is lost when we act on that side, and the loss is of such a nature that we cannot simply dismiss it as a regrettable though justifiable result of the right decision. This is no mere psychological phenomenon of being torn between different possible ways of addressing value conflicts. It is a problem in moral epistemology. We see that reasonable and knowledgeable people could have made different decisions, and any prior convictions we might have had about the superiority of our own decisions get shaken. Such conflicts between values in our own moral traditions help us to understand how other traditions might have embodied different priorities in similar conflicts.

And lest we think that this sort of ambivalence within a society is just an outcome of the heterogeneity and pluralism of modern Western democracies, consider an example from Samoa given by the anthropologist Brad Shore. Following the violent murder of his father, a young man receives public counsel from a village pastor in formal Samoan that he must resist the temptation to avenge his father's death, and keep in mind the values of peace and harmony and forgiveness. Yet later this same pastor, this time in colloquial Samoan, warned the young man that if he *failed* to kill the murderer of his father, he would not be his father's son. Shore doesn't draw the conclusion that the pastor is a hypocrite or confused. Rather, he concludes that the pastor's two pieces of conflicting advice illustrate the difficulty that any society has in making rigid choices between competing values. The pastor expresses both the value of

32. Philippa Foot, "Morality and Art," *Proceedings of the British Academy* 56 (1970): 133.

social harmony in a community threatened by civil war and the value of filial piety and evening scores. What is culturally particular is the way each society attempts to partially resolve such conflicts between values by emphasizing one or the other value. The value not emphasized may recede into the background but may nevertheless appear in ethical discourse.[33]

Another example concerns the contrast between moralities oriented toward rights as a basic source of value and moralities oriented toward relationships and community. Rights as a basic source of value have in the West come to be conceived as owed to individuals independently of their potential contributions to any community. That is why a central kind of right protects against interference from others. A characteristic justification for rights is the idea that the individual's morally legitimate interests should be protected in case of conflicts with communal interests. Let me associate the value of "autonomy" with these ideas that rights have an independent justification apart from the individual's contribution to community and that rights are needed to protect the individual's morally legitimate interests in case of conflict with communal interests. In contrast to autonomy, the value of community concerns the goods of a shared life of relationships and what is required of individuals to maintain that shared life. A morality centered on the value of community need not be construed as denying that individuals have morally legitimate interests, but the individual's welfare is conceived as lying in proper relationship to the community, in a kind of harmonization between the individual and the community.

Autonomy and community often function as counterpoints *to each other,* in that one value is asserted against the other value because it is seen as addressing the liabilities of asserting the other value strongly. Autonomy gets asserted against the sort of collective responsiveness to individual need that can be a great benefit of community when that responsiveness turns into the liability of oppressive suffocation or an alienating exclusion of those who fall from good standing. On the other side, community gets asserted against the barriers to intervention afforded by autonomy when this benefit blocks responsiveness to need. The U.S. moral tradition, I believe, exhibits this kind of dynamic between autonomy and community, and compared to many Asian traditions, gives far greater priority to rights as the expression of individual autonomy, but the presence of the value of community is nevertheless real even if relatively recessive. Indeed, much of the appeal of communitarian critiques of the U.S. tradition lies in its pointing to the receding nature of community and its alleged result of decreasing responsiveness to individual need.

Sometimes "cultures" are thought to be rather simple affairs in which people share the same values and practices and ways of making meaning of their worlds. I want to suggest that a culture can to some extent consist of commonly recognized values, but

33. Brad Shore, "Human Ambivalence and the Structuring of Moral Values," *Ethos* 18 (1990): 165–79.

that these values provide a counterpoint to one another. The identity of a culture is in part defined by which values are the most salient and which ones serve as counterpoints to others. A shared culture just is this dynamic configuration of values, but the configuration typically leaves a significant degree of openness and ambiguity in how conflicts between values are to be resolved. This is one important reason why moral ambivalence exists not only across different moral traditions but also within a single moral tradition. Values correspond to compelling human needs and derive much of their force from the satisfaction of those needs. But because human beings are many-sided and not necessarily harmonious wholes with respect to their needs, there will always be uncertainty and fluctuation as to how the needs and corresponding values are to be balanced against each other.

Cultures in part differ from one another to the extent that they provide at least partial value priorities. American culture, as I have suggested, contains both autonomy and communal themes. For example, civil liberties receive an autonomy-oriented interpretation when conceived as owed to people as individuals and are claimed against the larger society as protections against intrusive measures to advance the public interest. Civil liberties also receive community-oriented interpretations when conceived as empowering protections enabling the individual to contribute to the governance of her society as an end in itself. Liberties under this interpretation are among those goods enabling people to be and perform as good citizens. However, the autonomy-oriented themes are more dominant in the United States when compared to many Asian societies. Japan is a society in which both themes are present and in which the democratic tradition receives both autonomy-oriented and community-oriented traditions, but the latter are dominant compared to, say, the United States.

For example, Kenneth Winston has observed that police and prosecutors in Japan have the power to hold a suspect for interrogation for extended periods, in some instances up to twenty-three days, before filing charges. The exclusion of confessions obtained under such circumstances is very rare and virtually unheard-of in cases where a guilty person would go free as a result. Such practices are at odds with the right to silence embodied in the new constitution adopted by Japan after World War II, a constitution largely written by U.S. occupation forces. The actual powers granted to police and prosecutors reflect social norms that make confession the morally expected form of conduct, a moral duty owed to other citizens and an expectation shared by the public at large, as well as police, prosecutors, and judges.[34] Indeed, as John Haley observes, the vast majority of accused criminals in Japan confess, display repentance, negotiate for their victims' pardon, and submit to the mercy of the authorities.[35]

---

34. Kenneth Winston, "On the Ethics of Exporting Ethics: The Right to Silence in Japan and the U.S.," *Criminal Justice Ethics* 22 (2003): 6–7.

35. John Owen Haley, "Confession, Repentance and Absolution," in *Mediation and Criminal Justice: Victims, Offenders and Community*, ed. Martin Wright and Burt Galaway (London: Sage, 1989), 195. Quoted in Winston, "On the Ethics of Exporting Ethics," 5.

Another example of difference in relative priorities appears in the film *A Great Wall*, in which a Chinese American takes his family to Beijing to visit his sister and her family. The two young people in this meeting of families, his son and her daughter, cross the cultural divide most easily, and the young woman learns the American concept of privacy, which she applies with indignation to her mother's opening and reading her mail before handing it to her. The mother reacts with incomprehension: why should she need permission to learn what is going on with her daughter? In a small and intimate way, this incident illustrates a conception of personal autonomy coming into collision with a conception of life as social relationship and shared fate. Immigrant families who have parents rooted in the mother culture and offspring rooted in a new home culture often experience a kind of ambivalence about what is gained and what is lost when new ways replace the old.

1.6 HOW MORAL AMBIVALENCE MAKES TROUBLE FOR UNIVERSALISM

Conflicts exhibiting moral ambivalence clearly constitute a challenge for universalist moral theories asserting a single true morality. The dominant response in universalist theory has rested on denying the underlying phenomenon of moral value pluralism. Much of the work of Kantians and utilitarians, for example, is aimed at showing that the apparently irreducible and potentially conflicting sources of value are reducible to one source, whether it be the goal of promoting the greatest happiness or respect for rational natures. Consider one such conflict. Philosophers working from the impersonal perspective, from which one's actions must be rooted in the recognition that no person is more or less morally important than other persons, have tried to subsume special duties under that perspective. They argue that impersonal values are best fulfilled through the recognition and performance of these obligations.

Peter Railton attempts to subsume special obligations to family under a sophisticated act consequentialism by arguing that certain goods are reliably attainable only if people have certain enduring motivational patterns, traits, or commitments (such as those that involve acting for the good of loved ones) that sometimes override acting for the best. He gives the example of a commuting couple; the husband must decide whether to make an unscheduled trip to see his wife, who is feeling depressed. He could donate extra money to Oxfam if he does not go and thereby produce better consequences overall. The act consequentialist can allow that the husband perhaps should have the kind of character that would move him to such actions as making the trip. His overall contribution to human welfare would be less in the end if he were less devoted to his wife, "perhaps because he would become more cynical and self-centered."[36] Furthermore, these impersonal

---

36. Peter Railton, "Alienation, Consequentialism and Morality," *Philosophy and Public Affairs* 13 (1984): 134–71, 159.

goods include a plurality of mutually irreducible goods such as knowledge, friendship, solidarity, and autonomy.

Such attempted reductions of the different sources of value to one supreme source must stand examination against the kind of justifications we are strongly inclined to give for different value claims. Persuasive considerations need to be given for a theory that requires radical revision of our conceptions of what seems most morally important to us. In this spirit, it is relevant to ask how many of us would say that the rightness of devoting more of our attention and resources to loved ones should depend on the long-term consequences of such devotion to human welfare in general. How many of us really think that the rightness of taking special care of our children should depend on the making the case that it's really better for everyone if we do such things? And how many of us think that the *reason* it is right to care for our children is that it is part of a general arrangement that promotes welfare? While Railton's theory recognizes these things as irreducible goods, the rightness of claiming them for ourselves depends on whether doing so ultimately promotes such goods for all. But the claims generated by our moral ties to family members and particular others such as friends seem more basic than this. Their pull on us seems independent of their justifiability by reference to the goal of promoting impersonal good. On the other hand, when we take the impersonal perspective and are not specially concerned to show how that perspective justifies every moral value we hold dear, we see as unjustifiable many of the mundane acts of care and devotion we direct to particular others. The unjustifiability emerges when we compare what is at stake for those close to us and what is at stake for millions of people elsewhere in the world: life itself, and some small measure of human dignity in the face of brutality and degradation.[37] Denials of moral value pluralism run up against the widespread sense that different value claims often require different kinds of justification.

More generally, Railton's theory connects moral rightness with what would be rationally approved were the interests (naturalistically conceived) of all potentially affected individuals counted equally under circumstances of full (and perhaps vivid) information.[38] The doubts just raised about his approach to special duties suggest that utility is just one among competing values and that we are ambivalent about its ranking with respect to the others. Furthermore, to generate a contentful morality this view needs to assume some controversial notion of human well-being or welfare, and this notion would correspond to some specific priority set among conflicting moral values. It is no accident, I think, that monistic theories contribute very little to the resolution of genuinely controversial normative issues. They give either

---

37. Peter Singer articulates an eloquent and lucid defense of this point of view in "Famine, Affluence, and Morality," *Philosophy and Public Affairs* 1 (1972): 229–43.

38. An example of this view is Peter Railton's, in "Moral Realism," *Philosophical Review* 95 (1986): 163–207.

vague advice that fails to favor one side or another or advice that is reasonably rejected outright by those who do not already accept a rather controversial interpretation of the alleged supreme value.

Other attempts to deal with this conflict stop short of assuming moral value monism and attempt to show that definite priorities between the plural values can be established. Samuel Scheffler has distinguished two moral ideals that correspond to this conflict. On the one hand, the "Ideal of Humanity" carves out a space for us to live our own lives and makes only a moderate demand on us to meet the needs of others. On the other hand, the "Ideal of Purity" requires us to act from the impersonal viewpoint from which our lives are no more important than the lives of other human beings. Both ideals, Scheffler grants, have roots in our morality, but Humanity has "broader and deeper" roots. He argues that the Ideal of Humanity better fits our belief in the legitimacy of a space in which to live our own lives. Very rarely, he claims, does anyone question our right to have this space, except when we purchase luxuries that could have gone to meet desperate need. Further, he argues, living our own lives generates personal relationships that in turn generate special duties, so it is not just that Humanity carves out a space of moral permission for the individual. That space of permission inevitably generates its own duties. Finally, Scheffler argues that the Ideal of Humanity can accommodate to some extent the Ideal of Purity, but not the other way around. From the perspective defined by the former, one can regard the latter as a supererogatory ideal.[39]

However, Scheffler cannot claim both that our special duties weigh in favor of the Ideal of Humanity *and* that we can view Purity as supererogatory. If, on the one hand, our special duties can override all other duties we have (for example, if the duty to care for our children well really does override duties we might have that require devoting most of our resources to the care of many other children in the world in desperate need) then Purity cannot be supererogatory.[40] On the other hand, if our impersonal duties to others override our special duties to particular people, then the primacy of Humanity appears implausible. Furthermore, people *do* question our right to live our own lives, and not just when our purchase of luxuries is in question. We help ourselves to goods that are hardly essential to human life, or even to a decent minimum, and some have questioned whether we ought to do so when others are in desperate need.[41] We in fact should expect such questioning in a moral tradition with deep roots in early Christianity, with its radical challenge to material comfort and to partiality.

However, Scheffler is right to resist giving priority to the Ideal of Purity. Such an option would conflict with the facts that he points out: that we do believe in a space

---

39. Samuel Scheffler, *Human Morality* (New York: Oxford University Press, 1992).

40. In fact, Scheffler provides a subtle discussion of such possible conflicts in "Families, Nations and Strangers" and "Relationships and Responsibilities," both in *Boundaries and Allegiances: Problems of Justice and Responsibility in Liberal Thought* (Oxford: Oxford University Press, 2001).

41. For example, Railton in "Alienation, Consequentialism and Morality," and Singer in "Famine, Affluence, and Morality."

for people to live their own lives; and that living in such a space generates special duties. The problem is that our tradition contains both strains of thought and there seems no compelling, deeper rationale for subordinating one to the other. There is, I believe, no determinate ranking within our tradition that orders these two values. On some occasions we do think there is a right answer as to how a conflict should be resolved, and we are pretty confident about what that answer is. However, we encounter troubling ambivalence often enough that theoretical attempts to provide some general resolution look unpersuasive.

Consider Richard Boyd's view that some sort of balance among plural values is at the center of the truth conditions of moral judgments.[42] The problem lies in supporting the claim that *balance* between competing values is what the moralities of all societies and cultures *are after*. If the maximization of some values is incompatible with the maximization of other values, then some selection of values to be emphasized must be made, unless the idea is that we somehow strive to moderately satisfy all values. Even if that were possible, it seems unlikely that all societies and cultures are aiming at *that*, and not at all obvious that they *should*.

So far, I have discussed views denying moral ambivalence through asserting general priorities among values. The assumption of such an approach is that if there are resolutions to be found for conflicts between values in particular cases, these resolutions can be derived from general principles that assert priorities among values over a significant range of cases. This emphasis on deriving conclusions about particular cases from general principles represents a dominant trend in modern moral philosophy. For all their differences, the Kantian and the utilitarian both conceive ethical reasoning to be governed from the top down by the most general and abstract principles. In what I have elsewhere called "top-down reasoning," ethical judgments get deduced from general principles or at least validated by their consistency with such principles, never the other way around.[43] While Kant's categorical imperative does not entail substantive and specific maxims of action, acting according to such maxims is only morally permissible when they are consistent with the categorical imperative, which applies to all rational beings a priori in the conception of pure practical reason.[44] For John Stuart Mill, specific moral judgments are deduced from more general

---

42. See Richard Boyd, "How to Be a Moral Realist," in *Essays on Moral Realism*, ed. Geoffrey Sayre-McCord (Ithaca: Cornell University Press, 1988), 181–228. Boyd's view is a sort of consequentialism like Railton's, but he assumes that what is to be promoted is a "homeostatic cluster" of goods such as love and friendship, autonomy, and intellectual and artistic appreciation and expression. By calling them homeostatic, he means that they are mutually supporting, at least in moderation. See "How to Be a Moral Realist," 203.

43. See David B. Wong, "Crossing Cultures in Moral Psychology," *Philosophy Today* 3 (2002): 7–10, and "Reasons and Analogical Reasoning in Mengzi," in *Essays on the Moral Philosophy of Mengzi*, ed. Xiusheng Liu and Philip J. Ivanhoe (Indianapolis: Hackett, 2002), 187–220.

44. Immanuel Kant, preface of the *Groundwork of the Metaphysics of Morals*, ed. Thomas E. Hill Jr. and trans. Arnulf Zweig (New York: Oxford University Press, 2003).

goals, and ultimately the most general goal of advancing social utility. The direction of ethical justification runs from general goals to particular judgments.[45]

Recently, a renewed interest in particularism has emerged in response to perceived shortcomings of the top-down models. Particularists of various theoretical persuasions share the view that moral judgments about particular cases are not primarily derived from general principles. Many particularists hark back to the Aristotelian notion of a *phronesis* or practical wisdom that depends significantly on knowledge of particulars acquired through experience. Good moral judgment, they argue, is more akin to good perception than it is to deduction from the right principles. John McDowell, one influential representative of this view, holds that we perceive irreducibly moral properties and requirements, as well as the priorities among them when they imply different actions.[46] To say that moral properties or requirements are irreducible is not to deny that one perceives nonmoral aspects of a given situation as morally salient, but following Aristotle, McDowell argues that articulable rules cannot capture the moral sensibility of a person of good moral character.

The idea that we simply perceive moral properties or requirements is most compelling when perceptions involve an unproblematic application of a "thick" ethical concept, to use Bernard Williams's phrase.[47] We apply such concepts as being kind and being courageous in virtue of complex sets of factual considerations. They are not prescriptive labels we can paste onto anything we like. It may seem that in applying these concepts we refer to properties that supervene on these factual considerations. It may seem plausible, when reflecting on a situation and concluding that kindness is required, that this requirement is really something we perceive in the situation.

However, serious conflict between important ethical considerations in a given situation can create the kind of moral ambivalence I have described. While I have considerable sympathy for particularism, as shall become evident later in this book, it remains unclear how it can help us deal with moral ambivalence. One might argue that in cases of conflict of ethical considerations there is a correct priority that can be perceived by someone with sufficient moral experience and whose vision is unclouded by passion or self-interest. But the ways in which priorities between conflicting values are systematically different across societies and cultures demand some deeper explanation. Of course one may claim that whole societies and cultures have made fundamental mistakes in setting their priorities, but moral ambivalence problematizes attempts to say which priorities are the mistakes.

45. John Stuart Mill, *Utilitarianism*, 4th (University of Toronto) ed. (Longmans, Green, Reader, and Dyer, 1871), 205.

46. John McDowell has formulated a formidable, contemporary version of such realism in articles such as "Virtue and Reason," *Monist* 62 (1979): 331–50; see also Mark Platts, *Ways of Meaning* (London: Routledge and Kegan Paul, 1979); and David McNaughton, *Moral Vision: An Introduction to Ethics* (Oxford: Blackwell, 1988), chap. 5.

47. *Ethics and the Limits of Philosophy* (Cambridge, Mass.: Harvard University Press, 1985), 129.

2

Pluralistic Relativism

I have argued for the necessity of accounting for moral value pluralism and moral ambivalence. I have further argued that these features of moral life make problems for universalism. In this chapter, I give an accounting of them within a naturalistic framework, leading to the conclusion of pluralistic relativism. The first task is to explain what I mean by a naturalistic approach.

2.1 DIFFERENT STRANDS OF NATURALISM

Naturalism is identifiable with a number of themes, only some of which are endorsed here. One very general root sense of naturalism often opposes belief in the supernatural—that which exists beyond nature and is not subject to nature's laws. A related sense of naturalism stands opposed to various forms of ontological dualism between the inanimate and nonhuman "lower" forms of life (rocks, trees, bugs, dogs and cats) on the one hand and human and "higher" nonhuman forms of life (spirits, ghosts, gods, God). Cartesian dualism between thinking and extended substance provides a paradigm of nonnaturalism in this sense. The root sense of naturalism that is opposed to the supernatural and the ontologically nonnatural is a belief in one single natural world, in which human beings and other purportedly radically different beings must be situated. This root sense of a single world (compatible with the existence of multiple perspectives of belief on that world) is accepted here.

More specific forms of naturalism derive from the root sense. The root sense is often interpreted as a view about what kinds of things there are. In line with the idea of

In my discussion of Hume, I have especially benefited from discussions with Aaron Garrett and Knud Haakonssen. I am indebted to Charles Griswold Jr. for bringing to my attention the similarity between Protagoras's account of morality and the one defended here.

one natural world, the view is that there is just one basic kind of thing. Most often, naturalism as a substantive, ontological view holds that there are only physical things. But it is not at all clear that such a view is true. Its potential conflict with the recognition of mathematical properties or entities, for example, is well discussed and not satisfactorily resolved, at least in favor of physicalistic naturalism. Mathematics resists reduction to logical or conceptual truths or truths about physical things. Moreover, twentieth- and twenty-first-century physics has destabilized our intuitively familiar notions of what a physical thing is like, leaving us nothing that can take the place of the "physical object" talk we employ in everyday life, and rendering unclear the contrast between the physical and nonphysical. If there is just one basic kind of thing, it has become unclear what kind that is.

The more specific naturalistic themes endorsed here are not substantive, ontological views, but are rather methodological[1] in character. One such methodological theme holds that philosophy should not employ a distinctive, a priori method for yielding substantive truths shielded from empirical testing. Another such theme holds that there is no sharp boundary between epistemology and the science of psychology. The two methodological strands of naturalism are related. Rejection of the a priori arises from the insight that powerful explanatory empirical theories have frequently overturned claims that seemed logically or conceptually true at the time. Consider for example the principle of sufficient reason, the Euclidean structure of space, or the restriction of mechanical interaction to local contact.[2]

The undermining of such claims by scientific theory does not rule out important and distinctive roles for claims founded on logical, mathematical, or conceptual analysis, but it does weigh against the idea that these claims can constitute self-evident, permanent foundations of knowledge. Jean Hampton holds that substantive, rather than methodological, naturalism is the more plausible version of naturalism, because the former but not the latter "accommodates the successful use of nonempirical methods of mathematics and logic within scientific practice."[3] However, methodological naturalism does not rule out the use of nonempirical methods, but rather insists that the deliverances of such methods cannot be taken as self-evident or permanent. Consider Philip Kitcher's point that the processes by which logicians and mathematicians apprehend axioms and construct proofs might not fulfill knowledge-generating functions against a "background of experiences that explicitly called their reliability into question."[4]

---

1. The distinction between substantive and methodological naturalism is articulated by Peter Railton, "Naturalism and Prescriptivity," *Social Philosophy and Policy* 7 (1989): 155–7.
2. Railton, "Naturalism and Prescriptivity," 156.
3. Jean Hampton, *The Authority of Reason*, ed. Richard Healey (Cambridge: Cambridge University Press, 1998), 21.
4. Philip Kitcher, "The Naturalists Return," *Philosophical Review* 101 (1992): 72.

Methodological naturalism is compatible with the sort of a priori status for mathematics defended by Michael Friedman.[5] He grants that even firm mathematical theories are revisable and that particular mathematical frameworks such as that presupposed by Newtonian physics, once regarded as unshakeable, have been superseded. However, he points out that a mathematical framework may still perform a distinctive constitutive function that makes possible the rigorous formulation and confirmation of empirical scientific theories. For example, the mathematical framework presupposed by Newtonian physics was replaced by the Kleinian theory of transformation groups and the Riemannian theory of manifolds, as these were presupposed by Einstein's general theory of relativity. As presuppositions of this theory, this new mathematical framework faced the Quinean "tribunal of experience," but not in the same manner as Einstein's particular field equations governing the relationship of mass-energy density and space-time curvature. Rather, the Riemannian and Kleinian framework made possible the modern conception of space-time, without which Einstein's theory could not be formulated and subjected to rigorous empirical test. A reasonable naturalism, in my view, need not dispute this sort of distinctive role, as long as a more indirect revisability in the face of experience is recognized even for "constitutive" mathematical frameworks.

Even if some claim seems constitutive of our concept of rationality, the very concept of rationality is subject to change and variation across different communities of inquiry. Rather than conceiving knowledge to rest simply on logical or conceptual truths, naturalists propose that it rests on its etiology, and consequently on psychological facts about the subject.[6] For example, perceptual knowledge depends on the right kind of relation between the knower and the facts known, and part of the task of epistemology is to specify what that relation is. Psychology offers an obvious contribution to that task.

Methodological naturalism also stems from the root naturalistic belief in one world. According to C. A. Hooker, the best science we have now tells us that we are situated in that one world as

> one evolved species among many inhabiting a world we did not make and only very imperfectly understand, finding our way about through the use of highly fallible sensory and motor capacities orchestrated by equally fallible theories we construct and are constantly forced to reconstruct as our experience extends

5. Michael Friedman, "Philosophical Naturalism," *Proceedings and Addresses of the American Philosophical Association* 71 (1997): 7–21.

6. See Kitcher, "Naturalists Return," 60. 'Causal' theories of knowledge have received influential formulations in the work of Alvin Goldman, *Epistemology and Cognition* (Cambridge, Mass.: Harvard University Press, 1986), and Fred Dretske, *Knowledge and the Flow of Information* (Cambridge, Mass.: Bradford Books, 1981).

across ever wider environmental conditions. From this point of view nothing is certain; cognition is as problematic as the world.[7]

Substantive and methodological naturalism are found together in Quine's seminal work, but I believe it best to embrace methodological naturalism as more open-minded and more expansive, while using it to evaluate the controversial hypotheses of substantive naturalism. It is more consistent with the fallibilism that follows from a view of ourselves as one species among many, learning more about the world as we continue probing it, and therefore not insisting on a fixed boundary around what there is. That boundary may need to be expanded in the course of inquiry, depending on what is needed to make sense of everything that is so in the world. Epistemic terms such as 'justification' are not necessarily eliminable in favor of or reducible to physical terms, any more than the vocabulary of, say, biology is necessarily eliminable in favor of or reducible to the vocabulary of chemistry or physics.[8]

It might be objected that methodological naturalism, as I interpret it, is *too* open-minded. Barry Stroud identifies the most plausible core doctrine of naturalism with a kind of open-mindedness, and then questions whether mere open-mindedness deserves to be labeled as a distinctive view.[9] Simply equated with open-mindedness, naturalism indeed seems trivial, until one recognizes how many philosophers have departed from it in the form of attempting to deliver certain foundations of knowledge and a priori truths. Methodological naturalism is anything but trivial in rejecting a priori methods of reasoning, the deliverances of which are taken to be self-evident and permanent. Even that which is the most intuitively self-evident may be called into question if the assumption of its truth renders us less able to account for certain empirical experiences. This goes for a priori formal logic. For example, C. A. Hooker points out the diversity of approach to the law of the excluded middle across classical, intuitionist, n-valued, relevance, supervaluation, and various quantum logics, and argues that there is no more hope of finding a foundational rule of inference than there is of discovering foundational evidence.[10]

The phenomenon of moral ambivalence, as described in the chapter 1, supplies reason to question whether there is a single true morality, even if the existence of such a morality seems self-evident to inquirers and their communities. Methodological

7. C. A. Hooker, *Reason, Regulation, and Realism: Toward a Regulatory Systems Theory of Reason and Evolutionary Epistemology* (Albany: State University of New York Press, 1995), 15. Hooker does not use the term 'methodological naturalism', but his version of naturalism seems to fit the definition, and the way the root sense of naturalism as belief in one single world and methodological naturalism are linked in his writing is especially instructive.

8. The analogy is found in Robert G. Meyers, "Naturalizing Epistemic Terms," in *Naturalism and Rationality*, ed. Newton Garver and Peter H. Hare (Buffalo: Prometheus Books, 1986), 142.

9. Barry Stroud, "The Charm of Naturalism," *Proceedings and Addresses of the American Philosophical Association* 70 (1995–96): 53.

10. Hooker, *Reason, Regulation, and Realism*, 23.

naturalism moves us further in the direction of questioning such self-evident claims toward seeking an explanation of moral ambivalence, rather than denying it whenever it conflicts with one's conception of the single true morality. In accordance with the idea that the a priori has often been overturned by empirically driven theories, an attempted explanation of moral ambivalence will make use of and cohere with well-supported scientific theories about human beings and our relation to the world.

Methodological naturalism would at least place under suspicion the view that moral properties or facts are sui generis—that they constitute an irreducible part of the fabric of the world. This is because it is unclear how such a view could account for moral ambivalence. Do supposedly reliable perceivers of such moral properties or facts arrive at clean and definitive resolutions of grave conflicts between values? If they do, how have those who disagree with these resolutions come to err in *their* perceptions? If these supposedly reliable perceivers arrive at uniquely correct resolutions to grave conflicts between special duties to family and duties to strangers in urgent need, for instance, the question is how they happen to have this accurate perception when others err. On the other hand, if there is no single correct resolution, it is unclear why we should buy into the idea of sui generis properties or facts.

John McDowell is concerned to address criticisms of such an account from a naturalistic viewpoint, so it would be appropriate here to discuss why I think he does not fully escape these criticisms and does not take seriously enough moral ambivalence. McDowell steers away from a "ghostly Platonism" when he suggests that moral properties depend for their existence on human sensibility in a way that is analogous to color properties being dependent on human sensibility.[11] Both kinds of properties are such as to elicit characteristic responses from human beings in virtue of their having certain sensibilities. As McDowell himself notes, however, there is an important disanalogy between moral and color properties. Color properties merely cause responses, while moral properties are such as to merit certain responses, such as admiration. The normative inheres in moral properties in a manner that undermines the analogy to color properties.

Simon Blackburn, in criticism of McDowell's sort of view, mentions other, important disanalogies between moral and color properties. For one thing, it is not a matter of incompetence in the ascription of color properties to fail to realize that they supervene on the primary qualities of objects, even though it is a matter of solid science that they do so supervene. By contrast, it would be criterial incompetence in moralizing to fail to realize that moral properties supervene on other properties (for example, that the wrongness of torturing a cat depends on the cat's being a sentient being who experiences pain and fear), even though there is no science that tells us of such supervenience. To mention another important disanalogy in the way that color

11. John McDowell, "Values and Secondary Qualities," in *Essays on Moral Realism*, ed. Geoffrey Sayre-McCord (Ithaca: Cornell University Press, 1988), 166–80.

properties are mind dependent and moral properties are not, Blackburn points out that that if human beings' color sensibilities were to change such that everything that previously looked blue instead looked red, the result would be the disappearance of all blue things; whereas if our moral sensibilities changed such that we all thought it permissible to maltreat animals, it would not be permissible, but rather our sensibilities would have degraded.[12]

In work that is subsequent to his theory of moral perception, McDowell has moved toward a discussion of moral properties not so much in analogy with color but rather in terms of the irreducibly normative, and in particular, reasons. He still is concerned to avoid a full-strength Platonism that puts human beings partly in nature and partly outside it.[13] The "space of reasons," the space of justifications and warrants, is not the realm governed by natural law but is still part of nature.[14] Aristotle, McDowell believes, held such a conception of nature, under which the rational demands of ethics are part of the "second nature" of human beings, acquired in the course of an ethical upbringing.[15]

I am sympathetic to certain aspects of McDowell's compromise between Platonism and naturalism: as will be discussed later, I too accept irreducible normativity of reasons, though not the irreducibility of *moral* reasons. I do not see, however, why merely asserting the idea of an ethical upbringing makes ethical demands any more a part of nature. Plato, no less than Aristotle, conceived an ethical upbringing to be crucial for proper initiation into the space of ethical reasons. McDowell's reticence about saying anything much more on the nature of ethical upbringing undermines any attempt to deal with moral ambivalence. As suggested earlier, positing reliable perception of sui generis moral properties (or reasons) may result in a flat denial of moral ambivalence and conflict.

Axel Honneth makes a similar point in arguing for the need to address serious differences in moral perception in a manner that goes beyond the "moral certainties of 'second nature'" to a more principled, reflexive examination of one's ethical upbringing that will bring one into a dialogue with those who have had somewhat different upbringings.[16] In responding to Honneth, McDowell writes that he is not persuaded by the idea of a "greater inclusiveness," on the grounds that including more claims will let in ones that "do not deserve to be respected."[17] But Honneth is not

12. Simon Blackburn, "Errors and the Phenomenology of Value," in *Essays in Quasi-Realism* (New York: Oxford University Press, 1993), 159–60.

13. John McDowell, *Mind and World* (Cambridge, Mass.: Harvard University Press, 1996).

14. McDowell, *Mind and World*, 4–5.

15. McDowell, *Mind and World*, 84.

16. Axel Honneth, "Between Hermeneutics and Hegelianism: McDowell and the Challenge of Moral Realism," in *Reading McDowell: On Mind and World*, ed. Nicholas H. Smith (London: Routledge, 2002), 262–3.

17. John McDowell, response to Axel Honneth, in *Reading McDowell*, 302.

suggesting all ethical claims to be deserving of equal consideration. The point is whether there are plausible and even compelling claims that are not given much consideration within one's own ethical upbringing. The point is whether one's ethical upbringing contains tensions between important values that remain partially unresolved, thereby suggesting to at least some of us the possibility of alternative and incompatible ways of resolving the tensions.

Perhaps, however, there could be a more inclusive version of McDowell's model. Suppose that reliable perceivers of sui generis moral properties do experience moral ambivalence, that they see grave and possible irresolvable conflicts between different moral properties. This is to preserve moral ambivalence, yes, but to leave the matter at the mere perception of ambivalence is to explain nothing as to why it exists. The mildness of McDowellian naturalism prevents any genuine explanation. A naturalistic approach of the kind defended here presses for such an explanation with the aim of gaining more clarity on our ambivalent moral situation. The path to more clarity, I shall suggest, leads to a refusal to treat moral properties as sui generis.[19]

2.2 METHODOLOGICAL NATURALISM APPLIED TO MORALITY

In accordance with the methodological naturalism adopted here, an account of morality need not reduce moral properties to natural properties such as the satisfaction of desire. Supplying a plausible explanation of the interactions with the world that supply moral knowledge or a plausible explanation of morality itself does not necessarily require re-duction. Gilbert Harman has pointed out that prescriptivist or emotivist accounts of moral terms are perfectly consistent with a naturalistic account of morality even though they do not offer naturalistic *definitions* of moral terms.[18] Also consistent with a natu-ralistic account are analyses of moral terms that are defended here—those employing concepts of standards or norms established to further social cooperation. The very concept of a standard or norm may not be susceptible to naturalistic definition in terms of nonnormative properties, and such a possibility is not problematic from the standpoint of methodological naturalism. Scientific activity, after all, involves evaluation of theories and data by reference to scientific standards and norms. Another concept crucial to the vocabulary of evaluation is that of reason, as in the reasons for and against accepting a hypothesis or reasons for and against a desire or action. Thomas Scanlon holds, correctly I think, that the concept of a reason will yield to no noncircular definition. One can only associate it with phrases such as "a consideration that counts in favor of."[19]

18. Gilbert Harman, "Is There a Single True Morality?" in *Explaining Value and Other Essays in Moral Philosophy* (Oxford: Clarendon Press, 2000), 80.

19. Thomas M. Scanlon, *What We Owe to Each Other* (Cambridge, Mass.: Harvard University Press, 1998), 17.

The language of evaluation might resist naturalistic reduction because it emerges from the internal and subjective viewpoint of human beings, and such a subjective viewpoint may not be fully translatable into physicalistic terms. At least, it might not be fully translatable by *us* because of limitations in the cognitive capacities that go into constituting our subjective viewpoint on the world, including limitations on the language we use to refer to the physical and the subjective. Even if it were true that the language we use to express our subjective viewpoint on the world were irreducible to physicalistic language (however that language evolves with the strange developments on the frontiers of physics and neuroscience), it would not necessarily contradict the claim that whatever is truly described within the language of evaluation is also given in a complete physical description of the world at the relevant time. It is just that we might not be able to say how the one kind of report maps onto the other. As Thomas Nagel has observed, we have some reason to believe that sensations are physical processes without being in a position to explain how a physical process accounts for the phenomenological feel of a sensation.[20] Perhaps we may never get into a position to provide such an explanation, but we may nevertheless hold that sensations are physical processes because no other hypothesis seems as reasonable in light of the intimate correlation between sensations and physical events within and without our bodies. Analogously, we might grant the possibility that the language of evaluation is irreducible to nonevaluative terms, but nevertheless hold that whatever can be truly reported in that language is given in a complete physicalistic description of the world. A naturalistic account of morality advocated here, then, need not be an eliminative or reductive account given in purely nonevaluative terms. In fact, I suspect that its basic terms will retain on the ground level the language of standards, norms, and reasons.

Then how can we avoid the explanatory dead end of treating moral properties as sui generis? My strategy is to explain moral evaluation through evaluative terms that are *not irreducibly moral though still evaluative and normative in character.* The idea is to seek an explanation of morality in terms of standards and reasons as these relate to human needs, desires, and purposes. Morality, as conceived here, arises from a particular kind of evaluation. Such an explanation, in accordance with methodological naturalism, will be responsive to our best theories of human beings. It will not rely on a priori moral truths taken as self-evident and foundational or as derived purely from logical or conceptual analysis.

By taking such a starting point, I do not mean to imply that naturalistic accounts can be seen from the outset as the only legitimate accounts of morality. Such an assumption may constitute a form of "scientism," as John McDowell has argued.[21] It is neither incoherent nor silly for others to deny that moral knowledge is wholly

---

20. Thomas Nagel, "What Is It Like to Be a Bat?" in *Mortal Questions* (Cambridge: Cambridge University Press, 1979), 178.

21. See John McDowell, "Virtue and Reason," *Monist* 62 (1979): 331–50.

explicable in terms of, say, social arrangements and their relation to human needs, desires, and purposes. Or as Thomas Nagel has argued, to assume that what is real is only what has to be included in the best causal theory of the world is to beg the question against the view that there are irreducible moral truths that are somehow causally inert with respect to the rest of the world.[22] Pluralistic relativism is presented here as one line of explanation, in the spirit of showing how far one can go with a naturalistic approach.[23] The decision between a naturalistic and nonnaturalistic account of morality is not a simple one, and it will depend at least in part on comparing the explanatory powers of each kind of theory. For example, it must be determined how well rival accounts accord with important features of moral discourse and argument, and if there is some degree of ill-fit with those features, an account must provide some plausible story as to why there is that lack of fit that is consistent with its central claims.

2.3 BUILDING ON PREVIOUS ACCOUNTS OF MORALITY AS SOCIAL CONSTRUCTION: PROTAGORAS AND XUNZI

In chapter 1, I explained why moral ambivalence makes trouble for universalist theories. A naturalistic approach to morality can ground in a pretty clear way a relativistic theory of morality that explains moral ambivalence better than universalist theories can. On the naturalistic conception defended here, morality is partly a system of norms and reasons that human beings have developed in order to work and to live together. One of its functions is to regulate cooperation, conflicts of interest, and the division of labor and to specify the conditions under which some people have authority over others with respect to cooperative activities.

A long tradition lies behind this account of morality as partly a social invention. Plato gives Protagoras the role of articulating such an account. In the course of defending his thesis that virtue is teachable, Protagoras tells a myth about the creation of human beings. Human beings needed to gather together in cities for their self-preservation against the beasts. Because they couldn't naturally govern their relations to one another, Zeus gave them the virtues of reverence and justice to order their cities and serve as the bonds of friendship and conciliation. All human beings had to receive these virtues because cities could not survive if only a few possessed them. The argument for the teachability of virtue is that human beings and their cities could not have survived without their all having some degree of receptivity to moral norms.

In the ancient Chinese tradition, the philosopher Xunzi (Hsün Tzu) articulated an account of morality as social invention. Morality for Xunzi includes not only

22. Thomas Nagel, *The View from Nowhere* (New York: Oxford University Press, 1987), 144.

23. Peter Railton presents his naturalism in a similar light in "Naturalism and Prescriptivity," *Social Philosophy and Policy* 7 (1989): 151–74.

conceptions of virtues such as care for others (*ren*) and reliably performing the right action (*yi*) but also dedication to the correct performance of rituals (*li*) that included ceremonies such as those honoring ancestors, burial and mourning, respectful and appropriate relations between parents and children, and in later expansions of its meaning, respectful and appropriate relations between people occupying various social roles.

On Xunzi's genealogy of morality, the ancient sage-kings saw the need to control the inborn tendency of human beings to seek gain, which consists in satisfying desires of the ear and eye. The fact that such desires have no natural limit makes for chaos when combined with scarcity of resources. The sage-kings invented within ritual and moral principles in order to apportion things, to nurture the desires of men, and to supply the means for their satisfaction.[24]

Those familiar with the Western tradition are often struck by Xunzi's anticipation of Hobbes's story of why human beings need to escape from the state of nature. However, Xunzi's story differs from that of Hobbes in his recounting of what happens after human beings recognize the need to restrain their search for satisfaction of desire. They see the need not only to restrain their behavior but also to transform their very characters through ritual, music, and the virtue of acting from a reliable sense of what is right.[25] Xunzi's conception of the requirements of enlightened self-interest implies not only that following morality is best for everyone concerned but also that love of morality should be cultivated for its own sake. And indeed, he rapturously praises the ennobling effects on human desire of observing the rites. On David Nivison's interpretation of Xunzi, the feelings given form through the rituals are "fitting and beautiful" and essential to one's full humanity:

> The vision is that the human world, centrally man's world of institutions, ideals, and norms, is the flowering of what is most fundamental in the entire world of nature, and is deserving of just that savoring, admiration, and reverence that the Taoist accords to his tao, the order of nature and all its manifestations; and like the Taoist, Hsün Tzu focusses his attitude of wonder on both the whole of his world and on its detail; but [un]like the Taoist, he does not exclude social and religious forms as being at best non-obstacles to realization; on the contrary they are the very substance of it.[26]

There is a line of thought in the chapter on ritual that helps to explain how realizing one's full humanity—coming to dwell in one's true home—requires ethical engagement.

24. *Xunzi*, ed. and trans. John Knoblock (Changsha, Hunan: Hunan's People's, 1999), bk. 19.1, vol. 2, 601.

25. This comparative point has been made by Bryan Van Norden, "Mengzi and Xunzi: Two Views of Human Agency," *International Philosophical Quarterly* 32 (1992): 161–84.

26. David Nivison, "Hsün Tzu and Chuang Tzu," in *Chinese Texts and Philosophical Contexts: Essays Dedicated to Angus C. Graham*, ed. Henry Rosemont Jr. (Lasalle, Ill.: Open Court, 1991), 139, 140.

Xunzi says there that the mourning rituals enable the expression of love for and grief and remembrance of lost parents. He suggests that love of one's own kind is natural to all creatures with awareness, and greatest among human beings. The three-year mourning period and sacrificial rites to deceased parents strengthen, refine, and direct the natural feelings of grief and remembrance. We can come to love ritual, despite our original insatiable desires for satisfaction, because ritual allows full expression of natural and deep human emotion. Indeed, Xunzi is quite insistent in claiming that the three-year mourning period, not longer, not shorter, is precisely the length of time appropriate to the grief human beings need to express. This is the line of reasoning, I suggest, that enables Xunzi "to see human customs, 'rites,' norms, as both products of human invention, and so 'conventional,' and yet as 'universal.'" As Nivison puts it, "they had to happen, come to be, in more or less the form they have, sooner or later; and the fact that we see they are humanmade does not insulate them from our commitment to them. Their 'artificiality' thus in no way renders them not really obligatory and normative."[27]

The Confucian ethic is essential to our humanity not only because it allows expression of natural feeling but also because it confers a needed order on the human psyche. This order replaces the original, self-destructive, and impulsive pursuit of natural desires for gain and sensual gratification while training and satisfying those natural desires that are more congenial to productive life in relationship to others.

Xunzi's genealogical story of morality contains two claims that also form the cornerstones of my own functional conception of morality. The first claim is that morality functions to promote beneficial social cooperation, not simply through requiring behavior that is cooperative and considerate of the interests of others but also through refining and giving expression to feelings and that make people promising partners in social cooperation. Xunzi is well known for his claim that human nature is bad, but this is not to be taken as the claim that human beings naturally and knowingly desire to do what is wrong, but rather the claim that human beings acting on impulse, independently of their intelligence and the cultural forms that they have devised through their intelligence, will act in ways that are harmful to others and ultimately to themselves even though they may gratify themselves in the short term.

Xunzi is not always clear in articulating his view of human nature, especially when he is concerned to emphasize his disagreements with Mencius, who famously claimed that human nature is good. When he is so concerned, Xunzi tends to focus solely on the self-interested and sensual desires of human nature. When he is concerned to explain how ritual and moral principle work on human nature, he refers to feelings such as love of one's own kind, feelings that seem be natural because ritual helps to strengthen and give expression to them. Both kinds of feelings, the kind Xunzi emphasizes when asserting the badness of human nature and the kind that is expressed

---

27. Nivison, "Hsün Tzu and Chuang Tzu," 141.

through ritual, are ultimately necessary for the kind of explanation Xunzi desires to provide for the role of morality in human life. Without the "bad" kind, he would not be able to explain how morality helps to promote social cooperation by restraining the feelings that can undermine cooperation. Without the kind that is expressed through ritual, he would not be able to explain how human beings could ever feel that they complete themselves through them in the way Nivison so eloquently describes.[28]

The second claim of Xunzi that I want to use in my own theory is that morality serves the function of promoting a psychological order within the individual, and not just between individuals who are cooperating with each other. Xunzi saw that the two functions of morality were interdependent. To promote social cooperation, one must make enough human beings who are sufficiently promising partners, and this requires that the jumble of natural human desires undergo transformation. Xunzi was not clear on whether he thought these natural desires were solely self-interested and sensual in nature (as he suggests in his chapter on the badness of human nature) or whether human nature is a mix of such desires along with feelings of concern for others (as he suggests in the chapter on ritual), but I believe that the most powerful version of this theory takes up the second possibility. Morality plays a role in producing a more coherent system of desires and feelings, strengthening the feelings of other-concern by affording them expression in respectful actions that are conducive to social cooperation. Morality strengthens, moreover, the compatibility between interests in self and interests in others by supporting systems of social cooperation that reward cooperators and punish violators of the norms.

Xunzi's idea that ritual and moral principle ennobles human nature indicates, however, that morality does more than restructuring human motivation for the sake of social cooperation. Some moral norms take the form of character ideals and conceptions of the good life, specifying what is worthwhile for the individual to become and to pursue, and such specification can go beyond what is required for social cooperation. This intrapersonal function of morality comprehends what has been called the "ethical," as opposed to what might be called the "narrowly moral."

Xunzi's recognition of the need to structure natural feelings and desires resonates with the anthropological conception of human beings as "self-completing" animals, to use Clifford Geertz's phrase.[29] On Geertz's view, our original equipment of natural drives is insufficient to give us a coherent practical orientation, and it is through the collective inventions of culture that we give ourselves a coherent set of "templates" for such an orientation. Cruder functionalist explanations of morality, such as Hobbes's,

28. I develop this argument in "Xunzi on Moral Motivation," in *Chinese Language, Thought, and Culture: Nivison and His Critics*, ed. Philip J. Ivanhoe (Chicago: Open Court, 1996), 202–23; reprinted in *Virtue, Nature and Moral Agency in the Xunzi*, ed. Jack Kline and P. J. Ivanhoe (Indianapolis: Hackett, 2000), 135–54.

29. Clifford Geertz, "Ideology as a Cultural System," in *The Interpretation of Cultures* (New York: Basic Books, 1973), 217–8.

rely solely on the idea that morality helps to change behavior for the sake of accomplishing its functions but leaves human psychology untouched. Xunzi recognized that a *stable* solution to the need to promote social cooperation requires that human psychology be shaped, that desires and feelings become moralized or embedded with moral norms and moral reasons for action. This point will become important later on for explaining what I shall call the "expressivist" dimension of morality.

In his story, exceptionally wise sage-kings played the role of the gods in Protagoras's story. They recognized that human beings tended toward self-destructive conflict because of their tendency to impulsively gratify urgent desires. The sage-kings devised ritual practices and norms of rightness not only to restrain impulsive action but also to retrain human nature itself so as to produce intrinsic motives to consider the interests of others and to act rightly by them. Here also appears the assumption that despite its natural liabilities, human nature is at least receptive to the inculcation of moral virtue.

I do not accept everything in Xunzi's genealogy of morality. To say that the sage-kings realized the need for something like a morality and accordingly invented it is more plausible than saying that Zeus gave morality to human beings, but implausible nevertheless. Sage-kings themselves seem to be the sort of human beings that are themselves a social achievement. Those who are capable of a reflective articulation and justification of a sophisticated set of moral values and norms and who moreover possess a firm commitment to these values and norms would have to emerge as the *outcome* of a long developmental process, rather than the *initiators*.

A more plausible scenario is that morality played a role in the biological and cultural evolution of humanity. Alongside their instincts for self-preservation, human beings developed capacities for sympathy and other capacities to feel and act in ways conducive to social cooperation because these capacities were also fitness enhancing. At the same time, if the human capacity for self-guidance through culture developed about the same time as these innate characteristics, human beings developed practices of social cooperation. Such practices need not have grown out of any sophisticated or self-conscious reflection.

2.4 THE CULTURAL EVOLUTION OF MORALITY

Later in the Western tradition, David Hume provides another naturalistic account of morality as social invention, without resorting to gods or sage-kings as the inventors. He retains the earlier themes that human beings have no secure place in nature except for the one they make through their social lives.[30] It takes but "slight experience" and "the least reflection" to lead human beings to make a convention with each other to

30. David Hume, *A Treatise of Human Nature*, ed. L. A. Selby-Bigge (Oxford: Oxford University Press, 1888), 2nd rev. ed., ed. P. H. Nidditch (New York: Oxford University Press, 1978), 485.

"bestow security on the possession" of external goods acquired through fortune and industry.[31] This elementary lesson is learned within the family, where "every parent, in order to preserve peace among his children, must establish the rule for the stability of possession."[32] Further, families naturally develop tribal loyalties and strong partialities against each other, and rules of justice are made to manage the friction between them.[33]

Though he is not always consistent on this matter, Hume's predominant view of how the conventions of justice are made is evolutionary, as opposed to rationalistic or contractarian, that is, that the rules are in some sense agreed upon by all members of a society. Hume's position is that the conventions grow out of practices and slowly increase in generality of scope. While these practices may gain widespread acceptance, there is no assumption that agreement to their "terms" is a condition of whatever normative force they have. As Knud Haakonssen points out, the overall thrust of Hume's discussion of justice certainly seems more consistent with the evolutionary account, and this is certainly the kind of account advocated here.[34]

In the spirit of the earlier constructivist accounts, contemporary game theory provides some conceptual apparatus for describing how conventions could develop out of practices that are mutually beneficial to their participants. Bryan Skyrms constructs some game-theoretic scenarios in which the players could eventually come to correlate in such a way that some begin acting on a particular strategy, in which others detect that they are doing so through observation of a number of instances, and in which each player is better off adopting that strategy if the others do so.[35] Such a scenario is of a "correlated equilibrium." Suppose, for example, that there are no traffic lights at an intersection. Two drivers meet at the intersection at the same time, going different directions. One sees the other on her right, while the other sees the former on her left. As far as the drivers are concerned, being on the right or being on the left is random, like the coin toss in the preceding example. One correlated equilibrium results from following the rule that the driver on the right goes first. In the United States this rule is taught in driving schools and handbooks; but suppose that no such rule is taught as standard practice and that some players simply start behaving according to this rule and that others detect that they are doing so. It is a correlated equilibrium, in the sense that they are better off following the rule if the other player follows it, too. The

---

31. Hume, *Treatise*, 492, 489.

32. Hume, *Treatise*, 492–3.

33. Hume, *Treatise*, 488–9.

34. Knud Haakonssen proposes a plausible and interesting interpretation as to why Hume got occasionally confused as to the nature of his own account. See *The Science of a Legislator: The Natural Jurisprudence of David Hume and Adam Smith* (Cambridge: Cambridge University Press, 1981), 20–5.

35. Bryan Skyrms, *Evolution of the Social Contract* (Cambridge: Cambridge University Press, 1996). I thank Alex Rosenberg for pointing out to me the relevance of Skyrms's work for my project, as well as some of the work in evolutionary theory on altruism that I discuss later in this chapter.

rule that the driver on the left goes first is another perfectly acceptable correlated equilibrium. The point is that one or the other coordinated equilibrium could become established within a population through the "players" learning and acquiring beliefs about what strategies the others are acting upon. This process need not involve an explicit contract in any sense, but only people adjusting their actions to the actions of others to produce mutually beneficial results. That equilibrium becomes a custom or convention that is learned by each new generation.

As practices get passed on, however, they may be articulated. Norms could be spelled out as to who is properly participating in them as opposed to those who were not. Since practices tend to vary over time and with the identities of the particular people performing them, questions were raised and sometimes answered as to what were acceptable forms of these practices. The articulation of the difference between acceptable and unacceptable practices perhaps led to the articulation of more general values and norms.

2.5 An Intrapersonal Function for Morality and Its Relation to the Interpersonal Coordination Function

The naturalistic account defended here holds that human beings complete themselves through evolving systems of moral norms and reasons that help make possible beneficial social cooperation. This does not mean that directly facilitating social cooperation is the only function of morality. Some moral norms take the form of character ideals and conceptions of the good life specifying what is worthwhile for the individual to become and to pursue. This intrapersonal function of morality comprehends what has been called the "ethical," as opposed to what might be called the "narrowly moral." Morality in the broader sense used here comprehends the ethical. This part of morality helps human beings to structure their lives together in a larger sense, that is, not just for the sake of coordinating with each other but also for the sake of coordination within themselves. Because the natural drives of human beings are diffuse and general, and because they are diverse and are liable to come into conflict with each other, there is a need for a shaping of these drives, and much of it comes from people telling each other just how these drives should be shaped and how internal conflicts should be regulated and resolved.

The interpersonal and intrapersonal functions of morality are necessarily related. It seems impossible to reflect on what kind of morality might adequately fulfill the interpersonal function without consideration of intrapersonal ideals. Even if a moral conception of right relations between people does not dictate a specific ideal of character or a specific set of ends, it will certainly limit the range of permissible ideals and sets of ends. From the other side, a moral conception of individual excellence of character will place limits on conceptions of justice and the right. Nevertheless, the intrapersonal function emerges from a distinct set of human desires to identify and to aspire to a way of being and living that is worthwhile and that can be recommended to or even required of others as deserving of their aspiration or at least admiration.

2.6 Constraints on the Adequacy of Constructed Moralities Deriving from the Intrapersonal Function

A distinctive feature of my naturalistic account is that it generates significant constraints on what could count as an adequate morality, given its functions and given human nature. Consider the intrapersonal function of morality that has to do with shaping character and specification of worthwhile lives. There are a limited number of goods that human beings seek, given their nature and potentialities. The satisfaction of their physical needs, the goods of intimacy, sociability, and social status and approval, perhaps the opportunity to discharge aggressive energy, "having some degree of variety and challenge in activities," and knowledge either of the physical world or of the human world are goods sought across many different cultures.[36] Morality is not *determined* by these deep human propensities, but if it is to serve an effective guide to action, it must be limited by these propensities. In identifying positive goods that human beings are to seek, it cannot identify something human beings have no propensity to seek.[37]

36. Barrington Moore Jr. suggests that aggression is a "human capacity which, if not instinctive, is aroused by such a variety of frustrations that it is bound to find expression somehow." See his *Injustice: The Social Bases of Obedience and Revolt* (White Plains, N.Y.: Sharpe, 1978), 7; quotation here is from 7.

37. This constraint is like Owen Flanagan's Principle of Minimal Psychological Realism: when constructing a moral theory or projecting a moral ideal, the character, decision processing, and behavior prescribed must be possible, or are perceived to be possible, for creatures like us. The clause "perceived to be possible" is meant to allow for ideals that might be realized not strictly by the present generation of moral agents but by distant descendants whose capabilities are made possible by a process of change initiated by the present generation. See Flanagan, *Varieties of Moral Personality: Ethics and Psychological Realism* (Cambridge, Mass.: Harvard University Press, 1991), 32.

In my version of such a constraint, I do not, at this point, mean to rule out perspectives from which an individual agent might *come to have* a propensity to seek out a certain good upon becoming persuaded that it really is a good. This issue involves the large issue of whether action must always be motivated by something we could broadly call a desire, as opposed to a belief. Those who take themselves to be Humean on this issue argue that where action appears motivated by belief there must always be some relevant accompanying desire that explains why the belief helps to motivate. For example, suppose I start reading poetry when a friend persuades me I have been missing something good. The Humean position is that I must have already have had a desire in order to be motivated by the belief that reading poetry is worthwhile, for example, the desire for some knowledge about the human condition I can only get from reading poetry. Those who oppose the Humean position would argue that I need not have any preexisting desire of this kind in order to become motivated by the belief that reading poetry is worthwhile. No position is taken on this issue here, though it will be discussed in chapter 7. At this point, I mean to be imposing a simple constraint on moralities that remains neutral on the Humean issue: moralities cannot require the pursuit of what human beings have shown no propensity to pursue, and I leave it open at this point just how it is that they come to have such propensities.

Indeed, moralities that effectively command allegiance to character ideals and conceptions of worthwhile lives answer to powerful human interests. Such interests often motivate behavior, even in the face of strong counter-motivations. They further manifest motivational power across a wide variety of cultures. Their frustration ramifies through individuals' lives and adversely affects their ability to achieve other highly valued ends. Further, we may have interests in things we do not desire in any ordinary sense (for example, may not be acknowledged by its possessor) though it is rooted in human nature and has motivational force because of that nature.

Garrett Thomson associates "interests" with that which underlies desire—its motivational force. The intuitive basis for such a distinction consists of all those cases (1) in which desire seems to shift from object to object but in which something associated with it—Thomson calls it motivational force—remains constant and in fact explains how the shifts are connected to each other; and (2) in which what seems to motivate a desire is not necessarily congruent with the object of desire. Consider a man who works hard in order to impress his friends. We might say that what he really wants is not so much praise but stable affection. He might not *desire* affection, because he might shun close ties, fearing rejection. He desires the kind of praise that comes from hard work and success, and he thinks that requires distancing himself from others. We might say, however, in interpreting his actions that he has an interest or a want for affection. The interest motivates the desire. Commanding character ideals and conceptions of worthwhile lives center on interests that are deeply rooted in human nature such that they can be identified as what human beings really want, that have powerful motivational force in overriding other interests, and whose satisfaction or frustration widely ramifies throughout a person's character and life.

2.7 How Constraints on the Adequacy of Moralities Follow from the Interpersonal Function

Consider the interpersonal function of promoting and regulating cooperative activity. My argument in this and the next two sections shall be that this function, when combined with recognition of features of human nature confirmed by some of the most currently plausible theories, generates significant constraints on what shape an adequate morality can take.

To explain how constraints on what could be a true morality follow from the functions of morality, let me consider a general objection to the procedure of determining what an adequate morality must be like if it is to promote the interpersonal function. It may be granted that moralities do as a matter of fact perform this function, and that some may perform them better than others. However, it may be objected that one cannot validly turn a sociological observation about what moralities do into a normative criterion for evaluating the adequacy of a given morality. How can the observation that, as a sociological matter of fact, moralities have the function of regulating and promoting social cooperation support the normative criterion that adequate moralities must contain duties that further this function? Am I not, the objection goes, trying to derive an 'ought' from an 'is'?

To explain why I am not doing this, let me introduce John Rawls's method of reflective equilibrium.[38] As summarized by Norman Daniels,

> the method of reflective equilibrium consists in working back and forth among our considered judgments (some say our "intuitions") about particular instances or cases, the principles or rules that we believe govern them, and the theoretical considerations that we believe bear on accepting these considered judgments, principles, or rules, revising any of these elements wherever necessary in order to achieve an acceptable coherence among them. The method succeeds and we achieve reflective equilibrium when we arrive at an acceptable coherence among these beliefs. An acceptable coherence requires that our beliefs not only be consistent with each other (a weak requirement), but that some of these beliefs provide support or provide a best explanation for others.[39]

I have been arguing that the conception of morality as fulfilling a function can play a role in achieving reflective equilibrium within various systems of moral beliefs to be found across different cultures.

Consider some of the most central moral beliefs likely to be found across different cultures: beliefs that specify the conditions for permissible killing of or aggression toward other human beings, beliefs about the right to assign and distribute the basic resources needed to sustain life, and beliefs that require reciprocation of good for good. There is a lot of variation in how these beliefs are filled in with specific content and in the nature of the particular restrictions and distributions, but a common point these beliefs could be said to serve is in fact the regulation and promotion of social cooperation. The principle that moralities should promote social cooperation organizes and systematizes these beliefs. Furthermore, the principle also fits with the phenomenon of moral ambivalence precisely because there can be different ways of structuring social cooperation that seem to satisfy the normative criterion equally well, setting aside judgments based on the values about which we experience moral ambivalence.

So I am not trying to derive an 'ought' from an 'is' but making a purely normative argument. I am proposing that the functionalist criterion is plausibly seen as providing an underlying justification for many of the firmest and widely shared moral beliefs.

---

38. See John Rawls, *A Theory of Justice*, 2nd ed. (Cambridge, Mass.: Harvard University Press, 1999).

39. Norman Daniels, "Reflective Equilibrium," in *The Stanford Encyclopedia of Philosophy*, last rev. April 28, 2003, available at http://plato.stanford.edu/archives/sum2003/entries/reflective-equilibrium/.

Moreover, I will be arguing in later sections that the criterion is consistent with many of the most troubling cases in which we tend to have ambivalent moral reactions or experience internal conflict over which is the right course. The justification of this criterion is purely within the "space of morally normative reasons," the space of moral justifications and warrants, to borrow the term that John McDowell has adapted from Wilfred Sellars.[40]

Though I do not seek to derive the normative from the descriptive, my account is "naturalistic" in another way: it seeks to show how moral norms and reasons play an intelligible role in human life; how they serve goals that a scientific understanding of human beings can justifiably attribute to them. As Xunzi and Hobbes point out, it is in each individual's narrow self-interest (interests in sensual gratification, the accumulation of material goods) to avoid the conflict and strife that results from everyone's acting on their natural impulses without restraint; it is in each individual's narrow self-interest to have a system of social cooperation in place; as Xunzi is also aware when he is not trying to emphasize his differences with Mencius, human nature has other-regarding natural impulses that can motivate adherence to the social invention of morality even when such adherence exacts a cost outweighing the benefits in terms of narrow self-interest. The latest research on human nature and social cooperation broadly confirms this picture while adding some depth and complexity. Some of this depth and complexity will surface in later sections of this chapter.

2.8 THE NECESSITY FOR A NORM OF RECIPROCITY

This section addresses the way that the strength of self-interest in human nature necessitates a norm of reciprocity in moralities that effectively perform the interpersonal function. Human nature is significantly plastic but at the same time determinate enough so as to make for better and worse ways of regulating cooperative activity. It contains very strong tendencies to prefer the satisfaction of self-interests when in conflict with interests of others, at least when self-interests are of roughly equal importance to those of the others. The claim here is not that self-interest is the only human motivation, just that it is a very strong one that constrains the form that can be taken by successful cooperative activity. Consider that some form of reciprocity is a norm for all cultures we know, where reciprocity is conceived as a fitting and proportional return of good for good.[41] Its universality suggests that preference for one's

---

40. McDowell, *Mind and World*; Wilfred Sellars, "Empiricism and the Philosophy of Mind," in *The Foundations of Science and the Concepts of Psychoanalysis*, Minnesota Studies in the Philosophy of Science, vol. 1, ed. H. Feigl and M. Scriven (Minneapolis: University of Minnesota Press, 1956), 127–96.

41. Of course, the specific forms of reciprocity, and what is counted as fitting and proportional, vary widely.

own interests plays a significant role in human cooperative activity. Reciprocation for the help that any human being needs, if it is a general feature of social interaction, reinforces helping behavior. The fact that it is a powerful element in sustaining the help we need suggests the strength of self-interest as a human motivation. And as Lawrence Becker has observed, *not* reciprocating, if it were a general feature of social interaction, would quite likely extinguish helping behavior.[42]

If one's help is not reciprocated in interactions with a particular person, that might very well lead to one's ceasing to help that particular person, which suggests another reason for the importance of reciprocity in facilitating human social cooperation. It is not just that reciprocation from the person one helps generally reinforces one's helping that person. It is also that one's ceasing to help in response to that person's failure to reciprocate generally acts as a negative reinforcement against such failure. One's cessation serves as a kind of "punishment" for failure to reciprocate.

Some theorists have held that under certain conditions, simple forms of reciprocal cooperation might evolve among purely self-interested individuals. This theme arose in research on so-called Prisoner's Dilemma games in which there are opportunities for cooperation or noncooperation with others. If the two players cooperate with one another, they mutually benefit, but each must consider the temptation of refusing to cooperate on the possibility that the other will cooperate, thus "free-riding" on the other's cooperation—reaping the rewards of the other's cooperation while paying none of the costs of cooperating. In the classical Prisoner's Dilemma, two burglars, Bob and Al, are captured near the scene of a burglary and are interrogated separately by the police. Each has to choose whether or not to confess and implicate the other. If neither man confesses (refusing to confess is the equivalent of "cooperating" with the other), then both will serve one year on a charge of carrying a concealed weapon. If each confesses and implicates the other, both will go to prison for ten years. However, if one burglar confesses and implicates the other, and the other burglar does not confess, the one who has collaborated with the police gets the free ride, while the other burglar will go to prison for twenty years on the maximum charge. In a one-shot playing of this game, the most self-interested rational strategy for each player turns out to be confessing ("defecting," or refusing to cooperate with the other player), even though the end result will be worse than the result of mutual cooperation.

The Prisoner's Dilemma illustrates a problem posed for individual rationality by certain opportunities for social cooperation. The circumstances are such that if

42. See R. Mark Isaac, Kenneth McCue, and Charles Plott, "Public Goods Provision in an Experimental Environment," *Journal of Public Economics* 26 (1985): 51–74. This study indicates that unless cooperation is reciprocated, it diminishes rapidly over time. See also Lawrence Becker, *Reciprocity* (London: Routledge and Kegan Paul, 1986), 90–1; also see 347–59 for an excellent bibliography of anthropological, sociological, and psychological works on the appearance of reciprocity in various cultures.

everyone cooperates everyone is better off than if everyone defects. However, no individual player can assume that everyone *will* act in the same way. Furthermore, each player upon reflection can see that if one cooperates and the others *don't*, then one ends up with the worst outcome for oneself. If one does not cooperate and others don't either, one still ends up with a better result. Noncooperation, therefore, seems the best strategy from the standpoint of each individual.

Axelrod and Hamilton surmised that this discouraging conclusion depended upon the one-shot nature of the game and asked what would happen in an iterated Prisoner's Dilemma, where each player faces every other player a certain number of times.[43] The feature of repeated plays better approximates interactions in relatively stable and small social groups where individuals will frequently encounter each other. A number of strategies are possible for players of the iterated game, such as always cooperate, never cooperate, and "tit for tat"—cooperate in the first game with any player and then in the next game with the same player do whatever she did the last time. When the dozen or so possible strategies are played on a computer a couple of hundred times, it turns out that tit for tat does best in providing its players with the largest total payoff at the end of the tournament. If one runs the tournament with the added feature of eliminating the least successful strategies after a certain number of rounds, then the victory for the tit for tat strategies is even clearer. Consider, then, that from the perspective of self-interested rationality, a strategy instantiating one form of reciprocity turns out to be the best over a series of repeated opportunities for cooperation between individuals.

Such a result prompted the sociobiologist Robert Trivers to propose that human beings evolved with genetic dispositions to engage in reciprocal exchange arrangements with others. The feature of the iterated game by which the least successful strategies are eliminated after a few rounds corresponds to those who lacked the genetic dispositions to reciprocate and who were thereby less reproductively fit. The eventual superiority of the tit for tat strategy supposedly corresponds to the spread of individuals with reciprocating genes throughout a population.[44]

Further research, however, has undermined the idea that a relatively specific form of reciprocal cooperation such as tit for tat is built into the human genetic program. For one thing, other strategies do better than tit for tat when the conditions of playing the Prisoner's Dilemma are varied. Consider when "noise" is introduced, that is, when players defect by mistake or are mistakenly perceived by the other player as defecting. Tit for tat would end cooperation when it seems that productive cooperation could resume if players were given an opportunity to "recover" from the mistake. "Generous"

43. Robert Axelrod and William D. Hamilton, "The Evolution of Cooperation," *Science* 211 (1981): 1390–6.

44. See Robert Trivers, "The Evolution of Reciprocal Altruism," *Quarterly Review of Biology* 46 (1971): 35–56. Trivers's label 'altruism' seems to this author to be highly misleading.

tit for tat has each player cooperate some of the time with others even if they defect.[45] "Contrite" tit for tat addresses the problem from the perspective of the player who initially defects. If the victimized player responds by defecting, the contrite strategy is to cooperate anyway, offering "contrition" for the initial defection.[46] Still another strategy, "Pavlov," operates on the philosophy, "If you were successful last time, repeat whatever you did; if not, switch your behavior." One cooperates unless on the previous move one was a sucker (i.e., one cooperated but the other defected) or the other player was a sucker. This strategy resembles tit for tat in encouraging reciprocal altruism, but it differs from tit for tat in more frequently taking advantage of other individuals, called 'suckers', who can be systematically victimized or exploited.[47] "Pavlov," then, does particularly well in populations of players that contain large numbers of suckers. Given the variation in the success of these various strategies under varying conditions, it seems unlikely that any single one could be genetically programmed into human beings. This makes sense given the cultural evidence. While reciprocity in a very general sense is the norm for human cultures, the specific form it takes varies a great deal across cultures.

Further research has yielded possible features of human nature that might have evolved to support the effectiveness of reciprocating dispositions. When real people play Prisoner's Dilemma games on a one-shot or a repeated basis, opportunities for face-to-face communication significantly raise the cooperation rate.[48] Perhaps one of the benefits of face-to-face communication is the increased opportunity to read facial expression and body language, allowing those inclined to cooperate a better opportunity to identify other cooperators and to avoid consistent defectors. Another factor cited by researchers in explaining the efficacy of face-to-face communication is that it helps to foster "we-group" feeling (a feeling of solidarity with other members, a preference for them over those outside the group).[49] Other experiments have demonstrated the ease with which "we-group" feelings are produced on the basis of

45. M. A. Nowak and K. Sigmund, "Tit-for-Tat in Heterogeneous Populations," *Nature* 355 (1992): 250–2.

46. R. Sugden, *The Economics of Rights, Co-operation and Welfare* (Oxford: Blackwell, 1986).

47. M. Nowak and K. Sigmund, "Strategy of Win-Stay, Loose-Shift That Outperforms Tit-for-Tat in the Prisoner's Dilemma Game," *Nature* 364 (1993): 56–8.

48. David Sally, "Conversation and Cooperation in Social Dilemmas: A Meta-Analysis of Experiments from 1958 to 1992," *Rationality and Society* 7 (1995): 58–92. Also see Elena Rocco and Massimo Warglien, "Computer Mediated Communication and the Emergence of 'Electronic Opportunism," rev. October 24, 1997, available at www.economia.unitn.it/publications. They report that subjects who had to reply on computerized communication did not achieve as high a rate in cooperation as those communicating on a face-to-face basis.

49. John M. Orbell, Alphons van de Kragt, and Robyn M. Dawes, "Explaining Discussion-Induced Cooperation," *Journal of Personality and Social Psychology* 54 (1988): 811–9; Elinor Ostrom and James Walker, "Neither Markets nor States: Linking Transformation Processes in Collective Action Arenas," in *Perspectives on Public Choice: A Handbook,* ed. Dennis C. Mueller (Cambridge: Cambridge University Press, 1997), 35–72.

apparently arbitrary ways of dividing people into groups.[50] It is quite possible that all these factors work mutually to reinforce one another in reciprocal cooperation, and they might have this effect even if there is no specific genetic disposition to reciprocate in a particular fashion. Indeed, the existence of these other factors helps to explain why some form of reciprocity might be the best strategy even if there is no such specific genetic disposition to reciprocate.

Constructivist accounts of morality often claim that the primary purpose for which morality is invented is to counteract the destructive effects of self-interest (for example, Hobbes) or the limitations on our sympathies for others (Warnock, Mackie).[51] The present discussion of the need for a norm of reciprocity implies a more complex functional picture that confirms the Xunist picture of morality as effecting a change in the structure of the human psychological economy. Moral norms need to take into account the strength of self-interest in order to accommodate that motivation and to encourage its integration with motivations that more directly lead to acting on behalf of others. Moralities, then, should not merely restrain actions from self-interest or encourage the development of opposing motivations, though they do these things. They should provide outlets for the expression of self-interest that can be consistent with the expression of other-directed motivations. The next section seeks to articulate this more general constraint on moralities that adequately perform the interpersonal function in the context of a partial theory of human nature.

2.9 CONSTRAINTS HAVING TO DO WITH THE NECESSARY TASK OF BALANCING SELF- AND OTHER-CONCERN

The argument for the importance of reciprocity based on the strength of self-interested motivation is consistent with affirming genuinely altruistic interests, in the sense of direct interests in the welfare of others that are not instrumentally derived from in-

---

50. H. Tajfel, "Experiments in Intergroup Discrimination," *Scientific American* 223 (1970): 96–102, brought a group of boys, who knew each other from school, into his laboratory. The boys were asked to estimate the number of dots flashed on a screen. Purportedly on the basis of their responses (but in fact randomly), the experimenter divided the boys into two groups: Half the boys were privately informed that they were "overestimators" and the other half that they were "underestimators." Then each boy was asked to specify how monetary rewards should be distributed to the other boys in the laboratory. Although their own reward was not in question, and although they did not know which boys belonged to their group, they gave more rewards to their own group than to the other group. A later experiment M. Billig and H. Tajfel, "Social Categorization and Similarity in Intergroup Behavior," *European Journal of Social Psychology* 3 (1973): 27–52, showed that it is not necessary to create a fictitious criterion for dividing up the groups; participants can explicitly be told that the group assignments are random and they will still favor their own group.

51. See Thomas Hobbes, *Leviathan*, pt. 2, chaps. 13–17; G. J. Warnock, *The Object of Morality* (London: Methuen, 1971); and J. L. Mackie, *Ethics: Inventing Right and Wrong* (London: Penguin, 1977), chap. 5.

terests in the self. In this section I review recent scientific and philosophical arguments for the existence of altruism, and I point out the need to make distinctions between significantly different forms of altruism. I argue that he interpersonal function of morality necessitates a balancing of self- and other-concern in its various forms.

Recent years have witnessed progress in explaining the existence of such interests even on evolutionary theory—a theory that might seem to portray all altruism as an illusion. Natural selection would appear to favor the evolution of creatures that look out for their own survival and not to act for the welfare of others at a cost to their own reproductive fitness. While the tit-for-tat or similar strategies might explain why purely self-interested individuals might in very small and stable groups opt for cooperation with each other, it does not do well experimentally even in somewhat larger groups where a small number of selfish individuals are capable of bringing cooperation to a halt.[52] Yet individuals do cooperate with one another in ways that can't be explained on the basis of purely self-interested calculation. Moreover, it is apparent that family members do act for the sake of each other at a significant cost to themselves, and the widely accepted hypotheses of inclusive fitness and kin selection have been forwarded to explain this phenomenon. These hypotheses add up to the idea that evolution favors maximization of reproductive fitness, not of individuals, but of their genes and their copies in kin. From the perspective of maximizing such "inclusive fitness," individuals who sacrifice themselves to save a sufficient number of relatives will be doing better than individuals who save themselves.[53]

Kin selection, however, is not directly a theory about the psychological motivations of individuals. Elliott Sober and David Sloan Wilson provide one way to fill in the gap.[54] They argue that direct concern for one's kin evolved because ultimate desires for the welfare of kin constitute the most efficient and reliable way of ensuring that individuals care for their kin. More controversially, Sober and Wilson defend the idea of group selection to explain cooperation and altruistic behavior between nonkin. The idea of group selection is that natural selection can operate not only on genes and individual organisms but also on hives, herds, and other aggregations of organisms, including groups and tribes of human beings.

Darwin himself (*The Descent of Man*) thought that natural selection sometimes operates on groups and not just individuals, so that in the case of human beings, a tribe with members willing to sacrifice for other members will prevail in competition with other tribes with no such members, or will do well in adverse natural circumstances, and will therefore gradually predominate among the human species. A problem for

52. See Robert Boyd and Peter J. Richerson, "The Evolution of Reciprocity in Sizable Groups," *Journal of Theoretical Biology* 132 (1988): 337–56.

53. See W. D. Hamilton, "The Genetical Evolution of Social Behavior," *Journal of Theoretical Biology* 7 (1964): 1–52.

54. Elliott Sober and David Sloan Wilson, in *Unto Others: The Evolution and Psychology of Unselfish Behavior* (Cambridge, Mass.: Harvard University Press, 1998).

Darwin's idea is that even in the group of altruists, there will almost certainly be a dissenting minority who refuse to make any sacrifice. If there is just one purely self-interested individual, prepared to exploit the altruism of the rest, then that individual seems more likely than they are to survive and have children. Each of these children will tend to inherit that person's selfish traits. After several generations of this natural selection, the "altruistic group" will be overrun by selfish individuals, and will be indistinguishable from the selfish group. In response to this problem, Sober and Wilson argue that altruism can evolve as long as an individual's cost is offset by benefits to his group.

A prime example they give is a desert leaf-cutting ant, *Acromyrmex versicolor*, which after a mating swarm forms new colonies with several females in each. Before the colony can get started, it needs to gather leaves on which to grow fungus to feed its offspring. In each such new colony, one of the females takes on the special risk of being a forager, and wanders off in search of leaves. This is good for the new colony, but the forager ant is much more likely to be eaten before she can have offspring. It's an instance, Sober and Wilson say, in which group selection is outweighing individual selection. And kin selection can't explain it since the ant queens are not related. Of course, ant queens within a colony may be competing against one another in other ways. Sober and Wilson do not quarrel with the idea of competition between individuals, but rather argue that it isn't the whole story of natural selection. Units of natural selection, in their theory, are nestled in one another like Chinese boxes. Genes compete with other genes within an animal; animals compete with other animals within a group; and groups compete with other groups; and megagroups made up of groups compete with other megagroups. To go back to the original problem raised for group selection, one reason that individuals who do have concern for others don't get wiped out by the purely self-interested in the evolutionary battle is that other-concerned individuals will find one another, forming successful groups.[55] This does not mean that a successful group with other-concerned individuals will contain only such individuals. It does mean that part of its success consists in minimizing the destructive impact of free-riding within the group so that it is successful in relation to competing groups. Such a hypothesis might be linked with complementary ones such as the hypothesis that people have more ability to read each other's intentions in face-to-face

---

55. A recent study suggests a possible mechanism by which human beings might be hard-wired for altruistic behavior: researchers who conducted magnetic resonance imaging on subjects playing Prisoner's Dilemma games found that those who cooperated with another human being displayed activation in parts of the brain associated with reward-seeking behavior. The researchers did not see comparable brain activity when the subject cooperated with a computer (thus eliminating the explanation that it was the monetary gain from cooperating that caused the rewarding brain activity). Roughly put, we might be hard-wired to feel good when we cooperate with other human beings. See James K. Rilling, David A. Gutman, Thorsten R. Zeh, Guiseppe Pagnoni, Gregory S. Berns, and Clinton D. Kilts, "A Neural Basis for Social Cooperation," *Neuron* 35 (2002): 395–405.

interactions, or hypotheses that posit innate tendencies supporting group solidarity, such as tendencies to ostracize or punish those deviating from a common behaviors within a group and the corresponding tendency to fear being ostracized.[56]

It must be noted that group selection theory is still controversial. In addition to kin selection, reciprocal altruism, and group selection, a fourth, alternative explanation is *sexual* selection of genuine concern for others as a sign of fitness. The underlying idea is that human ancestors were motivated to find mates with good genes. "Fitness indicators" indicate an animal's general health and well-being, which in turn indicate evolutionary fitness. Large, bright, many-eyed tails function as fitness indicators of peacocks for peahens, precisely because having such tails requires a lot of energy to grow, to preen, and to carry around. Unhealthy and unfit peacocks can't afford them, and that is why the cost reliably indicates the fitness of a peacock that has one. Surprisingly, sympathy and kindness can function as fitness indicators for human beings, again because of the potential costs to the individual bearing them. Of course, traits that are incompatible with altruism might also function as fitness indicators because of the cost they impose on their bearers, but the advantage of altruism is that it benefits the group containing its possessors in ways that other fitness indicators might not. For example, hunters who share meat with others in the group display fitness that attracts mates, but they also give their group an advantage over other groups whose individuals display fitness by, say, beating up their rivals.[57] Strikingly, David Buss found that "kindness" was the single most important feature desired in a sexual partner by both men and women in every one of the thirty-seven cultures he studied.[58]

Finally, it is quite possible that cultural selection also helps to explain altruistic behavior. That is, groups can be more or less successful in competition with others in virtue of shared cultural traits that distinguish them from the other groups, and what is selected in this competition is not genes but cultural traits such as ones that promote cooperation and altruism among group members. As in the story of natural group selection, traits are replicated because they enable their possessor groups to be more successful, but the manner of reproduction is not biological but cultural transmission. Of course, the way that cultural traits come to be commonly shared by members of a group will depend on individual traits that do have a genetic basis. Boyd and Richerson, for example, argue that groups acquire common cultural traits through tendencies to imitate the most common traits or ones possessed by the most

56. The tendency of a majority within a group to collectively enforce a norm of behavior upon deviant minorities plays a crucial role in Christopher Boehm's theory of the origin of morality, which will be discussed later in this section.

57. For an excellent statement of the sexual selection theory and its application to moral traits, see Geoffrey Miller, *The Mating Mind* (New York: Anchor Books, 2000).

58. David Buss, "Sex Differences in Human Mate Selection: Evolutionary Hypotheses Tested in Thirty-seven Cultures," *Behavioral and Brain Sciences* 12 (1989): 1–49.

successful individuals, tendencies genetically selected at the level of individual human beings.[59]

It seems plausible that all the forces mentioned—individual natural selection, group natural selection, sexual selection, and cultural group selection—have played their roles in shaping human nature and behavior and have mutually reinforced and shaped one another (it is now widely accepted, for instance, that human genes and culture coevolved, making it possible for genetically based prosocial tendencies and prosocial cultural norms to have evolved together and mutually influenced their specific content). The virtue of allotting some sort of role for natural group selection or sexual selection of altruistic tendencies is that it confirms and provides an explanation of tendencies that from common-sense observation do seem to have psychological reality in individuals—people do make sacrifices to help their neighbors, compatriots, and sometimes complete strangers, just as they can sometimes astound and horrify us by their gratuitous cruelty. Neither kind of behavior can be completely explained on the assumption of psychological egoism (the view that human nature is purely self-interested) without considerable strain and speculative assumption.[60] Though common-sense observation is notoriously corrigible, surely it has some weight in situations where experimental evidence is scarce and cannot decide between competing theories more or less compatible with firmly established theory and explanation.

Furthermore, some experimental study has confirmed, if not decisively, common sense on this matter.[61] C. Daniel Batson has obtained interesting experimental results based on a sophisticated conceptual analysis of ways in which psychological egoism seeks to explain away apparently altruistic acts motivated by an empathetic focusing on the plight of a person in need. For example, they note the common suggestions that such acts are motivated by egoistic need to eliminate the unpleasant feelings caused by empathy, or to avoid the unpleasant feelings of shame and guilt should one fail to

---

59. See Robert Boyd and Peter J. Richerson, *Culture and the Evolutionary Process* (Chicago: University of Chicago Press, 1985), and *Not by Genes Alone: How Culture Transformed Human Evolution* (Chicago: University of Chicago Press, 2005).

60. Sober and Wilson claim that none of the direct arguments against psychological egoism are decisive and that a far better argument is to derive the denial of psychological egoism from the theory of group selection. They go so far as to defend the hedonistic form of psychological egoism—the theory that the good one seeks is ultimately one's own pleasure and avoidance of pain. While very few major views in philosophy have ever been "decisively" defeated in any strict sense, there are theories that require strenuous defense simply to avoid decisive defeat, theories, for example, that presuppose a necessarily thin and abstract entity such as "pleasure" as the ultimate positive object of an incredibly diverse range of human striving. While Sober and Wilson have made a strong case for natural group selection, it seems to me that their theory gains credibility as an explanation of the existence of altruism. The credibility relation does not run the other way.

61. See C. Daniel Batson, *The Altruism Question: Toward a Social-Psychological Answer* (Hillsdale, N.J.: Erlbaum, 1991). Also see the exchange between Sober and Wilson and Batson in *Evolutionary Origins of Morality*, ed. Leonard D. Katz (Bowling Green, Ohio: Imprint Academic, 2000), 207–10, 266–7.

help, or to avoid social punishments administered by others, or to reap pleasant feelings of self-esteem enhancement or social rewards of praise and prestige. Batson designed experiments in which his subjects were offered opportunities to satisfy the postulated egoistic needs without having to help the person they perceive to be in distress. The results confirm the reality of altruistic motivations.

Recent studies of the primates most closely related to human beings also provide some indirect evidence for the reality of altruistic motivations. Frans de Waal has found in monkeys and apes motivations to reduce conflict within groups, such as breaking up fights without choosing sides, and he argues that such impartial interventions are not satisfactorily explained by the standard methods put forward by psychological egoists. De Waal sees succoring behavior that includes care giving and provision of relief to distressed individuals who are not kin. This is a kind of behavior, he argues, that involves attachment to and concern for others, and sometimes even understanding of their needs and emotions. De Waal is not claiming that nonhuman primates have morality, but that they have some of the conative and cognitive building blocks of the morality we see in human society. If there are such building blocks that consist in a concern for the social life of the community as a whole and in capacities for sympathy and attachment to others, it would be surprising (as well as extremely depressing) if human beings lacked such building blocks.[62]

It must also be noted that altruistic motivation can take a wide variety of forms. Herbert Gintis argues that an empirically confirmed alternative to *Homo economicus*, who cooperates only when it serves his self-interested purposes and is basically indifferent to the well-being of others, is *Homo reciprocans*, who comes to new social situations with a propensity to cooperate, responds to prosocial behavior (i.e., behavior that positively contributes to social cooperation but does not necessarily exact a cost or require sacrifice by the agent) on the part of others by maintaining or increasing her level of cooperation, and responds to selfish, free-riding behavior on the part of others by retaliating against the offenders, even at a cost to herself, and even when she could not reasonably expect future personal gains from such retaliation.[63]

62. See Frans B. M. de Waal, *Peacemaking among the Primates* (Cambridge, Mass.: Harvard University Press, 1989); also Jessica C. Flack and Frans B. M. de Waal, "Any Animal Whatever," in Katz, *Evolutionary Origins of Morality*, 1–30. See also the commentary discussion by others and Flack and de Waal's response, 31–78. See also Owen Flanagan, "Ethical Expressions: Why Moralists Scowl, Frown, and Smile," in *The Cambridge Companion to Darwin*, ed. Jonathan Hodge and Gregory Radick (Cambridge: Cambridge University Press, 2003), 377–98.

63. Herbert Gintis, *Game Theory Evolving* (Princeton: Princeton University Press, 2000). Robert Trivers, in "The Evolution of Reciprocal Altruism," identified a crucial role for "moralistic aggression" (negative reactions to perceived violations of reciprocity) in helping to reduce the incidence of free-riding. However, it is Gintis who correctly points out that in many instances there is an altruistic element to the willingness to retaliate against free-riders. De Waal sees the capacity for retribution and revenge in some primates as a precursor of moralistic aggression. See Flack and De Waal, "Any Animal Whatever."

Gintis points to the results of experiments that involve the "public-goods game," designed to illuminate such problems as the voluntary payment of taxes and the restriction of one's use of an endangered environmental resource. In the early stages of the game, people generally make contributions that average about halfway between the perfectly cooperative and the perfectly selfish levels. In the later stages of the game, contributions decay until, at the end, they are close to the *Homo economicus* level. Further analysis indicates that the reason for the decay is that the cooperators want to retaliate against the free-riders, and the only way available to them is to cease cooperating altogether. Such "strong" reciprocating behavior (as opposed to forms that are based only on self-interested calculation) need not have a specific genetic basis but could be culturally selected or the joint result of genetic and cultural selection (e.g., culturally transmitted punishment of free-riders might deter other potential free-riders who would otherwise genetically overrun group members with altruistic traits). Some evidence for the role of cultural selection arises from game experiments in which advice from players who previously participated in the experiment increases altruistic punishment (and rewarding).[64]

In assessing the plausibility of genuine altruism, then, it is important to recognize that such forms need not be extreme and unconditional. In a similar vein, it is important to note that some of the most urgent human interests are ones that are neither clearly interests in only the self nor purely other regarding. The affection and love people have for their family members, for example, certainly has a strong other-regarding dimension, but is typically mixed, sometimes inextricably so, with the satisfactions people derive from a life with these others. It is not just that they want their sons and daughters to thrive, for example, but also that they get deep satisfaction in *themselves* being the persons who help their children to thrive and in being recognized by their children as doing so. This class of interests also comprehends interests in advancing the welfare of a community with which one has some deep identification. The satisfaction people get from contributing to that community is typically not reducible to a pure other-regarding interest but partly tied up with the satisfaction of knowing that one has made a difference to something larger than oneself and hence that one's existence has that larger significance.

If individual and group forms of natural selection have shaped human nature, then an intuitively plausible result is not only pluralism of motivation but profound ambivalence in human nature. The force of selection on the individual can be expected to have produced a strong dose of egoistic motivation, a significant capacity to take into account the welfare of others and to contribute to that welfare at varying levels of cost to the self, and various extremely familiar and frequently occurring motivations that seem to fall in between pure forms of egoism and altruism. Moreover, a mixture of

64. A. Schotter, "Decision Making with Naïve Advice," *American Economic Review* 93 (2003): 196–201.

such motivations is probably the norm for human beings. In one-shot game inter-actions, strongly reciprocal individuals punish and reward the cooperation of others, a result suggesting altruistic traits. But they also increase their punishments and rewards in repeated interactions or when their reputations with other players (as cooperators and as strongly reciprocal individuals) are at stake. It seems that a good dose of self-interest induces them to increase punishments and rewards in the second type of situation.[65]

Such features of human nature bear on what shape a normative system needs to take if it is to effectively perform the function of promoting and facilitating social co-operation. Self-interested motivation can clearly have undermining effects on social cooperation when it motivates free-riding and aggression against others. That is why the familiar moral injunctions to consider the interests of others for their own sake are entirely necessary from the standpoint of the interpersonal function. However, in the right circumstances self-interest can support, rather than oppose, other-interested motivations. Jane Mansbridge has suggested that while other-interested motivations such as those stemming from empathy do exist in most individuals, they do not have infinite value. Gintis's portrait of *Homo reciprocans* suggests the same qualification. If the costs of benefiting others are very high, many will simply decline to pay. Ar-rangements that generate some self-interested return to other-interested behavior can create an "ecological niche," Mansbridge suggests, that helps to sustain that behavior. By making that behavior less costly, these arrangements can increase the degree to which individuals feel they can afford to indulge their concerns for others.[66] Rather than saying that an effective morality should always constrain self-concern and rein-force other-concern, it should often attempt to accomplish a productive balance or reconciliation between those types of concern.

Moral norms requiring reciprocity play a crucial role in such reconciliation, and that is why they are universal elements of adequate moralities. The need to reconcile self- and other-concern appears first in family relationships. Across widely different cultures there are duties to respect and to honor parents and others whose roles involve raising and nurturing the young. Performance of such duties constitutes a kind of return of good for good, though what is returned, of course, is not always the same kind of good that was originally given. Sometimes the return is similar to the original good, as in the case of children's care of aged parents. But most other times, the return is a good that is fitting to the nature of the relationship to those who have cared and nurtured: obedience and receptiveness to what is taught, for example. Some might not

65. See R. M. Isaac and J. M. Walker, "Group-Size Effects in Public-Goods Provision: The Vol-untary Contributions Mechanism," *Quarterly Journal of Economics* 103 (1988): 179–99; see also Ernst Fehr and Urs Fischbacher, "The Nature of Human Altruism," *Nature* 425 (2003): 785–91, for a very useful survey and review of the recent literature.

66. Jane Mansbridge, "On the Relation of Altruism and Self-Interest," in *Beyond Self-Interest* (Chicago: University of Chicago, 1990), 133–43.

think of obedience in itself as a good return for care and nurture. It might not always be a good to those who are obeyed, but neither is it a good only for those who enjoy having power over others. However much we may value independence in our children, there are times when we greatly treasure their simply doing what we ask them to do, and if they do, or express gratitude for what we have given them, that helps us to continue to give them the care we owe to them. Perfectly selfless parents might not need such reinforcement, but profoundly ambivalent beings might not be able to do without it.

Moreover, the different mechanisms that result in the various forms of altruism—kin, group, sexual and cultural selection, and reciprocal altruism—help to explain the plurality of basic value. Kin selection and reciprocal altruism, plus forms of cultural selection, help to explain obligations to others based on special relationship to them, while the kind of altruism that does not depend on special relationship or on conditions that create expectation of reciprocation helps to explain impersonal values such as general rights or the promoting of social utility. These various forms of altruism, and the attendant obligations and values, serve well the function of regulating and facilitating social cooperation. The more limited and conditional forms of altruism, and those forms that sit pretty squarely between the purest forms of self- and other-concern, are the kinds of motivations that can be invoked and cultivated by moral norms and reasons to form cohesive smaller groups. The forms of altruism that are closest to pure other-concern are the ones that can be invoked and cultivated to facilitate cooperation between the smaller groups and to limit conflict between them.

2.10 THE CONSTRAINT OF JUSTIFIABILITY TO THE GOVERNED

Consider now another constraint on moralities that derives from the interpersonal function, the strong self-interested component of human motivation, and a widely shared feature of the concept of morality. As a system for promoting cooperation, morality works through a large degree of voluntary acceptance of its norms and the reasons it provides to act in this or that way. If conformance to its norms and reasons depended solely on the threat of force or coercion, the costs would detract greatly from the benefits of social cooperation itself. It makes sense that human beings evolved a system for regulating and promoting cooperation that governs in this way. A further step in the evolution of morality also makes sense for creatures who explain and justify their actions to one another: voluntary acceptance of moral norms came to be seen as based on their justifiability to those governed by them. Hence another constraint on moralities is that justification for following the norms and reasons of an adequate morality cannot crucially depend on falsehoods. In particular, when moral norms and reasons call for the subordination of the interests of some to the interests of others, the justification of such norms and reasons cannot crucially depend on falsehoods.

This constraint gains much of its bite when it is recognized that justification of subordinating norms and reasons typically takes the form of arguments that the interests of the subordinated are being satisfactorily addressed, even as they are being subordinated to the interests of others. And this should not be surprising if it is true that self-interest is a powerful human motivation, if not the only one. Arguments for subordinating norms and reasons often involve the theme of reciprocity among the subordinated and the subordinators. Even extremely hierarchical systems in which some have much more power and material means than others contain reciprocity of certain kinds. As Barrington Moore Jr. has observed, there are certain mutual obligations that generally link rulers and ruled, those in authority and those subject to authority. The ruler generally owes to the ruled contribution to security against foreign and domestic aggression and against threats to the material supports of customary daily life.[67] Michael Walzer has made a related point in observing that on a Marxist account, every ruling class "is compelled to present itself as a universal class." Even if the prevailing social norms of a society favor their interests over those of others, these norms purport to serve the common interests.[68]

In his book on the nature of political power, Thomas Wartenberg points out that a dominant group standing in a coercive power relationship to a dominated group has an interest in making that relationship into one also based on "influence." By "influence" Wartenberg means a power relationship in which the dominated agent does something because she accepts what the dominating agent tells her. Influence contrasts with a purely coercive power relationship in which the dominated agent submits because of fear of harm. So long as the dominating agent maintains a purely coercive relationship, there will be a tendency for the subordinate agent to resist and, thus, a need to use force to realize the threat upon which the dominating agent's coercive power rests. Such uses of force, Wartenberg observes, are costly in terms of resources, hence the dominating agent has an interest in avoiding cases of resistance.

Some instances of influence are morally justified. Others are not. Human beings have a long and tragic record of having accepted cruel subordination. But when they have accepted it as morally required, they have done so on the basis of justifications that purport in some way to satisfactorily address their interests. Subordination is often justified by reference to the necessity of a kind of paternalism: some people must be taken care of by other people. And this paternalism is justified by false characterizations of the capacities of the subordinated, such as their capacities for practical reasoning or self-control. As Wartenberg observes, there is "an inherent tendency" for dominating agents "to secure their position of dominance by developing misunderstandings among the dominated about what is happening to them" and "somehow to

---

67. Moore, *Injustice*, 22.
68. Michael Walzer, *Interpretation and Social Criticism* (Cambridge: Mass.: Harvard University Press, 1987), 40–1.

convince the subordinate group that it is not being dominated."[69] Other kinds of justification for subordination may rest on metaphysical claims. The caste system in India, for example, rests on the claim that one's place in the social order is necessitated by *karma*, by one's deeds in a past life. This sort of justification averts the need to satisfactorily address the interests of the subordinated by making subordination a kind of metaphysical and moral necessity.

The cultural anthropologist Christopher Boehm has a theory about the origin of morality that fits with the story just told about the moral requirement to justify subordination. Boehm hypothesizes that early manifestations of morality among no-madic bands of hunter-gatherers involved the collective suppression of behaviors likely to cause intragroup conflict. Boehm thinks that such bands were relatively egal-itarian, at least with respect to the main political actors, and he contrasts their structure with ones in which there is substantial social competition for a limited number of positions at the top and in which the leaders have substantial legitimate authority or coercive force at their disposal. Morality first arose from attempts to label as deviant and to collectively sanction competitive or predatory behaviors by indi-viduals that threatened to cause conflict within the band. The labeling and sanctioning of bullying behavior as deviant is an especially important instance of social control through morality, Boehm thinks, because human beings have strong natural pro-pensities to try to dominate others and to avoid domination by others. Boehm sees similar natural tendencies and at least some of the makings of collective sanctioning of bullying in chimpanzees and bonobos, with whom we share a common ancestor. For example, female chimpanzees in captivity have been known to collectively exercise such control over males who are individually dominant over them.[70] If Boehm is right, most of us have departed from the egalitarianism of our ancestors, but we still act on the desire to avoid domination in requiring a justification for subordination. If mo-rality began as a norm-based sanctioning of domination, it could be expected to retain the requirement of justification for subordination even as human social structures in most instances evolved toward much more hierarchical forms.

It may be objected that this story I have told about the necessity to justify sub-ordination in terms of the interests of the subordinated group depends on one con-tingency: that human beings have strong enough tendencies to resist that it eventually becomes necessary for their dominators to rely on something other than brute force to obtain enough of their cooperation. It might be thought that the way my story rests on

69. Thomas Wartenberg, *The Forms of Power: From Domination to Transformation* (Philadelphia: Temple University Press, 1990), 127.

70. See Christopher Boehm, "The Evolutionary Development of Morality as an Effect of Domi-nance Behavior and Conflict Interference," *Journal of Social and Biological Sciences* 5 (1982): 413–22; see also "Conflict and the Evolution of Social Control," in Katz, *Evolutionary Origins of Morality*, 79–102, where Boehm's article is followed by a very useful commentary discussion by a number of others and finally by a response to the commentary discussion by Boehm, 103–84.

this contingency is unacceptable: what about those who do not have tendencies to resist subordination? Is a morality that subordinates them unjustifiable in terms of their interests going to be adequate nevertheless, because they are not in a position to "fight back"?[71] Keep in mind, however, that the kind of resistance that can undermine dominance need not be armed rebellion. It can consist of attempts to escape or sabotage or the passive resistance of doing as little as possible when the master or the overseer is not looking. In the broader senses of resistance, human beings in general have the capacity to resist if they are not persuaded that they must accept their position. A morality that does not imply recognition of the need for justification of subordination would not be an adequate morality for human beings.

2.11 MORALITIES WITH AND WITHOUT UNIVERSAL SCOPE

Let me now turn to the different question of whether all moralities have principles with a universal scope of application, as is true in several Western moral traditions, according to which principles of conduct apply to all human beings. On the naturalistic approach defended here, the presence of such universal principles is not required in all conceivable adequate moralities, if such principles go beyond the constraints derived from human nature and the functions of morality. The functions of morality, after all, may be served by principles that apply only to a certain group or society and the internal relations within it. Members within the group or society may accept moral directives in their relations with each other, but not in their relations to those outside. However, most actual moralities do have a universalistic element.

The presence of such an element may have to do with the common conception of morality that naturalism must reject: that moral properties are somehow an irreducible part of the fabric of the world. If moral properties are "out there" as an irreducible part of the cosmic order, it is natural to think that they apply to everyone capable of acting on their recognition. Further, it may be in the interests of a group within a society to sustain such a view of the moral order, if the rules of that order are to its benefit. There is, however, a less pessimistic story to tell. Groups with fluid boundaries, or groups that have significant and fairly regular interaction with other groups, have good reasons to extend the scope of their moral rules outward.

Take moral rules that originally were intended to regulate and define family and kin relationships. When different families and clans cooperate to fulfill their needs, they must have rules to structure their cooperation and to resolve their conflicts. A natural solution is to extend some moral rules that previously applied only *within* the family

---

71. Nicholas Sturgeon might be making such an objection in his "Moral Disagreement and Moral Relativism," in *Cultural Pluralism and Moral Knowledge*, ed. Ellen Frankel Paul, Fred D. Miller Jr., and Jeffrey Paul (Cambridge: Cambridge University Press, 1994), 93 n. 40.

or clan to relations between the different families and clans. Similarly when larger groups interact, moral rules that previously applied only within each group are extended to relations between groups. To the extent that two groups cooperate voluntarily, they will need to regulate their interactions by rules (e.g., keeping agreements made, reciprocating aid) that both acknowledge as binding. Even when one group conquers another, there usually comes a time when the dominating group needs some degree of voluntary cooperation from the dominated. As pointed out earlier, domination through sheer force takes up too many resources for policing, and there are important tasks one cannot be forced to do but that require one's enduring and voluntary (to some degree at least) commitment.

The two stories, pessimistic and optimistic, are probably both true and in fact intertwine. Because dominating groups need the voluntary cooperation of those they dominate, they extend their in-group moral rules to the out-group. But these rules usually will be interpreted so that the interests of the out-group are subordinated. This dynamic, however, sets up a possible reexamination of the moral tradition. While the founders may have been content to limit application of the moral rules to their own group, the heirs of the tradition will recognize that at least some of the moral rules apply to out-groups. The heirs will usually want to maintain superiority of status, but once *some* of the moral rules, however interpreted to their disadvantage, apply to out-groups, the question can arise as to what justifies the difference in moral status. Since the dominating group does not present its position as justified by pure force, it must defend the difference. Kinship or belonging to the in-group by themselves are no longer valid justifications, since they did not bar the partial inclusion of the out-groups. Claims of superiority on behalf of the dominating group (members are more capable of moral virtue; they are more advanced and therefore must take on the burden of leading others out of the cave), when based on grounds both kinds of groups can recognize, can be scrutinized and refuted. Something like this process has led, I believe, to the impersonal elements of many modern moralities. This process is historically contingent and not mandated by the very idea of an adequate morality because there is no necessity in a group's reaching out beyond its boundaries to interact with others, nor in the initial application of moral rules to out-groups. Or if there is an initial necessity, it is not a moral one but more of a pragmatic one related to the ends the group has in desiring to interact with other groups or in dominating them.

The story I have told of the origin of universalistic, impersonal elements of morality may not seem to confer an exalted status on them. It may seem unsatisfactory to those who believe that the undistorted application of these elements to increasing numbers of people has constituted much of what one would call moral progress. Yet something like my story will have to be told, unless one declares by definitional fiat that morality simply *is* a set of principles with universal scope or alternatively shows that the universalistic elements derive from other criteria for an adequate morality. Furthermore, this story does not make it "optional" for us to retain the universalistic element. There is no going back from interaction between different global communities. We are more interdependent than we ever were before. More than ever before, no one community is capable of dominating the others without some background of consensual norms.

2.12 A Constraint Requiring Accommodation

The last constraint to identify may be somewhat surprising. I have argued that moral conflicts spring from plural values and the accompanying phenomenon of moral ambivalence will occur within societies and their moral traditions. We should expect that within cultures there occurs serious disagreement about the meaning of important values and the relative priorities among these values. Of course, there will be a significantly greater degree of agreement on these matters within a culture. That is partly how we individuate cultures. But cultures can have a sufficient degree of agreement in order to be differentiated from other cultures and yet leave plenty of room for disagreement within. As Alasdair MacIntyre has pointed out, moral traditions are not static systems of propositions but are constituted by continuing dialogue and debate.[72] Disagreement within a cultural tradition need not be as dramatic as disagreements between traditions. And yet it can be as serious. In the United States, for example, there is serious disagreement over the meaning and requirements of equality as a social value, and this disagreement is expressed in opposing philosophical theories such as libertarianism, liberal welfarism, and socialism. Of course, there are some who say that serious disagreement is no surprise in modern Western societies because these societies have lost their coherence, their traditions now incomprehensible mixtures of different cultural strands. But the ancient Chinese Confucian tradition, which is as coherent and as stable as we have any right to expect, shows serious disagreement over fundamental questions such as the extent to which the ruler should be limited in his power over the people, and whether the son should obey the father even when the father requires that he do something wrong.

Given the inevitability of serious disagreement within all kinds of moral traditions that have any degree of complexity, a particular sort of ethical value becomes especially important for the stability and integrity of these traditions and societies. Let me call this value "accommodation." To have this value is to be committed to supporting noncoercive and constructive relations with others although they have ethical beliefs that conflict with one's own. Why is this value important? From the standpoint of the integrity and stability of a society, this value is important given the regularity of occurrence of serious ethical disagreement. If such disagreement always threatened to become the source of schism, no society could survive for very long without brutal repression.

---

72. See, for example, Alasdair MacIntyre, *Whose Justice? Which Rationality?* (Notre Dame, Ind.: University of Notre Dame Press, 1988), chap. 28.

Consider the constraints on an adequate morality derived in this chapter from the functions of morality, human psychology, and the nature of human cooperation: requiring human beings to seek only that which they have some propensity to seek; inclusion of norms of reciprocity in light of strong self-interest; in specification of norms and reasons, balancing self- and other-concern in ways that include putting less pressure on other-concern through provision of some "payoff" in terms of self-interest; justifiability of norms and reasons to the governed in terms of their interests when presented without falsification; and finally the value of accommodation of moral disagreement. This is a diverse set of constraints, the validity of each one contingent on a variety of factors. When investigating what these criteria might be, I believe it is important to expect them to be of diverse natures, because of the internal complexity and diversity of morality itself. Any system of belief that could be considered a morality today is the product of a long and complex evolutionary (biological and cultural) process. As a society's circumstances change, old practices and customs that regulate intra- and interpersonal conflicts die off or transform, and new ones emerge. Settlers and immigrants bring customs and practices to new places where they may not only permute but also combine with other traditions. Those who live in large and heterogeneous societies such as the United States are the heirs of a long and complex moral tradition that contains many different strands with histories of different lengths, derived from different places and cultures. A common mistake of moral philosophy is to treat a morality as a homogeneous whole, to be justified as adequate on the basis of one *kind* of criterion. Given the internal complexity and diversity of a morality, it would be unrealistic to expect that we could justify through just one sort of argument a conception of the moral life, even if there were universally valid criteria for adequacy. As we have seen, special duties toward those who care for us may have their source in universal aspects of the human condition and human nature. The universalistic, impersonal elements may have their roots in a historically contingent process that nevertheless is firmly grounded for us, at this historical moment. As we shall see in chapter 6, the particular shape that impersonal requirements take for us may have much to do with where we have arrived at this historical moment and less to do with the human condition and human nature per se.

2.13 PLURALISM WITHIN THE CONSTRAINTS

Pluralistic relativism accounts for the plurality of values and for moral ambivalence by holding that the universal limits on adequate moralities do not narrow the range of such moralities to just one. The possibility of setting different priorities among values corresponds to different ways of regulating interpersonal conflict of interest and providing direction to the individual.

Consider moralities that differ over the priority to be given to individual rights versus social utility as summed over all the individuals affected. One effective way of promoting social cooperation is to assure to each individual protection of her fundamental interests, even if greater social utility can be gained through the violation of those interests. A morality that gives high priority to this deontological value will answer to the powerful human motivations described earlier. The substantial degree of self-interest that can be generally expected of human beings will generally place a limit (though highly variable according to culture and perhaps to individual genetic endowment) on the willingness to make too large a sacrifice on behalf of others. Furthermore, altruistic motivations might easily be shaped, again through moral socialization, toward the form of identification with and concern for each and every individual. On the other hand, a morality that gives a higher priority to social utility answers to the force of reasoning that goes by numbers: promoting the greatest happiness of the greatest number, for instance, can also be an effective way of promoting social cooperation. A utilitarian morality might have to take into consideration the effect on the security of individuals and their willingness to cooperate if they are not assured inviolable protection of their fundamental interests, and if indeed this turns out to render social cooperation unstable, some adjustment would have to be made, as some utilitarians, of course, have suggested. Even so, there are bound to be important differences between moralities that give a higher priority to individual rights as a basic value and those that give a higher priority to social utility. I do not see how universal constraints on adequate moralities rule out either kind of morality.

With regard to other kinds of differences over value priorities, we can, of course, attempt to give economic, sociological, and anthropological explanations of why a given society adopted a certain set of priorities, and such explanations may constitute the basis for the Kohlbergian argument that such a society is simply at a lower stage of moral progress than other societies with the "correct" set of priorities. For example, Jack Donnelly, an advocate of applying universal human rights to the less developed nations, has observed that traditional societies, which often strongly emphasize values of community, are linked to premodern modes of production that ensure only a precarious survival for many people. He grants that the ideal of a close-knit community answers to such a condition. He further grants that the best forms of such communities provide one with a range of personal and social relationships that provide material and nonmaterial support. They make available to their members regularized social protections of many of the values and interests that in the modern West are protected through individual human and legal rights. However, Donnelly goes on to argue, when traditional forms of community are disrupted for whatever reason, and where modernization means some forms of and some degree of capitalism, there is a need for individual rights.[73]

However, community-based ethics have remained in situations where the level of resources to satisfy basic material needs is adequate or much more than adequate. Asian societies that have undergone rapid growth and development still show in surveys a

73. See Jack Donnelly, *Universal Human Rights in Theory and Practice* (Ithaca: Cornell University Press, 1989), 59.

markedly greater concern for social harmony and correspondingly lesser concern for personal freedom than Western societies.[74] At such high levels of resources, and where members of the community have a choice as to whether to introduce changes of modernization, that choice becomes an ethical choice where there is awareness that modernization may undermine the supports for a community-based ethic.[75]

For example, a question of crucial importance in much of Asia today as nations modernize is whether Western-style democracies are appropriate for them, given their indigenous traditions that are oriented toward relationship and community. Among the people asking this question, of course, are self-serving autocratic political leaders. But this does not make it any less of a real issue for various peoples of Asia. A leader of an opposition party and former political prisoner in Taiwan admits that even he "would not advocate as many rights" as Americans, for example, hold dear. He says: "Harmony is more important in our society, so people do not put so much value on equality or personal freedom."[76] Some Asians perceive that Western individualism has costs they are unwilling to accept. A night watchman in Hong Kong makes the point vividly: "If New York City or Los Angeles are examples of democracy, I don't want it."[77]

It seems likely to me that a moral emphasis on individual rights will gradually grow within many Asian societies, and if so, there will be some hard choices as to how to balance and prioritize that emphasis with the more traditional emphasis on relationship and community. I suspect that many Asian cultures will remain distinctive in the emphasis they give to communal values and the needs they address, even as they incorporate Western political and economic forms and even some of the language and concerns of individual rights. At the same time, there will have to be reflection and debate over how the value framework of rights is to be balanced against communal values. I suspect that numerous forms of balance in different parts of Asia, not necessarily like

74. David Hitchcock, for example, conducted a 1994 survey of the value preferences of officials, business people, scholars, and professionals from the United States and eight East Asian societies. He found that a strong majority of Asian respondents preferred an 'orderly society' and 'harmony', which were values given little attention by Americans. The reverse result occurred, it should be added, in respect of the value of 'personal freedom'. See *Asian Values and the United States: How Much Conflict?* (Washington, D.C.: Center for Strategic and International Studies, 1994). See also Donald K. Emmerson, "Singapore and the 'Asian Values' Debate," *Journal of Democracy* 6 (1995): 101–2.

75. In 120 interviews with middle-class Malays, Joel Kahn found that almost all respondents stressed concerns about the "threat posed to Malay culture by modernisation" and criticized the West for its "lack of family values, individual and selfishness, a lack of cultural values, permissiveness, secularisation and uncaringness." See "Malaysian Modern or Anti-anti Asian Values," *Thesis Eleven* 50 (1997): 29–30.

76. Yao Chia-wen, a leader of Taiwan's Democratic Progressive opposition, as quoted in "Asia's Different Drum," *Time*, June 14, 1993.

77. "Asia's Different Drum," *Time*, June 14, 1993. Of course, not all that might repel the watchman about New York City or Los Angeles is necessarily attributable to values anyone in the West is willing to defend.

anything that appeared in Western traditions, will be the result. And why does there need to be a single correct balance? More discussion of the possible permutations and of one permutation in which rights are given a communal basis is forthcoming in the next chapter.

2.14 Commonalities and Differences across Moralities: Overlapping but Different Truth Conditions for Moral Statements

My version of pluralistic relativism implies that there will be such commonalities and differences in moralities across societies and within them. Much of what is moral will be the same for, say, Asian and Western societies, because of the common functions of moralities, human nature, and similar conditions across human societies. The commonalities form a shared core that includes duties arising from special relationships, including duties to care for the young and to instruct them so that they can become full-fledged moral agents, norms of reciprocity, and the other norms and reasons necessary for accomplishing the functions of morality.

The shared core also includes a common conceptual apparatus for transmitting moralities and deliberating over moral matters. Every society with a morality will have concepts of the morally ought to do and morally right to do. The different sources of moral value described in chapter 1 can be construed as sources of different kinds of reasons for doing or refraining from certain action types, for seeking or refraining from seeking certain kinds of things. Moral statements as to what a person ought or ought not to do or as to what is right or wrong for that person to do can be construed as statements as to what relevant moral reasons specify for that person. Sometimes these statements are concluding, deliberative statements about what the balance of all relevant moral reasons specifies for that person. Sometimes these statements are about what action or attitude is supported by a certain kind of reason, without purporting to provide an overall judgment as to what the balance of all relevant moral reasons specifies.

Moral reasons are those considerations weighing in favor of or against an agent's doing something.[78] We may think of a moral reason as a three-place relation between an agent A, an action X, and a feature in the agent's situation F that weighs in favor of

---

78. In *Moral Relativity*, I analyzed "A ought to do X" statements in terms of the performance of X following from the correct moral system of rules. I now think this particular way of analyzing 'ought' judgments is too wedded to a particular (and I now think mistaken) model of moral reasoning as invariably deducing particular conclusions from general rules. Standards for assessing actions or persons and their traits, and reasons for doing or not doing actions or for being this or that kind of person are weighed in moral deliberation in ways not captured by simple deduction from the general to the particular. My current language of being permitted, required, or prohibited by the relevant standards or the balance of reasons is meant to correspond to this revised conception of moral reasoning.

A's doing X. We may think of a morality as a configuration of (partially) ordered values that specify what situational features are relevant moral reasons and also what constitutes a correct balance of reasons in cases where more than one situational feature is relevant and the different features weigh in favor of different and incompatible actions. We may think of a reason defined in this way as *justifying* reason. F is the feature that purportedly justifies A's doing X. A justifying reason is not necessarily one that would motivate A to do X. It is not a motivating reason, though moral theory does owe an account of when a justifying moral reason can become motivating (the subject of chapter 7).

On the theory of pluralistic relativism, morality's functions of promoting and sustaining interpersonal cooperation and of guiding individuals toward worthwhile lives operate to constrain the identification of situational features as moral reasons. That is, a genuine moral reason is such that acting on it under the appropriate circumstances contributes to the functions of morality (the contribution that any single reason might make to morality's functions might have to be assessed according to the ways in which it works with other reasons recognized within that morality). Receiving the help of another person, for example, would constitute a reason to reciprocate according to the argument offered in section 2.8. The moralities of particular societies would evolve a diverse and rich set of moral reasons that operate on much more specific levels (the forms of help that would create duties to reciprocate and the appropriate forms of reciprocation would be specified more concretely), but to have a chance at being true, the reasons specified within these moralities must satisfy the general constraints.

How does a set of diverse and specific moral reasons get established as part of the morality of a given group? I approach this question as a question about the concepts of moral reasons and how they acquire the reference they have. Much recent work on the nature of concepts has undermined the 'classical' model that posits necessary and sufficient conditions for their application. One of the proposed replacements for the classical model is prototype theory, according to which concepts include features possessed by their instances, the features embodying the average or most typical instances. To take a frequently used example in the prototype literature, the concept of dog includes features making up a kind of composite "everydog" (has four legs, a tail, emits barking sounds) and an object that is a candidate for falling under that concept is more likely to qualify the more it resembles the composite typical dog. Exemplar theory, on the other hand, holds that having concepts involves the ability to call up particular instances that serve as the standards of comparison for candidate instances. Having the concept of a dog involves the ability to call up from memory particular dogs one has encountered, and one compares dog candidates to the closest exemplars to see if one gets a close-enough match.

I follow those who believe that concepts need not be limited to one structure. Indeed some concepts might acquire prototypes that are constructed on the basis of exemplars. A child might acquire her prototype of everydog on the basis of encounters with Sadie, Gus, and Pepper, particular dogs she knew while growing up.[79] She might call up the dog prototype to categorize most dogs she encounters, but if she were to encounter a difficult case, she might recall an atypical dog exemplar that most closely resembles the present animal.

Concepts of moral reasons seem to exhibit this kind of versatility. Consider the concept of a reason to help another person. In acquiring this concept, we might have had certain concrete situations identified as exemplars of a reason to help: a parent demonstrates for us what is to be done when a sibling falls down and hurts himself; the experience of the exchange of gifts or favors is in many cultures an occasion ex-emplifying a reason to reciprocate. On the other hand, people can construct prototypes of such reasons that generalize over these exemplar cases, giving rise to a conceptual representative of a "typical" reason, say, to help or to reciprocate. On many occasions of classification, we might call up a prototype if the current situation seems typical, but in novel or borderline cases, we might call up from memory the closest exemplar and try to determine whether there is a close enough match. Peter Singer's argument that the relatively affluent have a strong duty to help famine victims drew much of its power from his analogy to the duty to save a drowning child if doing so merely required wading into a shallow pool and ruining one's clothes.[80] A situation may present itself as falling under two prototypes that direct us to incompatible actions, and we may turn to exemplars to get a sense of which exemplar most closely resembles the current situation. Much moral argument is over the question of whether an exemplar is really the closest one available. In *Mencius* 4A17, Mencius accepts that to save the life of one's drowning sister-in-law, one of course suspends the customary rule of propriety prohibiting the touching of one's sister-in-law. A rival philosopher, Chunyu Kun, wants to apply this idea of suspending the usual rules of propriety to save the entire country. Mencius replies that one saves one's sister-in-law with one's hand but cannot save the world with one's hand. The world can only be pulled out by the Way (the implied argument being that the Way requires a respect for propriety that is violated by Chunyu Kun's sweeping and casual readiness to set it aside).

One worry about both the prototype and exemplar theories is that they do not ensure sufficient publicity of concepts: people are liable to have somewhat different prototypes or exemplars and therefore different concepts. I think that people are likely to have somewhat different moral concepts, but their prototypes or exemplars can largely overlap as a result of stories about acts of moral heroism, decency, kindness, and corresponding forms of moral failure that are transmitted widely throughout a

79. See Andy Clark, "Connectionism, Moral Cognition, and Collaborative Problem Solving," in *Mind and Morals: Essays on Ethics and Cognitive Science*, ed. Larry May, Marilyn Friedman, and Andy Clark (Cambridge, Mass.: Bradford Books, 1998), 109–3. Jesse Prinz's "proxytype" model is supremely eclectic in incorporating prototype, exemplar, and other models of concepts. See *Furnishing the Mind* (Cambridge, Mass.: Bradford Books, 2003).

80. Peter Singer, "Famine, Affluence, and Morality," *Philosophy and Public Affairs* 1 (1972): 229–43.

group and often in the socialization of the young. Moreover, there seems a great deal of plausibility in Boyd and Richerson's aforementioned (in sec. 2.9) suggestions that human beings have naturally selected tendencies to copy the majority or the successful, both of which would tend to produce significance degrees of convergence or overlap in concepts as prototypes or exemplars.

Moral norms or principles may bear several different relations to such reasons and the conception of the correct balance. Sometimes they simply articulate a kind of reason, such as reasons to do things because one has promised or agreed to do them, or reasons to tell the truth in communicative contexts where there is a standard expectation of truth telling. Sometimes norms provide guidance in cases of value conflict, as in the case of the norm that permits killing in self-defense. Sometimes a norm marks the relative centrality of a value to a morality, such as the norm requiring respect for individual liberty and autonomy or the norm that emphasizes the realization of one's humanity in relationship to others.

The moral norms accepted within a group specify the way that they go about determining the correct balance of reasons given an agent or agents, given an action, and given a situation. In accordance with the constructivist account of morality outlined in this chapter, the moral norms that emerge and get accepted within a group establish the truth conditions for moral statements as made by its members, but the truth conditions are subject to the universal constraints on adequate moralities that spring from human nature and the functions of morality. The set of commonly accepted moral norms that a group has, then, are not reliable indicators of what is true for that group; but some corrected version of that set, if it is not fatally incoherent or beyond redemption from its mistaken presuppositions, can be a reliable indicator of the truth conditions of that group's moral statements.

Because the universal constraints merely specify some of the general contours a morality must take, the truth conditions will reflect not just the requirements that any adequate morality must impose but also the kinds of values a group takes to be central and to have high priorities, as reflected in the kinds of reasons and moral norms it takes to be most central. In other words, there are not only universal criteria for the adequacy of moralities of the kind I have described but also locally contingent criteria. From the standpoint of a community-centered tradition, such criteria will be tied to whatever most promotes and sustains certain kinds of community. Its contingent criteria for determining what is moral will display a distinctive emphasis on communal values, even if these values enter into an uneasy and somewhat indeterminate relation to values having to do with individual autonomy and rights. From the standpoint of such a tradition, another tradition can go wrong in emphasizing individual rights at the cost of communal values. The cost will be not only to community but also to individuals, who find their human fulfillment in community. Thus even if another tradition emphasizing individual rights were to satisfy the universal constraints outlined in this chapter, it would still lead its adherents to make false moral judgments according to the lights of a communally oriented tradition.

The universal constraints do not narrow the range of adequate moralities to just one kind (for example, one that gives primary emphasis to rights as opposed to community). The plurality of adequate moralities constitute different ways of satisfying the functions of morality—of regulating interpersonal conflict of interest and providing intrapersonal ideals and practical orientations. Why are all these different kinds of moralities adequate? Because they satisfy the universal criteria for moralities, the constraints that any morality would have to satisfy in order to adequately promote and facilitate social cooperation. Each such adequate morality places additional conditions on what social cooperation and a worthwhile life must be like, in accordance with the distinctive priorities among values it has set. As a result, what is true within different moralities about what ought to be done or what is right may vary because the meanings that establish the truth conditions may vary. The result is a kind of conceptual relativity wherein the meanings of moral concepts across different societies or groups within a pluralistic society will overlap enough so that it is reasonable to call them the meanings of the same concept but at the same time differ enough so that what is morally true on a significant range of issues will vary. What is true for us, given the meanings we attach to moral concepts such as the right thing to do, may not be true for others, given the meanings they attach to those concepts. The relativity of moral truth comes down to our having somewhat different meanings for moral concepts and the terms we use to express those concepts.

Then how, it might be asked, can people with different moralities be talking about the same thing—what morally ought to be done or what is morally right, for instance— if they mean somewhat different things by these concepts and terms? The answer is that noncognitivists' analyses of moral concepts are partly correct. In order for moral concepts to have somewhat different sets for their truthful application, there must be preservation of meaning along some other dimension than truth conditions. The other dimension is illocutionary and pragmatic. All moralities guide action, specify acceptable forms of social cooperation, and at least to some extent specify what lives are worth living. All of them specify relevant sorts of reasons that pertain to social cooperation and the living of worthwhile lives, and all of them specify what correct balances of reasons are under this or that set of conditions.

Noncognitivists such as Hare and Stevenson, however, tended to treat the nondescriptive dimension of moral meaning as primary and whatever descriptive content constituted the conditions for correct application as secondary.[81] In fact the implication of their analyses is that just about any descriptive meaning could be attached to a moral term as long as it retained its primary nondescriptive meaning (in Hare's case, a meaning that was prescriptive, and in Stevenson's, a meaning that tends to influence pro and con attitudes of the audience). What they cannot explain is how the

---

81. See R. M. Hare, *The Language of Morals* (Oxford: Clarendon Press, 1952), and C. L. Stevenson, *Ethics and Language* (New Haven: Yale University Press, 1944).

nondescriptive dimension of meaning is rooted in the descriptive meanings of moral terms, meanings that make it possible for them to be used prescriptively (as Hare emphasized) or to influence the audience's attitudes (as Stevenson emphasized). It is because moral terms concern the conditions for promoting and facilitating social cooperation and help to guide people in living their lives that they have the kind of prescriptive and emotive force they have. And that is why, as Philippa Foot argued, one cannot stipulate just any set of conditions for the correct application of a term and preserve its status as a moral term.[82] It is only because different moralities have a common core of overlapping descriptive meaning that bears on the conditions necessary for social cooperation and the effective guidance of persons in fashioning their lives that they can all be *moralities* and prescribe and influence attitudes.[83]

This completes my preliminary sketch of pluralistic relativism. The next chapter is a defense against typical objections to any form of relativism, but let me straight-away address some major ways in which my pluralistic relativism differs from the straw relativism that universalists love to pillory. It is commonly thought that relativism simply regards the popularly accepted moral norms in a society as determinative of the truth conditions for moral statements in that society. This crude and uncritical conventionalism does not follow from pluralistic relativism, since moral norms are subject to evaluation according to the universal constraints on morality. When one uses one's own norms to evaluate the truth of a moral statement, one is presupposing that these norms are not defective in light of any such constraints.

Moreover, as just asserted, members of a particular moral tradition may, without logical or other epistemological flaw, use their locally contingent criteria for the adequacy of moralities to judge mistaken the members of other traditions. Typically, moral language users use their own norms to judge the actions of others, even others who are members of different moral traditions. Pluralistic relativism, therefore, does not imply that moral language users apply the moral norms adopted in a different moral tradition to judge the conduct of members of that tradition. Nor does pluralistic relativism imply that moral language users would refrain from judging what others

82. She argues, for example, that one cannot say meaningfully that clasping the hands three times an hour is a good action unless one gives a special background connecting this action to relevant forms of benefit and harm. See Philippa Foot, "Moral Beliefs," in *Theories of Ethics*, ed. Philippa Foot (London: Oxford University Press, 1967), 91.

83. In *Wise Choices, Apt Feelings: A Theory of Normative Judgment* (Cambridge, Mass.: Harvard University Press, 1992), Allan Gibbard has recently developed a very sophisticated "expressivist" theory in the tradition of Hare and Stevenson, according to which morality is tied to the function of social coordination and the transformative effect of judgments on human motivation. Where I depart from his view is in giving a truth-conditional analysis of moral language that is based on the function of social coordination, along with the expressivist use of moral language that his analysis emphasizes. In *Thinking How to Live* (Cambridge, Mass.: Harvard University Press, 2003), however, Gibbard seems to be moving closer to something like a truth-conditional analysis, or at least an analysis that makes moral judgments behave *as if* they had truth values.

ought to do if they become aware that these others have adopted moral norms very different from their own. Granted, a sophisticated, and not a straw, relativist has adopted the latter position.

Gilbert Harman, in "Moral Relativism Defended," analyzes "A morally ought to do X" statements as specifying what the balance of reasons supports, given an implicit agreement to which both the speaker and the subject of the judgment, A, are presupposed to subscribe.[84] "Inner" moral ought judgments, as Harman calls them, reveal the commitments to action that follow from implicit agreements made within moral communities. Such judgments are not properly made *across* moral communities. As Harman famously, or perhaps notoriously, claims, most of us cannot say that Hitler ought not to have killed all those people because he was obviously not a party to any implicit agreement to which we subscribe. Therefore, on Harman's analysis of these kinds of moral judgments (though not necessarily on his analysis of other kinds of moral judgments, it must be noted), we cannot even appropriately make the kind of "A ought to do X" judgments that would come into practical conflict with judgments that Hitler would have made about what he himself morally ought to have done.

I disagree with Harman's analysis and hold that many of us do not limit such ought judgments to people we assume to share our moral commitments. On my view, there is nothing in the logic or meaning of such judgments per se that implies that the people we judge share those conceptions. That can bring us into *practical conflict* with these others when we say their actions are wrong or that they are doing what they ought not to do, even if the reference of their concept of adequate moral systems differs from ours in such a way that they can say truthfully that they are doing what they ought to do. On a deeper level, I disagree with Harman's conception of morality as constituted by implicit agreements that properly govern only those who are parties to the agreements. Moralities play a crucial role in socializing and in shaping the characters and motivations of people who are not already members of any implicit agreement. Part of the point of such shaping is to "induct" or "recruit" new members into existing communities of shared norms. The prescriptive level of moral meaning makes such shaping possible.[85]

It therefore does not follow from my analysis that people are simply saying what follows from their adopted moral norms when they make a moral statement. They can be aware that they might have mistakenly adopted the moral norms they happen to have, and they can be aware that others may be mistaken in adopting the moral norms

---

84. Gilbert Harman, "Moral Relativism Defended," *Philosophical Review* 84 (1975): 3–22.

85. In his contribution to *Moral Relativism and Moral Objectivity*, Harman recognizes this kind of difference between his analysis and mine, and not surprisingly perhaps, chooses to call his view "a pure version" of relativism, because his implies that real moral disagreements can exist only between those who share the same implicit agreements (or "frameworks," in the language of *Moral Relativism and Moral Objectivity*). See Gilbert Harman and Judith Jarvis Thomson, *Moral Relativism and Moral Objectivity* (Cambridge, Mass.: Blackwell, 1996), 32–46.

these others have. Having a morality in a reflective and self-critical way means the readiness to be critical about established or accepted norms, whether they are one's own or others'. But pluralistic relativism holds that in stepping back and being critical about moralities, people must ultimately rely on substantive moral ideals—locally contingent criteria for the adequacy of moralities that go well beyond the universal constraints on moralities.

Nor does it follow from pluralistic relativism that in making moral statements people are merely saying what is required by moral norms that satisfy universal and their own locally contingent criteria, where these locally contingent criteria are being *mentioned as locally contingent criteria.* For one thing, they may not even be aware that there are locally contingent, as opposed to universal, criteria for moral norms. More important, however, the truth conditions of moral statements only require the *use* of locally contingent criteria, not the *mention* of such criteria qua locally contingent, that is, *not any awareness* on the part of the typical moral language user that some of the criteria she invokes are locally contingent as opposed to universal. People are not necessarily aware that there are fundamental differences in the moral ideals that human beings use to judge the adequacy of moralities, even as they invoke their own ideals to judge others. They may suppose that other people differ from them because of bad faith, moral self-deception about what the norms of true morality require, or that real disagreement cannot exist on the level of fundamental values, which all share, but only on the level of how to apply these values. This kind of mistaken impression is quite intelligible if what I argued in chapter 1 is true: that moral differences are not typically differences between moralities that have nothing in common with each other but differences between moralities that significantly overlap with one another in general features and shared values and norms. When people call something right or wrong, they merely invoke the moral ideals they have without necessarily being unaware that at least some of them are not required by universal criteria for the adequacy of moral norms.

3

Objections and Replies

In this chapter I consider several important objections to pluralistic relativism. Some of these objections are ones that defenders of any version of
relativism must address:

- Relativism makes it impossible to explain moral disagreement.
- Relativism undermines confidence in one's moral commitments.
- Relativism makes constructive discourse between different moral traditions
  impossible.

Other objections concern distinctive features of my particular version of relativism:

- My "local" criteria of adequacy for moralities cannot be regarded as criteria
  at all.
- My theory is not a form of relativism but rather a form of pluralism *simpliciter*.
- There is nothing like the fixed human nature I have presupposed.
- My functionalist conception of morality is biased toward consequentialist
  moralities.

In the case of some of these objections, I will be able to provide a complete
response (or at least as much of a response of which I am capable) within the confines
of this chapter. In other cases, I will state a main line of response that will receive
further development in several subsequent chapters.

3.1 EXPLAINING THE NATURE OF RADICAL MORAL DISAGREEMENT

A standard objection against all forms of relativism is that such views are incapable of
accounting for conflict or disagreement between people with different moralities. In
particular, my pluralistic relativism may seem to entail that in one sense, people with

different but equally adequate moralities are talking about somewhat different things, because they have different sets of truth conditions for applying moral concepts and terms. If the problem comes down to people "talking past one another," then there is no real disagreement; but, the objection goes, there is real disagreement. Meeting this challenge begins with distinguishing between two types of moral conflict or disagreement.

One type is conflict over what moral judgments are claimed true. This sort of conflict occurs only when those who disagree use moral terms with the same reference, at least with respect to the disagreement at hand (in case the references as a whole differ but overlap). The other type of conflict is illocutionary and pragmatic and is made possible by the action-guiding functions of morality. That is, conflict can occur between prescriptions to do certain things or to become a certain kind of person in the sense that conforming to one prescription necessarily precludes conforming to the other, and this conflict can occur even when the prescriptions are both true.

In ordinary moral discourse, people typically construe their disagreement with one another not just as pragmatic conflict but also as disagreement over when moral terms are truly applied. They may construe it this way even when, according to the pluralistic relativist, that disagreement is pragmatic and not a disagreement over truth. For example, let us suppose that two people who disagree over the morality of abortion really cannot resolve their disagreement because each holds different truth-conditional criteria for applying the term 'wrong' to the issue. Suppose that the moral status they each accord to the life of the fetus differs fundamentally because each attaches a different moral weight to the potentiality for sentience, self-awareness, and reasoning (a potentiality they both agree the fetus possesses at the relevant stage of development).[1] Under the relativist analysis, they are in real pragmatic conflict, but if they also conceive themselves to be in disagreement over what is true, as they very well may, they are in error. The relativist must give a plausible explanation of how such an error could be made.

Any explanation must refer partly to ancient and frequently unarticulated assumptions about morality: that it is about some irreducibly prescriptive part of the fabric of the world, or that we have certain natural ends in life that determine what is right action for us. Such assumptions still operate explicitly in the moral reasoning of many individuals. Even if they don't operate in the reasoning of others, they have played a role in creating the widespread if not unanimous expectation that all or virtually all moral problems have a uniquely true solution. One could have the expectation without being able to supply a particular basis for it.

---

1. Some will argue that such a disagreement over the moral weight to be given to certain kinds of potential traits may not reflect a fundamental disagreement for application of the moral term to the abortion disagreement. They may argue that there are grounds on which to correctly decide for both parties the weight to be given. I do not dismiss such a view and do not mean to suggest that it is obvious that the disagreement I have described is too fundamental to be decided by further argument. I do not think such an argument exists, but one's position on this matter, I believe, is ultimately based upon reflection on the adequacy of the arguments that have been given.

Note, furthermore, that fundamental differences among sets of criteria for applying a moral term are accompanied by broad similarities and overlapping among these sets. The similarities and overlapping, together with pragmatic similarities of use, obscure the differences and make it easy to conflate purely pragmatic disagreement with disagreement over the correct application of moral terms. Given a considerable degree of overlap among sets of criteria for the same term, moral disagreement frequently *will* be disagreement over moral truth, and it may be no easy matter to come to the realization that a considerable degree of agreement on criteria is consistent with some fundamental differences. In fact, the nature of overlap may be such as to make it difficult to ascertain whether disagreements are or are not susceptible to resolution through determination of truth. Advocates and enemies of abortion rights will typically overlap considerably on what counts as a person in the sense of morally deserving protection against harm, but on the question of a three-month fetus, for example, their relevant concepts of the person will have different boundaries, and there will be no truth of the matter that will decide the issue between them. Given that their concepts overlap considerably on other questions as to who counts as a person (even if they disagree on the morality of the death penalty, for example, they may both agree on who counts as a person in that area), both sides may mistakenly continue to think that there is but one concept and one true principle requiring the protection of innocent persons from harm.

That is why it may be difficult for two people to recognize that they actually do not disagree over what is true but only on the pragmatic level in what they want the world to be like. It is one reason why people may misconstrue pragmatic disagreement as disagreement over moral truth. They overgeneralize from those frequent cases in which settling an issue *is* possible by appealing to commonly held criteria to all cases of moral disagreement. And if one comes to assume that all moral disagreements are resolvable in this way, it becomes easier to hold the view of morality as part of the fabric of the world, since it would supply the common criteria for resolving all disagreements. Notice that the error attributed under this relativist analysis is not necessarily attributable to all competent moral language users, because quite a few, especially in pluralistic societies such as the United States, do not assume that all their criteria for applying moral terms are universally valid.

Sometimes there is a third possibility in addition to the possibilities that the opposing sides have different criteria of correct application for a moral term and that they differ over how common criteria are to be applied. Sometimes there are *no* relevant criteria that can be reasonably attributed to opposing sides, even though they think they have such criteria. The last possibility arises when beliefs about a moral issue seem to be inchoate or incoherent to such a degree that it is impossible to impose any order upon them through attribution of relevant criteria of application. For example, in the United States today, it may be indeterminate as to whether many people hold beliefs on distributive justice that are consistent with something like Rawls's difference principle or a rather minimal liberal welfarism that acknowledges that a society has responsibilities to safeguard the satisfaction of only the most urgent material needs of its members. Some of their beliefs may imply one possibility while others of their beliefs imply the other possibility. Or their beliefs may be too vague and general to settle the issue between the two possibilities. It is all too human to be unaware of such inconsistencies or vagueness, and even more human to have one's position on more particular issues of distributive justice be shaped by other factors, including one's personal stake in how these issues are resolved. Therefore, two parties who do not really disagree over the moral truth of a particular issue may nevertheless conflict pragmatically over how they want the issue to be resolved and mistakenly assume that their conflict is over the truth. ←

A different objection arises from the foregoing analysis of moral disagreement. If people mean to be referring to a moral fabric of the world, or at any rate to some set of moral facts that would constitute a uniquely true solution to moral disagreements, then aren't they wrong not only in holding those beliefs but in attempting to refer to anything at all when using moral terms? That is, the objection goes, if my arguments succeed, they fail to establish a pluralistic relativism of moral truth, and succeed in establishing moral nihilism—the absence of any moral truth.

The answer to this objection must begin with the observation that failure of reference need not result from a false belief about the putative referent. Not all beliefs about that referent contribute to their truth conditions. Such truth conditions may center on the satisfaction of constraints on normative systems promoting and regulating social cooperation. The fact that many believe these systems to have deeper roots in the fabric of the universe may lead them to think that there is a single true morality, but that mistake may not prevent them from making moral judgments that can be true. In other words, mistakenly thinking that one's morality is the *only* true one may not prevent it from being true.

On the other hand, there is no necessary and absolutely clean separation between the truth conditions of moral judgments and the belief in a uniquely correct morality. The nature of the separation depends on the centrality of the belief in one true morality to one's conception of morality. There is probably no uniform answer for all people to this last question. However, reflection on the nature of morality and on questions about its universality is by no means restricted to professional philosophers or other academics. Nor is rejection of a single true morality limited to academic relativists or beginning students in introduction to philosophy, as so many moral philosophers suppose.

The more important question is whether the false belief in a single correct morality is *separable* from other beliefs about the nature of morality that can make for successful reference. Perhaps a comparable case involves beliefs that many people have (at least in the United States and some other parts of the world) that connect religion and ethics. For at least some of these people, the true moral imperatives are imperatives that come from God. Perhaps this connection is so tight that their moral beliefs turn out to be false if moral imperatives do not have a divine source or if turns out that they incoherently have other moral beliefs that presuppose a status for moral imperatives independent from any divine being. Should we be moved to adopt a skeptical or nihilistic position about morality if it turns out that the moral beliefs of some turn out to be based on a false or inconsistent presuppositions? I don't see why. We need not adopt such a position if we could give a naturalistic account of morality like the one I have offered. Such an account could endorse many moral beliefs that people currently have, even beliefs of those who do hold in a tight connection between religion and ethics. Such an account might very well undermine some moral beliefs that they have, such as the immorality of homosexuality, but it is instructive to remind ourselves that many people have undergone profound changes in some of their central moral beliefs with a change or loss of religious faith. Yet we call them changes in *moral* belief. The separability of a belief in a single true morality from the rest of one's moral beliefs might be like the separability of belief in moral imperatives as coming from God.

3.2 AN OBJECTION TO THE IDEA OF LOCAL CRITERIA OF ADEQUACY: WHY NOT JUST GO WITH UNIVERSAL CRITERIA?

A second objection can be posed as a question about my claim that there are both universal and local criteria for the adequacy of moralities. Some criteria are rooted in the combination of functions that all moralities must perform, human nature and the human condition. Other criteria are not so rooted in such common features and are rather expressions of the contingent value priorities that differentiate one morality from another. The question about my claim is why one should regard these local criteria of adequacy as criteria at all. Why not rather hold that the only criteria for adequacy for moralities are justifiable on the basis of the functions of all moralities and of human nature? If more than one morality satisfies such universally valid criteria, then more than one morality is permissible to adopt. The result is not conflicting moral truths, as I would have it, but a plurality of moralities that are "optional" within the universally valid constraints on moralities. Where the choice between different sets of moral norms is underdetermined by reference to the functions of morality, human nature, and the human condition, why not say that the choice is optional for the individual?

The crucial assumption of this objection is that moral norms apply to individuals only if it is possible to offer them some rationally compulsory justification for guiding their behavior by those norms. Perhaps the justification need not compel them if they have no concerns to act morally, but at least it should be one that individuals could acknowledge to be rationally compulsory if they *did* have an overriding concern to act morally. However, from the standpoint of pluralistic relativism, this assumption begs the question. It begs the question to stipulate that the truth conditions for moral statements are constituted only by those criteria for adequate moralities that are universally valid and that stem from the nature of morality and the human condition. According to pluralistic relativism, the truth conditions for moral statements include local criteria that express certain kinds of priorities among human values, priorities that do not violate canons of rationality. However, it is incumbent on the pluralistic relativist to explain why the truth conditions include such local criteria.

The reason is that universally valid criteria yield merely a skeleton of a morality, insufficiently rich in content to be action guiding. Consider the question of which priorities to place on the kinds of values mentioned earlier: perfectionist versus egalitarian values; individual rights versus some form of group flourishing; individual rights versus utility; and obligations arising from special relationships versus impersonal obligations requiring, for example, respect for rights or promotion of utility. Within a moral tradition, there is room for a significant degree of indeterminacy in the priorities specified, as I believe is the case for rights versus utility in the traditions of the contemporary United States. However, no society could afford to make these matters entirely "optional" in the sense of leaving to individuals the choice of what priorities to impose on each of these possible conflicts of values. The function of morality to facilitate and regulate social cooperation depends on a substantial coordination of expectations between individuals, and this coordination in turn depends on common expectations as to how others will decide to behave when important values conflict. However, the selection of specific priorities among conflicting values is underdetermined by such a general function of morality and by the relevant features of human nature and of the human condition. That is why specific priorities must be established by local criteria within the truth conditions for moral judgments.

At this point, it is natural to raise the following question about the rationale given for local criteria for the adequacy of moralities. If local criteria are needed to produce moralities rich enough in content to be action guiding, then why can't these moralities be regarded simply as different ways of life that are optional for societies, if not for individuals? We have our way and the Romans had their way, but as long as both ways satisfy the universal criteria and are sufficient contentful to fulfill the coordination function, then neither the Romans nor we can make reasonable objection to the other way. Consider an analogy to laws governing the operation of motor vehicles. The rationale for having some fairly specific laws governing which side is the "right" side for forward motion is in some perfectly good sense "universal": people need to have common expectations as to how others will drive, for example, on the right or the left side of a two-way road. However, we are content to let different countries decide the content of those specific laws in different ways. The fact that British law directs drivers to the lefthand side while U.S. law directs them to the righthand side provokes no pondering over which is really the correct side. The scope of moralities would then be limited, with respect to local criteria, to the communities that have adopted those criteria. In other words, permissibility gets transferred to the societal rather than the individual level.[2]

Pluralistic relativism does allow for this kind of attitude toward other moralities and the societies that have adopted them, and I suggest that this is an explanatory virtue. To a certain extent, some people in a variety of different historical periods

---

2. Permissibility on the individual level can reenter on this scenario if people have the ability to move into those societies with moralities to which they assent.

and societies *have* broadened their conception of the range of permissible moralities, and in many cases this has been an eminently reasonable and enlightened attitude to take. Surely we are better off having left behind the days when someone could unreflectively assume that something called "Western European civilization" represented in most of its particularities the form of life to which all human beings should aspire.

A different objection, however, is that it becomes disturbing to extend this acceptance of moral diversity to ways of life that differ in the importance placed on, say, individual rights versus group flourishing, or on side-constraints on the means taken to achieve desirable ends versus consequentialism. It can be difficult to think of our criteria with respect to these kinds of cases as simply local. The choice between these criteria seems momentous. What turns on the acceptance of one or the other is the most serious kind of human harm and benefit. It seems extremely difficult to accept that one's criteria for the correct priorities are simply matters of what direction one's culture happens to have taken in giving us a sufficiently contentful guide to action. Yet on pluralistic relativism there exists no principled boundary between the acceptance of relatively unproblematic cases of pluralistic broadening of one's morality and other cases in which one is greatly reluctant to accept the relative validity of local criteria. This might be posed, therefore, as a problem for pluralistic relativism.

In dealing with this apparent problem, one first of all needs to distinguish between various possible sources of the reluctance. The fact that much seems at stake in how some priorities between values are set might lead one to assume that the choice between priorities should be made according to universal criteria for the adequacy of moralities. One might assume this because of the expectation mentioned earlier: that a true moral judgment is necessarily a sufficient guide to action, at least if one is committed to morality as a guide to action. Given this expectation, one becomes reluctant to accept that especially momentous moral choices might have multiple true resolutions that are pragmatically incompatible. If this is the source of our reluctance, then we need first of all to determine whether the choice of priorities is indeed something that can be resolved by reference to universal criteria (and of course, my theory allows that this is sometimes the case). If it is not, then we might simply have to broaden our view of what other ways of life are acceptable. We might have to accept such a broadened view, however reluctant we are to take it, as the price of a plausible naturalistic account of morality that is consistent with the phenomenon of moral ambivalence.

3.3 FIRST-ORDER NORMATIVE ISSUES RAISED BY THE IDEA OF LOCAL CRITERIA

However, a different source of the reluctance to accept other ways of life is simply that these other ways of life severely violate norms of the way of life we ourselves hold dear. From the purely metaethical perspective defined by the tenets of pluralistic relativism, one is not rationally *required* to take the sort of attitude illustrated by the rules-of-the-road case, though one is *permitted* to take it. From a metaethical perspective, one can accept another way of life in the sense of recognizing it as based on true moral judgments (i.e., satisfying universal criteria and satisfying at the same time its own local criteria). However, from a first-order, normative perspective, one is entitled to reject that other way of life on the grounds that at least some of its norms are morally repugnant. One makes that judgment on the basis of one's own criteria, however local some of those criteria might be. This is a first-order normative judgment one can make only on the basis of one's values, which is the only way to make such a judgment.

In making a judgment as to how one morally ought to react to other ways of life, one needs to consider the importance of the values and the priorities in conflict. The range of possible and reasonable reactions is varied, depending on the nature of the particular case at hand. In some cases, one may feel that one's own values are so deeply violated by others that one cannot fail to defend those values and at the same time think of oneself as committed to them. The fact that others could deny the importance we place on these values does not rationally require *us* to attach less importance to these values. On the other hand, there will be cases in which understanding another group's moral perspective might enrich one's sense of moral possibility. One might not be able to endorse the other perspective, but one also might be reluctant to condemn it. Moral difference, as I argued in chapter 1, is not typically the result of brute confrontation between mutually unintelligible ways of life but a confrontation between ways of life that significantly overlap with respect to some important values. Moreover, if one makes an effort to understand another moral tradition's capacities for self-criticism, one might see that it has resources to acknowledge at least some of the concerns that are most important to one's own tradition, even if the grounds for such acknowledgment in the other tradition are different. The attitude one takes might therefore have to be somewhat more complex than complete endorsement or rejection. In chapter 9, I discuss the controversy over female genital cutting, which displays all the complicating normative factors I have mentioned. In this chapter, I discuss the conflict between moralities that emphasize the good of community life versus those that emphasize individual rights, which may seem one of the most severe conflicts.

3.4 THE CASE OF COMMUNITY-CENTERED VERSUS RIGHTS-CENTERED MORALITIES

How can those who deeply believe in individual rights accept that community-based moralities are false only on their own local criteria for adequate moralities? How can they accept that rights to freedom of thought and of expression are only required on local criteria? On the other side, how can those who believe in the good of community accept that the rights of the individual can override that good on the basis of local criteria accepted in other moralities?

This sort of conflict can soften upon recognition of the need for communitarian moralities to recognize rights to dissent and criticism. Communitarian moralities such as Confucianism have the core value of a common good at their center.[3] This common good consists in a shared life as defined by a network of roles specifying the contribution of each member to the sustenance of that life. This type of morality contrasts with a rights-centered morality, which gives no comparable emphasis to a common good. Rather it emphasizes what each individual, qua individual, is entitled to claim from other members. Rights-centered moralities spring from a recognition of the moral worth of individuals independently of their roles in community. As I use the term "rights-centered," it therefore includes a conception of the characteristic ground for the recognition of individual rights, as well as a generic conception of rights. We may think of the individual's generic moral rights as that to which the individual is legitimately entitled to claim against others as her moral entitlement. But a rights-centered morality typically assumes as a basis for such entitlements that the individual has substantial domain of morally legitimate personal interests that may conflict with the goal of promoting public or collective goods. Rights constitute constraints or limits on the extent that individual personal interests may be sacrificed for the sake of public or collective goods. Let me call this kind of ground for the recognition of rights "the autonomy ground."

There is, however, another possible ground for the recognition of rights that may exist alongside the autonomy ground. Rights may be recognized on the basis of their necessity for promoting the common good. Community-centered moralities can and should recognize this sort of "communal ground" for rights. Rights-centered and community-centered moralities, then, need not differ because one recognizes rights while the other does not. They must differ in the sort of basis they offer for the recognition of rights. Consider the case of Confucianism.

3.5 THE COMMUNAL GROUND FOR RIGHTS

Heiner Roetz has very usefully identified some themes in the Confucian canon that could serve as the basis for what I have called a communal ground for rights to dissent and freedom of speech.[4] Consider the following translation by Roetz of a passage from the *Zi dao (The Way of the Son)*, chapter 29 of the *Xunzi*.

---

3. In *Moral Relativity* (Berkeley: University of California Press, 1984), I labeled communitarian moralities 'virtue-centered' moralities, because historically the concept of a virtue has been conceived as a quality needed by members to contribute to the common good of community. However, it now seems to me at least theoretically possible that virtues can become uncoupled from a common good and be deemed desirable qualities on some basis other than their necessity for a shared life. I therefore avoid the association of communitarian or community-centered moralities with virtue-centered moralities.

4. Heiner Roetz, *Confucian Ethics of the Axial Age: A Reconstruction under the Aspect of the Breakthrough toward Postconventional Thinking* (Albany: State University of New York Press, 1993).

Zigong said, "If a son follows the order of the father, this is already filial piety. And if a subject follows the order of the ruler, this is already loyalty. But what is the answer of my teacher?"

Confucius said, "What a mean man you are! You do not know that in antiquity, if there were four frank ministers in a state with ten thousand war-chariots, its territory was never diminished. If there were three frank ministers in a state with a thousand war-chariots, that state was never endangered. And if there were two frank subordinates in a clan with one hundred war-chariots, its ancestral temple was never destroyed. If a father has a frank son, he will not do anything that contradicts propriety. If a scholar has a frank friend, he will not do anything unjust. *How, then, could a son be filial if he follows the order of his father? And how could a subject be loyal if he follows the order of the ruler? One can only speak of filial piety and loyalty after one has examined the reasons why they follow the order.*[5]

The implication of this passage is that one has a duty to speak frankly when the violation of propriety and justice is in question, even if it is the ruler who is about to violate them. While the passage does not identify a right to speak, as opposed to a duty, we may infer such a right as a necessary presupposition of the duty. One has a justified claim to be allowed to speak and to dissent where one has a duty to do so. The interest of this passage lies in its suggestion that a communal ground exists for rights of free speech and dissent. It is in the interests of having a community that realizes propriety and justice that we should recognize such rights.

It is of further interest that the contemporary Western debate between communitarian and rights-centered theorists has given rise to the same idea of a communal ground for individual rights of free speech and dissent. Allen Buchanan, for example, has suggested that

individual rights can play a valuable role even in societies in which there is unanimous agreement as to what the common good is and a universal commitment to pursuing it. For even in such a society there could be serious, indeed violent, disagreements either about how the common good is to be specified concretely and in detail or about the proper means and strategies for achieving it. Individual rights, especially rights of political participation, freedom of expression, and association can serve to contain and channel such disagreements and to preserve community in spite of their presence.[6]

In other words, one could argue from the common good for the recognition of basic civil and political rights, or at least the rights to freedom of expression, religion,

---

5. Xianqian Wang, *Xunzi jijie*, trans. Heiner Roetz, chap. 29, in *Zhuzi jicheng*, vol. 2 (Hong Kong: Zhonghua, 1978), 347–8; 63–4.

6. Allen E. Buchanan, "Assessing the Communitarian Critique of Liberalism," *Ethics* 99 (1989): 877.

association, and political participation. The argument would be based on the "need to protect and allow for the peaceful transformations of communities."[7] A similar idea underlies the notion of controlled "liminality" spaces in the work of the anthropologist Victor Turner. These are spaces each culture provides outside the everyday positions in the established social structure that allow people to engage in critical reflection on features of their way of life. This liminality may be essential to cultural survival in leaving space for criticism that leads to culturally beneficial reform and revision of existing standards.[8]

A communal grounding for rights could be given within a contextualist and postmodernist interpretation of Confucianism, provided that such an interpretation still leaves room for criticism of the tradition. Hall and Ames, despite their vigorous defense of Confucianism, observe that "the most serious failings of Confucius's philosophy are due to the provincialism and parochialism that seem inevitably to result from the institutionalization of his thinking." This parochialism, they charge, retards "cross-cultural communication" and fosters abuses that cross the "fine line that keeps social order beginning at home separate from nepotism, personal loyalties from special privilege, deference to excellence from elitism, appropriate respect from graft," and, finally, "appropriate deference to the tradition and a cultural dogmatism that has too frequently been in the interests of particular groups."[9] Again, one could argue that part of an appropriate remedy for these failings is recognition and vigorous protection of rights to free speech and dissent.

One could argue, in fact, that the idea of rights as a means of promoting the common good is already part of the Chinese tradition. This is confirmed not only by Roetz's reading of passages such as the one from Xunzi but by a historical reading of the tradition as it has evolved. Andrew Nathan, in his study of Chinese conceptions of democracy, identifies in Chinese thinking about democracy just this very idea of rights. Early in this century, the influential political thinker Liang Qichao saw rights as consisting of that which it is appropriate for the citizen to do. As Nathan describes his thinking, "the duties of citizens are to love and be concerned about the nation. Hence political participation should unleash energies that will contribute to the collective welfare; it would not—as a Westerner might see it—enable individuals to pursue personal interests that might be competitive with that welfare."[10]

Later in this century, some democratic thinkers following in Liang's footsteps argued that China's problems in modernizing stemmed from the "systematic overconcentration

---

7. Buchanan, "Assessing the Comunitarian Critique," 881.

8. Victor Turner, *Dramas, Fields, and Metaphors: Symbolic Action in Human Society* (Ithaca: Cornell University Press, 1974).

9. David Hall and Roger Ames, *Thinking through Confucius* (Albany: State University of New York Press, 1987), 308–9, 310.

10. Andrew Nathan, *Chinese Democracy* (Berkeley: University of California Press, 1985), 51.

of power," yet they very rarely put forward a line of reasoning central to the Western democratic tradition: "that the individual's interests are separate from the group's, that certain of them are so basic as to have the status of 'rights,' and that democracy is first of all a system that protects these rights."[11]

Having roughly outlined the case for the possibility of communally grounded democratic rights, let me note that a communal grounding is different from a utilitarian grounding for rights, though both groundings are consequentialist in character. A utilitarian grounding of rights would make the case for their utility, where the sum total of utility is a function of the welfare of individuals. For most utilitarians, anyway, the character of the relations between individuals does not in itself necessarily count as part of the total good to be promoted.[12] But it is precisely the character of the relations between individuals that is the primary focus of community-centered moralities. Underlying this focus is a normative and descriptive conception of persons as constituted by their relationships to others and whose good is constituted by relationships that fulfill a moral ideal of appropriate respect and mutual concern. A community-centered morality must, of course, concern itself with some of the same goods with which utilitarianism is concerned. Both Mencius and Xunzi, for example, knew full well that their moral ideals of community could not begin to be fulfilled without a minimal level of material security for the people. And that has remained a preoccupation for Confucians up to the present. But a community-centered morality locates the importance of individual welfare within the larger context of a common good. In fact, the individual's good and the common good are inextricably linked.

Having noted the possibility of providing a communal ground for rights, however, we must note what such a ground does not provide. Rights grounded in community will not be precisely the same as rights grounded in autonomy. As Buchanan notes, if one were to justify individual rights only by reference to the moral requirement of autonomy, one might justify a "rather broad, virtually unrestricted right to freedom of expression." If, however, we allow the value of community "independent weight as a factor in determining the scope of the right of freedom of expression, we might find that only a more restricted right of freedom of expression can be justified." Therefore, concludes Buchanan, "in the justification of individual rights, the traditional liberal and the [rights-minded] communitarian may travel the same path for some time, but eventually the path may fork and they may be forced to part company."[13] Indeed, it might be that the rights-minded communitarian and the traditional liberal will part

11. Nathan, *Chinese Democracy*, 104.

12. An exception would be the "ideal" form of utilitarianism such as G. E. Moore held. This form counts certain states of affairs or relationships of a certain character as part of the total good to be promoted. More recently, Peter Railton has developed a theory that in some respects resembles Moore's ideal utilitarianism, in that he also counts certain kinds of relationships as part of the good. See his "Alienation, Consequentialism and Morality," *Philosophy and Public Affairs* 13 (1984): 159.

13. Buchanan, "Assessing the Communitarian Critique," 881.

sooner rather than later, and quite dramatically, depending on what the communitarian perceives as necessary for the common good.

But what is important to note in this context is that the gap between community-centered and rights-centered moralities is not as wide as it may have first appeared. Even if rights with a purely communal ground do not have the same scope as rights with a strong autonomy ground, the area of overlap will not be insignificant. A rights-centered moralist may find within a community-centered morality a basis for condemning severe violations of rights even if that basis is not the same as hers. In advocating the protection of these rights, she need not self-righteously assume that a community-centered morality is necessarily defective because it fails to ground rights in individual autonomy. Rather, she may succeed in finding a basis for condemning rights violations in the moral terms of a communal ground.

The aim of this discussion is not to acquire complete approval of community-centered moralities from those who have been committed to rights-centered moralities, or vice versa. The aim has been to suggest that a more complex attitude different from either complete approval or rejection might indeed seem appropriate. In the end, if we are making first-order normative judgments about the acceptability of another group's morality, we are making these judgments on the basis of our own values. But such judgments can be made with nuance and in light of the recognition that moral difference and commonality are frequently found together in the most serious cases of moral disagreement. For example, those who are committed to a rights-centered morality can acknowledge the good of community as an important human value, and indeed, as I shall suggest in section 3.7 and chapters 4 and 5, they have reason to recognize the good of community as a necessary support for nurturing commitment to individual rights. Yet they may at the same time reject the kind of priority placed on that good within community-centered moral traditions. Yet again, they can find upon closer examination that certain protections for the individual they have previously associated only with rights-centered traditions are provided, to a certain extent and on different grounds, with the other kind of tradition. While a more complex attitude toward the other tradition is not rationally required, it seems pretty reasonable in light of the points of connection and disconnection that can be made with that other tradition.

3.6 COMMUNITY-CENTERED MORALITIES AND THE PROBLEM OF HIERARCHY

This is another way in which the gap between community-centered and rights-centered moralities may not be as large as some may think. Some may associate community-centered moralities with objectionable hierarchy, with the "common good" masking the dominance of certain groups or social roles over others. But anthropology provides examples of nonhierarchical communal moralities. The G/wi (the oblique stroke represents a click consonant) Bushmen of the central Kalahari desert in Botswana have a community-centered morality that is egalitarian. "In G/wi exchanges," remarks George

Silberbauer, "the service or good to another was evaluated by the recipient's need for it, discounted by the donor's capacity to give." Such exchanges were in the service of establishing and maintaining harmonious relationships. Further, in G/wi bands (of hunter-gatherers) "there were as many valued social positions as there were those who sought them. Statuses were not ranked (with the exception of the culturally limited authority which parents had over their children)."[14] Of course, the moralities of small-scale societies such as that of the G/wi have limited generalizability to moralities for large-scale societies, but whatever hierarchy is needed in large-scale societies does not require justifications by reference to natural hierarchies among people or claims about innate differences.

It further is relevant to note that many traditional forms of community have been for all intents and purposes destroyed. The rise of the modern nation-state and capitalist economic practices have undermined the fabric of communities so that many of them no longer provide individuals with the kinds of protections and satisfactions they once did. In such cases, human rights advocates have a case in arguing that individuals need the protection that individual rights afford. Further, these communities have become internally diverse, with some espousing notions of individual rights with an autonomy ground. Others believe some fundamental change is necessary but resist the idea of importing Western moral notions wholesale. It remains to be seen whether new forms of community could evolve that afford the same sorts of protections and satisfactions the traditional ones provided and that do not depend on indefensible forms of hierarchy. It is clear that some thinkers in areas of the world with eroded traditional forms of community have had such a third possibility in mind. They hope to contribute to the evolution of new forms of community compatible with modernization but without what they see to be the individualistic excesses of Western liberalism and the oppressiveness of traditional structures.

There is already evidence from Japan and India that modernizing an economy does not require the wholesale elimination of traditional attitudes that support a community-oriented morality, though it must also be said at the same time that the record of evidence is still very much in the making.[15] Consider Henry Rosemont's reflections on the question of whether the conceptual framework of human rights is appropriate to the present Chinese situation. He argues that the classical Confucian heritage is still

14. George Silberbauer, "Ethics in Small-Scale Societies," in *A Companion to Ethics*, ed. Peter Singer (Oxford: Blackwell, 1991), 20.

15. For a description of this work on India, see Alan Roland, *In Search of Self in India and Japan: Toward a Cross-Cultural Psychology* (Princeton: Princeton University Press, 1988), 90–104. For a description of Japan and the relation between community-oriented attitudes and modernization, see George DeVos, *Socialization for Achievement* (Berkeley: University of California Press, 1973), and "Dimensions of the Self in Japanese Culture," in *Culture and Self: Asian and Western Perspectives*, ed. A. J. Marsella, G. DeVos, and F.L.K. Hsu (London: Tavistock, 1985), 141–84. See also Roland, *In Search of Self in India and Japan*, especially 130–7.

what makes the millions of people Chinese. That framework, he thinks, is the better one from which to address the evils of imprisonment and torture for political beliefs—evils that require, according to most in the West, the assertion of human rights. Granting that the classical Confucian heritage has shortcomings such as its endorsement of patriarchy, Rosemont argues that it is possible to excise them from the tradition. He argues that the centrality of the family that is the core of the Chinese tradition may be combined with the ideal of sexual equality and the acceptance of different sexual orientations: "the conceptual framework of Confucianism would surely be impoverished by their [gays and lesbians] exclusion, enriched by their inclusion."[16]

As in the case of rights to dissent and freedom of speech, we may find a different kind of basis for advocating the value of equality in a community-centered tradition. There may be in another strongly community-centered tradition no basis for equal individual rights if such rights are conceived with an autonomy ground. Hence there can be no such basis for condemnation of the subordination of women in that tradition. On the other hand, one could forcefully argue from within the tradition that the subordination of women unnecessarily restricts the ways in which women can make a contribution to the common moral ends of the community and deprives them of the dignity that would come from making such a contribution.

The story "White Tigers" by Maxine Hong Kingston can be read as bringing home just such a point.[17] Kingston retells the traditional Chinese ballad of a young woman who takes the place of her aged father when he is called into the army. In the course of that retelling, she juxtaposes the valor and resourcefulness of the woman warrior with the subordinate place allotted to women in the traditional culture. Other Asian American writers, mostly male, have criticized Kingston for forsaking the tradition, but her story can be read as a protest rooted within the tradition—the protest that women have not been allowed to contribute to the community in ways in which they are fully capable of contributing. The story gains its power from its juxtaposition of the woman warrior's satisfaction in demonstrating her "perfect filiality" on the one hand and on the other hand the contemporary narrator's inability to win from her family appreciation for any of her worldly achievements.[18] The appeal is to the core values in the Chinese tradition of community and filiality and the demand that women be given a full opportunity to realize those values. Within Chinese philosophy, Sin Yee Chan has argued persuasively that foundational Confucian texts (the *Analects* of Confucius and the *Mencius*) provide no basis for the exclusion of women from aspiration to become a *junzi* (the character ideal of the superior or noble person who is often depicted as aspiring to or occupying

---

16. Henry Rosemont Jr., *A Chinese Mirror: Moral Reflections on Political Economy and Society* (LaSalle, Ill.: Open Court, 1991), 76.

17. Maxine Hong Kingston, *The Woman Warrior: Memoirs of a Girlhood among Ghosts* (New York: Knopf, 1976).

18. The term "perfect filiality" is from Kingston, *Woman Warrior*, 45.

political office).[19] Enduring moral traditions have the sort of internal complexity that allows for significant change that is at the same time in accordance with at least some of their core values. A recent study of Asian attitudes toward the relations between the sexes indicates that change is taking place. A psychologist and a historian found that love matches—versus arranged alliances—and egalitarian families, versus patriarchal, hierarchical arrangements, are gaining ground in Asia.[20]

Consider another example of change toward greater egalitarianism within a communal ethical tradition. An anthropological study of the Greek community of Ammouliani revealed interesting ways in which people have adapted the traditional conception of marriage and household to new conditions of modernization—ways in which women are respected as essential and nonsubordinate partners in the family enterprise. The ethical ideal in that community is economic independence (as opposed to wage labor) for each household. Both men and women there retain the traditional belief that primary fulfillment of the individual is found in the family and tied to the socially desirable goals of marriage, childrearing, and the building of a future for one's children. What is untraditional in that community is the departure from the conception of women's role in the family enterprise. Women have an equal voice in capital expenditure in the family business, may initiate and manage their own expenditures, and, in short, possess prestige and power equal to or greater than that of their husbands. It is financial and managerial skill, rather than beauty, intelligence, cleverness, or housekeeping acumen, that both men and women of the community feel are essential for women to possess. And yet this unusual status for women is not achieved through recognition of rights that women have against the family or their husbands. Rather, it is through recognition of the ability of women to contribute to the enterprise that is the primary fulfillment of both men and women. One woman from the community illustrates this point:

> If a woman has her own household, her man, her children, if her children are healthy, it's her whole life. Those are the most important things to her. What kind of life would she have if she went out merry-making alone and came back to find her husband had made some great mistake and her daughter was out who knows where?[21]

This sentiment is often associated with subordination to men, but the study indicates that it is not so associated in this case.

---

19. Sin Yee Chan, "Gender and Relationship Roles in the *Analects* and the *Mencius*," *Asian Philosophy* 10 (2000): 115–31.

20. Elaine Hatfield and Richard Rapson, *Love and Sex: Cross-Cultural Perspectives* (Boston: Allyn and Bacon, 1996), 30, 49–51, 240–2.

21. Interviewed by Stephen D. Salamone, in "Tradition and Gender: The Nikokyrio: The Economics of Sex Role Complementarity in Rural Greece," *Ethos* 15 (1987): 216. Jill Dubisch reaches similar conclusions about the status of women on the island of Tinos, in "The Domestic Power of Women in a Greek Island Village," *Studies in European Society* 1 (1974): 23–33.

3.7 THE INTERDEPENDENCE OF RIGHTS AND COMMUNITY

So far I have discussed ways in which community-centered moralities must come closer to rights-centered moralities in offering some important protections and opportunities for individuals, even if the moral ground for such protections and opportunities is not the same. But it goes the other way also: rights-centered moralities must recognize the importance of community. Some United States political theorists have recently worried about the lack of an infrastructure of politically effective associations that could serve as channels of communication and influence between the family and local forms of community on the one hand and the national levels of government on the other.[22] These theorists see Tocqueville as prescient about the dangers of an atomistic individualism that leaves citizens isolated, pursuing their purely private interests, and quite ineffective in making their voices heard in the political sphere because their voices are single.

The problem for the American tradition goes beyond the problem of alienation from the political process for average citizens. Consider Tocqueville's definition of individualism as a "calm and considered feeling which disposes each citizen to isolate himself from the mass of his fellows and withdraw into the circle of family and friends," such that "with this little society formed to his taste he gladly leaves the greater society to look after itself." Such people, Tocqueville observed, form "the habit of thinking of themselves in isolation and imagine that their whole destiny is in their hands." They come to "forget their ancestors" and also their descendants, as well as isolating themselves from their contemporaries. "Each man is forever thrown back on himself alone, and there is danger that he may be shut up in the solitude of his own heart."[23]

Tocqueville's prescience concerning our isolation from our contemporaries and our descendants is reflected in the national unwillingness to address the problem of a potentially permanent class of the severely disadvantaged beset by poverty, crime, and drugs. It is not just political participation at stake here but more basically a question of moral agency and integrity (a problem about which I will have more to say in chapters 4, 5, and 6). This brings me to the mirror image of the truth that community-centered moralities should move closer to rights-centered moralities, at least in recognizing some of the most fundamental democratic rights. So, too, must rights-centered moralities recognize the indispensability of community for the realization of democratic values of self-governance and social justice. Rights and community are interdependent.

22. See, for example, Robert N. Bellah, Richard Madsen, William M. Sullivan, Ann Swidler, and Steven M. Tipton, *Habits of the Heart* (Berkeley: University of California Press, 1985).

23. Alexis de Tocqueville, *Democracy in America*, trans. George Lawrence, ed. J. Mayer (New York: Doubleday, 1969), 506, 508.

3.8 THE PLURALITY OF WAYS TO REACT
TO MORAL DIFFERENCE

I hope that what has been shown here is that we do not need rights with an autonomy ground to condemn torture of political dissidents or the subjugation of one group by another group on the grounds of the former's alleged inferiority. It is presumptuous to assume that others can make moral progress only if they adopt Western liberal values. It also is mistaken from a strategic viewpoint if one is truly interested in promoting some of the same protections and opportunities for individuals that are required by those same Western values. A plurality of adequate moralities prohibits cruelty and self-interested domination. On the other side, many institutionalized rights-centered moralities rightly receive criticism for their lack of community, but one need not be a Confucian to recognize the force of such criticism.

Of course, not everything we want to condemn will fall into this category of wrongs sanctioned by all adequate moralities. There will be cases where we want to condemn an action or policy or practice of another society, but where no basis for condemnation is present in what constitutes an adequate morality in that society. In such a case, we must make a choice, but the range of options and of considerations to be weighed is typically more complicated than is usually supposed by the critics of relativism. For one thing, there is the value of accommodation (discussed in sec. 2.12), which should be common to all adequate moralities. Such a value weighs against the option of unilateral intervention into the affairs of the other society in order to compel in one fashion or another conformance to those of our values in question. There is the value we have of respect for other peoples. Together with the recognition that their culture and moral values, in particular, may confer meaning and dignity on their lives, just as ours do on our own, this value also weighs against unilateral intervention. A related value we have is respect for the freedom of other peoples. We do not wish to impose on them a course of action that they themselves could not see to be justified or required. In *Moral Relativity*, I traced this theme of not wishing to impose without rational assent to the liberal contract ethic that forms so strong a part of the Western moral tradition. Samuel Fleischacker finds a similar theme in Aquinas and the doctrine of "invincible ignorance," which refers to a lack of knowledge that the person in question has done everything in her power to overcome. According to Aquinas, invincible ignorance serves as a complete excuse for all wrongdoing, including offenses against natural law and failure to accept Christianity.[24]

On the other side, the values in question may be so important to us, and the other society's violation of those values so grave, that we may feel we would fail ourselves, turn our own commitment to those values into a sham, if we did nothing.

---

24. Fleischacker, in *Integrity and Moral Relativism* (Leiden: Brill, 1992), 193, cites Thomas Aquinas, *Summa Theologica* 1–2, ques. 94, art. 4.

As Fleischacker has observed, the actions of another individual or group may constitute

> an affront to our specific norms...so deep that if we were to tolerate such behavior, we could not maintain our belief that we ourselves have respect and charity for all human beings: that tolerance in this case would destroy our values as much as intolerance might in other cases.[25]

In opposing the practices that deeply violate our values, we could be honest in stating that the reason for our interest is our own values and a concern for our own integrity (indeed, this may be less offensive to others than the claim that we are correcting some practice of theirs that they should know to be wrong). Further, as noted earlier, some non-Western communities have become more diverse, with some members advocating Western notions of individual rights. In such cases, any kind of intervention into the affairs of a community is not entirely an intervention from the outside.

One's response to serious moral difference need not be complete passivity and acceptance of what others believe and do, nor need it be a categorical refusal to give weight to what they believe and do. There is no simple general principle for deciding exactly what to do, but the kind of deliberation necessary in such cases is of a similar nature to deliberation in other cases in which important values one holds conflict with each other. I return to these normative issues in chapter 9.

3.9 IS PLURALISTIC RELATIVISM A KIND OF RELATIVISM AT ALL?

As noted in the introduction, relativism has typically been defined as the view that any morality is as good (i.e., as true or as justified) as any other. One possible reaction to my theory, therefore, is that it is not "real" relativism and is more properly labeled pluralism *simpliciter*. Indeed, it might be argued that by labeling my theory a kind of relativism, I draw unnecessary controversy by associating it with a name of such low repute.

Let me first grant that if someone insists on defining relativism as an extreme subjectivist view of morality that refuses to make any distinctions between better and worse moralities, then of course my view is not relativistic. However, simply pasting the label "pluralism" onto my view carries its own potential for confusion. The label has had its own problems and has carried an incompatible range of meanings that are too often blurred together. Consider the thesis I have called in chapter 1 "moral value pluralism"—that there are plural moral values that are basic in the sense of not being derivable from or reducible to other values. This is the minimal core meaning of any

25. Fleischacker, *Integrity and Moral Relativism*, 186.

view I would call 'pluralist'. Add to moral value pluralism Isaiah Berlin's claim that there can be no utopia in which the maximal realizations of these different sorts of value are made compatible with each other. Pluralists typically accept this claim, even though there is no relation of entailment holding between it and the first claim. Aside from these two standard and widely accepted meanings of pluralism, there is a great deal of ambiguity.

Consider the fact that Nagel, who is a pluralist in the first two senses, also holds that conflicts between the realizations of values are generally resolvable through the exercise of judgment. There are no master rules for resolving all conflicts, say, between rights and utility, but on individual occasions of conflict between these values, there is the possibility of making objectively correct judgments as to how the conflict should be resolved. Which judgments are objectively correct depends on the circumstances and nature of the conflict of values on the particular occasions. It is a matter neither of the identity of the individuals making the judgment nor of the standards of judgment they actually utilize. Nagel's pluralism is consistent with a view that deserves to be called a form of universalism.[26]

Another view that might deserve the label 'pluralism' is a Kantian view that is pluralistic about the ultimate (nonmoral) goods to be sought but holds that there are universally valid principles of right action. John Rawls's pluralism of "thick" conceptions of the good, combined with his argument for a liberal democratic interpretation of justice that is supposed to be neutral toward any particular conception of the good, at one time looked like it might be a version of this Kantian universalism.[27] As his view has evolved, however, he seems to intend his theory of justice to be a political theory that allows for a reasonable range of different theories of the right and the good to overlap in agreement on principles that govern the basic structure of social cooperation in a pluralistic society. These principles are not addressed to the sorts of ultimate questions about moral truth that are the subject of "comprehensive doctrines." Indeed, the whole point of political liberalism, as Rawls came to conceive it, is to provide a set of political doctrines on which conflicting comprehensive doctrines converge.

Isaiah Berlin, the most influential of pluralists to address the ultimate questions about moral truth, articulates an especially problematic form of this view. He characterizes the fundamental idea of pluralism as a rejection of a Platonic ideal—the belief

---

26. Thomas Nagel, "The Fragmentation of Value," in *Mortal Questions* (Cambridge: Cambridge University Press, 1979), 139. However, Nagel grants as a possibility that "real values will yield mutually inconsistent orderings, leading to conflicts between individuals who justify their choices and order their lives or their societies by reference to these conflicting choices." See Thomas Nagel, "Pluralism and Coherence," in *The Legacy of Isaiah Berlin*, ed. Ronald Dworkin, Mark Lilla, and Robert B. Silvers (New York: New York Review of Books, 2001), 109.

27. Rawls, *A Theory of Justice* (Cambridge, Mass.: Harvard University Press, 1971), might reasonably be read in this way, as Rawls himself grants in *Justice as Fairness: A Restatement* (Cambridge, Mass.: Belknap Press, 2001), xvii, 186.

that all genuine questions must have one true answer and one only; that there must be a dependable path toward the discovery of these truths; and that the true answers must necessarily be compatible with each other and form a single whole.[28] Berlin's rejection of the Platonic ideal suggests a pluralism that goes beyond the two core meanings, but he insisted that it was not relativism, which he defined as a kind of emotivism or subjectivism about moral judgments that deprives them of truth value.[29] In discussion of Vico's and Herder's views, Berlin appears to associate pluralism with the claim that the many kinds of happiness, beauty, goodness or visions of life "all respond to the real needs and aspirations of normal human beings; each fits its circumstances, its country, its people; the relation of fitting is the same in all these cases."[30] Berlin cites with approval certain sixteenth-century Reformers who "insisted on the equally objective validity of different sets of values for dissimilar societies and conditions; and believed that the appropriateness of a particular code to a particular society and form of life could be demonstrated by universally valid, that is non-relativist, factual and logical considerations."[31]

Without further qualification, such a view threatens indiscriminate generosity toward all actual codes and forms of life. Surely, if appropriateness of code or way of life is to have any bite as a normative concept of evaluation, some codes or ways of life should turn out to fail the test. Furthermore, Berlin does not explain how he can make good on his claim that the appropriateness of each actual code could be established on purely logical and factual considerations, where presumably such considerations are distinguished from judgments based on values that cannot be fully reconciled. What would these decisive and universally valid considerations show? If society A's circumstances make its code appropriate for A but inappropriate for society B, is it because their different circumstances are such that different codes produce the same *desirable end states* for both societies? And how are such end states judged to be desirable? It would seem that if each and every actual code is appropriate for its society, and "fitting in the same way," there must be some overarching normative framework within which such determinations of appropriateness are made. In this case, Berlin's form of pluralism morphs into a higher order universalism. Berlin gives no clue as to what such an overarching framework could be, and if in the absence of such a framework we interpret him to mean that each and every moral code is appropriate for its society, his pluralism seems to have collapsed into the kind of relativism he emphatically rejected. Berlin's pluralism turns out to be a confused mix of universalism and relativism rather than a legitimate alternative.

28. Isaiah Berlin, *The Crooked Timber of Humanity*, ed. Henry Hardy (Princeton: Princeton University Press, 1990), 5–6.

29. Berlin, *Crooked Timber*, 80.

30. Berlin, *Crooked Timber*, 84.

31. Berlin, *Crooked Timber*, 83.

To add to the confusion, Berlin sometimes states that a pluralism of true answers to the same question entails the superiority of the ideal of "negative liberty" to choose among the plurality of true answers: "Pluralism, with the measure of 'negative' liberty that it entails, seems to me a truer and more humane ideal than the goals of those who seek in the great, disciplined, authoritarian structures the ideal of 'positive' self-mastery by classes, or peoples, or the whole of mankind."[32] The problem is that this positive ideal is embodied in many of the actual moral codes that Berlin presumably wants to say are demonstrably appropriate for their societies on the basis of logical and factual considerations. A way of life that upholds negative liberty to choose within a range of ways of life is competitive with other ways of life that do not allow that latitude. Much criticism of Berlin has centered on the apparent tension between his acceptance of a plurality of true answers and his belief in the superiority of liberalism and its ideal of negative liberty.[33] The way he differentiates pluralism from relativism seems to confuse rather than to clarify the matter, and this may in part have stemmed from an understandable desire of pluralists to claim for a way of life that values pluralism a kind of singular truth or justifiability that usually is associated with universalism.

The theory defended here does not deliver such singularity, but it does provide an objective, naturalistic basis for universal judgments about the adequacy of moralities. It in fact avoids the pitfall of indiscriminate generosity toward any moral code that has been adopted by a society, but it does not declare the liberal morality of negative liberty to be any truer than the others that can be judged adequate according to the functions I attributed to morality in the previous chapter. In the latter sense, my pluralism is more relativistic than Berlin's.

Let me return to my immediate point in reply to the objection: the label 'pluralism' is by no means unproblematic. The fact is that once one gets beyond the core meanings of pluralism, which are clearly too weak to answer the fundamental issues between relativists and universalists, one encounters a variety of views, some of which deserve to be called universalistic, such as Nagel's, and some of which fall into conceptual confusion, such as Berlin's. I fail to see how adopting the terminology of 'pluralism', minus the 'relativism', helps to clarify matters.

Furthermore, use of the term 'pluralism' *simpliciter* can be deceptive if used to imply that rejecting the extreme subjectivist forms of relativism will leave us on unproblematic grounds with respect to our moral commitments. If we reject as implausible, as I think we should, the idea that the moral code adopted in a given society turns out to be uniquely appropriate to that society, then we must face disquieting questions about the particular

32. Isaiah Berlin, "Two Concepts of Liberty," in *Liberty: Incorporating Four Essays on Liberty* (Oxford: Oxford University Press, 2002), 216.

33. See for example John Gray, in *Berlin* (London: Fontana, 1995); Richard Rorty, *Contingency, Irony, and Solidarity* (Cambridge: Cambridge University Press, 1989); and Michael Sandel, ed., *Liberalism and Its Critics* (Oxford: Blackwell, 1984).

choices we have made at any given time. Perhaps much of the worry over relativism has stemmed from anticipation of these disquieting questions. If so, those who assume that being able to limit the range of true or acceptable moralities answers these questions are engaging in wishful thinking. The questions do not go away with the rejection of the extreme subjectivist forms of relativism, and they do not go away by labeling the more tempered views 'pluralism' *simpliciter*. In this sense, to retain the term 'relativism' in combination with 'pluralism' seems a more honest choice to me.

Putting to one side the question of what to call my view, I should mention others who have articulated some of the broad themes with which I am in general quite sympathetic. Stuart Hampshire, John Kekes, Charles Taylor, and Michael Walzer in particular have articulated with great depth and eloquence the Berlinian theme that there are irreducibly plural sources of value, that there is a plurality of justifiable ways of life combining these values. The ways in which they articulate this theme and some of the conclusions they draw from it differ from mine. My approach is explicitly committed to a naturalistic understanding of morality, and as I show in chapter 2, the combination of moral ambivalence and a naturalistic approach generates a particular way of understanding why there is no single true morality but also of the basis for certain broad constraints on the range of true moralities.

Much of Richard Brandt's work has expressed an acceptance for the plurality of moral practices across culture, and in *Ethical Theory* he distinguished a stronger and a weaker form of metaethical relativism. The weaker, which he cautiously accepts, holds that there is a "unique rational method" in ethics that leaves one unable to decide between conflicting judgments. The stronger form holds that there is no unique rational method.[34] The language of a common rational method is one I prefer not to use, but the spirit of Brandt's proposal is compatible with the position of pluralistic relativism defended here. Unfortunately, Brandt seems to have been alone among his contemporaries in suggesting that the more limited kind of relativism deserves further consideration.

Martha Nussbaum has defended an ethic based on the Aristotelian idea that human capabilities have a claim to be realized.[35] She therefore opposes antiessentialist views about human nature that deny a substantial common humanity, but declines to found her own essentialism in a metaphysical realism that supposes there is some determinate way the world is, apart from the interpretive workings of the cognitive faculties of living beings. Rather, she emphasizes that as an empirical matter, general and common capabilities have appeared in all kinds of human societies and historical periods.

34. Richard Brandt, *Ethical Theory* (Englewood Cliffs, N.J.: Prentice-Hall, 1959), 274–5. See also Judith Wagner DeCew, "Moral Conflicts and Ethical Relativism," *Ethics* 101 (1990): 27–41, for a clearheaded discussion of the meaning of relativism as it occurs in the work of Brandt, Hampshire, Harman, and myself.

35. Martha Nussbaum, "Human Capabilities, Female Human Beings," in *Women, Culture, and Development: A Study of Human Capabilities,* ed. Martha Nussbaum and Jonathan Glover (Oxford: Oxford University Press, 1995), 61–104.

Because this is an empirical matter, she emphasizes, the list of common capabilities should be tentative and open-ended. Moreover, different societies might to some extent construct items on the list differently. The capabilities are vague and general enough to allow for plural and local specification. Plural specification corresponds to different ways of fleshing out the realization of the capabilities according to local traditions or individual tastes. Local specification allows for different ways of realizing them according to context, to the character of the agents and their social situation.

I have already articulated my own reasons for agreeing with Nussbaum's claim that general and common features of human nature help to constrain the range of true moralities, and with her claim that within this range the content of different moralities can answer to such common human features in different ways. My disagreement concerns the specifics of her list and some of the moral requirements she derives from them. I shall expand a bit on a representative case of disagreement I have with her, partly because the particular case is important and is of broad practical interest but also because it illustrates the more general point that much of the interesting theoretical work needs to descend from highly abstract debates about relativism, universalism, and pluralism, as these are defined as general views, and get down to particular cases as to which ways of life might indeed fall in the range of justifiable or truly permissible ways.

The case I have in mind revolves around Nussbaum's argument that individual human life is characterized by a strong form of separateness. Not only does one die one's own death and not anyone else's, but one has a peculiar context and surroundings in the form of objects, places, history, particular friendships, locations, sexual ties, and these are not the same as anyone else's. Separateness means being able to live one's own life and nobody else's. From this characteristic, Nussbaum derives guarantees of noninterference with certain choices that are personal and definitive of selfhood— marriage, childbearing, sexual expression, speech, and employment. Strong separateness for Nussbaum implies freedom of association as well as freedom from unwarranted search and seizure.[36]

This is one of the crucial places at which Nussbaum's pluralism begins to resemble a fairly stringent universalism. There seems little room for plural and local specification of the separateness of individual human life when it is taken to imply a familiar list of Western liberal rights. In chapter 1, I have pointed to differences between moralities that have to do with varying emphases on communitarian values. Moralities distinguished by relatively high emphasis on these values tend to have complementary notions of the self and its separateness from others. It is quite true in the literal sense that one has to die one's own death, but one's relationship to particular others or to a community may be so important that the death of others or that of a community may inflict as much damage to one's welfare as one's own death, if not more so. Again,

36. Nussbaum, "Human Capabilities," 79–80, 85.

one's context, surroundings, and personal ties may be quite unique, but a good part of that uniqueness may lie in the distinctive quality of one's relationships to certain others or to a certain community. The point here is that dying on one's own and the uniqueness of one's circumstances and ties are compatible with placing great importance on relationship and community, and such a priority does not necessarily lead to an emphasis on the sort of individual rights Nussbaum mentions.

One thing Nussbaum might reply is that rights are the sorts of things that need only be assured and not necessarily exercised if an individual chooses otherwise. However, the question is how rights are to be grounded in a tradition that emphasizes the compatibility between individuals' most important interests and the interests of communities to which they belong. Though Nussbaum is not explicit about the way she derives individual rights from strong separateness, it would seem from the list of rights she derives that she has in mind a conception of separateness that emphasizes the potential incompatibility between individuals' interests and communal interests. If one is to make room for "plural and local specification" of human capabilities, one should, in my view, make more room for variation in the interpretation of separateness. This is not to say that communitarian moralities can have no basis for individual rights, but, as I explained earlier in this chapter, the basis of those rights and their scope of protection is different.

3.10 OBJECTIONS TO A FIXED HUMAN NATURE AS A SOURCE OF CONSTRAINTS ON ADEQUATE MORALITIES

Consider Max Horkheimer's rejection of a fixed human nature:

> The term 'human nature' here does not refer to an original or an eternal or uniform essence. Every philosophical doctrine which sees the movement of society or the life of the individual as emerging out of a fundamental, ahistorical unity is open to justified criticism. Such theories with their undialectical method have special difficulty in coming to grips with the fact that new individual and social qualities arise in the historical process. Their reaction to this fact either takes the form of mechanical evolution: all human characteristics which arise at a later point were originally present in germ; or it takes the form of some variety of philosophical anthropology: these characteristics emerge from a metaphysical 'ground' of being. These mutually opposed theories fail to do justice to the methodological principle that vital processes are marked by structural change no less than by continuous development.[37]

---

37. Max Horkheimer, "Authority and the Family," in *Critical Theory*, trans. M. J. O'Connell (New York: Herder and Herder, 1972), 66.

Horkheimer is right to point out that new individual and social qualities arise in the historical process and that not all human characteristics arising at a later point are originally present in germ. My use of the concept of human nature is not meant to deny this, but it does reject the claim that human beings are wholly plastic. Horkheimer does not believe this either. For example, he believes that "men's drives and passions, their characteristic dispositions and reaction-patterns are stamped by the power-relationships under which the social life-process unfolds at any time," and that the reason for this is their tendency to accept authority, a tendency manifested over the "whole time-span embraced by historical writing."[38] Horkheimer explains the emergence of genuinely new traits against an assumed background of the constant tendency to accept authority. At the same time, Horkheimer accepts a limit to that tendency that appears equally present in the span embraced by historical writing. Arguing that some degree of coercion must always be present in the raising of children, Horkheimer remarks that "the development of every human being from self-centered infant to member of society is, despite all modifications, essentially an abbreviated repetition of a thousand-year-long civilizing process which is unthinkable without an element of coercion."[39] Indeed, much of Horkheimer's criticism of the bourgeois family presupposes a Freudian theory of human nature.[40]

Consider that the figure in the history of philosophy from whom Horkheimer takes inspiration in denying a permanent essence for human beings is Friedrich Nietzsche. Horkheimer refers to the theme in *The Genealogy of Morals* that the ability to keep promises and in general the regulations of life in common was not a natural ability but something that had to be burnt into memory through horrible pain.[41] This very claim, however, presupposes that something *is* natural to human beings, and that it must be overcome through conditioning and pain.

With this much said against Horkheimer's objection to "human nature," let me point out that I have no need for the very strong conceptions of human nature Horkheimer probably had foremost in mind. I have no need for an Aristotelian conception of whatever makes human beings *distinctively* human. My aim is to derive constraints on moralities based on traits commonly possessed by human beings, and for this purpose I need not deny that other animals might have similar traits to some degree. Moreover, I need not insist that traits important to understanding human beings as a species are possessed in equal degree or even possessed at all by all members. Consider altruism, which enters into chapter 2's picture of a human nature that helps

---

38. Horkheimer, *Critical Theory*, 69.

39. Horkheimer, *Critical Theory*, 111.

40. Monogamy, he says, presupposes the devaluation of purely sensuous pleasure and banishes every sensuous element from the son's tenderness for his mother. This results in a "forced separation" between "idealistic dedication and sexual desire, tender mindfulness and simple self-interest, heavenly interiority and earthly passion." See *Critical Theory*, 121.

41. Horkheimer, *Critical Theory*, 56, referring to essay 2, sec. 3, of *The Genealogy*.

make social cooperation possible. I do not need to assert that altruism is a universal human trait. Indeed, I suspect that the capacity for various forms of other-directed concern varies widely across individuals, both in terms of the genetic basis of such concern and in terms of the degree to which this capacity is actualized in response to varying cultural and other social influences. Consider, furthermore, the theory of group selection offered by Sober and Wilson (and described in sec. 2.9), according to which altruism might been selected because it increased the fitness of some groups over other groups. Such a story does not require the "winning" groups to have nothing but altruists, but only a relatively high concentration of altruists compared to their competitors. Finally, I have no need to assert that common human traits are "fixed." If significant numbers of human beings came to have these traits through natural selection, we can expect the process to continue, and that its course will partly be determined by the actions human beings take and the effects they have in creating new environments to which they evolve adaptations. The naturalistic approach to morality undertaken in this book only requires a conception of common human traits as they have evolved to the present, and for the foreseeable future.[42]

Another kind of objection against claiming a structure for human nature is based on the Foucauldian insight that claims about the content of human nature are never purely disinterested but must always be understood in terms of relationships of power and dominance. Claims that moral dignity are based on certain kinds of human powers or traits have always and are always liable to help rationalize the subordination of certain others on the grounds that they possess not at all or in lesser degree the relevant powers or traits. If human beings derive their dignity from powers of rationality, then it will be said that human rationality is possessed in lesser degree by slaves, the chronically unemployed and on welfare, and unreasonable women. And the particular standards and models for rationality will turn out to favor precisely the ones who have the most to do with the articulation of those standards and models. Against such an objection, I must first of all plead that no such use here has been made of

42. My use of evolutionary theory in this book should not be confused with an endorsement of some of the most prominent theories of evolutionary psychology that do hold in central, universal psychological adaptations that evolved in the Pleistocene era and remain unchanged to this day. See John Tooby and Leda Cosmides, "The Psychological Foundations of Culture," in Jerome H. Barkow, Leda Cosmides, and John Tooby, eds., *The Adapted Mind: Evolutionary Psychology and the Generation of Culture* (New York: Oxford University Press, 1992), 19–136. Moreover, Tooby and Cosmides argue that human hunter-gatherers developed adaptations that are extremely task specific. They are most famous for the argument that human beings developed "cheater-detection" modules that equip them to ferret out potential free-riders in situations of social exchange. Another prominent evolutionary psychologist, David Buss, argues that different preferences for certain types of mates between men and women (men look for youth and attractiveness, while women look for resources and high status) evolved during the hunter-gatherer days. See *The Evolution of Desire: Strategies of Human Mating* (New York: Basic Books, 1995). No argument in this book presupposes the truth of such assertions. For a criticism of these prominent theories, see David J. Buller, *Adapting Minds: Evolutionary Psychology and the Persistent Quest for Human Nature* (Cambridge, Mass.: MIT Press, 2005).

human nature claims. I am not seeking to found moral dignity on a particular set of powers and traits.

Another, perhaps too easy reply is to point out the difference between the way a claim about human nature is sometimes, even often, used and the broader set of ways it *can* be used, and sometimes *is* used. It is certainly the case that invidious comparisons involving powers of rationality have been used, often and very destructively, to rationalize subordination. Also, criticizing the basis for those comparisons typically plays an important role in the struggle against subordination. Such criticism does not presuppose that rationality is irrelevant to moral dignity. On the contrary, it often presupposes that it is, and that claims about the rationality of subordinated groups are simply false or are perversely self-supporting, since acceptance of these claims helps to ensure that subordinated groups will be treated in such a way that their full powers of rationality might never manifest themselves. At the same time, it must be granted that powers of rationality, however they might be defined, are probably possessed in varying degrees by different people, even if they are not possessed in varying degrees according to the established categories through which some groups have been subordinated and oppressed. Founding moral dignity on rationality *is* dangerous, even when we have brushed aside the obviously dishonest uses of this idea.

It may be that, in general, claims about human nature have dangerous uses, and true also that we will not always be aware of what these uses are. Even though I make no use of human nature as a ground for human dignity, it could be said that I do use it to defend a notion of adequacy for moralities and thus for cultures. Surely, arguments to the effect that certain cultures do not measure up to the standard of adequacy can serve and have served oppressive ends. I agree with this point, and with Foucault's warning that "truth isn't outside power, or lacking in power," and that contrary to myths, it is not "the reward of free spirits, the child of protracted solitude, nor the privilege of those who have succeeded in liberating themselves." I agree with him so long as he defines truth as the "system of ordered procedures for the production, regulation, distribution, circulation, and operation of statements."[43] Our institutions and practices that constitute such a system do not lie outside power. I disagree with him if he thinks there is no truth apart from how he defines it, but I surely agree with his point "not that everything is bad, but that everything is dangerous," and that we must remain vigilant about what purposes our statements serve.[44]

We can put Foucault's warning to good use if we become more vigilant about some specific dangers that come with judging other cultures. A common pitfall is premised

---

43. Michael Foucault, in an interview with Alexandro Fontana and Pasquale Pasquino, "Truth and Power," in *The Foucault Reader*, ed. Paul Rabinow (New York: Pantheon, 1984), 72–4.
44. Michael Foucault, in an interview with Paul Rabinow and Hubert Dreyfus, "On the Genealogy of Ethics: An Overview of Work in Progress," in *The Foucault Reader*, 343.

on an unreflectively organic and holistic conception of what a culture is. When one is inclined to be unsympathetic toward a culture, one tends to take a practice one sees to be unjustifiable as reflective of the culture as a whole. On the other hand, one tends to treat an unjustifiable practice as an aberrant or at least separable part of a culture that one is interested in defending. Practices that are frequently taken to subordinate or oppress women, for example, can be viewed in either light. They can be taken as a symptom of a much more general and pervasive oppression embodied by the culture, or as things that can be corrected while preserving most of what confers an identity on the culture. Either judgment might be warranted with further study and reflection on the practice and the culture in question, but the point is that it usually takes considerable study and reflection to make an informed judgment, and people usually leap to their judgments with a wholly inadequate basis.

3.11 Can a Functional Conception of Morality Accommodate Deontological Moralities?

The present objection is that conceiving morality (in part) to serve the function of facilitating and regulating social cooperation is conceiving it in consequentialist terms. And given that I use that functionalist and consequentialist conception to derive universal constraints on adequate moralities, it might seem that only consequentialist moralities could qualify. This result, the objection goes, is contrary to the way I argue for and apply pluralistic relativism. I point to the conflict between deontological moralities centered on the notion of individual rights and utility-based moralities as part of my argument for a plurality of true moralities.

Consider the Kantian imperative of treating each person as an end, of owing to each a certain way of acting without regard to maximizing a sum total of satisfaction or welfare taken over a group of persons. Part of my reply to the objection is that acting on such an imperative is precisely a way of facilitating and regulating social cooperation. There is nothing in the notion of social cooperation itself that requires it to take the form of aggregating satisfaction, welfare, or value over persons. Social cooperation is facilitated when egoistic motivation is restrained or channeled so as to point in the same practical direction as concern for others, and inculcation of the Kantian imperative can help accomplish these ends. As explained in section 2.9, rights conceived as basic and as deontological in nature can answer in effective ways both to strong self-interest and to altruism.

It is true that the defense just offered for the Kantian imperative is consequentialist in a broad way, and this is certainly a defense inconsistent with Kant's theory of what morality is, but this theory is separable from his conception of the normative content of morality, even if he weaves that theory into his derivations of the content of the categorical imperative. And while it is true that the defense offered is one that Kant would reject, it is not consequentialist in the way that a standard teleological theory of the right means it to be. The standard teleological theory begins with the notion of a good that can be fully specified independently of the right and then determines the right in relation to what conduces to that good. The defense offered here presumes a notion of a function of morality that acts as a constraint on what could serve as an adequate morality. It does not assert that anything resembling a fully contentful notion of the right could be derived from that function. In fact the Kantian idea of owing to each person a way of acting that cannot be set aside for the sake of maximizing aggregated satisfactions or welfare is an idea that expresses a local criterion for adequacy of morality. The account of morality defended here is functionalist in the way David Hume's account is, but not in the way a classical utilitarian theory such as Bentham's is. Remember that Hume conceived morality as arising from conventions people make with each other in the course of their life together. His story also presupposes a function for morality, but the function is not to promote some ultimate and predefined ethical good but rather to promote the mutual satisfaction of interests. This is to facilitate and regulate social cooperation, but not in such a way as to presuppose a standard teleological theory of the right in the way Bentham presupposed one.[45]

3.12 WORRIES ABOUT THE CONSEQUENCES OF ACCEPTING PLURALISTIC RELATIVISM: CONFIDENCE AND LEARNING FROM OTHERS

One possible objection based on the consequences of accepting pluralistic relativism holds that relativism undermines confidence. If the standards we use to decide conflicts of basic values have no deep justification that makes them more correct to use than others' standards, are we not left without a reason to keep standards we have been using? Consider the objection when formulated in terms of the driving laws analogy. Saying that there must be local criteria for the true morality because they are needed to make morality action-guiding is like saying that these criteria are like the rule of driving on the righthand side of the road. The rule is needed, but there is no justification in the end for that rule rather than the British rule of driving on the left. The only justification is for having it one way or another. I argued earlier that one can still make first-order normative judgments about other ways of life that satisfy universal criteria for moralities but differ in local criteria. These judgments, I argued, can be completely accepting, completely rejecting, or considerably more nuanced than either, but in any case the judgments are based on our own moral values. However, the objection now under discussion points to a problem in the maintenance of our commitment to our

---

45. For informative discussions of this aspect of Hume's theory of morality, see Knud Haakonssen, *The Science of a Legislator: The Natural Jurisprudence of David Hume and Adam Smith* (Cambridge: Cambridge University Press, 1981), chap. 2, and Geoffrey Sayre-McCord, "Hume and the Bauhaus Theory of Ethics," *Midwest Studies in Philosophy* 20 (1995): 280–98.

own values. If the kinds of priorities we have in place for deciding deep conflicts between fundamental values have no justification except for the need to have it one way or another, doesn't this very thought undermine our moral commitments?

This thought certainly does undermine one's commitment if it presupposes something like the view that morality is part of the fabric of the world and provides objective, universally valid reasons for all to act. If a commitment to moral values is at bottom a search for such a morality, then such a commitment is futile. As I noted earlier, such a presupposition is not uncommon and is reflected in not only the strongest forms of objectivist views about morality but also the most radical forms of subjectivism ("Right and wrong is a matter of what one feels and chooses"). Radical subjectivism merely constitutes the other side of the coin of the strongest forms of objectivism: when one is committed to morality on the basis of believing it to be some irreducible part of the world's fabric that gives one objective and universally valid reasons to act, and when one becomes disillusioned with that conception, one is likely to fall into the other extreme. However, the entirely justifiable desire to refute radical subjectivism should not move us toward the traditional view. What we need are plausible alternatives to these equally untenable views.

A start to establishing a plausible alternative lies in seeing that we can be deeply committed to an ideal even while granting that not everyone needs to be so committed. In making this point, Edmund Pincoffs asks us to imagine that he has made a promise to a friend to meet him to attend a concert. He has broken a previous promise to this friend, and so it is important to him to keep this one. However, a neighbor calls him to remind him of his agreement to attend a meeting of the school board to argue that a proposed desegregation plan is inadequate. This meeting is the same time as the concert. Pincoffs argues that in making his decision, he should take into account considerations that are in a sense personal but are relevant to the question of what he morally ought to do. These considerations have to do with "what the agent will allow himself to do and to suffer in accordance with the conception that he has of his own moral character."[46] If he decides to keep the agreement rather than his promise to his friend, Pincoffs suggests, he must try to justify it to his friend by using "principles that I set for myself, but not necessarily for other people, and of moral ideals that I have but that I do not necessarily attribute to other people."[47] The point is that he cannot attempt to justify his decision by talking only about what anyone should have done in the same circumstances. He would have to talk, for example, about his lifelong commitment to desegregation and about his particular interest in the development of school policy in his town. He might talk about the ways in which both his self-

---

46. Edmund Pincoffs, *Quandaries and Virtues: Against Reductivism in Ethics* (Lawrence: University Press of Kansas, 1986), 21.
47. Pincoffs, *Quandaries and Virtues*, 22.

conception and the conception that others have of him are such that he would have to question his own integrity as a person if he missed the meeting.

The lesson to be taken from Pincoffs's example is that one's commitment to a moral ideals and principles need not be a commitment to a value one believes to be compulsory for everyone, yet one can still imagine maintaining one's commitment in light of a more particular relationship to that value. This is not to say the value is purely personal. But the place it has in one's life, the priority one acknowledges it to have in one's life, is not something one expects it to have in the lives of others, nor does one necessarily think it ought to have the same place. Still, it might be asked: "Isn't our confidence in our commitments undermined by the analogy to rules of driving?" Doesn't it undermine our confidence to recognize that nothing except the conventions of our culture determine our specific commitments? I reply that it is not just convention that determines these commitments. The choice of one path or another in the face of fundamental conflicts of value has definite moral liabilities as well as deep satisfactions. Taking a different path means a different set of liabilities and satisfactions.

There is another reply to the worry raised by the analogy to rules of driving. We could easily imagine switching sides for driving; it is considerably more difficult, if not impossible, to imagine ourselves *not* having any of the values mentioned in chapter 1—values that are responsible for our moral ambivalence. These values form part of the boundaries of a way of life. To the extent that our lives take meaning and substance from them, we will not be able to imagine *ourselves* having other kinds of commitments, even though we can perfectly well imagine and even observe that others have these other kinds. There may be, with respect to many of our basic standards, no psychologically real question of whether we should adopt different standards or have none at all. Further, there is real substance to our shared commitments in the sense that we can hold each other to them.

Charles Taylor has put the point well:

> We have become certain things in Western civilization. Our humanitari-
> anism, our notions of freedom—both personal independence and collective
> self-rule—have helped to define a political identity we share; and one which is
> deeply rooted in our more basic, seemingly infra-political understandings: of
> what it is to be an individual, of the person as a being with 'inner' depths—all
> the features which seem to us to be rock-bottom, almost biological properties
> of human beings, so long as we refrain from looking outside and experiencing
> the shock of encountering other cultures. . . . Do I want to be born a Sung dy-
> nasty Chinese, or a subject of Hammurabi of Babylon, or a twentieth-century
> American? Without a prior identity, I couldn't begin to choose. They incarnate
> incommensurable goods (at least prior to some deep comparative study, and
> conceivably even after this). But this is not my/our situation. We have al-
> ready *become* something. Questions of truth and freedom can arise for us in

the transformations we undergo or project. In short, we have a *history*. We live in time not just self-enclosed in the present, but essentially related to a past which has helped define our identity, and a future which puts it again in question.[48]

The argument, then, is that our commitments are so deeply rooted in who we are that recognition of the contingency of our moral identities need not undermine them. There is something to this argument. In fact, I shall argue in chapter 7 that moral values are deeply embedded in practical rationality. They constitute some of the most important reasons we weigh and act on in practical deliberation. However, I think that such an argument will take us only so far in addressing the problem of moral confidence.

For one thing, our commitments imply that we must act to realize certain values, and this seems to inevitably mean undermining the realization of other values embodied in other true moralities. There seems a conflict between the project of realizing our own commitments and expressing in our actions the recognition that other moralities may be as true as our own. Furthermore, Taylor's argument from psychological impossibility may rule out our adopting the specific commitments of a Babylonian or a Sung Dynasty Chinese, but surely there are significant alternative possibilities that are in closer psychological proximity. Thoroughly cosmopolitan, secular parents give birth to and raise children who then adopt traditional forms of life from which these parents fled. We therefore still have the task of dealing with conflicts between acting on our own values and recognizing the validity of others, but I argue in chapter 9 that this task is not so different from the one we face every day in trying to balance the plurality of values within our own moralities.

There is another reason why Taylor's argument does not address other sources of challenge to confidence in our moral commitments. We may be deceived, by others or by ourselves, in having our particular commitments. We must determine whether our commitments and the ways we attempt to realize them are founded on "ideologies" (in the pejorative sense of mystifying or concealing domination) that we have been deceived into accepting, perhaps for the unconscious purpose of justifying either our domination of others or simply our lack of concern for them. It seems to me that we may very well deceive ourselves about the possibilities for acting on a fundamental moral value we have: that other human lives are no more nor no less important than our own. We attempt to justify considerably less than maximal efforts to act on this value by citing what it is "realistic" to expect of human beings who have strong interests in their own lives and in those close to them. This matter I will treat in chapter 6.

---

48. Charles Taylor, "Foucault on Freedom and Truth," in *Philosophy and the Human Sciences: Philosophical Papers*, vol. 2 (Cambridge: Cambridge University Press, 1985), 181–2.

Another challenge to our moral confidence is posed by Freud's naturalistic conception of morality as a system of norms needed to tame our deepest and most basic impulses for the sake of civilization but not for us as individuals. Much of Freud's explanation of the growth of the moral sense, Richard Wollheim observes, paints a rather unhappy picture of our relation to morality. As children we experience anxiety and terror at a parent or someone upon whom we are utterly dependent. We perceive that figure as obstructing or threatening the satisfaction of our sensual desires. We internalize the demands of the external figure as a way of dealing with our terror:

> the gain in tranquillity outweighs the crippling loss in satisfaction, but the sacrifice has nothing independently to recommend it. . . . A happier interpretation of morality would be deserved if it could be shown that there are needs, some desires other than the avoidance of fear, and not shallow ones, that the establishment of the superego satisfies.[49]

To meet such a challenge, we need to show how some deep needs are satisfied by establishment of the "superego" and that morality is not merely something imposed by society on the individual. That certain types of moral duties are necessarily part of a way of life that we generally need to flourish is an upshot of chapter 4. There I argue that effective human agency needs to be nurtured and sustained within the context of particular relationships governed by special moral duties obtaining between the parties. My argument is based on the evident truth that we are social beings, in the sense that we require a great deal of teaching and nurturing in order to develop into agents capable of effectively pursuing our ends. Such a truth applies not just to children, as is commonly recognized in our culture, but to our adulthood as we learn to navigate through new social worlds.

Since this argument legitimates the presence of special duties toward particular others, the question arises as to the status of what have been called "impersonal" values, motivated by the moral theme that other human beings are no more nor less important than oneself or ones to whom one stands in a special relationship. Not all adequate moralities, I have argued, must contain such values, but they can be well grounded values for *us* now and in almost all parts of an increasingly interdependent world. Not all moral values that are well grounded for us need to be well grounded for all human beings in all ages and places. It will be argued in chapter 6 that values can be grounded in such a way that they are suitable for human beings under certain sets of broadly defined circumstances, though not necessarily for human beings under all historically known circumstances, much less all conceivable circumstances.

---

49. Richard Wollheim, *The Thread of Life* (Cambridge, Mass.: Harvard University Press, 1984), 205.

However, showing that adopting our moral values is one way to flourish requires us to meet certain challenges, such as those raised by Foucault, who describes a social reality that belies the claim that the modern Western capitalist democracies are freer, more equal, and permit a richer individuality than societies that have gone before. In an important sense, Foucault challenges the belief that our way of life has the benefits we claim for it, and argues that it has deeper costs than we are willing to admit. There is much in his critique, I think, that must be accepted.

However, his unrelenting pessimism is grounded in an excessively global and undifferentiated theory of the ways in which an omnipresent and impersonal power oppresses us. These assertions will need to be cashed out later in chapters 7 and 8. My point here is that this is the sort of task we must engage in if we are to sustain confidence in our moral commitments. It is a task that many moral philosophers have thought to be irrelevant to confidence, opting instead for very abstract universalistic justifications of our morality.[50] If I am right, moral philosophy needs to take a different direction, one that is more closely related to political theory and to certain versions of poststructuralism and critical theory.

Another objection based on the consequences of accepting a relativistic view is that it cannot allow us, or not very often at least, to try to incorporate what is right in perspectives that compete with ours. Relativism, it is charged, does not force us to ask what might be right about other perspectives because it encourages us to suspend judgment, to accept other moralities on their own terms. It is only when we see other moralities as competing with ours with respect to capturing *the* moral truth that we are led to ask what truth in these other moralities we ought to recognize and incorporate into our own viewpoints. I do think that this is a charge that holds considerable force against many relativistic views, but not pluralistic relativism.

Pluralistic relativists can point out that there are issues that admit of an objectively unique solution. They can encourage people to find out whether this is the case on a given issue. Further, given a distinction between ways in which a judgment may be more or less locally true, it becomes important to find out whether a disagreement could be resolved on the basis on some standard that is shared by the parties even if that standard is not derivable from the nature of morality. A third reply is that discussion and trying to understand the basis of other people's views is important because we need to get along with one another in spite of deep disagreements. Often we get along by attempting to accommodate other peoples' views in the political process. I will say more on this in chapter 9.

Finally, there is a way to learn from other cultures that does not consist in slavish imitation or rejecting one's own values. Because of the overlapping of necessary elements in any adequate morality, we can learn from the way that other societies have

---

50. For example, see Alan Gewirth, *Reason and Morality* (Chicago: University of Chicago Press, 1978).

embodied these elements in their cultures. In chapter 6, I will argue that we must be wary of estimates of what is "realistically possible" for human beings to do and to become, and of calls to tailor our moral requirements to these estimates. We can learn from other cultures about the limits of realistic possibility. More specifically, I argue, we can learn from some of these other cultures about the constructive role of moral identities based on membership in community and their efficacy in supporting the performance of other kinds of moral commitments that we ourselves have.

Constraints on Natural Moralities

Identity, Flourishing, and Relationship

This chapter begins the project of part II: to look more closely at the ways that the functions of morality, human nature, and the particular circumstances of a group at a given time all work together to impose constraints of varying levels of generality on what constitutes an adequate morality for that group.

4.1 THE MORAL IMPLICATIONS OF OUR SOCIAL NATURE

The argument starts with the subject of section 1.6—the conflict between personal and impersonal values. Taking the impersonal point of view that attaches equal weight to the interests of all persons, one acts on reasons that do not depend on one's particular identity as an agent. Taking the personal point of view that attaches greater weight to one's own interests and to personal relations to particular people, one acts in ways that are justified and motivated by one's particular identity as an agent. I argued in section 1.4 that special duties emerging from the personal perspective, such as those to friends and family, resist subsumption under the impersonal perspective and that conflicts between values arising from the two perspectives resist any universalist ordering.

This chapter draws from my essays "On Flourishing and Finding One's Identity in Community," *Midwest Studies in Philosophy* 13 (1988), special issue, *Ethical Theory: Character and Virtue*, ed. Peter A. French, Theodore E. Uehling Jr., and Howard K. Wettstein: 324–41, and "Aspects of Identity and Agency," coauthored with Amélie Rorty, in *Identity, Character and Morality: Essays in Moral Psychology*, ed. Amélie Rorty and Owen Flanagan (Cambridge, Mass.: MIT, 1990), 19–36. Owen Flanagan and Ruth Anna Putnam have given me useful comments on the *Midwest Studies* piece, some of which I have tried to incorporate here. Discussions with Laura J. Weisberg improved my understanding of psychological theories such as those of Kohut and Klein.

Pluralistic relativism holds that there is a range of adequate resolutions to resolving conflicts between these viewpoints.

This chapter seeks to explain why there must be a personal perspective and the duties arising from it. It is a universal constraint on adequate moralities that they must contain such a perspective and its attendant duties. The source of such a constraint is our social nature as human beings. Two philosophical traditions in particular have illuminated this subject: Chinese Confucian ethics, and the Western communitarian tradition having its roots in Aristotle and Hegel. In both traditions it is argued that our identities and our flourishing as social beings require our having certain sorts of re-lationships. The character of these relationships with others is partly defined and partly sustained by certain duties we have to them. Therefore, it is claimed, the reason for performing some of our most important ethical duties lies in our own identities and in our flourishing. This argument seems plausible to me, but it needs clarification on the relevant sense in which we have a social nature.[1]

The communitarian and neo-Aristotelian line of thought is usually coupled with a criticism of liberal ethical theory. By "liberal" theory, I mean one based on three claims: first, that there is a significant plurality of conceptions of the good life that are equally valid, or at least, a significant plurality of ones that reasonable people accept; second, that principles of right action and of justice should be neutral with respect to this significant plurality insofar as their justification does not depend on accepting any one conception of the good life; third, that a necessary feature of a right and just social order is that it respect the autonomy of all its members, where autonomy includes the freedom to choose among competing conceptions of the good life and to act on one's chosen conception within boundaries specified by principles of right and justice. The criticism is that liberal theory, with its toleration of competing conceptions of the good life, its separation of the right from the good, and its emphasis on autonomy, cannot recognize the way that our social nature determines what can be a good life for us and the way that the social content of a good life for human beings grounds some of our most important duties to others. I hold that the social nature of human beings does place constraints on what constitutes an adequate morality. In particular, I shall argue in this chapter and the next that the communitarian insight into our social nature requires liberal theory to pay greater attention to the necessity for cultivating those kinds of community that are compatible with liberal principles of the right and of justice.

1. Parts or the whole of this argument are found in the work of Alasdair MacIntyre, Charles Taylor, and Michael Sandel. See Alasdair MacIntyre, *After Virtue*, 2nd ed. (Notre Dame, Ind.: University of Notre Dame Press, 1982), and "Is Patriotism a Virtue?" Lindley Lecture (Lawrence: University of Kansas, 1983); Charles Taylor, *Hegel* (Cambridge: Cambridge University Press, 1975), and "The Nature and Scope of Distributive Justice," in *Justice and Equality Here and Now*, ed. Frank S. Lucash (Ithaca: Cornell University Press, 1986), 34–67; and Michael Sandel, *Liberalism and the Limits of Justice* (Cambridge: Cambridge University Press, 1982). This argument is also found in the works of Confucius and Mencius. See the references hereafter.

4.2 WHAT DOES IT MEAN TO HAVE A SOCIAL NATURE?

It might mean that our characters are "social products." That is, the complexes of traits, habits, cognitive and behavioral dispositions, and ends, needs, and desires that make up our characters are the results of our interactions with particular others and, more generally, of the communities and cultural traditions to which we belong. However, it is unclear why this claim would support some conception of the good life or some restricted range of conceptions. Perhaps this claim grounds our duties to others without determining specific notions of flourishing. The thought may be that we should be grateful to those who have shaped us and that we should repay them in some way. But it remains to be shown why gratitude is the required response to the simple fact that others have shaped us. It is most natural to speak of our having a debt of gratitude when we have received benefits. And while particular others and even the culture of a community may shape our characters in beneficial ways, not all shaping is beneficial. A related objection is that simply being grateful for having been shaped by others is to abdicate our responsibility to critically evaluate the norms of these others and of the culture around us.

Still another possible meaning for the claim that we have a social nature is that we are at least partly "constituted" by our relations to others. Critics of liberal theory sometimes charge that it is "atomistic" and neglects the fact that our identities are at least partly defined in relation to community. The language of constitution and definition implies something stronger than the causal claim that our characters are social products. And there does seem to be something plausible about this claim in light of the fact that people do say it is part of their identities to be fathers, Jews, Chinese, or Southerners.

However, it remains unclear what kind of identity is at stake. One possible meaning is that my metaphysical identity as the particular person I am is partly defined by my relations to others. That is, the relevant sense of 'identity' is the one that is the usual topic of contemporary metaphysics, concerning the properties that constitute us as individuals and permit our reidentification at different times as the same individuals. The claim about identity would then mean that the relevant identifying properties include the relational properties of being a member of certain groups, or having some relation to certain others. Thus construed, the claim is not obviously true and in need of defense.[2] Even if such an identity can be clarified and made plausible, it is unclear what follows from such a claim concerning my duties to those others who "enter into my identity." It might be suggested that being a father is to have certain duties toward one's children, and that in general, having a social role means having certain duties. But then the claim amounts to the assertion that the properties that make me who I am include the properties of having certain duties toward others, and this looks like the conclusion of the argument, not a premise to which we can readily assent.

---

2. I suggest a way to understand relational identities in "Relational and Autonomous Selves," *Journal of Chinese Philosophy* 31 (2004): 419–32.

Sometimes the word 'identity' is used in a nonmetaphysical sense to embrace individuals' ways of understanding and interpreting the world, their characteristic ways of behaving and relating to other people, their views as to what is most important and valuable in life, and what are in fact their most important ends and desires. In this case, the meaning of 'identity' is familiar and philosophically unproblematic, even if quite diffuse and vague. But the problem remains in explaining what it means for an identity to be *defined* or *constituted* by one's relations to others. It is plausible to say that identity in this sense is fundamentally shaped by others, not just particular others but the cultural traditions of our communities. But the language of shaping recalls the causal-origin claim discussed earlier, along with its problems. Still another problem is that our duties to others do not seem to flow straightforwardly from whatever identifications we make. People who identify themselves as Southerners in the United States might feel that they have a duty to display the Confederate flag and support states' rights against the encroachments of the national government, or they might think that being Southerners requires acknowledgment of a moral burden created by slavery and segregation, or they might think that being Southerners involves no special moral significance.

Another possible meaning of the claim that we have a social nature is that one of our most important *needs* is to have certain sorts of relationships with others. The advantage of this possible meaning is that it seems quite relevant to the claim that our flourishing must be social in nature. To make the claim under this possible meaning does seem to affirm the social nature of flourishing. The disadvantage of this possible interpretation is that it may be *too* close to the claim about flourishing. The relevant sense of "important need" seems to denote some objective requirement for human welfare such that it forms part of a definitional circle with "flourishing." One flourishes when one's important needs as a human being are fully met, and important needs are the various conditions that must be fulfilled for flourishing to obtain. If there is a circle here, the claim about need provides no independent support for the claim that our flourishing requires certain sorts of relationships with others.

Without further explanation, the claim about flourishing cannot be accepted straight off. Any further explanation must include a specification of the sort of relationships we need. Here the task is to steer a course between making the required relationships so general that nothing much of significance follows and making the required relationships so specific that the notion of flourishing seems unreasonably monistic. The latter possibility is a general danger for communitarians and neo-Aristotelians. Liberalism, as a doctrine that accepts a broad range of conceptions of flourishing, is deeply rooted in a culture that embraces many different cultural strands. "That is part of the problem," it may be replied. But the counter-reply is to ask for a practical and morally acceptable alternative to theories of right and of justice that attempt to occupy a neutral ground with respect to a broad range of competing conceptions of the good life. From the standpoint of pluralistic relativism it seems reasonable to allow for such a broad range, since (as argued in sec. 2.13) the universal constraints on adequate moralities still allow for a range of different ways for regulating interpersonal conflict of interest and for providing direction to the individual in the pursuit of worthwhile lives.

A clearer and more vivid idea of our social nature, however, may specify for all adequate moralities certain grounds for our duties to others, though the preceding analysis suggests that such grounds will be more indirect, complex, and qualified than is often suggested by communitarian critics of liberalism. These grounds still allow for significant pluralism in conceptions of flourishing. Let me define "effective agency " as the set of abilities that allow us to formulate reasonably clear priorities among our ends, and to plan and perform actions that have a reasonable chance of realizing our ends, given all the conditions beyond our control. The strategy will be to interpret the social-nature claim as meaning that the necessary conditions for effective agency include the possession of certain relationships with others that in turn are partially defined and sustained by duties we have toward them. The chain of reasoning is that flourishing requires effective agency, which in turn requires relationships of a certain sort, which in turn require moral duties of a certain sort. This chain of reasoning incorporates some of the claims discussed earlier. It makes use of the conception of character as inherently social in origin. I also will explain how the required sorts of relationships lead effective agents to have identities in relation to others, in a sense of "identities" that is neither metaphysically controversial nor simply a claim about the social origins of character. I will be affirming the idea that we *need* to have certain kinds of relationships to flourish, but in such a way as to allow for a reasonable pluralism regarding competing conceptions of flourishing.

4.3 IDENTITY AS PRACTICAL ORIENTATION

To show how the notion of effective agency connects with the notion of identity, I must clarify the relevant sense of 'identity'. Let me start with the kind of identity that covers individuals' characteristic ways of understanding and interpreting the world, their characteristic ways of behaving and relating to other people, their views as to what is most important and valuable in life, and what are in fact their most important ends and desires. I shall focus on the way this kind of identity seems connected with effective or ineffective agency. When people go through an "identity crisis," they express confusion, uncertainty, and disorientation. Their confusion about who they are involves confusion as to what they stand for and how to act toward others. They may be unclear about what is important to them, or on what their most important ends and desires are. Another possibility is that they may be unable to connect their actions (their job, their family life, their presence in school) with what they *believe* is important to them. And when they "find who they are," they achieve greater clarity and certainty about what they do stand for and how they are to act toward others. They know better what is important to them and what their most important ends and desires are. Or they may have a better sense of the connection between what they are actually doing with their lives and what is important to them. Or they may change what they are doing with their lives so that it is more congruent with their sense of what is important.

My suggestion is that we may view this broad kind of identity in the light of its practical thrust, as constituted by those traits of character that fix a person's practical orientation toward the world. Call the configuration of features "practical identity." The traits going into practical identity need not remain constant throughout an individual's lifetime. However, they typically make a systematic law-like difference to people's lives, to the habit-forming and action-guiding social categories in which they are placed, to the way that they act, react, and interact. The kinds of traits that form identity may vary culturally, across class and gender lines, and indeed, individually. A trait can be central to identity along numerous dimensions, and it can be central for one dimension without being central for others.

More specifically, Amélie Rorty and I have argued that a trait can be central to identity with respect to the degree

of its objective ramification, the extent to which other traits (that is, dispositions to beliefs, desires, habits, attitudes, and actions) are dependent on it;

of its contextual or regional ramification, that is, the extent to which a trait is exemplified across distinctive spheres (e.g., public and private domains, work and leisure) and across different types of relationships (as they are differentiated by gender, status, class, age, etc.);

to which it is difficult for a person to change the trait (which is often a function of its temporal persistence);

of its objective ramification, the extent to which other traits (that is, dispositions to beliefs, desires, habits, attitudes, and actions) are dependent on it;

of its social ramification, the extent to which the trait affects the way the person is categorized and treated by others;

to which it is dominant in situations that require coping with stress or conflict;

to which it is dominant when it conflicts with other traits (e.g., when generosity conflicts with vengefulness);

to which it is appropriated as important, in that the person regards herself as radically changed if the trait is lost or strongly modified. Such appropriations may, but need not be, explicitly articulated; they can be sporadic or contextualized; a person can appropriate a trait without succeeding in acting from it habitually. Sometimes what matters to identity is that the person centrally strives to strengthen and exercise a trait. Important traits are often also the focus of self-evaluation and self-esteem.[3]

---

3. Rorty and Wong, "Aspects of Identity and Agency," 20.

While many of these dimensions of the centrality of a trait can be correlated with one another, there is no necessary connection among them. For instance, a trait can be highly ramified without being considered important; it can be dominant as a coping strategy without being central to a person's self-evaluation. A trait can be accorded a high degree of centrality by a culture without its having a correspondingly high degree of either subjective or objective centrality in the configuration of an individual's character. It can, for instance, figure significantly in a culture's practices of praise and blame without actually being strongly ramified.

4.4 ASPECTS OF PRACTICAL IDENTITY AND HOW THEY AFFECT ACTION

How do the varieties of central traits enter into the formation of actions and into their individuation? How do such traits affect a person's values, beliefs, and motivations—the patterns of practical deliberation? Answering these questions requires differentiating distinctive aspects of identity and of action.

Somatic, proprioceptive, and kinaesthetic dispositions such as deftness or awkwardness, excitability, calmness, and quick or sluggish are prelinguistic in origin and need not be articulated or appropriated, but can often individuate the modality of an action as graceful, sluggish, or abrupt, for instance. Somatic dispositions can also affect a person's beliefs, motives, and plans. People with a low sense of somatic self-confidence can feel alienated or unempowered, act in a tentative and anxious way, limit their desires, avoid confrontational situations, expect failure, and so on.[4]

Central temperamental or psychological traits include aggression or friendliness, shyness or gregariousness, generosity or parsimony, trust or distrust. These affect the individuation of actions by modifying the manner in which they are performed and described, for example, by such adverbial modifiers as "He closed the door sullenly (apprehensively, expectantly)," "She voted enthusiastically (cynically, carelessly)." Central temperamental traits also dispose a person to develop certain sorts of motives and habits, but they can also affect actions directly, contrary to a person's desires.[5] While shy people might, for instance, prefer to avoid social occasions, they could also sincerely desire companionship but find themselves unable to move toward it. Because

---

4. See Hilda Bruch, *Conversations with Anorexics*, ed. D. Czyzewski and M. A. Suhr (New York: Basic Books, 1988).

5. As a philosophical term, 'desires' has a broad and a narrow sense. In its broad or philosophically technical sense, it refers to any and all motivating states and dispositions. The narrower and more common sense of 'desire' refers to a specific subclass of motives: wants and wishes that are directed to particular satisfactions. Acting out of unreflective habit counts as acting out of desire in the broad but not the narrow sense. In claiming that habits and identity traits can form actions independently of beliefs and desires, we are referring to the narrower sense of 'desire'. There will be more discussion on the subject of desire in chapter 7.

temperamental traits standardly and widely elicit specific patterns of social responses, they often tend to ramify to form clusters of mutually reinforcing dispositions. For instance, an aggressive person is likely to generate very different sorts of interactive action scenarios than would standardly be generated by a friendly or gentle person. But temperamental traits can also generate conflicting or erratic patterns of behavior: an aggressive person can also be shy.

Social role traits are acquired and entrenched by people being placed (or placing themselves) in socially defined institutional roles or being cast to play a certain kind of role in the unfolding of social dramas. Social-role channeling tends to occur early within the family's cast of characters.[6] Somatic factors often influence role casting: tall people with deep voices are often seen as reassuring, whether or not they initially have the desires or the skills for that kind of leadership. When people are constantly channeled by the interactive minutiae of cooperation and interaction, they tend to develop habits of perceptual salience, emotion, and motivation that are appropriate to the role in which they have been cast. When they are strongly socialized, reinforced, or rewarded, such habits can become central traits.[7] But there can also be a dramatic mismatch between social role casting and people's somatic or temperamental traits. While mismatches of this kind can produce pathologies of cognitive dissonance or conflicted identities, they can also lead to a critical evaluation of existing social practices or to the development of new coping traits.[8] Social role casting can also provide norms for deliberation. For instance, parents are pressed into socially defined forms of practical reasoning, beliefs, and desires by virtue of being held responsible for the welfare of their children.

Socially defined group traits such as race, class, age, gender, nationality, ethnicity, or occupation tend to be associated with stereotypic traits that often set directions for role casting. Like role casting, group identity can be socially attributed without being subjectively appropriated or being objectively central. Ethnic groups often have distinctive child-rearing practices, many of which also direct the formation of gender- and class-specific traits and habits. Members of groups are often socially channeled into specific sorts of habit-forming institutional roles. Women, for example, have been channeled into certain sorts of action-guiding institutional positions (nurses, secretaries), and immigrants often are streamed into certain sorts of ethnically stereotypic occupations. A person's group identity further tends to generate specific sorts of social interactions. The elderly or disabled are, for instance, stereotypically constrained and channeled in ways that can become strongly habitual, even to the extent of affecting beliefs and desires.

6. See Murray Bowen, *Family Therapy in Clinical Practice* (New York: Jason Aronson, 1978).

7. See Sara Ruddick, *Maternal Thinking* (Boston: Beacon Press, 1989); and Nancy Chodorow, *The Reproduction of Mothering: Psychoanalysis and the Sociology of Gender* (Berkeley: University of California Press, 1978).

8. See L. Festinger, *Theory of Cognitive Dissonance* (Stanford: Stanford University Press, 1965).

Ideal traits set directions for the development of actual traits. Sometimes this involves imitating an idealized figure—an Eleanor Roosevelt or Mahatma Gandhi. Sometimes it is envisioned from the acceptance of moral principles or ideology. People's conceptions of ideal selves can affect both the types of actions they perform and their manner of performing them. Because the ideal self defines a set of general ends and values, it affects the details of practical deliberation and the directions of choice, often by determining what is salient. But it is frequently difficult to integrate the habits required to actualize an ideal identity with the rest of a person's central traits, particularly when the ideal involves a commitment to a relatively undefined long-range projects. The extent of people's success in appropriating an ideal as part of their action-forming identity is generally a function of the sources of their commitment to that ideal, its attraction for them, and the extent to which the habits required to realize the ideal can be integrated with the rest of their character. Sometimes when an ideal cannot be fully or successfully realized, the focus of their identity can lie in their continuous striving toward it. The ideal of rationality might, for instance, be expressed by continuously attempting to entrench intellectual habits of disambiguation. Similarly, an ideal of empathy might be expressed by attempting to enrich habits of imagination.

While these aspects of identity are independent, they are often mutually reinforcing, constraining, or conflicting. Somatic and temperamental traits tend to affect the range of social roles in which people are cast. (For instance, an aggressive person is likely to be cast in the role of an explorer rather than that of a peacemaker.) On the other hand, the social roles into which people are cast can cause them to develop temperamental traits that might otherwise have remained relatively recessive. (For instance, a man who was not particularly nurturing can become so when he is centrally role-cast as a father.)

Similarly, a person can be unaware of, and even sometimes mistaken about, the connections among her central traits. For instance, the young woman who appropriates Madonna as an identity ideal may be unaware or mistaken about the ways that her own somatic dispositions and those she acquired as a result of social role (e.g., class) casting will resist her attempts to be like Madonna. Individuals are normally presented with a relatively limited repertoire of appropriate ideals, as defined by their social roles and groups. Both the ramification of her early traits and the dynamic force of their social interactions channel the aspiring Madonna in other directions. If she has a persistent and independent temperament, she may indeed move Madonna-ward. But attempting to free oneself from social norms—or attempting to change those norms—often exacts social and sometimes psychological costs.

Depending on the type and the degree of their centrality, then, there are a number of different ways in which practical identity traits affect actions.

> They affect what is (perceptually, imaginatively, emotionally, and cognitively) salient to agents. In directing interpretations of situations and affecting the associations that such interpretations generate, central identity traits form

(what might be called) the problematic of their experience. They propel
agents into certain sorts of situations and problems, and they provide a
relevance selector among the relatively indefinite number of action routines
that might be elicited in any given situation.

They affect the dynamics of social interaction, eliciting responses—sometimes
supportive and cooperative, sometimes antagonistic—that set constraints
and directions on agents' actions.

By affecting patterns of child-rearing and socialization, they direct the formation of habits.

They can affect systems of beliefs and desires. Ideals are often the best explanation
of a person's having acquired or developed a pattern of desires, even when
those ideals were initially socially inculcated. Similarly, group or role identity
can often provide the best explanation of a person's holding certain beliefs.

They can set ends and values that direct practical deliberation.

4.5 Relative Centrality of Aspects across Culture

Just as traits vary in degrees of centrality within a single individual, so, too, there are
considerable individual variations in the degree to which different aspects of identity
are central. One person might stress her role identity as a teacher, importing her ped-
agogic traits into a wide variety of contexts and according them priority in cases of
conflict. Another might stress temperamental traits, leaving role relatively recessive.
Similarly, there are cultural variations in the relative centrality of different traits. One
culture might stress the ramification of such temperamental traits as austerity and
asceticism, while another might focus on channeling social roles.

Anthropologists have claimed that there are systematic differences in the ways that
societies tend to weight the centrality of aspects of identity. Some have claimed that in
certain societies the social role aspect has a centrality it does not normally have in our
culture. K. E. Read reported that "social role is an intrinsic constituent of each man's
identity" among the Gahuku-Gama of New Guinea. Members of that congeries of
tribes do move in and out of social roles and "thereby in a somewhat paradoxical
sense, they lose or forfeit [what we would call] their identity." They note each other's
idiosyncrasies and conceive of one another as distinct personalities, but these differences "are like a shimmer which overlies their social identity." They chiefly regard
each other and themselves as "figures in a social pattern."[9]

9. K. E. Read, "Morality and the Concept of the Person among the Gahuku-Gama," *Oceana* 25
(1955): 278, 276.

Read notes that moral reasoning among the Gahuku-Gama is "primarily contextual, dependent, that is, on the nature of specific social ties." The condemnation of homicide, for example, varies with the social status of the agent and victim. It is seriously wrong to kill a member of one's own subclan, but commendable to kill a member of opposed tribes, even in peacetime.[10] Reid contrasts the views of the Gahuku-Gama with the Western doctrine that human beings are owed respect because they possess intrinsic value independently of their social status or role.[11] This, he concludes, amounts to a systematic cultural difference in the relative centrality accorded to the social ramification of role identity.

Clifford Geertz makes a similar point in contrasting Western with Balinese identity. The Balinese control interpersonal relations by a highly developed system of conventions and proprieties, and define the "substance of the self" by a person's roles.[12] Commenting on the connection between identity and social role in Balinese public life, Geertz says that political and religious leaders become absorbed into their roles. "We, focusing upon psychological traits as the heart of personal identity, would say they have sacrificed their true selves to their roles; they, focusing on social position, say that their role is of the essence of their true selves."[13]

George DeVos holds that Japanese society accords a high degree of subjective and objective dominance to role identity, particularly in cases of stress and conflict. He believes that the varieties of identity tend to be absorbed into role identity in societies where roles are socially channeled and widely ramified.[14] Richard Shweder and Edmund Bourne hold that the traditional "sociocentric" conception of the person does not differentiate the individual from his group and role, while the modern Western "egocentric" conception accords value and assigns duties to individuals independently of their social roles.[15]

The distinctions drawn here between dimensions and aspects of identity suggest that the wholesale contrasts that many anthropologists have drawn between traditional sociocentric and modern egocentric conceptions of identity are too stark.[16] The sharp

10. Read, "Morality and the Concept of the Person," 262–4.

11. Read, "Morality and the Concept of the Person," 263, 260, 259–61.

12. Clifford Geertz, "From the Native's Point of View: On the Nature of Anthropological Understanding," in *Culture Theory: Essays in Mind, Self, and Emotion*, ed. Richard Shweder and Robert Levine (Cambridge: Cambridge University Press, 1984), 129.

13. Clifford Geertz, "Person, Time, and Conduct in Bali," in *The Interpretation of Cultures* (New York: Basic Books, 1973), 386.

14. See George DeVos, *Socialization for Achievement* (Berkeley: University of California Press, 1973).

15. Richard Shweder and Edward Bourne, "Does the Concept of the Person Vary?" in *Culture Theory: Essays in Mind, Self, and Emotion*, ed. Richard Shweder and Robert Levine (Cambridge: Cambridge University Press, 1984), 166–8.

16. Alasdair MacIntyre, in chap. 3 of *After Virtue*, 2nd ed. (Notre Dame, Ind.: University of Notre Dame Press, 1983), seems to make the same stark contrast. His most recent book, *Whose Justice? Which Rationality?* (Notre Dame, Ind.: University of Notre Dame Press, 1988), especially chap. 20, moderates the contrast.

contrasts that Shweder and Bourne, along with some other anthropologists, have emphasized might be better understood as distinctions of degree and of domains of life activity. Traditional cultures have some identity-defining ideals and duties that are universally prescribed, independently of social roles. In India, certain ideal identities—those modeled on the Buddha—are prescribed across socially defined caste and class divisions.[17] More recent work on the Japanese self has suggested a more complex and balanced portrait. Nancy Rosenberger, for example, characterizes that self as able to freely move between dimensions of thought, feeling, and behavior associated with both sociocentrism and egocentrism. Different modes of behavior (e.g., disciplined effort for the sake of group ends, relaxed and spontaneous expression of "inner feelings") are deemed appropriate for different contexts (e.g., the workplace, home).[18]

On the other hand, while social mobility in modern Western society is greater than it is in traditional societies, twentieth-century North Americans also have social identities; they too are group-cast along race, class, and gender lines. While Western societies tend to give more subjective centrality to role-independent temperamental and ideal traits than they do to role and group identity, the latter aspects normally have much greater objective centrality than is usually subjectively acknowledged. This is not to deny a significantly lesser degree of centrality of social identities in the West. This could hardly be otherwise, given the dissolution of many traditional communal ties in the postmodern West and the resulting social mobility. But the difference, as suggested in chapter 1, is one in the relative emphasis of commonly shared themes. Many Americans seem reluctant to recognize their social identities, and perhaps this is more a reflection of the fact that some of the most powerful social identities that persist in American society are not supposed to exist in it (class and racial identity being foremost in this category).[19]

Even when ideal traits are specifiable independently of any particular social roles, social contexts place significant objective and subjective constraints on their development and exercise. An individual's attempt to discount the centrality of group identity

17. For example, the ideals of noninjury, truth, purity, not stealing, charity, forbearance, self-restraint, tranquility, generosity, and asceticism, as stated in the *Arthasastra*. See Wendy Doniger O'Flaherty, "The Clash between Relative and Absolute Duty: The Dharma of Demons," in *The Concept of Duty in South Asia*, ed. Wendy D. O'Flaherty and J. Duncan M. Derrett (New Delhi: Vikas, 1978), 96–106, for an interesting discussion on attempts to resolve conflicts between role-specific duties and common duties.

18. Nancy R. Rosenberger, "Dialectic Balance in the Polar Model of the Self: The Japan Case," *Ethos* 17 (1989): 88–113. See also Jane M. Bachnik, "The Two 'Faces' of Self and Society in Japan," *Ethos* 20 (1992): 3–32; and Hisa A. Kumagai and Arno K. Kumagai, "The Hidden 'I' in Amae: 'Passive Love' and Japanese Social Perception," *Ethos* 14 (1986): 305–20.

19. See Samuel Bowles and Herbert Gintis, *Schooling in Capitalist America* (Boulder, Colo.: Perseus Books, 1977), for a telling characterization of the ways in which working and middle-class schoolchildren are channeled in their work habits, attitudes toward authority, and goals in life, according to their class.

can often fail. The attempt to diminish the significance of race, ethnicity, or gender is often treated as itself a focal expression of the very identity whose centrality is denied. For example, African Americans are often called upon to give race relative dominance over other aspects of their identity.[20] Even if individual African Americans subjectively attempt to discount race and to stress their ideal identities, their refusal to privilege race identity is often socially interpreted as a form of racism. They may be charged with identifying with the oppressor; and they are likely to be continuously role-cast in ways that can override the centrality that they attempted to accord to their ideal identities.

There can be deep conflicts between the various aspects of identity. As we saw in section 4.2, aspects affect action in several direct and indirect ways. Different aspects can direct an agent toward incompatible courses of action: a person's ideals can direct a course of action that is countermanded by her temperament or her social roles; similarly, traits that have become widely ramified as the result of social channeling can be more dominant than traits of the ideal self. An observer or theoretician can diagnose such conflicts by tracing the distinctive patterns of centrality accorded to various aspects. But agents can also experience them when they find themselves conflicted between different plans of action, as these plans might be generated by distinctive configurations of their identity traits.

4.6 THE SOCIAL NATURE OF PRACTICAL IDENTITY

I have implicitly touched upon several senses in which practical identity is social: one's social role and group identities may profoundly shape one's practical orientation in a dominant and widely ramified manner. They may be objectively central even if one fails to recognize or to subjectively appropriate them. But if one does appropriate these identities or significant parts of them, one's ideal identity may incorporate the values and ends embedded in social role and group identities. Established social roles carry with them duties, privileges, powers, and rights. They also may carry ideals of the motivations and traits that are to be had by a person who performs them well. Group identities may in fact overlap with social role identities, but they may independently contain shared habits, perceptual saliences, general ends and values that may be objectively central and/or subjectively appropriated. Sometimes communitarians argue, correctly, that even we in the "individualistic" postmodern West have social identities. But then some of them conclude that the existence of social role and socially defined group traits is sufficient to show that flourishing is somehow social in nature.

20. Terminology often becomes centrally important to group identity. Whether a person is prepared to accord centrality to his racial identity will of course depend how the race is characterized and how it is related to his other group identities (e.g. to class or subculture). The differences between 'black', 'Afro-American', and 'African American' are significant; they affect an individual's decision about whether to appropriate or to discount race as central to his identity.

The mere fact that having these social identities is virtually inevitable, even for "individualistic" societies, does not mean these identities are necessary for flourishing. Social identities can severely conflict with other aspects of identity, as argued earlier. A severe conflict between social and ideal identities, for example, would hardly seem conducive to flourishing. The same holds true for a conflict between temperamental or psychological central traits and the requirements of a social role identity. If flourishing requires fulfillment of one's social nature, it must be found in a closer examination of the prerequisites for flourishing and their relation to social identity. In the next section, I will discuss three properties necessary for effective agency, without pretending they are the only ones. But the three do form a series, in the sense that one becomes more effective as one adds each property. Having these necessary properties requires having a social identity of a certain *sort*, not just having a social identity.

4.7 A Conception of Effective Identities

An "effective identity" is a practical identity with an adequate degree of effective agency. Such an identity must contain the trait of being able to determine what social norms require. This would be true even if its possessor had no consistent intention to conform to the norms and instead intended to manipulate and work around them to achieve his ends. One cannot manipulate people by playing on their expectations if one does not know in a given context what these expectations are.

An effective identity also possesses an appropriate balance among its component aspects. Balance includes a degree of congruence between the different aspects of identity. As we saw earlier, severe conflict between different aspects can hinder or completely obstruct the effective pursuit of one's ends. However, the notion of appropriate balance is wider than that of reasonable congruence because sometimes there is no more effective alternative than to have aspects of identity that *do* conflict in some degree. One context in which such conflicted identities may seem appropriate is a complex society in which individuals must perform roles that make very different demands on them. These demands may require for their effective execution different temperamental traits or different ideal identities, or social identities that conflict with either of the former. Consider a woman who must function both as a mother and an executive in a highly competitive business. Or consider those societies undergoing modernization and in which traditional communities and household structures coexist with new industrial enterprises. Individuals who must live and work within both realms show a capacity to switch back and forth between the traits, attitudes, and expectations required in each.[21] To some extent, people can mitigate the conflict between different aspects of identity by contextualizing their operation—by limiting

---

21. This seems to be the case in India, for example. See Alan Roland, *In Search of Self in India and Japan: Toward a Cross-Cultural Psychology* (Princeton: Princeton University Press, 1988).

their ramification to certain domains. However, these aspects cannot always be easily delimited in their ramification and are liable to conflict at least sometimes. Yet it may be better to live with a limited degree of conflict than to fail to have those aspects of identity needed to navigate in different domains of action. That is why the notion of appropriate balance between aspects of identity must include a measure of conflict as well as congruence.

Another property of an effective identity is that it contains the particular trait of self-esteem, which involves a belief in one's own worthiness and in the merit of one's primary goals and desires, and also a confidence in one's ability to satisfy the goals and desires if given a reasonable opportunity to do so. As John Rawls has emphasized in *A Theory of Justice*,[22] one will be unable to realize one's ends, whatever they are, unless one accepts oneself as worthy of having one's ends satisfied, and has confidence in one's abilities to achieve them.[23] Self-esteem can be seen to depend, at least in part, on some possible properties of identities already mentioned. It would be undermined if one saw serious incongruence between one's normative beliefs on the one hand and one's primary goals, desires, and traits on the other.

If we look more closely at what is involved in producing practical identities with adequate knowledge of social norms, reasonable congruence, and self-esteem, we can begin to see the necessity of certain sorts of relationship with others. To have a practical identity with any shape at all, we take from others who raise us. The child's tendency to imitate others is well known, but the tendency seems to go way beyond outward imitation of behavior. That is why the Confucians gave the most emphasis to the family in their ethic. The Confucian ethic prescribes that one ought to have care and concern for all people, but when it considers how this care is to be made a reality, it focuses on the family. This institution provides the first context in which love of others is learnt, and the habits of thought, feeling, and acting that compose this love form much of the foundation of the individual's character. Mencius believed that we have an innate capacity to love and care for others, but he also believed that that capacity could turn into something very different unless it is given the appropriate nurturance (*Mencius* 6A7, 7A15). Security is needed, and by "security" Mencius did not mean merely the provision of basic material needs. There is a wonderful translation by Wing-Tsit Chan of a passage in *Mencius* 7A15: "children carried in the arms all know to love their parents."[24]

22. John Rawls, *A Theory of Justice* (Cambridge, Mass.: Belknap Press, 1971), 440.

23. Belief in one's worthiness in my sense is consistent with self-criticism and awareness of one's inadequacies. Indeed, in Chinese traditional culture, having an inflated sense of one's accomplishments or admirable traits is one of the worst defects of character. Similarly, confidence in one's abilities to achieve one's ends is not inconsistent with the assumption that one will have to work very hard to achieve them.

24. Wing-Tsit Chan, *A Sourcebook in Chinese Philosophy* (Princeton: Princeton University Press, 1963), 80.

4.8 Evidence for the Necessity of Nurturing Effective Identities

Much common sense confirms such a view. Scientific evidence is limited because controlled experiments on human beings are unfeasible and/or ethically impermissible. However, experiments on the closest genetic relatives point in the direction of the Mencian view. In Harlow's celebrated experiments, infant rhesus monkeys were fed by "artificial" mothers made of wire or wood covered with soft cloth.[25] The infants developed abnormal behavior patterns such as clutching themselves, rocking constantly back and forth, and excessive and misdirected aggression. When they became mothers themselves, they tended to be indifferent or abusive toward their infants.

Many studies have found that low serotonin levels in adult human beings are linked to aggression, alcohol abuse, and mental illness. A team led by Stephen Suomi and Dee Higley studied the link between behavior, serotonin, and environment in rhesus monkeys. They found that the monkeys who are unusually impulsive and aggressive are the ones with the comparatively lowest levels of serotonin, tend to become loners, are unable to win acceptance into the troupes they try to enter, are unsuccessful at mating, and often die within a year. Low serotonin levels tend to run in families, but Suomi and Higley's research indicated that low serotonin is also influenced by environment. They took monkey infants away from their mothers and raised them almost completely among other monkeys their age. In their socially inept behavior they resembled those mother-reared counterparts who were born shy and easily frightened. Moreover, they started showing the low serotonin levels associated with aggression. Suomi and his colleagues attributed many of these characteristics to the fact that peers aren't as good at comforting each other as are mothers, and in new situations they become as scared as their partners. In addition, peer-reared monkeys drank significantly more alcohol than mother-reared monkeys, with a correlation between low serotonin and heavy drinking. But that difference disappeared when the researchers separated all the monkeys from their social group—a highly stressful situation for monkeys. Both groups drank heavily.[26]

25. H. F. Harlow and R. R. Zimmermann, "Affectional Responses in the Infant Monkey," in *Foundations of Animal Behavior: Classic Papers with Commentaries*, ed. L. D. Houck and L. C. Drickamer (Chicago: University of Chicago Press, 1996), 376–87.

26. J. D. Higley, P.T. Mehlman, R. E. Poland, D. T. Taub, S. J. Suomi, and M. Linnoila, "Aggression, Social Dominance, Serotonin, and Causal Relationships," *Biological Psychiatry* 42 (1997): 306–7; J. D. Higley, S. J. Suomi, and M. Linnoila, "Excessive Alcohol Consumption, Inappropriate Aggression, and Serotonin: A Nonhuman Primate Model of Alcohol Abuse," *Recent Developments in Alcoholism* 13 (1997): 191–219; J. D. Higley, S. J. Suomi, and M. Linnoila, "A Nonhuman Primate Model of Type II Alcoholism? Part 2: Diminished Social Competence and Excessive Aggression Correlates with Low Cerebrospinal Fluid 5-hydroxyindoleacetic Acid Concentrations," *Alcoholism* 20 (1996): 643–50; J. D. Higley, S. J. Suomi, and M. Linnoila, "A Nonhuman Primate Model of Type II Excessive Alcohol Consumption? Part 1: Low Cerebrospinal Fluid 5-hydroxyindoleacetic Acid Concentrations

The team found that nurturing mothers could buffer infants from their genetic inheritance. There is a long and a short form of the gene that regulates serotonin turnover in rhesus monkeys. Monkeys raised by nurturing mothers showed fairly normal serotonin metabolism, regardless of which gene type they had. But gene type made a huge difference in peer-reared monkeys. Those with the long version looked normal. Those with the short version had problems with aggression. In another experiment, the team took highly reactive monkey infants—those most likely to grow up anxiety-prone—and gave them to foster mothers that were extremely nurturing. Most of these infants rose to assume dominant positions in their troops. The females became nurturing mothers themselves. They calmed themselves down much more quickly than other highly reactive individuals, bringing their heart rates down faster, lowering their level of the stress hormone cortisol more quickly, for example. It seems that their experiences with nurturing mothers altered not only their behavioral propensities but their physiological patterns as well.[27] Suomi's results strongly parallel a human study led by Avshalom Caspi and Terrie Moffitt in which children from New Zealand were followed over the course of twenty-six years. Children were much more likely to be aggressive and antisocial if they inherited a short version of the gene MAOA, but carriers of this gene who had good mothering were usually quite normal.[28]

There are several theories that emphasize the influence of caregivers on the development of human children. In object-relations theory, an offshoot of classical psychoanalytic theory that is rooted in the clinical experience of therapists, Melanie Klein has written of the way in which children come to internalize or incorporate the others who are caring for them. Richard Wollheim, drawing from her work, outlines a crucial stage of incorporation that he calls "identification." This is an imaginative activity whereby the child imagines another "centrally." The activity is analogous to an audience empathizing with the character of a play. As the audience represents the thoughts, feelings, and experiences of a character as though they were its own, so does

---

and Diminished Social Competence Correlate with Excessive Alcohol Consumption," *Alcoholism* 20 (1996): 629–42; J. D. Higley, "Use of Nonhuman Primates in Alcohol Research," *Alcohol, Health and Research World* 19 (1996): 213–6; J. D. Higley, P. T. Mehlman, D. T. Taub, S. B. Higley, B. Fernald, J. Vickers, S. J. Suomi, and M. Linnoila, "Excessive Mortality in Young Male Nonhuman Primates with Low CSF 5-HIAA Concentrations," *Archives of General Psychiatry* 53 (1996): 537–43; J. D. Higley, P. T. Mehlman, R. E. Poland, I. Faucher, D. T. Taub, J. Vickers, S. J. Suomi, and M. Linnoila, "A Nonhuman Primate Model of Violence and Assertiveness: CSF 5-HIAA and CSF Testosterone Correlate with Different Types of Aggressive Behaviors," *Biological Psychiatry* 40 (1996): 1067–82; J. D. Higley and S. J. Suomi, "Effect of Reactivity and Social Competence on Individual Responses to Severe Stress in Children: Investigations Using Nonhuman Primates." In *Intense Stress and Mental Disturbance in Children*, ed. C. R. Pfeffer (New York: American Psychiatric Press, 1996), pp. 3–57.

27. Stephen J. Suomi, "Gene-Environment Interactions and the Neurobiology of Social Conflict," *Annals of the New York Academy of Science* 1008 (2003): 132–9.

28. A. Caspi, J. McClay, T. E. Moffitt, J. Mill, J. Martin, I. W. Craig, A. Taylor, and R. Poulton, "Role of Genotype in the Cycle of Violence in Maltreated Children," *Science* 297 (2002): 851–4.

one who "centrally imagines" another. Children imagine what parents would do if faced with a certain kind of situation. They imagine what the parents would think, feel, and experience in that situation, and they imagine these as if they were their own. In doing this, they alter their internal lives, because they find themselves in the condition in which thinking, feeling, and experiencing those things would have left them. That is, they fashion, to some extent, their internal lives after the imagined internal life of the others. They enlarge their emotional range, acquire new objects of care, new ideals.[29]

John Bowlby proposed that an infant's behavior toward its primary caregiver is under the control of an "attachment behavior control system" that is encoded in the core of the human central nervous system.[30] A possible evolutionary explanation lies in the vulnerability of our human ancestors to predatory attacks. An innate system in infants that worked to maintain a degree of proximity or access to adults reduced the likelihood of falling prey to such attacks. Inspired by Bowlby's theory, Mary Ainsworth and her colleagues have identified three major attachment patterns based on infants' behavior in a reunion with the mother after a brief separation.[31] "Secure" infants, in the mother's presence, explore actively and use the mother as a base for their adventures. They are upset when separated from the mother, and seek bodily contact and comfort when reunited. "Anxious/ambivalent" infants, upon the mother's return, show desire for proximity, but also anger and resistance. They display intense emotional protest and an inability to be comforted into normal play. "Avoidant" infants ignore and avoid interaction with the mother by turning away to other things such as playing with toys. Ainsworth and her colleagues have also found sets of parental behaviors that correspond to the infants' attachment styles. The secure mothers are sensitive and responsive. The anxious mothers are inconsistent, unpredictable, and intrusive. The avoidant mothers are rejecting and rebuffing.

Traits on both the mothers' and the children's sides contribute to the achievement of a secure base attachment. On the mothers' side, the most powerful component is early, sensitive care, characterized by accurate reading and interpretation of infant cues

29. See Richard Wollheim, "The Good Self and the Bad Self," in *Rationalism, Empiricism, and Idealism*, ed. Anthony Kenny (Oxford: Clarendon Press, 1986), 151–76. See also his *The Thread of Life* (Cambridge: Harvard University Press, 1984), 78–82, 123–5. A recent study shows that children as young as one year can be influenced by and emulate emotions of an adult they see on television. The study had one-year-olds watch a videotape of an adult actress displaying positive or negative emotions toward a toy. After watching, the infants were observed to show similar emotions toward the same toy. They also appeared to display different reactions toward other toys not shown in the video, so the signals they picked up from the actress in the video appeared to be rather specific. See Donna L. Mumme and Anne Fernald, "The Infant as Onlooker: Learning from Emotional Reactions Observed in a Television Scenario," *Child Development* 74 (2003): 221–37.

30. John Bowlby, "The Nature of the Child's Tie to His Mother," *International Journal of Psycho-Analysis* 39 (1958): 350–73.

31. Mary D. Ainsworth, *Infancy in Uganda: Infant Care and the Growth of Love* (Baltimore: Johns Hopkins Press, 1967).

and signals, letting the child's signals, rather than the parents' needs or wishes, set the agenda, and consistency or predictability over time. Silverman and Ragusa found a connection between negative (anxious or avoidant styles) maternal behavior and difficulty in control of delayed gratification behavior in children between the ages of two and four. In addition, Rodriguez and Mischel tied delay behavior of preschoolers to the interactive quality of the parent-child interaction. Jacobsen, Edelstein, and Hofmann observed that children without secure attachment (such that they are able to accept the short absences of parents) were found to have difficulty in frustration tolerance, behavior control, aggression, and later with reflective thought.[32] Secure attachment infants are commonly found to establish closer attachments with others in their same age group. Sroufe and Fleeson suggest that the formation of primary, maternal relationships affect peer relations. Consequently, if the attachment type is known, a prediction can be made in the area of future peer relations. Kerns observed that early childhood relationship goals are oriented toward establishing coordinated interactions. The child must have the ability to respond to others and to resolve conflicts. Dishion discovered that aversive parenting practices are reflected in antisocial behavior in grade-school children.[33]

32. All studies in this paragraph were cited in M. Fendrich, M. Huss, T. Jacobsen, M. Kruesi, and U. Ziegenhain, "Children's Ability to Delay Gratification: Longitudinal Relations to Mother-Child Attachment," *Journal of Genetic Psychology* 158 (1997): 411–27; and in Jonathan C. Wildman Jr., "Elements of Infant-Mother Attachment," *New Perspectives: A Social Sciences Journal* (1999–2000) available at www.ycp.edu/besc/journal2000/article1.html.

33. All studies in this paragraph are cited in B. Fagot, "Attachment, Parenting, and Peer Interactions of Toddler Children," *Developmental Psychology* 33 (1997): 489–500; and in Wildman, "Elements of Infant-Mother Attachment."

It is assumed, of course, that genes have a very significant impact on whatever character traits eventually develop in a person. Studies of identical twins raised in different families sometimes indicate remarkable similarities in attitudes and preferences despite significant differences in child-rearing environment. See Thomas J. Bouchard Jr., David T. Lykken, Matthew McGue, Nancy L. Segal, and Auke Tellegen, "Sources of Human Psychological Differences: The Minnesota Study of Twins Reared Apart," *Science* 250 (1990): 223–9. Sometimes, such studies get cited as evidence that nature "beats" nurture as the primary determinant of character and behavior. However, twin studies such as Bouchard's may rather indicate that most families supply "good enough" parenting for their children, and that the similarities in this parenting are more important than the differences that coexist with them. For the notion of "good enough" parenting, see D. W. Winnicot, *The Family and Individual Development* (London: Routledge, 1989). Moreover, the "nature wins" conclusion not only conflicts with the studies previously cited but also overlooks ways in which dramatic conclusions based on twin studies are hasty. As Wendy Doniger points out, "twins raised together often make a conscious effort to differentiate themselves, more than twins raised apart. On the other hand, identical twins raised apart may be treated similarly by their adoptive families because of their physical similarity (ugly ones teased, pretty ones praised etc). Then again, there is often a negative correlation between similarities in personality or ability: the twins who look most alike are least alike in their behavior. Besides, the 'separated' factor is often corrupted by shared environments, always shared in the womb (prenatal influences) and often in early childhood, or by unrecorded meetings during the adult testing period." See Doniger, "What Did They Name the Dog?" review of *Twins: Genes, Environment and the Mystery of Identity*, by Lawrence Wright, *London Review of Books*, March 19, 1998. Simon Blackburn, in a

Such empirical work provides some support for the common-sense view that others have a deep effect on the formation of our characters, and in such a way as to shape many of the fundamental attitudes we carry into our relationships with others and into the projects of achieving our most important ends.[34] This fact did not escape the American sociologist Charles Horton Cooley. Cooley emphasized the importance of interactive process between group and individual in the formation of individual human nature and the development of norms and ends. He called "primary" those groups most influential in the process, such as the family, the household group, and the old-fashioned neighborhood. Such groups facilitate insight into the moods and states of mind of others, and tend to result in a "certain fusion of individualities in a common whole, so that one's very self, for many purposes at least, is the common life and purpose of the group."[35]

The penetration of others into our identities can take place through their influence on the acquisition of those properties necessary for effective agency. Consider the path to knowledge of social norms. The Confucians believed that the knowledge and ability to respond rightly to particular situations can be acquired only in the context of the daily practices and institutions that shape our lives, and the family is the first and most influential. Often the best way to teach the application of a general principle or concept is to give examples until the learner knows how to go on in the right way, where that way cannot be spelled out except in a very general and deliberately vague fashion. Within the family, the child learns that going on in the right way depends on the situation, on the particular character of the parties involved, and on the nature of their relationship at the time. Children learn this through interaction with family members and being shown in particular instances what they did right or wrong. After having acquired a fund of such experience, they may know *how* to go on in the right way, without an explicit and specific knowing *that*, to use Ryle's distinction.[36] There may not even be an explicit

---

review of *The Blank Slate: The Modern Denial of Human Nature,* by Steven Pinker, points out that measures of heritability are highly contextual, such that in a world of clones, the heritability of properties is zero, while in a world of absolute sameness of environment, it goes to 100 percent. He also points out that heritability also has little or nothing to do with the malleability of the trait in question. He cites Swedish twin studies that give heritability estimates for regular tobacco use that ranged from zero to 60 percent in three different age cohorts for women, presumably because of changing cultural pressures on female smoking. See "Meet the Flintstones," *New Republic,* November 25, 2002, 28–33.

34. For an interpretation of Aristotle's view of the importance of modeling, see Martha Nussbaum, *The Fragility of Goodness: Luck and Ethics in Greek Tragedy and Philosophy* (Cambridge: Cambridge University Press, 1986), 363. For an interpretation of Confucius's view, see my "Universalism versus Love with Distinctions: An Ancient Debate Revived," *Journal of Chinese Philosophy* 16 (1989): 252–72.

35. Charles Cooley, Robert C. Angell, and Lowell J. Carr, *Introductory Sociology* (New York: Scribner's, 1933), 55–6, quoted in Charles Loomis and John C. McKinney, introduction to Ferdinand Tonnies, *Community and Society (Gemeinschaft und Gesellschaft),* trans. Charles Loomis (New Brunswick, N.J.: Transaction, 1988), 14–5.

36. Gilbert Ryle, *The Concept of Mind* (Chicago: University of Chicago Press, 1984), chap. 2.

consciousness of learning or teaching, for these activities to be going on. For good or ill, many of the ways we model after others or model for others is not deliberate.

Parents have the common experience of having to correct a child's too-literal application of some elementary social norm, and they know that explicit explanation of why their child's application is too literal can only go so far. Consider the task of teaching a child the line between acceptable friendliness to strangers and being overly familiar. Sometimes the best way to teach the content of a general norm is to give examples of what is to be done in this or that situation, or to point out when the child has got it right or wrong in a particular situation. In her study of Inuit conceptions of identity, Arlene Stairs discusses the way in which the introduction of formal schooling from the majority culture contrasts with traditional learning, which is "a way of passing along knowledge through observation and imitation embedded in daily family and community activities, with integration into the immediate, shared social structure and ecology as the principal goal."[37] Beatrice Whiting and Carolyn Edwards, in a comparative study of child-rearing in different cultures, conclude that the universal task of the mother and other caregivers includes the teaching of norms of social behavior. Like Stairs, they contrast the explicit instruction of formal schooling with the "much less rationalized" form of feedback and information about social roles. They are conveyed less by explicit instruction, observe Whiting and Edwards, and more by implicit moral messages that "children can and must abstract from what happens in everyday social interaction." The consequences of interaction include frequent commands, suggestions, threats, and punishment, received from adults and other children. "From this feedback, children appear to construct a working knowledge of the complex conditions surrounding the 'do's and 'don't's of interpersonal aggression, the distribution of resources, social roles, task assignment, damage to property, etiquette, hygiene, and other matters of proper social behavior."[38]

To have a minimally adequate knowledge of social norms, then, requires that we enter into a learning relationship with others, in which the "right way" is shown throughout various situations over an extended period of our lives. Learning how to go on in the right way is acquiring judgment. The relationship in which judgment is cultivated must be regular and extend to many domains of our lives, given the extensive scope of social norms. Where learning and teaching are deliberate and self-conscious, a certain degree of trust is presupposed between learner and teacher. The learner must believe that the teacher intends to and is in fact cultivating the relevant abilities, by and large.

Now consider appropriate balance between identity aspects. We are not simply given practical identities with such a property. We must form our important commitments

37. Arlene Stairs, "Self-Image, World Image: Speculations on Identity from Experience with Inuit," *Ethos* 20 (1992): 116–26.

38. Beatrice Blythe Whiting and Carolyn Hope Edwards, *Children of Different Worlds: The Formation of Social Behavior* (Cambridge, Mass.: Harvard University Press, 1988), 253.

with an eye to their possible balance with other of our traits, and to the extent that we can alter or develop our own traits, we should alter or develop them with an eye to their possible congruence with our ends. An effective identity, therefore, requires the ability to judge the congruence between our commitments and other identity aspects, and that requires a substantial degree of self-knowledge. Others play an essential role in the acquisition of this knowledge. This is not just because it can be difficult by ourselves to judge what we are, as opposed to what we would wish to be, but also because we are often liable to blame others and the world for our failures, rather than to look for some conflict between what we want to achieve and what our traits enable us to achieve. If achieving an appropriate balance within our identities requires us to change our commitments, we often need to understand why they were important to us in the first place, and that can be a difficult task. We need the perspective of others to correct for self-deception and lack of self-perspective. And getting such help and being able to use it again presupposes a substantial degree of trust. We must believe that others are giving objective information about ourselves. What is more, we sometimes are unable to accept negative information unless we believe that the one who is giving it to us is also one who thinks well of us, overall, and wishes us well.

Others not only provide self-knowledge in the project of achieving balance but also can help to shape and crystallize traits and desires that are especially congruent with our most important ends. Or rather, there are often times when increased self-knowledge merges with the crystallization of a trait or desire—when, for instance, understanding oneself better is at the same time making more determinate tendencies and impulses within one's character that are in some degree inchoate. I have in mind ways that others can help us through some insight as to what our "real" feelings and motivations are, where that insight is partly an accurate portrayal of what is already there but also helps to reinforce and make more determinate what those feelings and motivations are. A friend who points out to a person that she is more compassionate than she understands herself to be, who points to certain recurring instances of compassionate behavior as evidence, may not just be pointing to what is already there but crystallizing and making more motivationally salient that trait in his friend.

Consider the question of acquiring self-confidence and self-esteem. Object-relations theory and "self psychology," another offshoot of classical psychoanalytic theory, have located the sources of healthy self-assessment in the interaction of the individual with others, especially in early life. This is a shift from the time when the sources were located in the purely internal dynamics of the individual's drives (as much of Freud's early work does), and surely something like the former view must be correct. For example, self psychologist Heinz Kohut emphasizes the need of the child for "mirroring," a process that involves expressing pleasure in the child's developing abilities and acceptance of the child's ambitions. Parents may fail to adequately mirror a child because of their own defects in self-confidence. Kohut gives the example of a girl who comes home from school eager to tell her mother of her great successes, but the mother, instead of listening with pride, talks about her own successes. This child may become a "mirror-hungry" personality, which is sometimes manifested in the demand for exclusive attention and reassuring praise from others to counteract the internal sense of worthlessness. Much of her psychic energies will be taken up by the attempt to compensate for the inadequate mirroring of her childhood. Kohut also stresses the need for parents to curb a child's grandiose ambitions and self-image at the appropriate moments.[39] To fail in this is to expose the child to a collapse of self-esteem when she inevitably fails to live up to her grandiose self-image.

Here again, the mirroring relation requires trust. The child must be ready to receive correction from the parents when they point out some incongruence between her ambitions and her traits, and to do that, she must trust in their motives and their judgment. We have arrived at a picture in which the individual develops in relationship to others not only a practical identity but also the properties of an identity that are necessary for effective agency. These relationships must involve trust if they are to contribute optimally to effective agency.[40] Where do we find these others who can be trusted? There must be others who are firmly committed to providing the required nurturing, and who will persevere despite the many frustrations and setbacks that inevitably accompany such nurturing.[41] Furthermore, one cannot reasonably expect human beings to make such commitments without some reciprocation from those they nurture.

That is why duties of care by parents and duties of gratitude and obedience by children define and sustain relationships that help to form effective identities. Reciprocation of care by children need not take the form of obedience, and certainly not unconditional obedience, but simple obedience is often appreciated and needed when no further reasons for the desired behavior can be given. Fortunately, there are deep satisfactions obtained from nurturing, and deep tendencies to reciprocate, even if these tendencies can be and are overridden. Whiting and Edwards, in their crosscultural study of child-rearing, find striking similarities across cultures in the way in which children and adults respond to very young children. In agreement with attachment theory, they conclude that these children "have the power to elicit positive responsiveness and nurturance even from children as young as two years of age, and from both girls and boys." The universality of this pattern suggests to Whiting and Edwards that infants are born equipped with physical features and behavioral systems that evoke positive behavior and nurturance from both adults and children (a suggestion

---

39. See Heinz Kohut and Ernest Wolf, "Disorders of the Self and Their Treatment: An Outline," *International Journal of Psycho-Analysis* 59 (1978): 403–25, for an introduction to Kohut's theory.

40. In emphasizing the importance of trust in relationships that nurture effective identities, I take myself to be confirming Annette Baier's claim that trust is a central but neglected concept for ethical theory. See her "What Do Women Want in a Moral Theory?" *Noûs* 19 (1985), 53–63.

41. MacIntyre, "Is Patriotism a Virtue?" points out the necessity for such a commitment for the nurturing of moral virtue, and reading his article set me on the line of thought that culminates here. See also MacIntyre's *Dependent Rational Animals: Why Human Beings Need the Virtues* (Perus, Ill.: OpenCourt, 1999), for a further development of this theme.

congenial to Bowlby's attachment theory).[42] But if young children have this genetic program, adults and older children must have a genetic program that disposes them to respond with positive behavior and nurturance. This should not be so surprising in a species in which the young are so completely helpless for a long period of time, and in which the specificity of instinctual behavior found in the lower animals is replaced by the ability to learn the cultural forms that make social cooperation possible. So duties of care and of reciprocation through gratitude and obedience find some hospitable soil in human nature.

Recall, however, the conclusion of section 2.9: that human beings are profoundly ambivalent beings in whom strong self-interest intertwines with various forms of other-concern. Moreover, the frustrations inevitably encountered in providing care and nurturing of others make it necessary for duties of care and reciprocation to be affirmed within communities in such ways that individuals are motivated to focus on the satisfactions and the urge to reciprocate. Nurturing and teaching roles must be relatively central to their identities. Only then do those they care for have a reasonable chance of receiving consistent and reliable help in the task of achieving effective identities. Duties of care and of reciprocity for care constitute, in fact, an especially important case of the theme cited in chapter 1: the need for reciprocation of aid. Human beings are of such a nature that one cannot reliably expect help from them unless one reciprocates that help.

We have arrived at the conclusion that the nurturing of an effective identity in an individual requires relationships with others that are partly defined and sustained by reciprocal duties. We have grounded certain duties to others in the requirements for effective agency. In particular, people have duties toward those who are helping them realize conditions for their effective agency, which are in turn necessary conditions for their flourishing. We may expect some variation in the specific content of those duties as we cross cultures (and here there is more room for pluralistic relativism), and in the structure of families and other groups charged with the task of nurturing agency. (Fraternal polyandry, or the practice of brothers marrying the same woman and raising their children together and sharing their material resources, appears in regions of Nepal and Tibet and China, and there is no a priori reason why such a practice would be inferior or superior to monogamy with regard to the task of nurturing the agency of children.) But the range of variation is constrained by the condition that performance of these duties be such that it contributes to the sustaining of the relationship. We would expect these duties to reflect a concern for the welfare of those nurturing the individual. This argument provides a way to understand why special duties to particular others have such a powerful hold on us. Moral agency must grow within the context of relationships governed by such duties.

---

42. Whiting and Edwards, *Children of Different Worlds*, 270.

The sort of argument I have just given would seem to require that there be relationships of such a type within the family or, more generally, within small groups that have taken on the task of raising children. As noted earlier, Confucianism has recognized and articulated the value of the family and given the reasons why it supports effective moral agency.[43] We in the contemporary West, with a culture so penetrated by the language and explanations of psychology, also readily recognize the significant effects of child-rearing.

The impact of early childhood rearing can be profound, but is not necessarily permanent. Brandt and Mitchell expanded on Suomi and Harlow's work with rhesus monkeys and managed to rehabilitate young monkeys who had been raised in isolation.[44] In a case that supports the same conclusion for human beings, Mary and Louise, aged two and a half and three and a half, respectively, spent their early lives in extreme deprivation with a mentally retarded mother. After extensive speech therapy and years of interaction, there was a huge improvement. Skuse concluded that victims of this level of privation still have excellent prospects.[45]

There is another way in which the effects of early childhood rearing might be overestimated. Many of us do not adequately recognize that effective identities need sustenance and further development as the individual achieves maturity and moves into the wider network of her society's institutions and practices. It is somewhat surprising that we, with our heavily psychologized culture, do not recognize the extent to which this is true. The reason for the lack of recognition may have something to do with a popular belief associated with the ideal of the autonomous individual: the belief that a good upbringing results in an independent person who is more or less fully equipped with the traits that will allow her to fulfill her own conception of flourishing.

But if we go back to the properties of effective identities, we will see how difficult it is to sustain such a belief. Surely the most ideal parenting does not ensure knowledge of norms that is necessary for acting effectively within institutions and practices beyond the family. Yasuko Minoura, in a study of Japanese children growing up in the United States, compares the influence of Japanese parents with the influence of American peers on the psychological development of these children. He finds that cultural norms and expectations get embedded much later than age six (the point in Freudian theory at which our personalities are basically formed). He finds further that peers have more power in "cultural learning" than parents.[46]

43. See my "Universalism versus Love with Distinctions."

44. E. M. Brandt and G. Mitchell, "Pairing Pre-Adolescents with Infants (Macaca Mulatta)," *Developmental Psychology* 8 (1973): 222–8, cited in E. E. Maccoby, *Social Development: Psychological Growth and the Parent-Child Relationship* (New York: Harcourt Brace Jovanovich, 1980), 94.

45. David Skuse, "Extreme Deprivation in Childhood: Theoretical Issues and a Comparative Review," *Journal of Child Psychology and Psychiatry* 25 (1984): 543–72.

46. Yasuko Minoura, "A Sensitive Period for the Incorporation of Cultural Meaning System: A Study of Japanese Children Growing Up in the United States," *Ethos* 20 (1992): 304–39.

Furthermore, the appropriate balance between aspects of identity is not achieved once and for all within the family. Indeed, given the complexity of identity and all the possibilities for enervating conflict described earlier, reasonable balance is a difficult and fragile achievement. This is not just because our ends change, and not just because different relationships may require different skills and abilities. We sometimes talk of character traits as if they were global properties that "stick" to us as we move from context to context. Yet many of our traits turn out to be more localized, in that they must be described with implicit reference to situations that elicit or suppress the relevant behavior. People we characterize as generally self-confident may not be so when they are taken from their familiar community and placed in a new social context. And it is not unusual to encounter persons who manifest certain traits to family and close friends, such as warmth and generosity, but who manifest very different ones to those with whom they work.[47]

---

47. Gilbert Harman has argued that we should dispense with talk of character traits altogether, given folk expectations about their global character. See Harman, "Moral Philosophy Meets Social Psychology: Virtue Ethics and the Fundamental Attribution Error," *Proceedings of the Aristotelian Society* 99 (1998–99): 315–31, and "The Nonexistence of Character Traits," *Proceedings of the Aristotelian Society* 100 (1999–2000): 223–6. Dispensing with the talk, he thinks, will draw attention to the influence of situational factors on behavior. I certainly agree that this is a beneficial result, but dispensing with the notion of character traits altogether would place all the emphasis on situational factors, with the exceptions Harman wishes to make for the existence of psychological disorders such as depression and schizophrenia and innate aspects of temperamental traits such as shyness. However, the existence of the systematic regularities that underlie psychological disorders and innate temperaments suggests that there are interesting and useful regularities that go under the heading of character traits, even if they are, as I have argued earlier, considerably more context-dependent than is usually assumed. Innate temperaments interact with situational factors in complex ways and are often self-consciously modified by individuals themselves, but regularities of perception and behavior relative to certain kinds of situations can result. The social psychologist Ziva Kunda has expressed skepticism about the existence of global character traits, but points out that the nonexistence of such traits is consistent with systematic differences between individuals such as someone's being quite extroverted in one-to-one interactions, moderately so in small groups, and not at all in large groups, whereas another person might display the reverse profile. See Kunda, *Social Cognition: Making Sense of People* (Cambridge, Mass.: MIT Press, 1999).

The philosopher John Doris has recently argued for a conception of "local character traits" that is in line with such context-dependence, or "situational sensitivity," as he calls it. See his *Lack of Character: Personality and Moral Behavior* (Cambridge: Cambridge University Press, 2002). However, Doris takes a kind of skeptical stance on the viability of virtue ethics that is not explained by his rejection of global character traits in favor of local traits. His main reason seems to be that local traits as found in most people show a kind of situation sensitivity that is ethically *undesirable or objectionable*. A good mood, prompted by finding a stray dime, renders most people much more likely to help a stranger. (See A. M. Isen and P. F. Levin, "Effect of Feeling Good on Helping: Cookies and Kindness," *Journal of Personality and Social Psychology* 21 (1972): 384–8.) In general, many of the situational factors that make a great deal of difference to the manifestation of ethical behavior are factors that from an ethical perspective *ought not to* make the kind of difference they make. To me, this is not a reason to be skeptical of the prospects for virtue ethics, but rather gives us a better idea of the distance between most people as we find them and virtue ideals. It also gives us a reason to identify and promote more specifically those local environments that help to cultivate and sustain the context-dependent traits that *are* ethically desirable.

It should not be surprising, after all, that many of our traits are context-dependent. We are relatively complex beings who have created for ourselves complicated social worlds. The context-dependence of traits suggests that qualities that promote effective agency for a person, and that may have been cultivated within the family with regard to circumscribed domains of action, cannot be assumed to transfer to social contexts outside the family and to domains of action other than the ones in which the qualities developed. If these qualities are needed for effective agency in the other contexts and domains, they may need to be developed there through further interaction with others. Let us also note that the specific form our actions take is determined through interactive process with others.[48] Many of those actions that flow from settled character traits are also elicited by the people with whom we interact, because our characters are configurations of traits. Different ones can be elicited by different people and by different interactive processes. It is often the case, therefore, that getting the best from ourselves means getting the right company. An important reason for the context-dependence of our character traits is that different people, and the nature of our relationships to them, make different contexts.

That is why we can be startled when we discuss with others the character of some common acquaintance, and may even wonder whether we are talking about the same person. The characters of others penetrate and shape our own traits to a significant extent, and this applies to the traits needed for effective agency. As to self-esteem, it is probably true, as many psychologists stress, that appropriate nurturing will provide a child a base of self-regard that she will carry throughout her life. Yet it is very unusual to encounter a person to whom the opinions of her peers made no difference at all. More important, such a person would have an unhealthy self-regard, for her indifference to the opinions of others would indicate a lack of awareness of her own fallibility in determining her strengths and weaknesses.

All these observations reinforce the conclusion that the qualities needed for effective agency require continual sustenance and development as we move through adulthood. We would expect the *nature* of the relationships that could provide such sustenance and development to be different from that of a child to her parents, but trust is required here, too. To learn from others, to receive their correction and support, we must trust them, even if our trust is much more qualified and limited than the sort that ideally obtains between parent and child. So there must be others outside the family who, for whatever reason, are committed to providing us what we need. Individuals vary in having the opportunity and ability to find those who can help. Undoubtedly some of the variation is rooted in the simple luck of circumstances and innate temperament, but differences in the ways people are raised within their families

---

48. See Amélie Rorty, "Virtue and Its Vicissitudes," *Midwest Studies in Philosophy* 13 (1988), special issue, *Ethical Theory: Character and Virtue*, ed. Peter A. French, Theodore E. Uehling Jr., and Howard K. Wettstein: 314–24.

also play a part in this. Some are well prepared to learn from and engage in fruitful interaction with others; others may be crippled in just these respects.

It is here where a great deal of plausibility is to be found in the communitarian argument for the necessity of associations other than the family, and smaller than the state, that bind individuals together in pursuit of a common end. In such "intermediate" associations, which are small enough to allow significant face-to-face interaction among its members, and which in our society include informal social groups, churches, business associations, unions, universities, cooperatives, and mutual aid groups, there will be greater opportunity for (though no guarantee of) the formation of ties in which each comes to have concern for others in ways that may contribute to their effective agency. Furthermore, if we keep in mind the context-dependence of character traits, we can note that the members of such associations may be able to help each other with the development of the traits necessary for effective agency, as those traits need to form relative to certain kinds of social contexts. Consider a graduate student trying to find a teaching style suited to her particular strengths, and receiving help from professors and her fellow students.

Finally, a common function of such associations is the communication of social norms, and these norms often pertain to institutions and practices that are far removed from the family. Working from the concept of the primary group developed by Cooley, Edward Shils describes some classic studies showing the importance of primary group loyalty for military morale. What emerged from these studies was

> the relative unimportance of direct identification with the total symbols of the military organization as a whole, of the state, or of the political cause in the name of which a war is fought, as contrasted with the feelings of strength and security in the military primary group and of loyalty to one's immediate comrades. The soldier's motivation to fight is not derived from his perceiving and striving toward any strategic or political goals; it is a function of his need to protect his primary group and to conform with its expectations. The military machine thus obtains its inner cohesion . . . through a system of overlapping primary groups. The effective transmission and execution of commands along the formal line of authority can be successful only when it coincides with this system of informal groups.[49]

In reflecting on this and other studies of the function of primary groups in larger social structures, Shils maintains that

---

49. Edward Shils, "The Study of the Primary Group," in *The Policy Sciences: Recent Developments in Scope and Method*, ed. Daniel Lerner and Harold D. Lasswell (Stanford: Stanford University Press, 1951), 64.

individuals who are members of larger social structures make their decisions and concert their actions within those structures, not by the direct focus of attention on the central authority and the agents who bear the symbols of that authority, but rather by identification with some individual with whom they have primary-group relationships and who serves to transmit to them ideas from and concerning the larger structure.[50]

4.9 HOW AN ADEQUATE MORALITY MUST FOSTER EFFECTIVE AGENCY

To see what constraints on a true morality emerge from this discussion, we must observe that moral agency is a species of effective agency. I define *moral agency* as the ability to formulate reasonably clear priorities among one's moral ends, and to plan and carry out courses of action that have a reasonable chance of realizing those ends. To the extent that a morality provides motivationally effective guidelines for accomplishing what I have characterized as the function of all moralities—the facilitation of social cooperation and the guidance of individuals toward worthwhile lives—it should promote relationships that involve identifications, trust, and reciprocal care. And, therefore, it should contain duties of the type I described earlier. Consider some of the features of nurturing effective agency that make relationships of trust and care necessary. People need to learn the application of social norms in the context of sustained relationships with others who show them in particular instances what is or is not a correct application of the norms. Moral norms, such as that of showing respect for persons, need to be learned in this manner. What it is to show respect, and how, and when, needs to be shown in a range of situations.

The current revival of interest in Aristotelianism and the even more recent comparative interest in Confucianism is partly fueled, I believe, by just such recognitions. I argued that people typically need the help of others to obtain a reasonable balance between aspects of their identity. This dimension of effective identity is especially salient for achieving effective moral identity. Morality facilitates social cooperation partly through requiring people to sometimes set aside some of their most pressing self-regarding interests for the sake of others. To do this, they need to develop traits that allow them to do so. Compassion, concern, respect, and deference are among the traits required by different moralities to fulfill this function. Such traits need to be reasonably balanced with other elements of an effective identity in order to be motivationally efficacious. Furthermore, I argued that a minimal degree of self-esteem was necessary for effective agency. One plausible consequence of inadequate self-esteem, I noted, was

50. Shils, "The Study of the Primary Group," 67.

a condition that results in excessive self-concern—the demand of the mirror-hungry person for exclusive attention and reassuring praise, for instance. The need for avoiding this condition for the sake of achieving an effective moral identity is obvious.

The claim that certain kinds of relationships, with the corresponding duty types, must go along with effective moral agency needs a qualification and clarification, however. Within the constraints provided by my broad description of the necessary relationships, there can be considerable variation in the content of the corresponding duties. And that is as it should be for a pluralistic relativist. Furthermore, the argument does not validate *any* duties flowing from the sort of identifications necessary for effective agency. Whether a particular set of such duties is valid from the viewpoint of any particular morality will depend on their consistency with other constraints on what counts as an adequate morality, and these constraints may be universal or particular to a given morality. But if the particular duties and identifications that we have, for instance, are not morally acceptable, it is *morally* necessary for us to find some that are, because morality requires effective agency.

Finally, remember that the argument that certain important duties flow from our identities and flourishing is sometimes used to undermine a certain conception of liberalism. Liberalism, as defined earlier, holds that the right is prior to the good, in the sense that a conception of right action or justice is and should be justifiable independently of any specific conception of the good for human beings.[51] Some communitarians then argue that the right cannot be prior to the good, given that certain duties flow from the social nature, the identities, and the flourishing of human beings. I have provided some confirmation of this communitarian argument against liberalism because I have argued for a partial schema of a flourishing life as a necessary element of a viable morality.

But just because I have provided only a *partial* schema, I have provided only partial confirmation of the communitarian argument. Clearly, many different kinds of flourishing lives are compatible with the broadly described relationships, identifications, and duty types I have argued for. A liberalism that accepts these elements as necessary for a viable morality can still remain significantly pluralistic in accepting a very broad range of conceptions of the good.

Still, a significant constraint on what a flourishing life must look like has emerged, and here again, pluralistic relativism turns out to be a limited relativism: not all coherent conceptions of the flourishing life are equally valid. And while my argument has force only against those liberal theorists who insist on complete neutrality with respect to conceptions of the good, it does require all liberal theorists to address the question of what social, political, and economic structures provide the most hospitable conditions for the growth of effective moral agency. While nothing I have said is

---

51. See, for example, Sandel, *Liberalism and the Limits of Justice.*

intended to undermine the viability of individual rights or of fair distribution of wealth and income, what I have said *is* intended to emphasize the need for examining the effects of social, political, and economic structures that may be formally consistent with individual rights and fair distribution but that may be inhospitable to the cultivation of persons capable of effectively acting on these liberal values. I will have more to say on this in the next chapter.

5

Community and Liberal Theory

I have argued that the social nature of human beings requires within an adequate morality the personal perspective and its special duties to others. Hence even moralities that give a prominent place to the impersonal perspective, such as those favored by liberal theory, must leave a place for the personal perspective and special duties. Moreover, I have argued, the very project of realizing the impersonal perspective requires the recognition of special duties and the way they help to nurture effective moral agency.

I have also argued that intermediate associations play a crucial role in the promotion of effective agency, and this leads to a criticism of liberal ethical theory: its characteristic lack of attention to such associations and to the whole complex of issues and problems that sustaining associations implies. To illustrate the way this criticism could be made out, I shall discuss the liberal theory that takes as much account of these associations as any such theory does: Rawls's theory of justice. The idea is to take the best existing case of the liberal treatment on the subject, and to show that there is serious lack of attention even here. I suspect that this lack of attention is supported by the assumption that liberal and communitarian values are incompatible. I argue against this assumption by taking the family as the paradigm context in which communitarian and relational values of care apply. I argue that liberal values of justice also apply to the family and in fact are related to communitarian and relational values.

The argument of this chapter brings together and extends arguments contained in two previously published articles: "On Flourishing and Finding One's Identity in Community," *Midwest Studies in Philosophy* 13 (1988), special issue, *Ethical Theory: Character and Virtue*, ed. Peter A. French, Theodore E. Uehling Jr., and Howard K. Wettstein: 324–341; and "On Care and Justice in the Family," in *In the Company of Others: Perspectives on Community, Family, and Culture*, ed. Nancy Snow (New York: Rowman and Littlefield, 1996), 91–101.

5.1 TAKING COMMUNITY SERIOUSLY IN RAWLS

In that part of *A Theory of Justice* concerning moral development in the ideally just society, John Rawls outlines three stages. The first stage imbues the individual with the "morality of authority," which essentially is the morality learned in a family in which the parents love and care for the child and affirm her sense of worth. The child reciprocates in love and trust. The second stage imbues the individual with the "morality of association." The individual becomes aware of herself as a member of a group, and conceives of the moral norms that apply to her as stemming from the role she plays in the group. The third stage brings the "morality of principles," in which individuals come to understand the most general and fundamental principles (including the two principles of justice) governing their society, and in which they come to understand the reasons for these principles.[1] Through his sequencing of the stages, Rawls certainly recognizes the necessity of at least some of the processes of nurturing and growth that I have described in the previous chapter.

One problem with his treatment, however, is that he seems to assume that the necessary associations will exist in a society that satisfies his two principles of justice. Yet if we look at the way Rawls himself describes the major political and economic institutions of the just society, there seems to be nothing to ensure that there will be associations able to perform the functions described earlier. Nor does Rawls address those social critics who see some of the forces typically present in capitalist, liberal democracies—increasing social and cultural homogeneity and the pervasive power of impersonal, large-scale political and economic entities—as forces *undermining* intermediate associations. There also is the increased tendency to treat all social relations as contractual ones, which, the critics say, undermines the sort of commitment and trust that should obtain within families and secondary associations. As a result, there are fewer such associations with which people can identify.[2] This trend seems to undermine the sort of role morality that characterizes Rawls's second stage, and which he sees to be a necessary condition of advancing to the third stage. According to the argument of the previous chapter, Rawls is right in characterizing that second stage as necessary. It is necessary for effective agency, which is necessary for effective moral agency. To the extent that a theory of justice must be concerned with effective moral agency, it must be concerned with the ability of people to identify with groups that nurture and sustain effective agency in them.

Concern for the conditions of effective agency needs to be wider in focus than the very genuine concern that Rawls shows. His two principles of justice primarily concern the distribution of goods such as liberties, wealth, and income. These goods surely are

---

1. *A Theory of Justice* (Cambridge, Mass.: Harvard University Press, 1971), 462–79.

2. See, for exaMple, Robert Putnam, *Bowling Alone: The Collapse and Revival of American Community* (New York: Simon and Schuster, 2000).

relevant to effective agency. But there is the question of the way that the nature and content of relationships between people affects the nurturance and sustenance of effective agency. This question relates to the question of distribution in complex ways but does not reduce to the question of distribution. Communitarian criticism of Rawls is sound to the extent that it strikes at Rawls's silence on the question of whether we are losing the social structures whose effect on agency is not reducible to distributional matters. It is true that Rawls talks about self-esteem, but mainly in connection with the question of how distribution of the other goods affects it.

I am not accusing Rawls of *endorsing* the alleged effects of these undermining forces. My point is his *neglect to address* forces that have consequences that bear on the viability of his theory of justice. The ideal of a just society requires effective moral agents. And to the extent that a theory is politically egalitarian in thrust, as Rawls's is, it requires widespread effective moral agency. In this respect, Rawls has more reason than other theorists, even some communitarian theorists, to be worried about the undermining of associations that nurture and sustain effective agency.

My point, then, is that liberal theorists are not so much guilty of holding some "atomistic" model of the person that *contradicts* any of the ways we depend on others for our effective agency as guilty of not fully attending to these ways and how they may or may not be realized. One standard reply to this objection is that evaluation of the seriousness of these potential problems is not the task of philosophers but one for, say, sociologists, social psychologists, and economists. There is no doubt that the philosopher will need help on these matters, but the practical result of such compartmentalization of tasks, in too many cases, is that philosophers ignore potentially serious problems with their theories. The compartmentalization is false on the other side, too. Treating such issues as if they were purely empirical is to neglect the substantial philosophical assumptions about value and human psychology that crucially underlie theories in sociology, social psychology, and economics.

False compartmentalization leads to neglect of other potentially serious problems. Take Rawls again, and assume that we do have the intermediate associations necessary for promotion of the role morality in the second stage. Rawls characterizes the transition to the third stage in the following terms: in the second stage, we develop ties of trust and loyalty with other members of the associations to which we belong; as we come to understand how the two principles affirm everyone's worth and work to everyone's advantage, we come to realize how they benefit the people with whom we have ties; we develop an attachment to the principles themselves.

This makes the transition to the third stage sound unproblematic and natural, but it is not unusual for people's loyalties to particular others to conflict with their sense of what constitutes impartial and fair treatment of all.[3] The role morality of associations

---

3. On this kind of conflict, see Alasdair MacIntyre, "Is Patriotism a Virtue?" Lindley Lecture (Lawrence: University of Kansas, 1984). For the way this conflict is played out in ancient Chinese

is not so easily subsumed under principles that are generated from choice under the veil of ignorance. When role morality penetrates practical identities, it binds agents because of their tendency and felt duty to reciprocate the care and trust that *particular* people have shown to them. Yet the two principles are founded on the idea that one owes certain things to others regardless of the special relationships one has. There need not always be a conflict between special loyalties and the ideal of impartiality, but there are enough occasions of conflict so that the commitment to impartial fairness cannot be seen as an unproblematic extension of the commitments underlying the special loyalties. One furthermore cannot assume that when there is conflict, the principles of justice take precedence—not if one's bonds to particular others help to promote and sustain one's effective moral agency. I do not mean to suggest that the conflicts are unmanageable, but they are an important feature of the moral landscape for human beings.

Liberals may retort correctly that the time of vital and relatively autonomous associations was also a time when hierarchy and privilege were acceptable to a much greater degree than they are now. If these associations provided the opportunities for nurturing and sustaining effective agency in their members, it is also true that some of them had the effect of restricting the life prospects of their members by confining them to certain social roles. Others may not have had this effect on their members, but were so powerful that they restricted the life prospects of members of other associations. These liabilities do not, however, cancel out the positive power that the more local forms of community exert over human beings. That power is rooted in the requirements for nurturing effective human moral agency. It is no accident that the reaction against modern liberal theories has taken a neo-Aristotelian and communitarian turn. It is an indication of the nature of what is lacking in these theories. It is sometimes admitted by liberals that they cannot, after all, be completely neutral toward competing conceptions of flourishing, because their own principles reflect the priority placed on autonomy. But if autonomy is to be combined with effective agency, that neutrality must be compromised further, in light of the ways in which our human nature is indeed a social nature.

Addressing the social conditions of effective agency requires more sophisticated attention to the way that egalitarian values are implemented in family and divorce law. Philip Selznick acknowledges that the recent trend toward no-fault divorce reflected and reinforced the movement for women's equality and independence. The idea of marriage as a contract between equals was translated into equal sharing in the allocation of marital assets. But this sort of equality, Selznick points out, often runs counter to the social reality of the economic vulnerability of women, the needs of children, and the opportunities of ex-husbands and fathers to avoid responsibility.

---

philosophy, see my "Universalism versus Love with Distinctions: An Ancient Debate Revived," *Journal of Chinese Philosophy* 16 (1989): 252–72.

The result, he concludes, was a retreat from the idea that our law should have special concern for institutions with the historic function of making males responsible for their families, and for creating units within which obligations stem not just from a contract but from identity and relatedness.[4] If intermediate associations are declining in their influence, there will be increased pressure on the family to perform the functions of nurturing and sustaining effective agency at the same time that progress in gender equality, the pressure of economic necessity, and welfare reform that often requires single parents to work all combine to shrink the family resources available for these tasks.

What I am proposing, then, is that liberal morality must incorporate the value of community in order to promote the effective agency it needs to promote its own values. Many communitarians and liberals alike will object to this idea. Advocates on both sides see incompatibility between their respective values. How can the value of community be combined with a morality that emphasizes individual rights and the freedom within broad limits to adopt and pursue one's own conception of the good? Aren't such freedoms incompatible with the idea of seeing one's good as intertwined with the good of others? Selznick's point about contemporary divorce law supplies an example of how the two ethics might appear to be incompatible. Liberal feminists will certainly decry the nonsupport of families by ex-husbands and fathers, yet neither will they want to endorse a renewal of a patriarchal conception of the family. It might seem to them that the right course is more vigorous enforcement of women's rights to support, without any attempt to strengthen a communal ethic of responsibility within the family. On the other side, communitarians such as Michael Sandel have used an ideal conception of the family to argue that liberal principles of justice are unsuitable to certain kinds of community.

I propose to examine the issue of the compatibility of liberal and communitarian values with regard to the family. The (ideal traditional) family is perhaps the paradigm of a community with a common good that is intimately connected with the individual goods of its members, and therefore might be thought to be an uncongenial home to liberal values. I shall argue that there is a greater degree of compatibility between liberal and communitarian values than these thinkers have supposed. Such a line of argument might be supposed to be contrary to the pluralistic relativism defended in this book. After all, it might be objected, I have relied in arguing for the significance of moral ambivalence on value conflicts such as the one between the values of community and relationship on the one hand and the values of individual rights and impersonal concern for strangers and friends and family alike on the other. I cannot have that cake and eat it, too, in arguing for greater compatibility between these values than some of their respective defenders have supposed. But I will show

4. Philip Selznick, "The Idea of a Communitarian Morality," *California Law Review* 75 (1987): 445–63.

how values within an adequate morality can come to interweave with each other and mutually support one another in some respects even as they conflict in other respects.

5.2 CRITICISMS OF LIBERAL JUSTICE FROM THE CARE AND COMMUNITARIAN PERSPECTIVES

Much recent literature about the family has been couched in the language of the "care ethic," as characterized by Carol Gilligan.[5] This ethic involves a concern for the well-being of particular others and for one's relationship to them. It involves highly contextualized reasoning that is directed toward the welfare of others and toward sustaining or mending relationships with and among them. Such an ethic seems appropriate to the family because family members frequently see their relationships as important goods, ones that may be essential to their identities. Much of what we do in the family is directed toward sustaining or mending our relationships with very particular others, and these actions cannot always be straightforwardly deduced from some general moral principles.

Gilligan contrasts the care ethic with one that emphasizes fairness, justice, and rights and that requires reasoning by deduction from general principles. The question arises as to whether justice applies to the family. Some have argued that justice does not fit the family, that it conflicts with the emphasis on harmony and affection within the family. It is here that communitarians and care ethicists join forces.

Michael Sandel has given a version of the argument that justice does not fit the family. In posing the question of whether Rawls's liberal theory of justice should be applied to the family, Sandel asks us to

> consider for example a more or less ideal family situation, where relations are governed in large part by spontaneous affection and where, in consequence, the circumstances of justice prevail to a relatively small degree. Individual rights and fair decision procedures are seldom invoked, not because injustice is rampant but because their appeal is pre-empted by a spirit of generosity in which I am rarely inclined to claim my fair share. . . . Now imagine that one day the harmonious family comes to be wrought with dissension. Interests grow

---

5. Carol Gilligan, *In a Different Voice: Psychological Theory and Women's Development* (Cambridge, Mass.: Harvard University Press, 1982); Carol Gilligan, Janie Victoria Ward, and Jill McLean Taylor, eds., *Mapping the Moral Domain: A Contribution of Women's Thinking to Psychological Theory and Education* (Cambridge, Mass.: Center for the Study of Gender, Education, and Human Development, Harvard University Graduate School of Education, distributed by Harvard University Press, 1988); Carol Gilligan, Nona Lyons, and Trudy Hanmer, eds., *Making Connections: the Relational World of Adolescent Girls at Emma Willard School* (Cambridge, Mass.: Harvard University Press, 1990). For an analysis of the distinctive features of the care perspective, see Lawrence Blum, "Gilligan and Kohlberg: Implications for Moral Theory," *Ethics* 98 (1988): 472–91.

divergent and the circumstances of justice grow more acute. The affection and spontaneity of previous days give way to demands for fairness and the observance of rights. . . . Parents and children reflectively equilibriate, dutifully if sullenly abide by the two principles of justice. . . . Are we prepared to say that the arrival of justice, however, full, restores to the situation its full moral character, and that the only difference is a psychological one?[6]

Susan Okin sees in this argument the presupposition that feelings of spontaneous affection are somehow incompatible with abiding by principles of justice. She rightly questions this presupposition.[7] According to Sandel, affection is "spontaneous" in the ideal family. Interests of family members are so united that questions of fairness and rights do not even arise. Well, affection in the best moments of families is spontaneous, but even then questions of fairness can arise. Children can question whether they are being treated fairly even though they may not question their parents' love for them. Spouses or partners may both prefer not to perform a necessary task, and they might have to discuss a fair division of labor. Such questions arise in the healthiest of families. In fact, I shall argue, caring about the health of a family may require thinking about justice.

5.3 How Care and Justice Can Interweave

To see this, we need to recognize what it is to care about a relationship. Under Gilligan's characterization of the care ethic, moral action is meant to sustain and mend relationships. When we act to sustain and mend, surely we sometimes do and in any case should act from an idea of what a good relationship is, at least what a good one is between the particular people at hand.

It is at this point that justice informs the care perspective. As Marilyn Friedman has pointed out, personal relationships providing intimacy, support, and concern are relationships that require effort by the participants.[8] When one member of such a relationship bears a greater burden in this effort, the question of unfairness arises. It arises along gender lines if, in Marilyn Frye's words, "men do not serve women as women serve men."[9] Justice is relevant to relationships of care, furthermore, not solely as an external constraint on how such relationships are to be conducted. Justice may be necessary to the health of the relationship itself, and in this sense *internal* to the care perspective. As Claudia Card as pointed out, lack of reciprocity is probably a major

---

6. Michael Sandel, *Liberalism and the Limits of Justice* (Cambridge: Cambridge University Press, 1982), 33.

7. Susan Okin, *Justice, Gender, and the Family* (New York: Basic Books, 1989), 32.

8. Marilyn Friedman, "Beyond Caring: The De-Moralization of Gender," *Canadian Journal of Philosophy*, supp. vol. 13 (1987): 100.

9. Marilyn Frye, *The Politics of Reality* (Trumansburg, N.Y:. Crossing Press, 1983), 9.

cause of breakup of friendship between peers.[10] And marriage, as a friendship among peers, would be threatened by lack of reciprocity in the bearing of burdens.

In looking more closely at the relationship of justice to care, however, we need to make a distinction between two conceptions of justice. On one conception of justice, deserts and responsibilities are determined by reference to the end of achieving a common good. This common good includes the good of participation in a common life, a network of relationships conceived to be an essential part of the flourishing of all participants. The virtues of justice under this conception are those virtues required to sustain and promote the common good. In the family, the common good includes an ideal set of relations between its members that may be called a good family life. When members are not doing their parts in sustaining and promoting that life, or when they take more of the benefits of that life than they deserve in accordance with their contribution, they are being unjust. Injustice in this sense threatens the common life of the family.

The contemporary advocates of communitarian traditions fear that these traditions are disappearing or weakening. They may be right, but the communitarian tradition as applied to the family still has some hold on us. Many of us still see our family life as a good essential to our flourishing, and as a common good for all members. Because this common good provides a basis for deciding questions about the fairness of the distribution of benefits and burdens within the family, much depends on the ideal of family life, and in particular, on the kinds of hierarchy and subordination accepted. It is important to remember that many traditions that exemplify a communitarian conception have had conceptions of a good family life that systematically subordinate women and devalue their contributions—conceptions, in short, that we can no longer justify. It is equally important to note, however, that a communitarian conception of a good family life need not subordinate women or legitimate their domination. We can value a family life constituted by relations of equality between men and women, mutual support, and reciprocity.

The liberal conception of justice focuses not on the good of a common life but on rights the individual possesses as a human being in society and on the question of fairness of distribution of important goods, where distribution ultimately is not determined by reference to the requirements for a common life and a common good but by principles that express the moral equality of persons. This conception focuses on the conflicts between the legitimate interests of individuals and seeks a fair way to adjudicate these conflicts.

This liberal conception also applies to the family, but in a way that is distinct from the way that the communitarian conception relates to the family. Even in families where individuals rightly see their well-being as depending on the common life of the

10. Claudia Card, "Gender and Moral Luck," in *Identity, Character, and Morality: Essays in Moral Psychology*, ed. Owen Flanagan and Amelie Rorty (Cambridge, Mass.: MIT Press, 1990), 205.

family, they will have conflicts of legitimate interests that cannot be resolved by appeal to what best promotes that common life. In families where members need protection, one way of providing them with it is through the recognition and enforcement of rights they have as human beings. A parent who beats a child is not only being unjust in the sense of undermining the common life of the family but in violating that child's rights as a human being.

The two kinds of justice provide different moral perspectives on the family. Communitarian justice focuses on the moral goods of relationship in the family. Liberal justice focuses on the moral status of family members as human beings, not as family members. But just as communitarian justice can inform the care perspective, so liberal justice can inform communitarian justice. It can, for example, support those conceptions of a good family life that reject subordination and domination. And liberal justice can inform care. For example, our notions of what it is to care properly for children have come in the twenty-first century United States to include the idea that they ought to be raised to know their rights, to be able to assert them, and to exercise them effectively. We would not care well for them if we did not.

Conversely, care informs both kinds of justice. Care requires attention to the particularity of each person's traits, needs, desires, and circumstances. Surely such attention is required to know how each family member can contribute to the common family life and how each is to be accorded what is deserved in light of that contribution, and it is required to know the best ways in which each particular child must be raised to know, assert, and exercise his rights as a human being as well as to respect the rights of others. In dominant moral traditions of the United States, the concerns of liberal justice, of communitarian justice, and of care can and should be interwoven in all these ways.

At the same time, these moral perspectives on the family can be in tension and sometimes outright conflict, depending on the family and the individuals in it. Caring for a family member may require intrusions that may not be justifiable from the standpoint of liberal justice. Liberal justice, when it emphasizes the rights of individuals to liberty, can conflict with demands made on the individual from other family members, and these demands may be justified from the standpoint of the common life of the family. No one type of consideration consistently outweighs the other in cases of conflict. A lot depends on what is at stake. Intrusions for the sake of care or restrictions of liberty for the sake of communitarian justice may be justified when what is at stake is an older child's drug use but not on other matters, even when a parent disapproves of what that child may be doing.

Even here we must allow for and accept a significant degree of cultural variability in what counts as intrusion. Traditional Chinese families, for example, allow for a sort of parental involvement in a child's affairs that would be widely considered unjustifiably intrusive in the United States. An example used in chapter 1 serves to make my point here. In the movie *A Great Wall,* a young Chinese American man, very assimilated, is shocked when he a Chinese mother opening and reading her daughter's mail without permission. The mother does not see her act as an invasion of privacy but merely as a rightful expression of her interest in her daughter's life. On pluralistic relativism, such differences fall within the range of the adequate moralities.

The perspectives of care, of communitarian justice, and of liberal justice, then, overlap, inform each other, sometimes reinforce each other and sometimes conflict. Each of these perspectives is but a partial perspective on the family and needs to be informed by the others. To reinforce this point, let me consider some criticisms of liberal theories of justice as applied to the family. The proper conclusion, I shall argue, is not that such theories fail to apply to the family, but that such theories must be taken as incomplete perspectives on the family.

5.4 Is Liberal Justice Ill Suited for the Family?

Sara Ruddick has argued that liberal theories of justice are ill suited to the family because they abstract from the particular identities of family members.[11] Consider Rawls's theory of the original position, in which the parties do not know their particular identities in deciding upon principles of justice. But this kind of abstraction does not make liberal justice ill suited to the family. It does make liberal justice incapable of accounting for the moral requirements that flow from particular identities. Such a theory cannot explain, for example, what is required of me in virtue of my identity as a father. Some of these requirements flow from a general conception of good fatherhood and, more generally, from a general conception of a good family. Other requirements flow from my wholly particular identity as father of Liana. That is, they flow from who she is, who I am, and from the way our relationship has evolved. The proper conclusion is that liberal justice is but a partial perspective on the family, a perspective that cannot account for all our moral duties and obligations.

But theories of liberal justice provide a distinct perspective on families precisely because they abstract from our particular identities and from communitarian conceptions of appropriate familial roles. Liberal justice provides a distinctive sort of critical distance from those particular identities and conceptions.[12] This perspective can move us to make the family relationships between adult women and men equal and reciprocal relations, ones that respect the (autonomy-based) rights of both women and men.

There is another way in which liberal theories cannot tell the whole moral story but in which they must be an essential part of the story in modern Western moral

---

11. Sarah Ruddick, "Justice within Families," in Snow, *In the Company of Others*, 65–90.

12. As I argued in section 3.6, however, I do not think that the conceptual framework of individual rights is the *only* way to gain a needed critical distance on traditional forms of community. From the communitarian perspective itself, one can criticize traditional ideas of the inequality between men and women by referring to the equal capacity of men and women to make contributions to the family good.

traditions. Liberal theories are based on the paradigm of the relationship between moral equals, where the ground of moral equality is the equal possession of some trait or capacity. In Kantian theories, the basis of this relationship is the possession of rationality. The question arises as to whether significant variations in the degree to which people possess such a capacity undermine the idea of moral equality. Some theorists address this problem by widening the notion of the relevant trait or quality. In Rawls's theory, the relevant basis of moral equality consists of capacities that need not be realized: the capacities to have a conception of one's good and to have a sense of justice, which he defines as a "normally effective desire to apply and to act upon the principles of justice, at least to a certain minimum degree." Rawls counts children and infants as meeting the minimal requirements, since they have the capacities. They therefore have basic rights to receive the full protection of the principles of justice. These rights, he says, are normally exercised on their behalf by parents and guardians.[13]

With the move of defining the relevant basis of equality in a broad enough manner, Rawls is able to preserve the notion of a moral equality in virtue of which a wide range of human beings with varied capacities have the same rights. And surely some rights are invariant over this range, such as the right against being assaulted, even if the violator is a family member. But the focus on the ways in which these human beings are the same should not mislead us into neglecting the ways in which we must treat them differently in light of their differences.[14] There might be some extended sense in which infants and children have exactly the same set of rights. But I wonder whether this sense serves as a useful guide to action. I'm not sure what exactly Rawls means when he says that parents and guardians exercise rights on the behalf of children. Whatever it means, it must be consistent with the fact that children, at least up to a certain age, have a capacity for a sense of justice that to some extent is actualized but is largely a set of potentials whose development very much depends on their subsequent relations with others. They are not full moral agents, and often this means that we cannot let them exercise some rights that most adults have.

Children do, at very early ages, begin to display a sense of fairness, but it is sufficiently crude and erratically effective that much of what parents and guardians should be doing is to foster a sense of justice. And to do that, children must be guided and just plain ordered at times. True, parents often assume that their children are much less capable of reason giving and reasoned consideration than they actually are. It is also possible to err on the other side of giving children "options" when these children are not capable of adequately considering these options, when what they need is direction instead of options. Another factor relevant to the treatment of children is their changing age. An appropriate intervention in a child's affair may become inappropriate at a later stage of maturation.

13. Rawls, *A Theory of Justice*, 505–9.
14. Ruddick made this point in "Justice within Families."

Consider also that the process of transmitting a religious tradition within a family sometimes requires that parents not give younger children options that they would be required to give adults or mature children. For example, we would not tolerate making adults go to Sunday school, but in the case of children this seems necessary if they are to be given a concrete understanding of at least one religious alternative and some sense of what it is like to live it. Here again, parents must recognize that their children's relation to a religion must change as their children mature and that their own relation with their children with respect to religion must change accordingly.

To say that children and adults have the same set of basic rights does not capture any of these complexities about the ways in which family members must act differently toward other members in light of significant inequalities—inequalities across members and inequalities across the life span of each member. The language of equal rights seems too crude an instrument to deal with these questions. Yet it seems to me that liberal justice is still relevant in bringing out ways in which family members are to be treated alike and in identifying the morally relevant respects in which a family can be a group of *potential* equals. The job of some family members, in fact, is to help make that equality a reality. Liberal justice provides a needed perspective on the family, but it needs to be informed by the kind of attention paid to the particularity of each individual that is at the heart of the care perspective, and informed by a communitarian appreciation of the ways in which individuals come to form meaningful identities through institutions, such as the family, that transmit traditions.

The care and justice perspectives identify sets of considerations—kinds of reasons—that go into the rich and complex moral reasoning people normally engage in. These perspectives are useful to the extent that they allow clearer and more careful thought about the ways in which different types of moral considerations bear on decisions to act in contexts such as the family, and on how they may sometimes interweave, reinforce each other, or conflict with each other. These perspectives are misleading if they are taken to exclude each other and the ways in which different types of moral considerations interweave and overlap.

There is danger in emphasizing care while tearing it away from its relations to justice, and there is danger in emphasizing one sort of justice while tearing it away from the other moral perspectives. Emphasizing liberal justice to the neglect of care and communitarian justice can lead to an impoverished family life and impoverished individual lives. When we are guided solely by a conception of the rights of individuals as human beings, we forget the moral considerations that help our most valued relationships to flourish. The absence of flourishing would not only make human life poorer but, as we saw in the previous chapter, also make it doubtful that there would be enough individuals who could act effectively on liberal justice itself. The best way we know to foster an effective sense of justice begins with a nourishing and just life of personal relationships. We know that the first relationships a person has are especially important, and that they often, if not always, affect a person's ability to be concerned about anyone.

What I have shown, of course, is not that community, care, and liberal justice are fully compatible. But they are incompatible in ways that other sets of our values are. And the degree of their actual compatibility depends greatly, as is usually the case, on the institutions and practices we have and on our willingness and ability to change them. The next chapter is both further argument that the value of community needs to be integrated with liberal values and an examination of another kind of constraint on adequate moralities.

It sometimes is said that adequate moralities must take into account what is possible for human beings to be and to do, given their nature. As we shall see in the next chapter, some forms of this argument are unsound. Such arguments are quite prevalent, however, and this raises the possibility that our present moralities can be criticized on the grounds that they presuppose false claims about what our human nature permits us to try to be and to do. As I noted in chapter 1, current social, political, and economic arrangements often strike us as natural and inevitable. But that may be because accepting such arrangements is more comfortable for those who benefit from them.

6

Does Psychological Realism Constrain the Content of Moralities?

I have argued that the personal perspective is rooted in human nature, and in a way that constrains how moral agency is to be nurtured and sustained. Moralities giving a central place to the impersonal perspective must recognize such constraints, and this is why the impersonal perspective will presuppose the personal perspective even when it comes into conflict with it. Apart from the ways specified in chapters 4 and 5, does human nature further constrain how we could balance the personal and impersonal perspectives?

6.1 ATTEMPTS TO RESOLVE THE CONFLICT BETWEEN PERSONAL AND IMPERSONAL VIEWPOINTS BY APPEAL TO HUMAN NATURE

Some have argued for the greater weight to be given to the personal perspective. One reason they give is the difficulty of conceiving human beings as giving *no* disproportionate weight whatsoever to their own interests and personal relations. Realism about the psychology of human beings suggests that moralities must take into account the content and strength of personal motives. The difficult question is *how* moralities should take this content and strength into account. There are at least two general ways for moralities to incorporate the content and strength of personal motives: there may be limits on the *manner* in which people ought to be required to give impersonal consideration to the interests of others; and there may be limits on the *extent* to which people ought to give such impersonal consideration. I shall argue that there are limits on the manner of requirement. But whether there are limits on the extent of requirement

The basic work for this chapter is contained in my "Psychological Realism and Moral Theory," *Nomos* 37 (1995), special issue, *Theory and Practice*, ed. Ian Shapiro and Judith Wagner DeCew (New York: New York University Press, 1995), 108–37.

is inconclusive and is related in complicated ways to the limits on manner. My argument begins with some recent attempts to relate issues of psychological realism to moral theory.

6.2 STRONG AND MINIMAL FORMS OF PSYCHOLOGICAL REALISM

Bernard Williams provides the clearest example of criticism of moral theory on the grounds that it does not give enough weight to personal motives. Williams includes within the personal those "ground" projects of individuals that make life meaningful for them, including long-term personal goals and relationships. Given their role in making life meaningful and coherent, Williams argues that it is unreasonable to require that the individual always set aside her ground projects if they conflict with impersonal principles. Modern moral theory in either utilitarian or Kantian forms, he believes, is committed to such an unreasonable requirement.[1] He calls for a rejection of modern theory in favor of an ethics (as held by the ancient Greeks) that embraces the importance of personal ends and relationships as well as the values of freedom and of social justice that are the genuinely valuable elements of modern moral theory.[2]

Owen Flanagan has characterized Williams as a "strong psychological realist" who, "given a life form which lies above some minimal standard of decency," sets his "standards of moral decency closer to, rather than farther from, the personalities of the agents to whom the theory is already addressed."[3] In response to his arguments, Flanagan points out that it is possible for agents, for example, in following Buddhism, to be committed to a highly impersonal moral perspective and that there is nothing necessarily unreasonable about such a commitment. To the argument that it is neither normal nor natural to be as alienated from one's personal relations and projects as impersonal morality requires, Flanagan points out that what is natural or normal deserves sometimes to be suppressed, modified, or transcended. Further, it is difficult to say what *is* a normal or natural way to be attached to the personal, given actual variations in attachment to it across individuals, cultures, and historical periods. Finally, Flanagan argues that it sometimes is possible and desirable to teach succeeding generations what one cannot oneself learn. For example, if one's upbringing places a limit on the extent to which one can care for distant persons, that may be a reason to raise one's children differently, not a reason to place a limit on what impersonal morality can demand.[4]

1. See Bernard Williams, "Persons, Character, and Morality," in *Moral Luck* (Cambridge: Cambridge University Press, 1981), 1–19.

2. Bernard Williams, *Ethics and the Limits of Philosophy* (Cambridge, Mass.: Harvard University Press, 1985), 198.

3. Owen Flanagan, *Varieties of Moral Personality* (Cambridge, Mass.: Harvard University Press, 1991), 56.

4. Flanagan, *Varieties*, 97–8.

In place of strong realism, Flanagan offers his Principle of Minimal Psychological Realism: "Make sure when constructing a moral theory or projecting a moral ideal that the character, decision processing, and behavior prescribed are possible, or are perceived to be possible, for creatures like us."[5] The principle rules out theories that require an individual to set aside all defensible aims whenever the nonessential desires of many others would be met by so doing.[6] In effect, this would rule out extreme consequentialist theories that require raw quantitative optimizing of agglomerated satisfactions with no deontological constraints whatsoever.

While Flanagan's principle is more plausible than strong psychological realism, the issue merits further exploration. Flanagan is right to warn against mistaking local, socially formed traits as universal, natural traits, and he is further right to point out that moral theory should provide a critical perspective on the most entrenched of our socially formed traits. One might grant that it is possible, in some sense of 'possible', that human beings can be motivated to conform to impersonal moral theory as minimally qualified by deontological constraints. One might grant all this but leave unaddressed some important issues about psychological realism.

One of the most important unaddressed issues is the distinction between the abstractly possible and the realistically or practically possible. It could be replied to Flanagan's use of Buddhism that the religion in its most popular forms imposes on its lay people rather modest requirements for action. To claim that Buddhism in some forms may require a far stronger and pervasive expression of concern for life is not to show that most people, maybe even most Buddhist monks, could actually live that way. Furthermore, teaching succeeding generations to be very different from us may amount to a mere abstract possibility, if it cannot be specified how that teaching would actually make people different. For example, we can stress to our children our obligations to distant persons more forcefully and more consistently than our parents did for us, but that does not mean that our children have a realistic possibility *of being* more concerned for distant persons and of acting on that concern.

6.3 THE COMPLEXITY OF REALISTIC POSSIBILITY

The distinction between abstract and realistic possibility seems ethically important, but at the same time talk about realistic possibility is dangerous. Being "realistic" about the possibilities for change may wed us to the cultural, political, social, and economic institutions that have shaped our current motivations. Those institutions shape not only our motivations but also our vision of what is possible. To some extent, we can mitigate this danger by taking the widest possible range of information—for example, from anthropology, sociology, psychology, and history—as our base for estimating the

5. Flanagan, *Varieties*, 32.
6. Flanagan, *Varieties*, 73.

extent of realistic possibility. From this base we judge whether we can reasonably expect to realize new institutions and practices that would effect the change in our actual motivations required by the impersonal point of view.

Notice that there are two dimensions to the notion of realistic possibility. To call something such a possibility is, first, to say that we have a conception of the *process* by which it could be realized; and second, that there is *evidence* for the relevant agents' ability to initiate and complete that process. By contrast, an unrealistic possibility may be one for which we have no conception of a realizing process or one for which there is no evidence (in the strongest case of unrealism there would be strong counter-evidence) that the agents could initiate and complete any purported path to realization. Pretty clearly, there are *degrees* of realism and unrealism. Conceptions of processes of realization will vary in the degree of their specificity. If we have only a vague and sketchy conception of a process of realization, we have a weaker case for the realism of the relevant possibility. Or our evidence for ability to initiate and implement may be sketchy, sparse, and even contradictory. Some possibilities will fall midway on the spectrum from the most unrealistic to the most realistic and hence will be neither realistic nor unrealistic.

What is a realistic possibility for human beings under certain circumstances, furthermore, is not necessarily a realistic possibility for *us* under our circumstances. Some of the circumstances that constrain our possibilities for change are unalterable, at least by us. Other constraining circumstances could be changed but should not be. Some alterable features of our institutions may render more difficult a desired change in our motivations, but they are so morally valuable or required that we should not give them up. Further, what is a realistic possibility for us may depend on which of "us" are in question. For example, there may be a relevant distinction between what is realistic to expect of most people and what is realistic to expect of a few, perhaps exceptional, individuals. The existence of a Gandhi or a Mother Theresa may show that exemplary commitment to an impersonal moral ideal is within the range of human possibility, but their existence does not show that such commitment is possible for most people.

6.4 Realistic Possibility and Equality

An argument by Thomas Nagel provides good material for discussing the complexities of realistic possibility and its relation to the personal and impersonal in moral theory, so I shall summarize it in some detail. Nagel argues that we do not yet have an acceptable political ideal because we do not yet have an acceptable integration of the impersonal and personal viewpoints.[7] The problem is to design institutions that do justice to the equal importance of all persons, without making unacceptable demands on individuals.

---

7. *Equality and Partiality* (New York: Oxford University Press, 1991).

The ideal, then, is a set of institutions within which persons can live a collective life that meets the impartial requirements of the impersonal standpoint while at the same time having to conduct themselves only in ways that it is reasonable to require of individuals with strong personal motives.[8]

What makes the task of finding realistic solutions especially difficult is that our ultimate aim in political theory should "be to approach as nearly as possible to unanimity, at some level, in support of those political institutions which are maintained by force and into which we are born."[9]

The approach to unanimity gets especially difficult when its task is to agree upon principles of aid to others. It is unacceptable to fall below a modest overall level of aid to others, but as we move above that level, we enter a region where we "cannot will as a universal principle *either* that one *must* or that one *need not* help the needy at that level of sacrifice to one's personal aims."[10] We cannot will that one must help because of the strength of personal motives and certain intuitions we have about the reasonableness of letting people live their lives within wide boundaries. But we cannot will that one need not help beyond that modest level because reflection from the impersonal viewpoint compels recognition of our duty to correct for the advantages or disadvantages that are out of people's control:

> What seems bad is not that people should be unequal in advantages or disadvantages generally, but that they should be unequal in the advantages or disadvantages for which they are not responsible ... whatever remotely plausible positive condition of responsibility one takes as correct, many of the important things in life—especially the advantages and disadvantages with which people are born or which form the basic framework within which they must lead their lives—cannot be regarded as goods or evils for which they are responsible, and so fall under the egalitarian principle.[11]

Nagel admits that a significant step toward equality might be embodied in constitutional guarantees for everyone of medical care, education, decent housing, unemployment insurance, child-care allowances, retirement benefits, and even a minimum income. But a strongly egalitarian system is beyond the reach of constitutionalization, and the prospects of realizing it through legislation are remote. In large, ethnically diverse societies such as our own, "a politically secure combination of equality with liberty and democracy would require a far greater transformation of human nature than there is reason either to expect or to require."[12]

---

8. Nagel, *Equality*, 18.
9. Nagel, *Equality*, 8.
10. Nagel, *Equality*, 50.
11. Nagel, *Equality*, 71.
12. Nagel, *Equality*, 90.

Evidence that human nature places limits on this project include the failed attempts to create a classless society through state ownership and control of the means of production. The evidence includes, on the other side, the kind of economies that do work:

> Going by contemporary evidence, the advantages of a significant private sector in the economy of a modern society are enormous, as measured by productivity, innovation, variety, and growth. The productive advantages of competitive market economies are due to the familiar acquisitive motives of individuals, which lead them to exert themselves most energetically to produce or supply what others need or want not from benevolence, but from the hope of reward and the fear of failure.[13]

Since "it does not belong to the socialized nature of modern man in general to be motivated by a concern for the good of all in most of his working, let alone private, life," a debilitating conflict of motives emerges:

> As acquisitive individuals they must force their socially conscientious selves to permit talent-dependent rewards as the unavoidable price of productivity, efficiency, and growth. As participants in the system they are expected, indeed encouraged, to pursue those advantages, but as citizens they are expected to allow them only reluctantly. They must regard it as legitimate and natural to want them, but in another light not legitimate to have them.[14]

On the possibility of substituting other personal motives for acquisitiveness, Nagel grants that

> people can of course be motivated to work hard at something they are interested in for its own sake, and sometimes this will yield a product which others also want. But it is a romantic fantasy to imagine the world run on such a basis. We cannot all be creative artists, research scientists, or professional athletes.[15]

He further argues that even if everyone were motivated to do his job well, design and manufacture must be motivated by economically expressed demand. Such decisions will not be motivated as a form of self-expression, and neither will benevolence provide a basis for them. And the most effective motive for responding to market information is

> a strong investment of personal ambition and desire for success in productive activities that pay off. It is hard to do without people who work hard and exercise their ingenuity for gain and competitive success; yet in a stable egalitarian

---

13. Nagel, *Equality*, 91.
14. Nagel, *Equality*, 115.
15. Nagel, *Equality*, 121.

society they would have to combine this with a desire to live under a system which made it as difficult as possible for them to achieve these goals.

While such a combination of attitudes is not contradictory, grants Nagel, it is "not strictly intelligible."[16]

I find compelling Nagel's case from the impersonal perspective for a strong form of equality. He is right in pointing out that many of the advantages and disadvantages with which people are born, and the basic framework within which they must live their lives, are not under their control. One could, of course, take the libertarian perspective and assert that it is freedom that matters and economic freedom without pervasive interference from government that matters especially. That is a coherent view, but a view that the vast majority of people have rejected in practice, however many times some of them bring it up when it is in their interests. The fact is that it is a core belief of modern moral traditions in the United States that we do have collective responsibility for the harms and absence of significant goods that befall people no matter what they do. Much of the political argument at present is over the question of how much control people do have over the harms and benefits that befall them. But much of the division on this matter, as I will note later, rests on myth. Nagel cannot be more right when he considers the serious effects of class advantage and disadvantage.

Nagel is certainly right in trying to find the fine line between a sensible realism and an undue pessimism that ends up legitimating the institutions, and motivations, already in place. However, he too frequently falls onto the side of undue pessimism. He does not take the widest range of evidence on what is realistic for human beings or even for human beings in modern, industrialized economies with democratic political structures. Nor does he distinguish the question of what is realistic given the "socialized nature" of modern human beings and what is realistic for people in the United States given their culture, current institutions, and dominant motivations.

6.5 THE DANGERS OF UNDERESTIMATING THE COMPLEXITIES OF REALISTIC POSSIBILITY

I do not find persuasive Nagel's worry about the intelligibility of combining impersonal motives with personal motives of acquisitiveness and competitiveness. People are sufficiently complicated to be able on the one hand to try to get the most out of an economic system, given its present rules, but on the other hand to think that the system ought to have different rules. Studies have shown that people in modernizing societies are able to retain traditional attitudes and beliefs that have been thought to be incompatible with their being able to function in developed economies. They contextualize their attitudes, so that one set is appropriate for work and another for life in the

---

16. Nagel, *Equality*, 117.

166 Constraints on Natural Moralities

family and the community.[17] The same contextualizing strategy applies to one's role in the economic system and one's role as a citizen. One can expect some degree of conflict because contextualization is liable to be imperfect, but as I observed in section 4.7, a manageable degree of conflict is to be expected in complex, effective identities.

Perhaps Nagel thinks that the desire for as much gain as possible would undermine the desire to live under a more egalitarian system. But even his version of strong equality would presumably not eliminate all rewards for ability or effort. It is just that the rewards would be smaller. Perhaps the worry is that people who exercise their ingenuity and work hard for gain and competitive success would not want to live under a system that provides them with smaller rewards. But should an academic not be struck by the extent to which people can be motivated to work hard for the sake of small monetary rewards and dubious competitive success? Sometimes Nagel treats such fields as exceptions to the rule, along with the arts, entertainment, and sports, where intrinsic satisfaction of the work itself or recognition and honor of some kind is sufficient to motivate great effort. But to hold these fields so much apart from all others is to neglect the evident fact that people in many of these other fields *do* get satisfaction from doing their jobs well and in having their accomplishments recognized by a very small number of peers, subordinates, and superiors.

More generally, Nagel's estimate of the realistic possibilities for strong egalitarianism seems too much influenced by his perceptions of the present situation in the United States. In particular, his emphasis on acquisitiveness as the primary personal motive in productive economies is culture-bound. The powerful achievement motivations displayed by many Japanese seems anchored not in acquisitiveness but partly in their identifications with family and the desire to reflect well on them and partly in the feeling of a debt owed to them for their care.[18] The desire to reflect well on one's family and community also seems a primary motive for high achievement in modernizing sectors of the economy in India.[19] Such work on other cultures suggests that modernization and economic competitiveness do not necessarily require the psychology of competitive individualism that is much more dominant in the United States at present and that seems to inspire Nagel's pessimism.

Consider also his pessimism about the prospects of reasonable agreement on a strong form of equality. Behind that pessimism lies the thought that the more advantaged can reasonably reject strong egalitarian principles requiring substantial sacrifice of their personal ends for the sake of the less advantaged, while the less advantaged can

17. For a description of this work on India, see Alan Roland, *In Search of Self in India and Japan: Toward a Cross-Cultural Psychology* (Princeton: Princeton University Press, 1988).

18. See George DeVos, *Socialization for Achievement* (Berkeley: University of California Press, 1973), and "Dimensions of the Self in Japanese Culture," in *Culture and Self: Asian and Western Perspectives*, ed. A. J. Marsella, G. DeVos, and F.L.K. Hsu (London: Tavistock, 1985), 141–84. See also Roland, *In Search of Self in India and Japan*, especially 130–7.

19. See Roland, *In Search of Self in India and Japan*, 90–104.

reasonably reject principles that require less sacrifice by the more advantaged. I am no more optimistic than Nagel is that this kind of agreement could be reached on the basis of universally valid principles of reason that somehow make it rationally compulsory to come to a certain agreement. However, I question whether such principles are a necessary condition for reaching agreement at a particular time and place. In fact, the problem of balancing the personal and impersonal can be more or less difficult to resolve, more or less subject to radical disagreement among people in a society, depending on the particular content and strength of personal motives that are dominant in a society. Ultimately, I shall be recommending that we seek consensus (or as much of it as we can achieve) on principles of distributive justice by examining the configuration of personal motives in U.S. society, and not by seeking a universal consensus that applies across all sorts of societies. In doing so, I hope to show that there is an alternative to the method of discussing particular moral disagreements and issues by trying to derive answers from universally valid moral principles. As indicated in earlier chapters, universal constraints on the adequacy of moralities do exist and do sometimes yield substantive conclusions on practical issues, but the existence of such constraints does not rule out other kinds of useful constraints the range of which are less than universal.

Nagel thinks that what is reasonable for the more advantaged conflicts with what is reasonable for the less advantaged. Is there anything that justifies that thought, other than intuitions of what degree of personal sacrifice is reasonable to demand of people? If not, we must ask whether these intuitions are deeply shaped by the norms of our particular culture here in the United States. Here again, in estimating the realistic possibilities for the "socialized nature of modern man," we must look to the broadest range of information about the actual range of attitudes. Relevant to this question is a study by Sidney Verba and his colleagues on the attitudes about equality held by leadership elites in the United States, Japan, and Sweden.[20]

Leaders (from business and labor groups, feminists, advocates for ethnic minorities, political parties, the media, and intellectual elites) were asked to choose between two definitions of a fair economic system—one in which all people would earn about the same and one in which earnings would be commensurate with ability. In the United States, all groups among the elites surveyed were on the conservative side of the scale, rejecting to a greater or lesser degree rough equality of earnings. In Sweden, by contrast, the issue was more open. Two leadership groups took positions on the equal-shares side. Japan fell at about the midpoint between the other two nations. Interestingly, almost all groups in the United States and Japan want to see some reduction in the income gap between the top earner and the skilled or unskilled worker (this was

20. Sidney Verba, Steven Kelman, Gary R. Orren, Ichiro Miyake, Joji Watanuki, Ikuo Kabashima, and G. Donald Ferree Jr., *Elites and the Idea of Equality: A Comparison of Japan, Sweden, and the United States* (Cambridge, Mass.: Harvard University Press, 1987).

less true in Sweden, but the cause was significantly greater equality of income than in Japan and especially in the United States).

No leadership group would reduce the income disparity completely, primarily for the familiar reasons of efficiency and productivity. In the United States, even the most radical groups would accept as fair a ratio of executive to unskilled worker earnings of between eight to one and ten to one. In Japan there is a tendency to favor a somewhat narrower income gap. Business and labor leaders favor ratios slightly more than half as large as those favored by their counterparts in the United States. Views of the Swedish elite are of a different order of magnitude. Each group in the United States and Japan favors ratios that are many times as large as those that their counterparts in Sweden consider fair. Further, there is no overlap between the preferred ratios among the Swedish groups and those of the groups in the other two nations. The *left* party leaders in Japan and the United States favor an earnings ratio about three times as large as that favored by the *conservative* leaders in Sweden. The *least* egalitarian group in Sweden, business leaders, consider fair a ratio of their income to that of the unskilled worker that is very close in magnitude to that of the *most* egalitarian groups in Japan and the United States. Views of Japanese leaders lie between those of other two, though they are, if anything, closer to those in Sweden than in the United States.[21]

There is, of course, the much observed phenomenon of "backing away" from the welfare state and equality in Sweden. Verba and his colleagues, however, remind us that this backing away must be understood within the context of an already well-developed egalitarian commitment. If some Swedish leaders would move back from that direction, the level of commitment to welfare and redistribution would still be greater than that to which the most radical of leadership groups in Japan and the United States aspire.[22]

In Sweden, a radical equality more stringent than Nagel's strong equality is still an open question, and the entire left-to-right range of attitudes is considerably to the left of those in the United States. Even a backing away from equality in Sweden on the matter of preferred ratio of income would leave the conservatives still to the left of the most radical groups in the United States. Consider that the study was conducted at a time of economic downturn, which seems to push people toward the conservative end of the spectrum. The broad range of *actual* attitudes (never mind possible ones) about equality, even among the democratic developed nations, and the significant influence of particular economic conditions on these attitudes, should make us wary about accepting any particular set of intuitions as to what the more advantaged could reasonably be required to sacrifice.

Even with respect to the United States, Nagel seems excessively pessimistic about the dominance of this psychology. It was not that long ago that the "organization man" was said to be the dominant middle-class character type, for whom making

---

21. Verba et al., *Elites*, 146.
22. Verba et al., *Elites*, 146.

money was fine but only a by-product of belonging to an organization where one could make a contribution, where one could be proud of the work one was doing.[23] Perhaps this way of being motivated appeared quite natural to people who had lived through New Deal cooperation to combat the Great Depression and the mobilization of the nation to fight World War II. On the other hand, it might seem that the time for dominance of such a character type is over, and Nagel's pessimism has a basis in the present situation. Even now, however, the children of the organization men may be motivated not primarily by acquisitiveness but by a search for self-fulfillment and self-expression.[24] This is not to deny the place of acquisitiveness as a powerful motivation. But if it is not the primary one or simply one among several primary ones, the case for pessimism about the prospects of strong equality weakens.

Furthermore, a closer look at the way that Sweden and Japan have achieved greater equality than the United States will lead us to question any overly simple contrast between commitment to personal values and commitment to impersonal values. As Verba and his colleagues tell the story, Sweden's course to making the strongest effort toward equality of any industrialized nation was set by a long tradition of acceptance of hierarchy (ironically enough) and of deference to governmental authority, a process of industrialization that promoted compromise and accommodation between established groups and the working class, the dominant political role of the Social Democratic Party, and a strong socialist party allied with strong unions. Compared to Sweden, the Japanese government has undertaken relatively few measures to promote equality (it does not, for example, use the tax-and-transfer system for redistribution as in Sweden). Rather, greater equality seems to have resulted partly from a group-oriented ethic and from the weakening (though certainly not disappearance) of the tendency to accept hierarchical statuses. These factors have contributed to shrinkage in the disparity of top and bottom wage earners within private firms.[25]

Shall we say that Swedish and Japanese commitments to equality are commitments to an impersonal value? The impersonal element is certainly there. But just as present in the Swedish case is the tendency to defer to governmental authority, and it is not clear on which side such a tendency falls in Nagel's contrast. If it belongs anywhere, it belongs in the personal. In the Japanese case, there is something that Nagel would classify as a personal commitment—personal allegiance to a "community of interest . . . larger than

23. See William H. Whyte Jr., *The Organization Man* (New York: Simon and Schuster, 1956).

24. See Paul Leinberger and Bruce Tucker, *The New Individualists: The Generation after the Organization Man* (New York: HarperCollins, 1991). See also Robert N. Bellah, Richard Madsen, William N. Sullivan, Ann Swidler, and Steven M. Tipton, *Habits of the Heart* (Berkeley: University of California Press, 1985); and Charles Taylor, *The Ethics of Authenticity* (Cambridge, Mass.: Harvard University Press, 1992). There are some reports that Japanese culture contains a trend of more younger workers choosing part-time, freelance work. See Stephanie Strom, "A Shift in Japanese Culture Aids Some Workers Who Want to Go It Alone," *New York Times*, November 16, 2000.

25. See Verba et al., *Elites*, 20–57.

those defined by family or friendship" but still "far less than universal." However, there is also the absorption of values of equality from the time of American occupation. In both cases, the personal and impersonal elements seem inseparable from the actual commitment that promoted equality.[26]

To return to the issue of whether the project of promoting the impersonal value of strong equality is a psychologically realistic one: this issue now becomes partly one about the realistically possible *ways* to link the impersonal value with sufficiently strong "personal" values, that is, ways to mediate the commitment to the impersonal through sufficiently strong personal commitments. In other words, the question of whether it is realistic to require a robust commitment to strong equality may depend on the *manner* in which that requirement is to be fulfilled. Nagel, I suspect, did not explore this aspect of the issue because of his implicit identification of the impersonal realm of values with public morality. Another reason, I also suspect, is his implicit assumption about the power of the acquisitive motive for most people, given the kind of work they do. At crucial places, where Nagel argues for his pessimism, the acquisitive motive stands in for personal motives. It has been argued here not only that commitments to impersonal values are typically mediated by commitments to personal values but also that significant distinctions must be made within the class of personal motives.

6.6 A COMMUNITARIAN COMMITMENT TO EQUALITY?

To some extent, the argument thus far has provided some support for communitarian criticisms of liberal political theory. Especially relevant is a criticism made by Michael Sandel of the liberal inability to provide persuasive justifications for principles of strong equality such as Rawls's Difference Principle. In the end, he argues, the better off will be able to accept the sacrifices required by such principles only if they see their individual good as intertwined with the common good. Sandel argues, for example, that when such a mode of self-understanding becomes widespread within a group, its members regard each other less as others and more as participants in a common identity, "be it family or community or class or people or nation." A consequence of such a self-understanding is that

> when "my" assets or life prospects are enlisted in the service of a common en-
> deavor, I am likely to experience this less as a case of being used for others' ends

---

26. Or consider Norman Sheehan, an Irishman currently living in Boston, who served as a relief worker helping the victims of famine and war in the Sudan, Liberia, Iraq, and Somalia. One might assume that such a person would exemplify the purest of commitments to impersonal values, yet he explained his initial decision to be a relief worker in a way that intermingles the impersonal, his individual ends, and his identification with a community: "I'm not religious. I'm the greatest rogue you ever met. It's just a calling. You feel as though you can do something, make a difference. We Irish, we love the underdog." Kevin Cullen, "Haunted by Death in Somalia," *Boston Globe*, July 15, 1993, 19.

and more as a way of contributing to the purposes of a community I regard as my own. The justification of my sacrifice, if it can be called a sacrifice, is not the abstract assurance that unknown others will gain more than I will lose, but the rather more compelling notion that by my efforts I contribute to the realization of a way of life in which I take pride and with which my identity is bound.[27]

Sandel's point about sacrifice becoming a contribution to a community with which one identifies, instead of an "abstract assurance that unknown others will gain," is close to the conclusion here that the most realistic possibility of realizing strong equality is by mediating commitment to it through certain kinds of personal values.[28] The mechanism of motivation here is something akin to the mechanism described in section 2.9: moralities must be fitted to deal with the profoundly ambivalent nature of human beings: a strong component of self-interest combined with other-interestedness, both arguably selected in the course of human evolution. One of the most effective ways to deal with this ambivalence is to set up incentives appealing to self-interest that mitigate the cost of acting on other-interestedness. Another effective way is for moralities to appeal to motivations that can bridge between the more purely self-interested and other-interested motivations.

The present conclusion also supports the type of ethic that attempts to connect the good or the flourishing of the individual with that individual's duties toward others. Consider Aristotle's attempt to link the flourishing of the individual with his participation in the political community, via the claim that human beings are political animals. Or consider the Confucian notion that human beings find their fulfillment in community with others, where the notion of community is less political in nature than in Aristotle's theory. Take note that the conclusion reached here does not confirm certain other themes sometimes found in communitarian philosophy: the categorical rejection of impersonal values, the claim (mistaken, as I argued in sec. 5.1) that liberalism must presuppose some queer metaphysical notion of the self as existing independently of relationship to others and to communities. Nor, of course, does the conclusion reached here reveal how we are to promote a mediation of impersonal equality through personal values.

---

27. Michael Sandel, *Liberalism and the Limits of Justice* (Cambridge: Cambridge University Press, 1982), 143.

28. It seems to me that Jonathan Kozol appeals to this very kind of commitment when he asserts in *Savage Inequalities* (New York: Crown, 1991), 173, that "the advocates of fiscal equity seem to be more confident about American potentials than their adversaries are. 'America,' they say, 'is wealthy, wise, ingenious. We can give terrific schools to *all* our children.' . . . Conservatives are generally the ones who speak more passionately of patriotic values. They are often the first to rise up to protest an insult to the flag. But, in this instance, they reduce America to something rather tight and mean and sour, and they make the flag less beautiful than it should be. They soil the flag in telling us to fly it over ruined children's heads in ugly segregated schools. . . . Children in a dirty school are asked to pledge a dirtied flag. What they learn of patriotism is not clear."

It does not seem realistic to think that most people in the United States would come to a stronger commitment to equality via a Swedish deference to governmental authority. Nor would most of us regard such a route as desirable. It would require a change in the political culture that most of us value highly. Yet, as Verba and his colleagues note, the American antipathy toward established authority limits the state's ability to lead its citizens toward a stronger commitment to equality.[29] If there are realistic prospects for a greater commitment to equality in the United States, they would seem to depend on a stronger and more pervasive commitment to community-oriented values. But is that a realistic prospect?

6.7 Is a Communitarian Commitment to Equality Realistic?

As noted earlier, strengthened commitment to equality emerged in certain historical periods. After World War II, according to J. R. Pole, minorities "who had long perceived themselves as having unfulfilled claims on the moral sense of the whole nation" were able to "exert an unusual degree of purchase on that moral sense and make it bear on the processes of law and law-making." This new ability was tied partly to the general recognition that members of these minorities had contributed, often at very great cost, to the collective war effort. It also was tied, observes J. R. Pole, to the clarification of American social and political values that resulted in fighting enemies representing "racial and religious hatred, tyranny over the spiritual, intellectual, and physical liberties of all individuals and associations that failed to conform to the state's prescriptions . . . fairly clear opposites to anything that Americans were willing to claim as their own inheritance."[30] The changed attitude toward minorities exemplifies the kind of mix of personal and impersonal values present in the Swedish and Japanese efforts toward equality: a recognition of minorities as contributing members to a collective effort of the greatest importance on the one hand and on the other a clarification and intensified commitment to impersonal values of liberty and equality that were (newly, in many cases) seen to be at the core of the national community's moral tradition.

Noting the effect of World War II, however, brings out a new issue about the realism of mediating a commitment to strong equality through a commitment to a national community. It is of course absurd and perverse to propose that we start a war in order to promote a greater spirit of community in the nation. But do we have alternative means of comparable efficacy? It is notable that political leaders often use the metaphor of war when they call on their people to make some sacrifice for a collective end. The

---

29. Verba et al., *Elites*, 55.

30. J. R. Pole, *The Pursuit of Equality in American History* (Berkeley: University of California Press, 1978), 256.

question is whether such calls are ineffective in the context of a strong cultural current of individualism, in which people are looking inward and increasingly reluctant to acknowledge that they have obligations to address the situation of the less advantaged. Furthermore, don't Sweden and Japan differ from the United States in a way that is crucially relevant to the question of whether it is realistic to try to promote equality through strengthening a community-oriented ethic? The former two societies are relatively homogeneous in ethnic and cultural terms, while the United States is heterogeneous in just these terms (remember Nagel's reference to the difficulties of establishing a "politically secure" combination of liberty and equality in "large, ethnically diverse" societies). Doesn't that make a strong community-oriented ethic (with the nation as community) an unlikely prospect?

These are the most frequently expressed criticisms of the call to strengthen the communitarian strains in the American moral and political tradition. There is a fair amount of tension between the different criticisms. On the one hand our society is too heterogeneous to be a genuine community, and on the other it is too homogeneous to become a community. The rising tide of individualism, after all, consists in more and more people adopting the *same* set of values. Whether or not these two sorts of criticism are compatible, I am more concerned about the conflicts generated by increasing homogeneity than about those generated by heterogeneity.

Those who associate harmonious community with shared values (both communitarians and their liberal critics make this association) should realize that it all depends on what values are shared. Groups that are otherwise heterogeneous can live together and even join in common projects if they share some values, including those of tolerance and accommodation with each other.[31] And groups that share many values can conflict severely. The values associated with individualism, after all, can and do generate conflicts of claims—competing claims for rights, opportunities, and material resources. The older and more established ethnic groups in the United States have learned this language of claims very well. The new groups may bring a different language, corresponding to a different political culture, but to the extent that they do, they seem less inclined or less able to even enter the political process of competing claims.

Nevertheless, there is a serious issue about the realistic prospects for implementing the ideal of a communitarian commitment to strong equality. The reasons for this differ importantly. One reason why the prospects are in doubt is a deeply entrenched *moral* belief held by Americans: a preference for the ideal of equality of *opportunity* rather than equality of *result*. Lawrence Blum has pointed out that what equality of opportunity has come to mean is equality of *competitive* opportunity—in the great majority of cases, opportunity to compete with a great many others for a few desirable positions. Blum

---

31. I discuss strategies of accommodating to serious disagreement with others in chapter 9.

has pointed out how deeply problematic this notion is (for one thing, competition results in winners and losers, and competitive advantages or disadvantages accrue, both to the winners and losers and those closely connected to them, such that equality of competition is undermined).[32] He also points out how far this current notion of equal opportunity differs from the original mythic notion when Americans had a genuine frontier, where something closer to equal life prospects seemed available.[33] But so far such arguments have not undermined the strength of belief in competitive opportunity and its equation with the original mythic opportunity.

At this point, however, we have reached another level of realistic possibility. We have descended from talk about realistic possibility for human beings per se to people in modern, industrialized democracies to people in the United States and now finally to people in the United States given certain entrenched moral beliefs. At this point we must ask whether moralities should be evaluated while holding constant certain entrenched though problematic moral beliefs. We must preserve the difference between moralities that should be adjusted to the realistic possibilities of what people can do and be on the one hand and moralities that on the other hand simply demand too little of people because of entrenched unreasonableness and the acceptance of myth. When realistic possibility is estimated on the basis of entrenched moral belief independently of its reasonableness, it cannot be used to evaluate moralities.

This is not to deny this kind of realistic possibility a proper place in influencing our pragmatic and strategic decisions concerning what to do now in addressing the situation of the less advantaged. The resistance of Americans to the idea of equal results, for example, can weigh in favor of pressing for universal entitlement programs instead of ones specially targeted at the less advantaged. It can weigh in favor of pressing for a more extensive and higher minimal floor of welfare in the short term. As Nagel says, perhaps it is too difficult to see our way to a distant goal such as strong equality until we have taken more intermediate steps. But it should be obvious by now that we are not evaluating the requirement of strong equality in *theory*. Instead of bringing realistic possibility to bear on moral theory from the *outside*, so to speak, we are now bringing it to bear from the inside, where it influences our considerations as to how best strategically to attempt to realize the values of the theory.

32. Consider Jonathan Kozol's statement in *Savage Inequalities*, 83: "Denial of the 'means of competition' is perhaps the single most consistent outcome of the education offered to poor children in the schools of our large cities." He notes that average expenditures per pupil in the city of New York in 1987 were some $5,500. In the highest spending suburbs of New York, funding levels rose above $11,000, with the highest districts at $15,000. Even within the city, there is gross inequity: the poor income schools need to use funds earmarked for computers to buy supplies like pen and paper. They have the worst teachers, when outstanding ones are needed to address diverse needs in overcrowded classrooms (84–5).

33. Lawrence Blum, "Opportunity and Equality of Opportunity," *Public Affairs Quarterly* 2 (1988): 1–18.

There is, however, another reason why the prospects for a communitarian commitment to strong equality are in doubt, and this reason is the progressive weakening of the apparent base for strengthening that communitarian commitment. As argued in chapters 4 and 5, smaller forms of community are necessary for nurturing effective moral agency and for fostering commitment to social norms, including that of equality, that apply far beyond their own boundaries.

Do these points weigh against the realism of a greater communitarian commitment to equality? Recall my point near the beginning of this chapter that the realism or unrealism of a possibility may fall somewhere on a spectrum between the most realistic to the most unrealistic, depending on the specificity of our conception of the process by which the given possibility could be realized and on the evidence for or against our ability to initiate and complete that process. In this case, we certainly cannot deem a sufficiently strengthened communitarian commitment a clearly realistic possibility for *us here and now*, but neither can we deem it a clearly unrealistic possibility. There are pockets where such a strengthened commitment exists. Such a commitment, after all, does not require the moral level of a Mother Theresa or a Gandhi. A fair number of people, far less than the majority but far greater than the number of exceptional moral exemplars, have demonstrated this kind of commitment. Thus we know it is possible under some circumstances. But whether it can take place under something like our circumstances on a sufficiently large scale is a question we simply do not know how to answer. What is the proper conclusion, then? In light of our inability to say that strong equality is a realistic possibility, shall we moderate the requirement to have impersonal concern for all? Or shall we retain that requirement simply because we are unable to say that it is an *un*realistic possibility?

To pose the question this way is reminiscent of Nagel's claim that we neither can will as a universal principle that one must help the needy (at a level of sacrifice that goes far beyond modest aid) nor that one need not do so. Unlike Nagel, however, I think we can will as a universal principle that one must help (beyond the level of modest aid). We must do that because we cannot take as a given the strength of acquisitive and competitive motives as found here in the United States. The fact that we do not know whether a communitarian commitment to strong equality is an *un*realistic possibility weighs in favor of retaining the requirement of impersonal concern. If nothing else, retaining that requirement serves as a spur to keep looking for genuine possibilities of change and to keep striving to make our local forms of community more consistent with the aspiration to strong equality. And if we do not know now the path to implementing strong equality on a large scale, the possibilities for actually aiding some number of people on smaller scales are real enough.

In chapter 4, I argued that human nature does place constraints on adequate moralities through the requirements of cultivating effective moral agency. In chapter 5, I argued that there was a way within a liberal moral tradition to fulfill those constraints, *contra* the alleged incompatibility between liberal and communitarian values. And in this chapter, I argued that the constraints of realistic possibility require institutions and practices that embody and facilitate on the individual level the mediation of impersonal values through personal values. These are local constraints that work through the claim that there are constraints on possible ways of realizing moral values, given human nature in combination with our other more particular circumstances. Interestingly, however, seeing that certain possibilities are *real enough* (if not realistic) also works as a constraint on adequate moralities. Those moralities that in some way depend for their acceptance on denying the reality of certain possibilities must also be ruled out as inadequate.

Having Confidence in Our Moral Commitments

Moral Reasons—Internal and External

In this chapter, I begin the project of part III: to address the potential problems for the firmness and stability of moral commitments that are raised by the recognition of a plurality of true moralities. In this chapter I begin with the most basic questions. How deeply do moral reasons relate to human motivation? To what extent is it rational to try to be moral? My approach is through the debate over internalism and externalism of reasons in ethics.

7.1 INTRODUCTION TO THE INTERNALISM-EXTERNALISM DEBATE

The contemporary debate dates back to David Falk's essay about the location of morality's authority. Externalism locates the authority outside the agent in holding that she can have a duty while having no reason or motive to do it.[1] Internalism locates it inside the agent in holding that she has a reason or motive that necessarily accompanies duty. Historically, wrote Falk, the first moral injunctions probably were demands from the outside, obeyed habitually and unreflectively. The other conception of duty closely accompanies the subsequent growth of reasoned choice by agents. Reflective agents deny the validity of external demands that they have no reason or motive to satisfy.

Falk used the term 'reason' as if it were equivalent to an existing motive of the agent. In more recent years, attention has turned to the nature of a reason itself. In part, this focus emerged from a desire to clarify the relation a reason for acting bears to the agent's motivations and then to draw out the consequences for the relation of duty to interest. Internalists on reasons hold that an agent's having a reason to act requires

---

Most of this chapter appears as "Moral Reasons: Internal and External," *Philosophy and Phenomenological Research*, forthcoming.

1. David Falk, "'Ought' and Motivation," *Proceedings of the Aristotelian Society* 48 (1947–48): 116.

that it be based in some motive that she already has, while externalists deny the necessity of this relation. Therefore, one can be an internalist about both duty and reasons, holding that a reason must be based on a motive and that such reason to do an action must be present whenever an agent has a duty to do it. One can be an externalist about duty and an internalist about reasons, holding that a reason must be based on motive and that an agent can have a duty without having such a reason to do it. One can be an externalist about duty and an externalist about reasons, severing any necessary connection between motive on the one hand and both duty and reasons on the other. Finally, one could be an internalist about duty but an externalist about reasons, holding that an agent who has a duty has a reason to do it but that the reason need not be based in the agent's motives.[2]

Internalism of duty is plausible. It seems odd to say that people morally ought to do something but that they have no moral reason to do it. And there is a way of understanding what a moral reason is that supports this intuition of oddity. A moral reason to do X, and in general any kind of reason to do X, just *is* a feature of the situation that calls for the agent to do X, for example, the fact that her not doing X would be an injustice or a piece of cruelty (see sec. 2.14).[3] A moral reason draws our attention to something that is very often outside agents and to their relation to that feature, not to what is inside the agents that might motivate them to act on it. And if this is what a moral reason does, there seems little gap between duty and reasons. Given such a connection, the issue is whether the reasons that are internal to moral duty are themselves internal or external.

Both internalism and externalism about reasons have some initial appeal. E. J. Bond has observed that reasons for action seem to be tied in some necessary way to motivation, for how can one speak about reasons that cannot move an agent to act? On the other hand, seeing oneself as having a reason for action seems to involve the recognition that something of value or worth would be realized by doing it or that there is a consideration that weighs in favor of doing it, and such language may suggest

---

2. In some of her earlier work, Philippa Foot seems to be an externalist about duty and an internalist on reasons, and her internalism about reasons holds them to be desire based. See her "Morality as a System of Hypothetical Imperatives," *Philosophical Review* 81 (1972): 305–16; and "Reasons for Action and Desires," *Proceedings of the Aristotelian Society*, supp. vol. 46 (1972): 202–10. In some of my previous work, I also defended such a position. I held an internalism about reasons because it was unclear to me what point was served by saying that an agent A has a reason to do an action X while admitting that such a reason has no base in A's motivations. At the same time it seemed to me that people do have duties even if they have no motivations that would support their doing these duties, and given my previous position of internalism about reasons, this required an externalism about duties. I thought, for example, that we do say of amoral or of evil people that they have duties to do what they have no motive-based reason to do. See *Moral Relativity* (Berkeley: University of California Press, 1984), 65; also "On Moral Realism without Foundations," *Southern Journal of Philosophy*, supp. vol. 24 (1986): 112. For the reasons I will outline here, I have reconsidered this position.

3. I was first impressed by this understanding in reading Kwong-loi Shun, "Moral Reasons in Confucian Ethics," *Journal of Chinese Philosophy* 16 (1989): 317–44.

a merely loose connection to any motivations we actually have.[4] Not having the relevant motivation, on such a perspective, might mean a blameworthy lack of sensitivity. The critical normative function of a reasons claim seems to put some distance between having a reason and already having the sort of motivation that prompts one to act on it. To say that someone has a moral reason to do something is to focus attention on the feature of the situation that calls on the agent to do a certain sort of action. It is not, on the face of it, to link some motivation the agent already has to the performance of that action.

In what follows, I develop a view that is by the literal definition an externalist view of reasons, but it specifies an intelligible relation between external reasons and the possibility of our acting on them. Understanding this relation, I will argue, will lead us away from stark oppositions between internal and external reasons and internal and external duty. I begin developing my view through consideration of a Humean theory that makes reasons internal. I identify the reasoning that underlies that theory and then discuss one of the most interesting criticisms of that theory.

7.2 A Problem for the Humean Theory of Internal Reasons

The debate over internalism versus externalism of reasons concerns justifying or normative reasons. These are reasons that bear on what an agent *ought* to do. On the other hand, we often use 'reason' to identify an agent's actual motivation for an action. The existence of a justifying reason for me to do X may not at all *explain* my having done X.[5] However, one might have a reason for doing X that both justifies and motivates doing X. A justifying reason also motivates when the agent recognizes it and acts on it. Both internalists and externalists, therefore, seek to show that their theories are compatible with plausible explanations of how agents could be motivated to act upon the recognition of such a reason. Consider a well-known variety of internalist theory of justifying reasons that purports to give a plausible explanation of how they can become motivating reasons. The theory starts from Hume's thesis that reason is motivationally inert and that preexisting desire is necessary for the production of action. This thesis implies that agents' recognition of a justifying reason cannot motivate them to do X (via rational processes) unless it reveals to them that X is appropriately related to their preexisting desires (desires, that is, that exist before the relevant rational processes; desires understood as contrasting with beliefs by way of the intuitive distinction between aiming to fit the world versus aiming to make the world fit). Advocates of the

---

4. E. J. Bond, *Reason and Value* (Cambridge: Cambridge University Press, 1983), 7.
5. See Michael Woods, "Reasons for Action and Desires," *Proceedings of the Aristotelian Society*, supp. vol. 46 (1972): 189–201; and Michael Smith, "The Humean Theory of Motivation," *Mind* 96 (1987): 36–61. Both make distinctions along these lines.

Humean theory claim that it presents a clear and intelligible picture of the way that a justifying reason can become a motivating reason. A justifying reason connects an action with the potential satisfaction of a preexisting desire of the agent. Once the agent recognizes the reason as making this connection, it can motivate her.

One of the most interesting critiques of the Humean theory contests its power to explain how justifying reasons can motivate. Stephen Darwall asks us to imagine a woman named Roberta who grows up in a sheltered environment. She sees a film about textile workers in the South and is shocked and dismayed by their suffering. She decides to promote a boycott of the goods of one company that is attempting to destroy a union. It is crucial to Darwall's example that Roberta has no desire prior to seeing the film that explains her decision to join the boycott. She has no general desire to relieve suffering, or to fight injustice wherever she finds it, for instance. Her decision to act seems based on her vivid recognition of the unjustifiable suffering of *these* workers as constituting a strong reason for her to support their cause.[6]

Bernard Williams's theory of internal reasons might appear to address the problem raised by Darwall. Williams defines the internalist position as requiring reasons to be based in an agent's "subjective motivational set," which includes "dispositions of evaluation, patterns of emotional reaction, personal loyalties, and various projects . . . embodying commitments of the agent."[7] Applying the Williams internalist model to the case of Roberta, one might say that while Roberta had no preexisting desires to relieve suffering or to fight injustice, her awakening to the plight of the workers is intelligible only if it can be related in some way to tendencies she already has, such as dispositions of evaluation or patterns of emotional reaction. If Roberta, even within her sheltered environment, had previously shown no response at all to the distress of those around her, no response to wrongs done to others, the story of her decision to become an activist would be an implausible one. Further, Williams takes a liberal view as to how action can arise from preexisting elements of an agent's subjective motivational set S. A reason to X need not arise from seeing X as a causal means to satisfy some element of S. A reason may arise from time-ordering the satisfaction of elements of S, or from assigning priorities among the elements where there is some irresoluble conflict, or from specifying in particular what constitutes the satisfaction of a desire.[8] Such deliberation from elements in one's S can involve processes of vivid imaginative projection, processes one can envision operating in Roberta's case.

However, there is a problem with Williams's strategy of broadening the notion of desire to explain hard cases of transformation. When "dispositions of evaluation" are invoked as elements of a subjective set, it appears that the distinction between belief and

---

6. Stephen Darwall, *Impartial Reason* (Ithaca: Cornell University Press, 1983), 39–40.
7. See "Internal and External Reasons," in *Moral Luck* (Cambridge: Cambridge University Press, 1981), 105.
8. Williams, "Internal and External Reasons," 104.

desire that is needed to formulate Hume's thesis about the motivational inertness of reason has become thoroughly obscured. Personal loyalties might also include beliefs or belief-like components, such as the belief that one owes quite a lot to a friend with whom one goes way back. If the subjective set includes beliefs or complex attitudes embedded with belief, then Williams's theory would allow for new motivations to arise in appropriate ways from beliefs. Williams's theory, intended to be a sophisticated Humeanism, fails to preserve the Humean position on motivation. What is worse, his theory fails to be Humean and still does not provide for the full normative function of reasons for action, at least on commonly held intuitions. One such intuition is that a man has moral reason to stop beating his wife, regardless of what exists or fails to exist in his subjective set S.

On the positive side, Williams's definition of internalism does answer to one of the intuitions I identified earlier as lying behind internalist positions: that reasons attributed to an agent are pointless without the possibility of their motivating her. Williams's responsiveness to this intuition is illustrated by his discussion of the protagonist in Benjamin Britten's opera, *Owen Wingrave*, who has no basis in his S for conforming to his family's tradition of military service. It would be browbeating Owen to insist that he nevertheless has a genuine reason to do so, Williams argues. Moreover, to insist that Owen has a reason is to falsely imply that he is somehow irrational not to recognize the external reason, given his subjective set S and the reasons to which it gives rise. Williams also seems right to insist that a theory of justifying reasons fit with a plausible explanation of how an agent comes to have a new motivation based on coming to believe a justifying reason. Finally, he seems right to ask what point a reason could have if it is not capable of motivating the agent who has it.

The alternative analysis of reasons proposed here contrasts with Williams's analysis by affirming externalism with respect to the individual's motivation, but, in a sense to be explained later, it affirms internalism with respect to *human* motivation. Indeed, the sense in which it is internal to human motivation will help explain why external reasons can have a point even if the agent to whom these reasons apply may not be capable of acting on them. The theory defended here avoids the claim that failing to recognize a genuine external reason is necessarily irrational. It is simply failing to recognize some reasons that exist. Finally, the alternative theory defended here proposes an explanation of how a person could come to a new motivation on the basis of coming to believe a reason applies to her. This explanation will be broadly Humean in spirit by denying that simply coming to recognize that one has a reason to do X is a sufficient explanation of one's doing X. To unfold this theory, I start with the last feature.

7.3 PROPENSITY, INTENTIONAL OBJECTS, AND REASONS

Thomas Scanlon holds that recognizing a reason to do X can be sufficient for explaining why one does X. Consider, he says, a case of drinking something because one is thirsty.

There are three elements in this case that could serve as the motivation for drinking: an unpleasant sensation of dryness in the throat; a belief that an action (drinking) would lead to a pleasant state in the future; and taking this future good to be a reason to act. It's this third thing that Scanlon believes to constitute the sort of ordinary desire that motivates action. That is, he treats the notion of a reason (for believing or for acting) as a primitive, and argues that desires motivate human agents precisely with respect to their being *perceptions of reasons* to do or to get things.

Scanlon considers the possible objection that his account omits the urge to drink and that this is what the desire consists in. He responds that when we isolate this urge from any evaluative element, it does not fit in very well with what is ordinarily meant by desire, pointing to Warren Quinn's example of a man who has a brute urge to turn on every radio he sees. Such an urge lacks a feature essential in the most common cases of desire: having a tendency to see something good or desirable about it. Having a desire to drink, asserts Scanlon, is similar in that it involves seeing drinking as desirable—for example, that it would be pleasant.[9] While most cases of desire do seem to involve this evaluative component of seeing something to be good or desirable, such a point does not show that all the motivational work is done by the evaluative component. The Humean point, I take it, is that even if ordinary desire involves this evaluative element, it must be accompanied by something like the urge to drink. Indeed, in a case such as drinking from thirst, the urge to drink and the future good of enjoyment have a common source in the biological requirements of animals in general and human beings in particular.

The Humean picture that reason alone cannot motivate action, I suggest, is best supported by the naturalized view of human beings as animals, especially wonderful and sophisticated animals, but animals nevertheless whose original motivational directions and energy derive from the imperatives of our biological being. Those basic directions can be rechanneled and reshaped in wondrous ways, and in particular by our learning what reasons there are for doing things. There are external reasons, but merely recognizing such reasons does not assure any motivational propensity to act accordingly. Recognizing such reasons becomes motivationally efficacious when it gets *embedded* in a propensity that ultimately derives from our physical being.

In using the term 'propensity', I mean to isolate that element in ordinary desire that is different from the evaluative, belief-like component, different from the taking of something as good or desirable or as something there are reasons to have or to do. It can take the form of a felt urge toward an intentional object, as in thirsting after a drink of cool water, but it need not have anything close to a determinate intentional object the realization of which is aimed at. The intentional object can but need not be a *phenomenological* content of a propositional attitude. That is, the object of such a

9. Thomas Scanlon, *What We Owe to Each Other* (Cambridge, Mass.: Harvard University Press, 1998), 38.

propensity or urge or impulse need not be an object of awareness for the agent. When propensities are construed as functional states grounding dispositions to act or to feel under certain circumstances, for instance, the propositional content is taken as reflecting the motivational direction of the dispositions and the way they can form an intelligible bundle of action and feeling tendencies.

To return to Roberta's case, she must have already had a motivational propensity of some sort that partly explains how her recognizing a reason to boycott motivated her action. This Humean position leads us to expect, for example, that Roberta must have displayed in the past some degree of empathy or inclination toward the suffering of others, even if only toward people within her sheltered environment. Such a propensity is only a partial explanation because it is likely to be significantly indeterminate in several respects. For example, there is likely to be no determinate answer to the question of *whose* suffering provokes a response from Roberta, or to what counts as sufficient suffering to provoke a response, or to what the nature of the response is likely to be. In fact, none of her preexisting propensities may be determinate enough to dictate an action of helping the workers, even when the appropriate beliefs about their unjustified suffering are in place.[10] As Darwall rightly points out, the vividness with which Roberta imagines this suffering has a lot to do with her reaction.

One of the *results* of her watching the movie and coming to recognize a reason to boycott may be a greater determination of the intentional object in one or more of the respects in which the propensity is indeterminate. It is crucial to the explanation I am proposing that Roberta *not* see the reason to boycott as somehow based on a desire she already has. The reason has an external focus in the sense I described earlier: it draws her attention to the suffering of the workers as calling for certain kinds of action. By drawing her attention to the suffering of workers in this way, the reason helps to make more determinate any preexisting propensities she had to respond to others' suffering. Another way to put my point is that Roberta's recognition of workers' suffering could *focus* and make more determinate that propensity. She may emerge from her experience with something closer to what we could call an ordinary desire (if such desires are ever ordinary) to relieve suffering or to right injustice. While the preexisting propensity may help to explain how recognition of the reason was motivationally efficacious, the recognition simultaneously plays a role in the further shaping of the propensity as it becomes focused on the case of the workers.

---

10. John McDowell makes a similar point against a Humean-style explanation of the virtue of charity as based on natural fellow feeling or benevolence. It is implausible, he argues, that any such natural feeling could, unmediated by the special ways of perceiving situations that are characteristic of charity, issue in behavior that would match that of charitable persons. See "Are Moral Requirements Hypothetical Imperatives?" in *Mind, Value, and Reality* (Cambridge, Mass.: Harvard University Press, 1998), 84; originally published in *Proceedings of the Aristotelian Society*, supp. vol. 52 (1978): 13–29.

This further shaping could have an *extended* set of consequences for future action. It may move Roberta to reflect on unjustifiable suffering of people other than the textile workers and on her previous lack of response to that suffering. The concept of a reason has an inherent generality. A reason to aid the textile workers implies a reason to help those in relevantly similar situations. Reflection on this may result in a wider scope of operation for the original propensity and in a wider scope for the intentional object of any resulting desire, in the ordinary sense of 'desire'. Such changes could ramify throughout her character. A good film, like good literature, can help to expand one's powers of empathy and imagination even as it draws upon these powers. If the textile workers are unlike her in economic background and social manners, her having penetrated beyond these features might lead to an ability to respond to other sorts of people who are unlike her. Whether these changes occur will depend on other aspects of her character. Traits such as openness and generosity of spirit involve perceptual habits concerning what becomes salient to a person in reacting to situations and other persons. If Roberta has such traits, they are likely to contribute to an expansion of her empathetic and imaginative powers, but they may also undergo transformation themselves.

Nothing in my description of the Roberta case is contrary to the general spirit of Humean naturalism with regard to the explanation of action. However, the interaction between Roberta's prior motivational propensities, her experience of the film, and her recognition of a reason to boycott seems much more complex and interactive than is pictured by the standard Humean explanation. Perhaps the dynamic character of this process has been neglected because of use of the term 'desire' in philosophical discussions of motivation. One of the dangers in using this term is that we may carry over from ordinary usage an assumption that there is a more or less determinate intentional object the satisfaction of which is being aimed at. And while it may be reasonable to include a propensity with an extremely general and amorphous intentional object in an explanation of the motivational force of a reason, the explanation often does not work as it does in the case of a desire with a determinate intentional object. In the sort of case that has become standard as the example of how desire and belief combine to motivate, the desire is specified in the major premise of a practical syllogism, and the minor premise is a belief identifying a means to fulfilling the desire through a certain action. There is a kind of channeling going on here of the motivational force of the original desire by the belief, but the channeling occurs through recognition of a deductive relation between the intentional object of the original desire and a description of an action that would promote realization of the object.

7.4 CONSIDERATION OF POSSIBLE OBJECTIONS

A possible objection is that Roberta's experience of watching the movie shaped her propensity to respond to suffering and injustice without the mediation of recognition of a reason to act. It could be argued, in other words, that her recognition of a reason to act is logically *subsequent* to the shaping of her propensity through watching the movie.

Only *after* watching the movie results in a further definition of that propensity, so that it does imply helping the textile workers, does she have a reason to respond to their suffering. Actions such as Roberta's sometimes could happen in the way the objection envisions. But if the objection is that it must always happen in such a way, this seems no more than a theoretical prejudice. It is based on a prior commitment to the claim that a motivating reason can only be based on some preexisting *determinate* propensity. It requires that we divorce the experience that further shaped her propensity from her deliberative experience of coming to see that the suffering and injustice done to the workers constituted a reason for her to help them. Such a divorce not only seems artificial but deprives us of a way to see how her social and cultural environment acts to shape her propensity.

Let us try to picture what would be some realistic background for Roberta's case. She is likely to have already absorbed the norms of her moral and cultural background that require her to respond to injustice and to the sufferings of others. She may have been raised in a sheltered environment and previously exercised her care and concern for others only within a very small circle of others who are like her, but she is not likely to have lacked beliefs that require her to exercise care and concern for others beyond that circle. She is likely to have learned that she has a *moral reason* to do so (and here again let us be clear that what she learns is that certain features of a situation morally call on her to do certain kinds of actions). What she lacks before viewing the movie is an experience that engages her recognition of such a reason so that it becomes motivationally efficacious. But in the very process of its becoming engaged, the recognition of a reason can play a vital role in channeling the propensity toward helping the workers. It is uncontroversial that the norms of our social and cultural environment profoundly shape our propensities. The influence of those norms is often transmitted, I claim, through our learning that certain things constitute reasons to act in certain ways. In fact, the structure of a reasons claim is well suited to aid in the shaping of a propensity in the sense of making it more determinate what activates the propensity and what specific behavior results. A reasons claim identifies an action type X to be performed by A that is required by a feature of a situation R in which A finds herself. A's accepting that R constitutes a reason for her to do X helps to anchor the relevant propensity in R, such that the propensity is more reliably activated by perception of R. Her acceptance of the reasons claim also helps to channel the relevant propensity toward actions of the type X.

It may be objected that indeterminate propensities cannot have the explanatory power that I attribute to them. The extent to which propensities are unfocused and diffuse, it may be said, is precisely the extent to which they fail to explain how action is produced. But even the sorts of propensities we call desires are not wholly determinate in their intentional objects. To be explanatory, it suffices that a propensity be determinate in the respect that is relevant to the action to be explained. On my reading of the Roberta case, her propensity to respond to injustice and suffering becomes determinate in a respect relevant to production of her action. And it becomes determinate in that respect through an experience that includes recognition of a reason for that action.

To forestall another possible objection, let me note that accepting the existence of indeterminate propensities is fully compatible with a deterministic naturalism on the explanation of behavior. To say that there are indeterminate propensities is not to deny that there are precise causes for diffuse and variable boundaries of an intentional object, nor is it to deny that any further definition of these boundaries will have precise causes. Furthermore, let it be noted that the determinateness of an intentional object is assessed relative to our expectations as to what *makes sense* as an intentional object for that propensity. For example, a propensity for responding to the suffering of others will be indeterminate to the extent that it manifests erratic tendencies to responding to similar cases of suffering. Sometimes a person with such a propensity responds and sometimes not. The person may be easily deterred from helping by minor obstacles. When her propensity becomes more determinate, it becomes less erratic and stronger with respect to her responses to suffering, but that does not imply that the propensity is literally undefined when *considered apart* from our expectations as to what makes sense as an intentional object for it. It simply is an erratic and sometimes weak propensity to respond to suffering. To make it a more determinate propensity is to change at least some its constitutive response tendencies. Making a propensity more determinate in this sense is made possible by the *plasticity* of such response tendencies.

The position defended here stands in contrast not just to Humean internalism but also to the kind of Kantian internalism defended by Thomas Nagel, who argues that reasons motivate because they represent certain moral requirements.[11] The British moral realists—John McDowell, Mark Platts, and David McNaughton—hold that certain moral beliefs, arising from perception of moral requirements in a situation, can motivate without the aid of preexisting desire, though there is a feature of McDowell's theory (on which I will comment later) that overlaps with my claim that while reasons are external with respect to the motivations of the individual agent, they are internal with respect to human nature.[12] The theory defended here differs both from the usual formulations of Humean internalism and from the competitors identified earlier because it has a role for preexisting motivational propensities that can be identified independently of ethical principles, even if it is not the standard Humean role.

11. Thomas Nagel, *The Possibility of Altruism* (Oxford: Clarendon Press, 1970), 7–17.

12. John McDowell, "Are Moral Requirements Hypothetical Imperatives?" and "Virtue and Reason," *Monist* 62 (1979), 331–50; Mark Platts, *Ways of Meaning* (London: Routledge and Kegan Paul, 1979), and "Moral Reality and the End of Desire," in *Reference, Truth and Reality*, ed. M. Platts (London: Routledge and Kegan Paul), 69–82; David McNaughton, *Moral Vision: An Introduction to Ethics* (Oxford: Blackwell, 1988). In some of her recent work, Philippa Foot has defended an internalism of duty and of reasons that also holds the recognition of resons to have motivational power independently of pre-existing desires. See her "Does Moral Subjectivism Rest on a Mistake?" *Oxford Journal of Legal Studies* 15 (1995): 1–14; and *Natural Goodness* (Oxford: Clarendon, 2001).

Underlying this theory is a picture of how preexisting motivational propensity and recognition of a reason to act can interact. This picture gives propensities with significantly diffuse or indeterminate intentional objects a much more pervasive role in motivation than is commonly recognized.

7.5 The Plasticity of Motivational Propensity

The degree of indeterminacy to which our motivational sets are subject is most apparent in children. This is not to deny what any parent knows: that at times a child's desires may be maddeningly definite and intractable. But certain strategies we take with children presuppose that their tendencies are, within a certain range, plastic and subject to channeling. There are times, for instance, when asking a child what she "really wants," that we voice interpretations or guesses about what she wants. These queries have a directive element to them. It is not just that we think she might want to play with another child and share her toys, for example, but that we would like her to, and in asking or suggesting that that is what she wants, we may be partly trying to bring that about. This kind of channeling need not be a matter of putting something in the child's mind that wasn't there in the first place, but can be more a matter of activating certain tendencies, making them more determinate in their intentional objects and therefore in specificity of behavioral tendency, by encouraging their realization in particular situations. The effect of advertising on consumer psychology, of course, is often through a similar process of channeling preexisting propensity.[13]

Ronald deSousa's picture of the way emotions develop from the association of instinctual responses with "paradigm scenarios" provides another way of thinking about such processes.[14] Paradigm scenarios include situation types that provide the characteristic intentional objects of the emotion in question. Compassion, for example, is distinguished from other emotions by certain perceived features of situations to which it is characteristically directed, primarily the perceived suffering of another sentient being. The development of compassion, then, involves a process in which another's suffering becomes salient to a child. Paradigm scenarios also include characteristic responses to the situation, which have a biological, instinctual basis, but quickly become culturally elaborated and refined. Innate tendencies to be compassionate may have intentional objects, but both the responses and the objects are likely to be extremely rudimentary and incomplete. What is to be perceived as suffering, *whose* suffering becomes salient, and the specific nature of the helping response at this point is still largely indeterminate. Cultural elaboration and refinement results in increased determinacy along these dimensions. The process may occur through repeated exposure to paradigm scenarios in

---

13. As pointed out to me by Geoffrey Sayre-McCord.

14. Ronald deSousa, *The Rationality of Emotion* (Cambridge, Mass.: MIT Press, 1987), see especially 181–3.

the daily lives of children, for example, in the fairy tales and stories read to them. It also occurs through modeling. Children emulate the mental focus of their caretakers, and, drawing from their instinctual responses, learn how to react to the relevant features of the situation.

7.6 THE ROLE OF REASONS IN SHAPING PROPENSITY

I have argued elsewhere that the development of compassion as a virtue involves learning that another's suffering is a *reason* to try to help.[15] That is, the development of compassion as an ethical virtue not only involves increased sensitivity to suffering as a salient feature of situations to which one emotionally responds, and not only increased regularity and specificity of response, but also integration of that emotional response into the agent's practical reasoning. This initially takes place in conjunction with learning the conceptual apparatus of practical deliberation. We initially learn what a reason to act is primarily through being given examples of what sorts of reasons there are. Another's suffering is one of the primary examples. This picture of development within a person's motivational set, then, involves a "material" conception of practical reason. Practical reason consists not only of formal principles, such as universalizability, and strategic principles, such as minimizing the greatest possible losses (maximin), but also of a value-laden substance, the beginnings of which are given when an individual is taught what sorts of reasons there are to act in what ways.

This picture of the development of practical reason is one way of specifying how a human being is a "self-completing" animal, to use Clifford Geertz's phrase. It is a way of spelling out how "the extreme generality, diffuseness, and variability of man's innate response capacities" get modified by "cultural templates."[16] More specifically, it depicts a way that the learning of reasons to act goes into the shaping of motivational propensities through the further definition of intentional objects for them. The shaping of intentional objects goes on throughout an individual's lifetime. Generality, diffuseness, and variability are not just characteristics of innate response capacities but continue to characterize in significant degree our culturally shaped propensities.

For example, let us go back to Roberta. The circle of human beings to which she is likely to actively respond has been enlarged, but it remains to be seen how much wider that circle will become in the future, and what the shape of her future responses will be. The intangible effects of the boycott may discourage her and prompt her to sink back into her smaller circles of active concern. She could sustain her commitment in various ways and extend the circle of her concern beyond the textile workers. No

---

15. "Is There a Distinction between Reason and Emotion in Mencius?" *Philosophy East and West* 41 (1991): 31–44.

16. Clifford Geertz, "Ideology as a Cultural System," in *The Interpretation of Cultures* (New York: Basic Books, 1973), 217–8.

doubt much depends on other aspects of her character and the multiple external contingencies involved in projects of this sort. The point is that there are infinitely more ways in which her propensities could go on to be shaped, both in terms of what becomes motivationally salient as a reason to act and in terms of what the likely response will be like.

Propensities other than the ones I've mentioned so far could become engaged in Roberta's further experience and reflection, and these other propensities could alter or reinforce the original ones. Suppose she follows her participation in the boycott with work as an organizer. She becomes increasingly committed to her work. Her situation could be like that of a political activist and community organizer who was interviewed by Robert Coles. This young man started working as a civil rights activist in the South of the 1960s, and at the point that Coles interviews him in the 1970s, he recounts the internal struggles he had as to whether to continue his life as an organizer, rather than "getting on with his life and making something of himself," as his friends and family put it. He now says,

> I've become immersed in this life, in the lives of the people I work with. I feel part of their existence. I really miss them when I leave; it's as if a big part of me is gone, and I'm floundering and helpless. When I come back, I see not only "them," I see myself: I'm reunited with what has become my life—me here working with people and getting a lot from them, not just trying to be of help to them . . . to leave them would be to leave a lot of myself. It would be like starting in all over again as a person![17]

This is an example of how a commitment that perhaps began as a response to injustice or suffering has become tied to other propensities and satisfactions in a person's life. The initial commitment has become a project that enters into the person's identity. In this case, he has discovered that his current life satisfies an impulse to seek belonging and contribution to a community. But if he had such an impulse before he went to south Georgia, it is likely to have been quite general and diffuse in its intentional object. What is initially sought is community of some sort, with satisfactions very generally conceived. Living in that particular community provided him with a more determinate idea of what it is he seeks, but I want to say it also *made* the object of that seeking more determinate.

Let this now remind us of the way in which the story I have told confirms the criticism of the standard Humean explanation of action done according to a reason. When the recognition of a reason to act does become effective in channeling a motivational propensity and in giving further definition to its intentional object, we have the explanation of how an action can flow from such recognition without the aid of a

---

17. Robert Coles, *The Moral Life of Children* (Boston: Atlantic Monthly, 1986), 167.

preexisting desire in the standard ways. Since the propensity is channeled through the recognition, the recognition acquires motivational efficacy. The motive force of the propensity is transferred through that which channels it. That we could have a motivating reason to aid others in suffering does not depend in any simple or straightforward sense on our having a preexisting desire that would be promoted by aiding them, but neither does the reason carry its own efficacy independently of our preexisting motivations.

7.7 How the Theory Is Supported against Its Competitors

It may be that the only way to decide among the competing theories of reasons and their implications for explanation of acting on reasons is by seeing how they fit our best science of mind and action. Previous philosophical arguments for and against theories of reasons have relied on stories such as Darwall's, stories that appeal to an intuitively plausible construal of the relevant motivational processes. The other sides to this debate are not lacking in their stories and their favored construals of the motivational processes, as has been demonstrated here. While I hope that my construal is more intuitively appealing than, or at least as appealing as, Darwall's, the issue will not and should not be decided on the basis of armchair intuitions about what is psychologically plausible.

The sciences of the mind seem not yet at the point where one sort of theory dominates and has definitive implications for philosophical theories of reasons. However, one promising scientific theory for the philosophical theory defended here is Antonio Damasio's, based on his studies of the way that practical reasoning goes wrong in those suffering certain kinds of brain damage. For example, one patient, Elliot, exhibited completely inappropriate decision-making on matters of practical import for himself. He would become distracted by one component of a task at work and become waylaid. He would make disastrous decisions that he should have known would be disastrous. He would do such things over and over, unable to learn from experience. Yet he tested normal and high on intelligence tests of reasoning and thinking concerning objects, space, numbers, and words. More remarkably, when tested on ethical dilemmas and financial questions (would he steal if he needed cash and could assume he would not be discovered?), Elliot showed normal ethical judgment. His financial decisions, when made in the abstract, seemed reasonable. Yet when called upon to act in real life in this areas, his behavior was a "catalogue of violations." Damasio observes that Elliot's impairment appeared to set in at the late stages of reasoning, "close to or at the point at which choice making or response selection must occur."[18] Elliot displayed one more striking characteristic: lack of affect. The damaged parts of his brain play roles not only

---

18. Antonio Damasio, *Descartes' Error* (New York: Avon Books, 1994), 50.

in planning and deciding but also in the processing of emotions. Damasio concluded that the apparatus of rationality, traditionally thought to be located in the cortical structures of the brain, engages not only those areas but also the subcortical structures associated with biological regulation and the basic drives and instincts. Practical rationality is built not just on top of the subcortical structures concerned with these aims but from these structures and with them.[19]

The sort of thing I have called a propensity in this essay has its roots on Damasio's theory in the drives and instincts associated with survival and biological regulation. Remember the biological urge to drink posited by the theory defended here as supplying the motivational force of judgments that there are reasons to drink. Emotions are combinations of mental evaluative processes, which would include seeing things as good or desirable or seeing reasons to have or do things, with dispositional responses of the body that have their roots in the drives and instincts associated with the subcortical areas. Emotions, Damasio theorized, form the crucial bridge between these areas of the brain and make it possible for the apparatus of rationality to be built from and with the lower structures. Emotions are a crucial part of rationality because they provide the valences in terms of which we are able to rank possible outcomes of our actions. Because they are combinations of mental evaluative processes and bodily dispositions, they help assure that our evaluations will be motivationally effective. Damasio's theory, then, is broadly consistent with the story told here. The higher reaches of rationality are built upon biologically basic drives and instincts, with emotions and their bodily dispositions serving to channel the motivational force of those drives and instincts. When this bridging structure between the apparatus of rationality and the drives and instincts is disrupted, rational judgments are disrupted in their power to guide behavior.

7.8 EXTERNALISM OR INTERNALISM?

The story I have told is externalist in the following sense: an individual can learn that a certain kind of feature of a situation is a reason to act in certain ways, but such a recognition may fail to become engaged with and channel a motivational propensity. When such failures are massive, and the reasons are ethical, we have a sociopath. As observed by Mencius in the Chinese tradition and Aristotle in the Greek tradition, character development can go so wrong that there may be nothing left for ethical decency to take root in. Some partial failure in moral decency, at least on occasions, is typical for most of us, which is also what we should expect if human beings have a plurality of basic motivations, including self-interest and various forms of altruism. The phenomenon of partial moral failure most typically involves giving weight to moral reasons but allowing other reasons to unjustifiably trump them on occasion.

19. Damasio, *Descartes' Error*, 128.

The story told here, therefore, excludes an internalism that *guarantees* a motivational propensity appropriately related to what one has reason to do. To serve the kind of channeling and shaping functions described earlier, the reason must be external to the individual's motivational system, precisely because recognition of an external feature of a situation as a reason helps to *shape* a motivational propensity when it becomes engaged with that propensity. Whether it becomes so engaged depends on many factors. One can imagine that a movie capable of shaping a person's motivation as it does in Roberta's case must be such as to activate the relevant propensity (e.g., feelings of compassion, a sense of indignation at injustice) at the same time that it focuses the agent's attention on the relevant reason. This is why purely didactic films or literature with a moral purpose often fail in that purpose. If so, this confirms the picture of moral education we get from Aristotle in the Greek tradition and Mencius in the Chinese tradition.

The story told here conflicts with the theories of reasons offered by Nagel and Scanlon or by realists such as Platts and McDowell insofar as their views deny the necessity of preexisting propensities for the recognition of reasons to be motivationally efficacious. It does honor a possible motivation for those positions: the perception that the Humean strains too much in trying to find exactly the right kind of preexisting desire behind all acting according to a reason—a propensity with the right kind of determinate object that in combination with the appropriate beliefs yields the action to be explained.

These positions, furthermore, have been motivated by the belief that reasons to act must provide a basis from which to criticize existing desire on the most fundamental levels. The sort of critical perspective provided by the recognition of valid reasons to act cuts deeper, it is believed, than any Humean internalism could allow. For example, John McDowell grants that sophisticated Humean theories such as Williams's do open up some critical distance between agents' existing motivations and what they have reason to do through allowing for the role of deliberation in correcting and enriching those motivations. Williams is right to argue that the internal reasons theorist need not say that the man who mistakes some petrol for gin and wants a gin and tonic thereby has a reason to drink the petrol. However, McDowell doubts that this is the right sort of critical distance. Humean desires, as we happen to have them and even as corrected by Humean reasoning, cannot unproblematically determine the shape of practical rationality for the individual agent who possesses them.[20] McDowell is right to suggest that agents can have reasons not to fulfill their desires even if such desires are not based on any garden-variety factual mistake such as mistaking petrol for gin. My theory allows for greater critical distance between the reasons we may have and our existing motivations through holding that moral reasons are external and that they come to play a role in the channeling and shaping of propensity.

20. See John McDowell, "Might There Be External Reasons?" in *Mind, Value, and Reality* (Cambridge, Mass.: Harvard University Press, 1998), 104–7.

Michael Smith's theory of normative reasons bears important similarities with Williams's theory, but is developed in a way that might appear to answer McDowell's criticism. Put in terms of what it takes for an agent to have reason to *phi* in circumstances C, Smith's analysis is that the agent would desire to *phi* in C were she fully rational. Thus Smith's analysis, like Williams's, construes the normativity of reasons to rest on correct deliberation on the agent's existing set of desires and beliefs. Smith emphasizes his difference with Williams, however, in holding that imagination is not the main way that old desires can be extinguished and new ones formed through deliberation. Rather, the system of desires can be transformed through striving to make the total system more systematically justifiable, by way of achieving a Rawlsian reflective equilibrium between one's specific and general desires. The aim is to have one's general desires explain and justify the more specific one in a systematic and unified fashion.

In the end, though, Smith has not gone much further than Williams in achieving the right sort of critical distance from an agent's existing desires. An agent will come to have a more coherent set of desires through reaching reflective equilibrium, but her conclusions about the desirability of *phi*-ing in C will still be based on what could be a pretty inadequate or unacceptable set of desires. The conclusions could not be guaranteed to stand up to the sort of critical reflection McDowell has in mind. Smith counters this criticism of his position by arguing that the way we discuss reasons to *phi* or not to *phi* presupposes that we are trying to reach agreement on the desirability of *phi*-ing in C. In trying to achieve reflective equilibrium among our desires, we are supposedly trying to get nonrelative reasons to *phi* in C (reasons on which we could agree were we fully rational). Of course, Smith admits, his analysis leaves it quite open as to whether there are any nonrelative reasons to *phi* in C. The fact that we presuppose that there are in normative discourse is consistent with the possibility that we are profoundly mistaken.[21] We have to see whether fully rational agents would converge in their desires about what is to be done in the various circumstances they might face. This seems to me to leave hugely open, if not highly dubious, whether there are any genuine normative reasons. At best, Smith's account allows us to say that there might be such reasons. He urges greater optimism by pointing to the degree of agreement we have now on moral questions, and by claiming that the best explanation of such agreement is convergence on what desires we would have with respect to these questions were we fully rational.[22] But a much more plausible explanation is, first, the necessity of fairly widespread agreement on moral norms and reasons given the function of morality in promoting social coordination, and second, the kind of moralization of desire that can be achieved in socialization and moral discourse described in this chapter.

---

21. Michael Smith, *The Moral Problem* (Oxford: Blackwell, 1994), 151–75.
22. Smith, *Moral Problem*, 187–8.

The last point explains why my theory is compatible with Quinn's and Scanlon's point that there is a significant evaluative component in the typical sort of *desire* that could be said to motivate action. Such a conception of desires, which goes back to Aristotle and Aquinas, and has an analogue in Mencius, is of an inclination toward something apprehended as good or desirable. If the story defended here is right, many of our desires must aim at what we have reason to seek, because their objects have been shaped and made more determinate through the recognition of such reasons. Reasons could in fact enter into the intentional object of propensities and emotions that initially have no such content. The propensity to respond to the suffering of others, for example, could become in part desire that involves seeing the sufferings of others as reasons to act. While under my theory, the mere belief that something is desirable cannot create a propensity toward it, a reason to seek it can appear in the intentional object of a propensity as a result of the processes of channeling and shaping. In that way the propensity can become a desire for what appears desirable.

Even if my theory of moral reasons is by literal definition externalist, however, it does admit of an important sense in which moral reasons have some necessary connection to, and in this sense are internal to, human *nature*, if not to every human agent's motivational system. If an important function of moral reasons is precisely to channel propensities rooted in that nature, then what we have moral reason to do is, in an important sense, dependent on what human beings are generally capable of being motivated to do. We cannot be morally required to be what has no relation to what human beings are or what they could be. Moral reasons would not serve their function as practical reasons unless some preexisting human propensities were not susceptible to shaping by them. There is some necessary *general* connection between reasons for action and what human beings are capable of being motivated by.

This is the feature of my theory that overlaps with a theme in John McDowell's construal of values as analogous to secondary qualities. On his construal, just as secondary qualities such as colors are powers to present certain kinds of phenomenal appearances to creatures endowed with certain perceptual sensibilities, so value qualities are constituted by objects being such as to merit the attention or admiration of creatures with certain sensibilities. McDowell offers this theory as a way to preserve the objectivity of value qualities while at the same time avoiding a construal of them as ghostly Platonic forms, existing independently of us while simultaneously laying a claim on us to act for their realization.[23] McDowell encounters a difficulty in reaching this desirable middle ground between relativity to human sensibility and Platonic objectivism because the analogy between color qualities and value qualities breaks down at the point where he must acknowledge that value qualities are such as to *merit* admiration from creatures with sensibilities such as ours. The normative dimension of

23. See John McDowell, "Values and Secondary Qualities," *Essays on Moral Realism*, ed. Geoffrey Sayre-McCord (Ithaca: Cornell University Press, 1988), 166–80.

value qualities finds no analogy in color qualities (such qualities are such as to elicit the appropriate color experiences), as McDowell himself notes.[24] The account of moral reasons defended here occupies that middle ground between radical subjectivism and ghostly Platonism without having to explain away the disanalogy between color and moral properties. The account implies that moral reasons exist independently of the motivational structures of particular individuals, but not independently of the motivational structures that human beings generally have or are capable of developing. Moral reasons that require consideration of the interests of others, for example, exist because human beings generally have the sensibilities that make it both possible and necessary for them to cooperate with each other.

The theme that morality is internal to human nature points to the ways in which the account defended here weighs against the opposition between externalism and internalism, rather than weighing in favor of one side. Recall that the motivation for the externalist position on moral duty, as Falk characterized it, was the perception that moral duty comes from outside the agent and her motivational structure. The motivation for the internalist position on moral duty was the conviction that for a reflective and relatively autonomous agent, reasons come from the inside. The metaphor of inside and outside creates a false dichotomy. The internalist position would be suited to creatures whose motivational propensities are much more determinate and less plastic to begin with. But as we are constituted, at least part of the substance of moral reasons must come from the outside of any given individual and her motivational structure. On the other hand, whatever substance does come from the outside of any individual must be suitable to the guiding of propensities that human beings generally have.

The opposition between internalism and externalism on reasons reinforces the false dichotomy between thinking of the individual as a being upon whom reasons are imposed from the outside or as a being from whom reasons can arise autonomously from the inside. The opposition draws our attention away from the possibility that without the channeling and shaping of motivational propensity through the learning of reasons such as the suffering of others, we would scarcely be recognizable as human agents. Reasons initially come from the outside, but if we abstract *all* reasons, what is left is someone who is not yet a human agent. Such an agent begins to exist only when some reasons are taken inside so that they can shape and even become embedded in the intentional structure of motivational propensity. Human beings complete themselves, to return to Geertz's phrase, not just through cultural forms but also through the forms that identify the substance of practical reason for them.

I said earlier that we learn what reasons to act are by learning what some of them are, such as another's suffering. Why are such conditions *reasons* at all for us? The argument of this book is that morality must be understood as having evolved in part to facilitate

---

24. McDowell, "Values and Secondary Qualities," 175.

and regulate social cooperation. As suggested in section 2.9, human genes and human culture coevolved, such that genetically based prosocial tendencies and prosocial cultural norms mutually shaped one another. Altruistic impulses, including empathetic ones, are possessed by many, if not all, human beings. We do have experimental evidence of the "infectiousness" of emotion in newborns and infants.[25] The human capacity for self-governance through culture and inculcated norms evolved in conjunction with the development of such primitive capacities underlying altruism. Within human culture, teaching that the suffering of others is a reason to act in certain ways would reinforce and channel whatever innate capacities we have for empathy.

Other sorts of moral reasons may help to channel and shape other deep propensities in human nature so as to further adaptive social cooperation. As argued in section 2.8, a moral reason that appears in all kinds of societies and cultures is the reason to return good for good that is voluntarily given, and its universality may reflect its roots in human nature. Often the most crucial forms of human cooperation involve helping behavior. Reciprocation for being helped, if it is a general feature of social interaction, reinforces helping behavior and is therefore a powerful element in sustaining that help. The absence of reciprocation, if it were a general feature of social interaction, would quite likely extinguish helping behavior. This would explain why some form of reciprocity is a necessary element of morality, for without it human cooperative activity could not get off the ground. For example, the requirement of reciprocating good for good along with the fact that the young need a great deal of physical care and teaching helps to explain the existence of duties to parents and others whose roles involve raising and nurturing the young. Performance of such duties constitutes a kind of return of good for good, though the kind of good returned, of course, need not be the same as the kind received. This line of reasoning matches nicely with the hypothesis of reciprocal altruism: that the tendency to reciprocate aid was selected precisely because of cooperative benefits. If such altruism was selected in human beings, it is likely to have been a diffuse and indeterminate drive in many respects, and the various reasons that identify occasions for reciprocation and appropriate ways of reciprocating that are to be found across cultures are the ways this drive was and is constantly being channeled and made more determinate.

7.9 The Point of External Reasons

At the beginning of this chapter, I said that internalism is motivated by puzzlement over what point there could be in saying that an agent had a reason to do an action when that action was not supported by any of the agent's motivations. What I have just said about

25. See M. L. Simner, "Newborn's Response to the Cry of Another Infant," *Developmental Psychology* 5 (1971): 136–50; and Alvin Goldman, "Empathy, Mind, and Morals," *Proceedings and Addresses of the American Philosophical Association* 66 (1992): 17–42.

the relation of morality to the structure of human cooperative life helps us to understand how there could be a point to external reasons. Unless they have a degree of independence from the actual motivations of individuals, they could not serve the kind of channeling and function that is plausibly attributed to them. Part of the naturalistic explanation of such channeling and shaping is that it forms part of a process for producing creatures adapted to cooperative life. This is not to say that the configuration of moral reasons will be the same across different forms of cooperative life. Different forms may be partly distinguished according to distinctive emphases that are given to a particular sort of reason. The feeling of a debt of gratitude for a kindness or a gift is something we all know, but in Chinese and Japanese societies that feeling is greatly magnified, corresponding to a difference in the priority given to this sort of reason relative to others.[26] Such differences are compatible with the idea that there are limits on what can count as a moral reason, given human nature and the nature of human cooperative life.

It may be asked whether the view defended here somehow makes it rationally necessary to be motivated by moral considerations. It might be thought that this is a consequence of the view, since it takes moral reasons to apply to individuals even if they have none of the relevant motivations. Recall that one of the original supports for Humean internalism of the sort defended by Williams is precisely a rejection of this consequence. I, too, want to reject the consequence that it is necessarily *irrational* to fail to be motivated by moral reasons. The term 'irrational' has a particularly strong sense, implying a disorder in reasoning processes, a violation of universally valid principles of reasoning that ought to be apparent to a normal reasoner.[27] But to point out to people what they have reason to do is not necessarily to hold the threat of irrationality over their heads if they do not take it into consideration. In particular, it is suggested here that pointing out a certain species of moral reason to a person has a point that is connected to the plea to be *reasonable*.

Reasonableness is neither equivalent to nor required by pure rationality. It is motivated by a willingness to enter into certain kinds of cooperative relations with other human beings. When we call people unreasonable, we often mean not that they are irrational in that very strong sense but that they are taking a stance that makes them unlikely partners in our joint enterprises. To refuse to take moral reasons into account is to refuse part of what makes our cooperative life possible—perhaps any human cooperative life or, at any rate, ours in particular. Saying that people have moral reasons, then, has a point, even if there is nowhere for that reason take hold in their motivations. It is to identify what they have to do to place themselves within the boundaries of fair cooperation, and if they have no motivation to do so, warning must be given to them and to others contemplating cooperation with them.

26. See David Nivison, "'Virtue' in Boné and Bronze," in *The Ways of Confucianism*, ed. Bryan W. Van Norden (Chicago: Open Court, 1996), 17–30.
27. On this matter I am in agreement with Scanlon, *What We Owe to Each Other*.

Jonathan Lear has suggested that the sorts of reasons most relevant to ethics are not derived from "a fixed structure revealed by transcendental argument" (as Kant thought), nor do they "Platonically exist totally independently of us." Rather, they may be part of a way of life that is "somehow constituted by our thoughts, actions, feelings of naturalness, perceptions of salience."[28] I would qualify this last remark of Lear. The reasons most relevant to ethics may not be merely constituted by our thoughts, feelings, and perceptions of salience, but in fact may infuse those things and give them the shape they have. That is why they help to define a way of life.

7.10   CAN WE ANSWER THE QUESTIONS "WHY BE MORAL?" AND "WHY OUR PARTICULAR MORALITY?"

Morality is not rationally compulsory. At best, it, or a part of it, is only a part of the reasonable. If reason includes not only the rational but also the reasonable, then it is against reason to refuse moral reasons. It is, however, the confusion between the reasonable and the rational, or the desire to make the reasonable compulsory upon pain of irrationality, that has fueled so many philosophical attempts to show that to knowingly do what is morally wrong is necessarily irrational. The confusion is understandable, given that the languages of reasonableness and of rationality both employ the terminology of reasons.

The theory defended here will remain disturbing to those who insist that our justifications for morality must engage the motivational structure of each individual. Nothing I have said here even promises an answer to the sociopath who asks the question "Why be moral?" And some may insist that ethical justification have an answer ready for all. Given the conclusions of this essay, it is relevant to point out that for most of us, ethical reasons may be part of what makes a human cooperative life possible, that such reasons have become deeply embedded in the structure of our emotions and propensities. These reasons are internal to human nature in general, if not to each individual's motivations. Moral reasons and the propensities in which they are embedded may go into our most basic ways of orienting ourselves in the world, into our most firmly rooted conceptions of ourselves, into our identities. An ethical justification that reassures and strengthens those of us in whom ethical motivations are deeply rooted, then, may point to who we already are, and to the difficulty of imagining who else we might want to be.[29]

---

28. Jonathan Lear, "Moral Objectivity," in *Objectivity and Cultural Divergence*, ed. S. C. Brown (Cambridge: Cambridge University Press, 1984), 148. Lear proposes his account in terms such that I am unable to say precisely how his account relates to mine, but I suspect there is significant affinity between them.

29. Bernard Williams has rightly suggested, I think, that providing such a justification is a worthy aim for philosophy that might be substituted for the futile aim of showing that even the most amoral of persons would be irrational to not strive to be moral. See his *Ethics and the Limits of Philosophy* (Cambridge, Mass.: Harvard University Press, 1985), 27.

Much the same answer can be given to worries about the stability and firmness of moral commitments raised by the recognition of a plurality of true moralities. A radical departure might very well be merely a notional alternative to us. It will be replied, however, that departures might fall short of radical and yet be significant. This is the subject of the next chapter.

8

Morality and Need

The previous chapter showed how morality deeply influences us, not just in the sense that it deeply shapes our characters before we are even aware of its influence but in the sense that it shapes what constitutes for us reasons for acting. However, if morality does not constitute an irreducible part of the world's fabric that simultaneously has prescriptive authority over us, why go on accepting the influence it has over us? I have suggested in chapters 3 and 7 that it may be very difficult to imagine a genuine alternative. Our identities are deeply rooted in our moralities (which is not to say that we cannot frequently fail to meet their fullest demands). On the other hand, this may not be the case for all of us, and even those whose identities are rooted in moralities may experience internal conflict or cannot absolutely rule out change within themselves, and so the question of continuing our acceptance arises. Further, we could be in the unhappy situation of not being able to be other than deeply influenced by morality, but unable to accept its influence as a good thing for us. If that is true, then perhaps we should simply acknowledge it. If it is false, then we should be able to say something persuasive to the moral cynics.

The aura of morality as an objectively prescriptive part of the world's fabric continues to hang over us, even those of us who reject it intellectually. We condemn, and want to be able to condemn, torture and unremitting cruelty as an offense against the world, somehow, and not just against the rules we need to live together and to make meaning out of human life. Perhaps that is so because we know that morality can call upon us, and that in its name we can call upon others, to make great sacrifice. We have a need to see that sacrifice as required by something greater than ourselves. If we cannot satisfy that need, perhaps we can connect morality with the satisfaction of other, central human needs.

The strongest possible answer along these lines is to show that an individual cannot flourish without living a moral life. In the next section I examine a contemporary version of this response and explain why I think it is too strong to be realized successfully.

8.1 Trying to Show That Flourishing
Requires Morality

Laurence Thomas is particularly concerned to undermine views of human nature as innately self-interested, and draws from recent evolutionary theory to argue that natural selection favored natural desires for the welfare of others.[1] Thomas further argues that we are favored to flourish if we realize our altruistic desires. Parental love, claims Thomas, is innate and "transparent" in being unconditional on its recipient's behaving in desired ways. Because children naturally reciprocate parental love, they learn to forgo benefits for the sake not only of their parents but also for the sake of others generally. Thomas assumes here that a generalized capacity for sympathy and empathy underlies the capacity to be moved by the weal and woe of particular others. The biological capacity for transparent love in particular, he argues, is the basis for developing the minimum respect that is owed to persons regardless of their personal attributes.

Morality arguably requires a measure of transparent concern for others, and tracing the root of that concern to parental love is an interesting and fresh one. The claim for the innateness of transparency seems questionable to me. Thomas apparently assumes that natural selection favored transparent love because it provides children the psychological security they need to flourish, but it is not clear why, from the perspective of our psychological armchairs, a measure of conditional love might have an advantage in motivating children to become better people. In any case, there is no general theoretical reason to assume that natural selection favors individual flourishing when it differs from maximizing one's genetic contribution to future generations. While natural selection plausibly selected parental love, its innate form is probably too variable, diffuse, and indeterminate to be called either transparent or conditional. The rest is culture and individual permutations of general innate tendencies. However, if Thomas is right about there being an innate basis for parental love (however transparent it is), and if he is further right about that love's containing at least the germ for a generalized capacity for sympathy and empathy, then we at least may conclude that the kind of altruism morality requires is not a *distortion* of human nature or something that is mysteriously imprinted entirely from the outside by social conditioning.

Thomas goes on to argue that the individual with a morally good character is thereby significantly favored to be happy and to live well. His argument depends on seeing the immoral as caring for their loved ones and friends on the one hand and on the other hand having to feign care for the rest of the people they manipulate. Effective dissimulation of an emotion involves producing in some measure the real emotion, through deliberately dwelling on the kind of thoughts that give rise to it.[2] Effective

---

1. Laurence Thomas, *Living Morally: A Psychology of Moral Character* (Philadelphia: Temple University Press, 1989).

2. Thomas, *Living Morally*, 222–7.

dissimulators are so good at this that they have more reason than others to question whether they are moved to do the right things for those close to them out of genuine care or self-interest. Because it is universally important to people to have secure knowledge that they are acting from the right motivations toward those close to them, immoral persons will be less happy.

The claim that effective dissimulators are so good that they are liable to fool themselves as well as others may capture a tendency, but it is difficult to see why it is believable as an invariable truth. Another problem with this argument is the intellectualistic assumption that one's happiness is necessarily lessened by the lack of the secure knowledge that one is acting from the right motives for one's loved ones and friends. But it is not clear why amoral persons should from the standpoint of promoting their own flourishing be seriously concerned to confirm to themselves the genuineness of their emotions toward those close to them. Thomas emphasizes the disconcerting effect that would accompany continual doubt about these matters, but the safest way to avoid such doubt may be to avoid reflection on them.

Thomas's general strategy is to start from the idea that one needs meaningful ties with some particular others to flourish, and then to argue that maintaining these ties and the ways they help one to flourish requires one to acknowledge duties to others generally. I agree that the starting point is plausible (as argued in chapter 4), but the line of argument to the conclusion is tenuous. There might be another way of getting to the conclusion from Thomas's starting point. For example, Hugh LaFollette has argued that satisfying personal relationships depend on morality because the quality of such relationships is deeply affected by the larger society that contains them. We cannot expect to have good relationships if the general climate of a society lacks certain moral virtues. He argues that in a generally amoral society, "relationships between non-moral people are at risk. Intimates must be honest with one another; any dishonesty will chip away at the foundations of the relationship. Yet people cannot be as honest as they need to be if they are immersed in a subculture built on dishonesty and deceit."[3] LaFollete makes a similar argument about trust. The trust needed in personal relationships cannot survive in a larger environment of distrust and hate.

The conclusion LaFollette wants to draw here is that even though there are conflicts between personal relationships and impartial morality, morality must allow some personal relationships because it depends on them; at the same time, because the quality of our personal relationships depends on the moral quality of the larger society, we should not regularly disregard the needs of strangers while heaping trivial benefits on close ones. Here again, it seems to me that the argument rests on a tenuous generalization. In the United States, for example, gated communities, private schools, the white middle-class flight to increasingly remote suburbs, and the de facto tracking system that exists even in

---

3. Hugh LaFollette, "Personal Relationships," in *A Companion to Ethics*, ed. Peter Singer (Oxford: Blackwell, 1991), 331.

the more successfully integrated (both in terms of race and class) urban public schools signify the widespread conviction that one can insulate oneself from the problems of the larger society. A just world would be one in which one could not succeed in this endeavor, but I see no evidence that the actual one is such a world. Closing the gates can work if one has enough money and if a moderate degree of luck holds.

I have seen no attempt to show that individual flourishing requires morality that is immune to these kinds of problems. Neither have I seen a persuasive demonstration that all such attempts would meet the same fate, but induction is enough to move me to a more modest project: showing that there are forms of flourishing that involve a moral life, even if not all forms of flourishing do.

8.2 THE ALTERNATIVE OF SHOWING THAT FLOURISHING IS COMPATIBLE WITH MORALITY

Both Bernard Williams and Jonathan Lear have suggested the modest project. To use Lear's formulation, we must avoid the Platonic project of taking "the reflective justification for a practice, say acting justly, to be a proof which eliminates all alternative possibilities for acting in one's interest other than acting justly," because "the mere construction of an alternative possibility will be sufficient to undermine the reflective justification."[4] Lear's proposal is to show a posteriori that a significant form of flourishing can partly consist in promoting human flourishing generally. One does this by pointing to actual cases of flourishing, where the flourishers are actively engaged in promoting the flourishing of others. After all, Lear suggests, people do find significance and fulfillment in acting to better humanity's lot and find frustration often when they live in a society or historical period in which they are prevented from doing so. What would this accomplish? Bernard Williams suggests that a reasonable aim of moral justification is to address people who are largely within the ethical world, to reassure and strengthen those who are disposed to listen, and to give them reason "to help in continually creating a community held together by that same disposition."[5]

8.3 CHALLENGES TO THE PURPORTED COMPATIBILITY BETWEEN MORALITY AND FLOURISHING

Even this more modest project is not immune from strong challenge, however. Michael Foucault's work contains one particularly subtle challenge to modern Enlightenment moralities. As Charles Taylor, in writing on Foucault, has observed, the Enlightenment self-portrait is self-flattering: we have overcome superstition and myth and as a

4. Jonathan Lear, "Moral Objectivity," in *Objectivity and Cultural Divergence*, ed. S. C. Brown (Cambridge: Cambridge University Press, 1984), 161.
5. *Ethics and the Limits of Philosophy* (Cambridge: Harvard University Press, 1985), 27.

consequence have adopted humanitarian values.[6] The modern view of the world contrasts with premodern notions of a cosmic order constituted by a hierarchy of beings that is also a hierarchy of goods. The cosmic order validates the political order. Certain kinds of crime, for example, parricide—offences against the cosmic order as well as the political order—tear things out of place. The order must be set right by what seems to the modern sensibility gratuitous cruelty and sadism. It seems so to us because the whole background notion of order has disappeared for us. Our modern identity is of free, self-defining subjects, says Taylor, whose understanding of their own essence or of their paradigm purposes is drawn from 'within', and no longer from a supposed cosmic order in which they are set. In addition, a new good has arisen. We have acquired since the eighteenth century a concern for the preservation of life, for the fulfilling of human need, and above all for the relief of suffering. This new humanitarianism is connected to the increased significance of "ordinary life," by which Taylor means the activities of producing and consuming, or marriage, love, and the family. Along with this comes a growing sense of the importance of *emotional* fulfillment in marriage—the whole modern sense that one's *feelings* are a key to the good life. The modern view, therefore, contains a critique of the older view as based on mystification, in the name of which human beings were sacrificed, and terrible suffering was inflicted.

Foucault rejects the Enlightenment-inspired reaction to the older order. For him, there are just two systems of power—classical and modern. He sees modern humanitarianism as reflection of a new system of domination. In *Surveiller et punir* and volume 1 of *Histoire de la sexualité*, Foucault portrays a constellation combining modern humanitarianism, the new social sciences, and the new disciplines that developed in armies, schools, and hospitals in the eighteenth century, all seen as the formation of new modes of domination. The new domination operates by universal surveillance. Computerized data banks are at the disposal of the authorities, whose key agencies are not clearly identifiable, and whose *modus operandi* is often partly secret. The new philosophy of punishment is not inspired by humanitarianism but by the need to control. The new forms of knowledge serve this end. People are measured, classed, examined in various ways, and thus made the better subject to a control that tends to normalization. Foucault focuses on the medical examination, and the various kinds of inspection that arose on its model. The modern notion of individuality is in fact one of the products of this new technology of control.

We have not seen this new technology because its relations of power are different from the older model of power in which some give commands and others obey. The modern forms are not concerned with law but with normalization—with bringing about a certain result, defined as health or good function. Law is infiltrated with this "normalization." Criminals are more and more treated as cases to be rehabilitated and

---

6. Charles Taylor, "Foucault on Freedom and Truth," in *Philosophy and the Human Sciences: Philosophical Papers*, vol. 2 (Cambridge: Cambridge University Press, 1985), 152–84.

brought back to normal. The new kind of power brings about a new kind of subject and new kinds of desire and behavior that belong to him. Power is no longer wielded by a subject but by a complex form of organization in which we all are involved. Foucault has written of the processes of subjection in order to indicate that the same processes that form a new kind of subject also form that individual as subjected to power. When being abnormal is defined as a social position that involves being denied goods that one seeks, then one will adopt certain courses of action that will allow one access to these goods. New subjects are created who adopt certain desires as their own as a result of being placed in a power structure over which they have no control. As Thomas Wartenberg has pointed out, this sort of interaction with a power structure causes the formation of subjects with skills and abilities and desires that fundamentally constitute character: "human beings come to be the sorts of beings that they are as a result of the presence of power relationships."[7]

Foucault doesn't accept the notion from Romantic and critical theory that there is some deeper self that social and political and economic structures can better express and refrain from dominating. There is no deep inner self, but only the relations of power. An example is how sexual desire came to play such a deep role in definition of the inner self. The centrality of sexuality is not some deep fact about us, says Foucault, but some construction that is intimately related to purposes of control. We seek to liberate our sexual selves, but become more deeply enmeshed in strategies of control. The very notion that we have a sexual nature such that a key element of the good life is sexual fulfillment is a stratagem of power. We now have to find our sexual nature, and set our lives to rights by it. Finding it requires the 'help' of experts, that we put ourselves in their care—the psychoanalysts and social workers. This makes us objects of control in all sorts of ways that we barely understand. We are not controlled on the old model through certain prohibitions laid on us. As Taylor remarks, "we may think we are gaining some freedom when we throw off sexual prohibitions, but in fact we are dominated by certain images of what it is to be a full, healthy, fulfilled sexual being."[8] The whole idea that we are sexually repressed and need liberation is itself a creation of the new kind of power/control. We see ourselves as escaping from the old kind of power but are in fact submitting to the new kind. Foucault reveals the contingency of our ideas of what is central to human nature by starting from a point of difference. As Mark Poster has remarked, Foucault addresses and analyzes a phenomenon that appears strange, discomforting, unfamiliar, and vaguely threatening to the modern sensibility.[9] In his *History of Sexuality*, Foucault begins with the Greek sexual practice of love between free,

---

7. Thomas Wartenberg, *The Forms of Power: From Domination to Transformation* (Philadelphia: Temple University Press, 1990), 160.

8. Taylor, "Foucault," 162.

9. Mark Poster, *Critical Theory and Poststructuralism: In Search of a Context* (Ithaca: Cornell University Press, 1990), 91.

adult males and boys. Love for boys was not merely a point of difference with regard to sexual desire. It also is different in that the sexual desire per se did not pose a problem for the Greeks ("Was it normal, healthy?" was not the question). Rather, the practice posed a problem for individual freedom and ethics. For most writers of the fourth to the second centuries B.C., Greek masters had no constraints on their sexual passion. Anyone could become a love object. To lead an ethical life a master need only actively decide on a course of action. He valued the active posture because it alone was commensurate with his freedom, and his freedom alone ensured the health of the polis. The moral issue for them was not the sexual desire for boys, but the propriety and possible harmful consequences of placing boys from the ruling class in a passive position during sexual relations with free adult males.[10]

Foucault combines his historical analysis of "points of difference" with a sophisticated view about the structure of power. Consider "micro" contexts in which power is internal to relationships such as doctor-patient. It is built into the very notion of that relation that one needs and the other knows. The former has an overwhelming interest in taking advice from the latter. Doctors can wreak their arbitrary and unrestrained wills on patients, but rarely do so. Both sides are constrained by a common understanding, the common activity. But within this relationship there is domination on the part of the doctor, a relation in which the dominated frequently cooperate in their subordination. The dominated often come to interiorize the norms of the common activity. These microcontexts must be understood in relation to macrocontexts, which involve institutions, classes such as the state and a ruling class. The grand strategies of the macrocontexts "form the context in which the micro-relations come to be, modify or reproduce themselves, while reciprocally these provide the soil and point of anchorage for the grand strategies.... There is an endless relation of reciprocal conditioning between global and micro-contexts."[11] Here Foucault rightly seems to reject the Marxist thesis that the global contexts are explanatorily basic.

Taylor finds much to admire in the subtlety of Foucault's analyses. However, he criticizes Foucault for the one-sidedness of his analyses:

> Foucault reads the rise of humanitarianism exclusively in terms of the new technologies of control. The development of the new ethics of life is given no independent significance. This seems to me quite absurdly one-sided.... The new forms of discipline have not only served to feed a system of control. They have also taken the form of genuine self-disciplines which have made possible new kinds of collective action characterized by more egalitarian forms of participation ... free participatory institutions require some commonly accepted self-disciplines.... There is a tremendous difference between societies which

---

10. Michel Foucault, *The History of Sexuality: The Use of Pleasure* (New York: Vintage, 1990), 245.
11. Taylor, "Foucault," 168.

find their cohesion through such common disciplines grounded on a public identity, and which thus permit of and call for the participatory action of equals, on the one hand, and the multiplicity of kinds of society which require chains of command based on unquestionable authority on the other.[12]

Taylor also criticizes Foucault's concept of power without a subject. He believes that aside from the particular conscious purposes that agents pursue in their given context, there is a discernible strategic logic of the context itself, but this cannot be attributed to anyone as his plan, as his conscious purpose. There are contexts in which purposefulness without a purpose makes sense. First, there is purposefulness to people's actions where their motivation and goals are unacknowledged, or unable to be acknowledged. For example, if some theorists are right, modern political terrorism is projected self-hatred and the response to a sense of emptiness. Second, there are unintended but systematic consequences such as 'invisible hand' theories—situations so constituted that individual decisions are bound to concatenate in a certain systematic way. There is Adam Smith's benign invisible hand where individual actors moved by self-interest benefit the social whole, and Marx's malign hand, where numerous individual decisions by capitalists and workers result in the impoverishment and misery of workers. Third, there are unintended consequences as the results of collective action and not just the combination of individual actions, for example, the Leninist model of mass mobilization results ineluctably but unintentionally in destroying the bases of devolved power and restricting participation.

Taylor's main point is that purposefulness without a purpose requires a certain kind of explanation to be intelligible. Undesigned systematicity has to be related to the purposeful action of agents in a way that we can understand. Foucault cannot supply such an explanation because he gives no priority of explanation in terms of the interest of some dominant class. Thus the first and third possibilities are ruled out. This leaves the second, which in principle is available to Foucault, but he does not begin to give an explanation along such lines. There are obviously lots of aspects of social life where the reciprocal play of micropractice and global structures each having largely unintended consequences for the other. The problem arises only when one combines this with the very strong claims to systematicity—that there are pervasive *strategies* afoot which condition the battle in each microcontext, that 'power' can retreat or reorganize its forces. This leaves us, Taylor points out, with a strange Schopenhauerian will, ungrounded in human action.[13]

There is something quite right about Foucault's theory of the power of social arrangements. Many aspects of the self we have come to regard as "natural" are in fact deeply cultural constructions of the person. Yet something has gone wrong in Foucault's

12. Taylor, "Foucault," 165.
13. Taylor, "Foucault," 172.

equation of the clearly dominating disciplines he finds in the clinics, hospitals, and prisons of the late nineteenth and twentieth centuries with all forms of the social constitution of the self. All attempts to constitute the self, for Foucault, are attempts to gain power over the self. This not only seems false but also diminishes and even trivializes the moral wrongness of the dominating strategies Foucault so rightly identifies.

On one interpretation, Foucault is committed to his conclusions because of his commitment to the Nietzschean view that all knowledge is valuation and that all valuation is a means of gaining power over others. According to Nietzsche, there is no such thing as truth that is independent of some perspective on reality. The particular perspective that has gained ascendancy determines the truth at any given time. Moral valuations are means that a social group uses to gain power over another group. Their use, however, is obscured by their presentation as objective truths. The way in which power is gained by use of valuations is different than gaining power through sheer force. In fact, Nietzsche's *Genealogy of Morals* is the story of the weak (in terms of those who are able to exercise force) gaining power over the strong by persuading them that the forms of behavior characteristic of their way of life were evil. As Thomas Wartenberg explains,

> It is simply not apparent to the strong that, under the influence of the priests, power has been exercised upon them. Because the power of the priests masquerades as a form of truth, the strong are unable to detect the presence of a "regime of power" as constituting their own "knowledge", their own "truth".[14]

If we wish to avoid this Nietzschean equation of knowledge with power and valuation with attempts to gain power, we must distinguish between relations of power over the self and relations of constitution of the self. We must distinguish the self that is made by others and by culture and the self that is controlled and dominated by others and by social structure. Domination must, as Taylor has pointed out, be related to purposeful action of agents in an intelligible way. To attribute human agency to power itself as Foucault does is mystifying. On the positive side of the Foucauldian ledger, however, we must allow that domination of one group by another may occur through the medium of thought, discourse, and knowledge, and that such domination may constitute human beings in a manner that allows them to occupy certain social positions in society. Finally, we must focus on domination rather than simply one agent's having power over another at a given time.

Wartenberg has usefully suggested that domination must be systematic and at the expense of the dominated.[15] Given such a concept of domination, we clearly see that not all constitutions of the self by social structure are instances of domination. Taylor has given us an illuminating critique of Foucault, as well as doing us the service of

14. Wartenberg, *Forms of Power*, 134.
15. Wartenberg, *Forms of Power*, 119.

clarifying Foucault's claims. However, the fact that not all constitutions of the self by social structure are instances of domination should not necessarily comfort us. Even if there is no one or no thing that is systematically, say, normalizing the contemporary self, that does not mean that whatever ways we are shaped are good. Nor does it mean that *we* are in control, even if no one else or no thing is controlling us. Furthermore, it is not the most generous interpretation of Foucault to have him positing no distance whatsoever between the truth and any particular dominating perspective. It seems difficult to make sense of his own project if this were to be the case for him. As I suggested in section 3.10, we should take Foucault as warning us against any established view of the truth as being dangerous, if not necessarily bad. This will not be taking him at his most dramatic moments, but perhaps at his most illuminating ones.

Therefore, showing that morality need not become embedded in human identities through domination does not show that morality is something to be accepted by us, nor does it show that our truth is really truth or good for us. In section 3.12, I briefly introduced the Freudian challenge to confidence in our values as expressed by Richard Wollheim. Morality may answer to the social need to tame the innate drives dangerous to civilization, but it may not answer to the individual's needs. To meet this challenge, Wollheim suggested, we must identify true needs of the individual that morality satisfies, and not insignificant ones at that. Interestingly, a similar problem arises for Xunzi.

8.4 Xunzi and the Problem of Morality's Relation to Human Nature

I introduced Xunzi in section 2.3 as one of the first great theorists of morality as social invention.[16] For him, morality is a system of rules devised by human beings to address problems created by their own nature. That nature includes the motive for gain, a self-seeking tendency to satisfy desires of the ear and eye and liking of sound and beauty. These desires and likings are responses to feelings such as pleasure, joy, anger, and sorrow, and they have no natural limit. This makes for conflict with others when combined with scarcity of resources. Realizing this, the sage-kings invented ritual and moral principles in order to apportion things, to nurture the desires of men, and to supply the means for their satisfaction.[17]

Many have observed that this story of morality anticipates Hobbes's story of why human beings need to escape from the state of nature. Xunzi's story differs from Hobbes's, however, in saying that the sage-kings saw the need not only to restrain

---

16. This section is based on my "Xunzi on Moral Motivation," in *Chinese Language, Thought, and Culture: Nivison and his Critics*, ed. Philip J. Ivanhoe (Chicago: Open Court, 1996), 202–23.

17. *Xunzi*, translated by John Knoblock (Changsha, Hunan: Hunan's People's, 1999), bk. 19.1, vol. 2, p. 601.

self-seeking behavior but also to transform human character through morality.[18] As David Nivison has observed, Xunzi held that enlightened self-interest requires not merely the belief that the Way is best for everyone concerned but also the cultivation of love for the Way.[19]

By contrast, Hobbes never expected the self-interested motivation of human beings to change in the transition from the state of nature to civil society.[20] His egoistic psychology allows the internalization of no standards other than that of direct concern with individual preservation and contentment. This psychology creates a problem for his theory that only the state can solve. The rules that curb the pursuit of desire are mutually beneficial to all, but individuals can benefit even more if they can cheat on them while others generally comply. Since everyone knows this fact, no one will have confidence that others will comply, and therefore no one will have a self-interested reason to comply. The solution to this problem is the state as the enforcer of the rules. It must create a risk of punishment that makes it irrational for any individual to try to cheat. Only with the state does it become perfectly rational for the egoist to obey the rules.

By comparison, Xunzi recognized force as a necessary means, but not the primary means: "One who knows the way of true strength does not rely on military strength."[21] While he may have been skeptical of most people's willingness and ability to become truly moral, he saw the need for a ruling elite to transform themselves so that they come to love and delight in virtue and morality. This elite, with supreme benevolence, righteousness, and authority, would attract the people and inspire them with respect. In this, Xunzi seems to affirm the Confucian belief in the ability of a ruler with the virtue (*de*, perhaps best conceived as a moral power and charisma) to win the hearts and minds of the people.

Hobbes's solution to the egoism of human beings has some serious disadvantages. As David Gauthier has observed, his use of the state to make it irrational for individuals to cheat is a political solution to the problem, not a moral one.[22] A morality that gives one reason to obey only by virtue of the threat of punishment is not a genuine morality. A moral reason to obey should be one that is more internal to the motivations of individuals. This is not to deny that compulsion may have some role to play. Ideally, we need enough enforcement of the moral rules so that we would not be

---

18. This comparative point has been made by Bryan Van Norden, "Mengzi and Xunzi: Two Views of Human Agency," *International Philosophical Quarterly* 32 (1992): 178.

19. David Nivison, review of *The World of Thought in Ancient China*, by Benjamin Schwartz, *Philosophy East and West* 38 (1988): 416.

20. He did believe, however, that our self-interest can become more expansive in civil society. Part of his account in *Leviathan* of the growth of civility and civilization hinges on an explanation of how we can come to appreciate the arts and sciences as answering to an expanded sense of self-interest.

21. "Regulations of a King," in *Xunzi*, trans. Knoblock, bk. 9, vol. 1, p. 223.

22. David Gauthier, *Morals by Agreement* (Oxford: Clarendon Press, 1986), 162–3.

fools to obey the rules. We would be fools if we obeyed while others did not. Xunzi assigns enforcement the role of creating enough security so that we feel safe enough to embark on the project of transforming our characters. But also crucial to that security is the character of the ruling elite. It is because they have transformed their characters that they can be trusted. Their moral influence, and not just their capacity to punish, affects the characters of others so that a general climate of security is created.

Xunzi, then, has in this respect offered a better solution to the problem of the self-interested behavior of human beings. His solution is a moral solution because it envisions an internal change in human beings that makes a reliance on force unnecessary. Moreover, in locating the greatest transformation in a ruling elite, Xunzi offers a solution to another problem Hobbes has. It has often been pointed out that Hobbes did not adequately address the problem of corruption of the state. His solution to the state of nature requires the assumption that the state will be an impartial enforcer of the rules. Given that human beings run the state, and that they have the same egoistic nature as their subjects, Hobbes seems not entitled to this assumption. By contrast, Xunzi avoids this problem by requiring a moral transformation of those who run the state. Therefore Hobbes's solution to the dangerous nature of human beings is unstable without an envisioned change in their motivations.

So both Hobbes and Xunzi begin with similar premises about human nature and its propensities to seek the satisfaction of desires that if unchecked would lead to chaos. But they end with very different visions of what people can become. For Hobbes, self-interested human beings accepted the authority and power of the state on the basis of their long-term interests. While the same is true for Xunzi, he also holds that one's long-term interests dictate a radical transformation in one's character. As we have seen, his vision can claim certain advantages over Hobbes's. But Xunzi's vision has its own problems in explaining how moral transformation is effected. The question is how one becomes a person who loves morality when one starts with a repertoire of "very unlovely" emotions that cause a man to neglect his parents once he acquires a wife and children, or to neglect his friends once he has satisfied his cravings and desires, or to cease to serve a sovereign with a loyal heart once he has attained high position and a good stipend.[23]

David Nivison has given another way to put the problem for Xunzi. "How could the sage-kings have created morality unless morality were already a part of their nature?"[24] Xunzi's answer seems to be that through their "superior creative intelligence," the sage-kings moralized themselves.[25] But just *how* did they use that intelligence to transform themselves? The question seems difficult to answer precisely because Xunzi shares with

23. *Xunzi*, trans. Knoblock, bk. 23.16, vol. 2, p. 769.
24. David Nivison, "Hsün Tzu and Chuang Tzu," in *Chinese Texts and Philosophical Contexts: Essays dedicated to Angus C. Graham*, ed. Henry Rosemont (La Salle, Ill.: Open Court, 1991), 129–42.
25. Nivison, "Hsün Tzu and Chuang Tzu," 142.

Hobbes a pessimistic (from the moral viewpoint) conception of human nature. How did they, with their "unlovely emotions" and self-regarding desires, turn themselves into beings who loved and delighted in morality? To accept rites and morality as not only necessary to self-interest but as part of the natural order is not yet to love and delight in them. It is not yet to make oneself willing to die for them, as Xunzi thinks the sage-kings were.[26]

Now Xunzi clearly seems to have believed in the power of the mind to override emotion and desire, to act contrary to their dictates.[27] However, he is clear in holding that the ultimate motive force of the mind's ability to override desire and emotion is ultimately derived from desire. He believes that we can override our more immediate desires in favor of our long-term interests:

> Who understands that risking death in carrying out a commission is how an officer cares for his life? Who understands that producing and supplying goods are how to nurture resources? Who knows that reverence and courtesy are how to nurture his security? Who knows that acting in accordance with ritual and moral principles and observing good form and reason are how to nurture his emotions?[28]

For Xunzi, then, any path to self-transformation must start from the preexisting impulses and emotions of human beings. We still have the problem of explaining how calculation of one's self-interest can lead to a transformation of one's selfish desires. How does one become a person who sacrifices himself for morality when the raw material for such a transformation is a self-interested nature? We can see the self-interested grounds for transforming our characters, but what remains unclear is how the transformation takes place, given the nature of what we have to start with. Of course, Xunzi is not trying to convince his audience to undertake the transformation from self-interest to morality. The audience, after all, has already been transformed to at least some extent. His account is a retrospective explanation of how we came to be the way we are. But the question is how to fill in the explanation.

Xunzi may have been grappling with this problem in the chapter entitled "Human Nature Is Evil." There he directly opposes Mencius in denying that goodness is part of the innate endowment of human beings. He turns to the question of the origin of goodness if it is not in human nature already. The answer he gives is quite curious:

26. Nivison identifies precisely this problem in a later essay, "Xunzi on Human Nature," in his *The Ways of Confucianism: Investigations in Chinese Philosophy*, ed. Bryan Van Norden (Chicago: Open Court, 1996), 203–13.

27. For an interesting study of this theme, see Bryan Van Norden, "Mengzi and Xunzi: Two Views of Human Agency," 161–84.

28. *Xunzi*, trans. Knoblock, bk. 19.3, vol. 2, p. 605.

As a general rule, the fact that men desire to do good is the product of the fact that their nature is evil. Those with very little think longingly about having much, the ugly about being beautiful, those in cramped quarters about spacious surroundings, the poor about wealth, the base about eminence—indeed whatever a man lacks within himself he is sure to desire from without. Thus those who are already rich do not wish for valuables nor do the eminent wish for high position, for indeed whatever a person has within he does not seek without. If we consider the implications of these facts, it is plain that man's desire to good is the product of the fact that his nature is evil.[29]

What could Xunzi mean by these odd claims? This passage occurs after the question is raised about the origin of goodness, and in particular, the question of how human beings can become good if they do not already have some goodness in them. Xunzi is attempting to show how human beings could transform themselves into moral beings when their original nature is to seek the immoral. The basis of transition is precisely this seeking after what they lack. The point of the passage is to show, *contra* those who think that goodness must come from goodness, that goodness can come from evil. And this would be an answer to the question of transformation I have been raising.

What is still very unclear is how the evil in human nature gives rise to a desire to do good. One might interpret Xunzi as attributing to human nature moral desires to be good, as some eminent scholars have.[30] On this interpretation, Xunzi thinks that human nature is bad, not because it lacks any good impulses, but because it is an anarchic mix of selfish and moral desires. Such an interpretation, however, does not square with Xunzi's naturalistic account of morality. If morality is born of the need to create a social order that will benefit all, then it seems to make no sense to do as Mencius does and posit an original desire to do good or a sense of duty in human nature. Goodness and right are determined by the rules created by the sages. They cannot be prior to the sages in the sense required by their having innate desires for these things. This must be true even if, as Nivison emphasizes, it was inevitable that the sages create such rules.

An alternative interpretation is that any desire to do good is not original to human nature for Xunzi but rather derived from calculation on what is in our self-interest. We come to have these things when we see in terms of our own long-term self-interest that we should have a certain character that we now lack.[31] This certainly would fit with Xunzi's story of why morality is necessary, and it is consistent with Xunzi's naturalistic account of morality. But if we are to interpret the desire to do good as derived from a desire to do what is in one's long-term interests, we still have no

29. *Xunzi,* trans. Knoblock, bk. 23.8, vol. 2, p. 753.

30. See, for instance, A. C. Graham, *Disputers of the Tao: Philosophical Argumentation in Ancient China* (La Salle, Ill.: Open Court, 1989), 248.

31. For this interpretation, see Fung Yu-Lan, *A History of Chinese Philosophy,* trans. Derk Bodde (Princeton: Princeton University Press, 1952), 1:294.

explanation of how self-interest turns into love of and delight in morality. How does one start with the attitude that "one has no alternative but to desire" morality and create within oneself a genuine love for and a delight in it?

It may well be that Xunzi was confused or ambivalent abut the status of the desire. And if this is true, there will be no determinate answers from Xunzi about the nature of moral transformation. What we can do, however, is to construct an explanation of moral transformation that is compatible with his theory. I will consider two possible explanations.

One explanation is suggested by J. S. Mill's answer to the question of why moral virtue came to be valued for its own sake. The question is a problem for Mill because he thinks people desire only various kinds of pleasure and the absence of pain. At first glance, it seems that he could only allow virtue to be a means to pleasure and the absence of pain, just as it may seem that Xunzi could only allow moral virtue to be a means to the optimal long-term satisfaction of desire. But Mill, like Xunzi, does not want this result. Mill's answer is an analogy: just as money is originally only a means to pleasure, so virtue is originally only a means; but the constant association of money with pleasure, and virtue with pleasure, results in money and virtue being in themselves sources of pleasure. In other words, we are *conditioned* to take pleasure in virtue.[32]

In order for this idea to help Xunzi, however, there must be explanation of how the sage-kings could have created in the first place the connection between virtue and pleasure. On Xunzi's account, morality can be a means to satisfying desire over the long term only when the sage-kings have internalized it and gained the following of the people. Only then will they be able to create the secure social order that benefits all, including themselves. But if that is the story, then the sage-kings cannot *first* condition themselves by associating pleasure with virtue. The constant connection between pleasure and virtue only comes after they have succeeded in transforming themselves and creating a social order that *makes* virtue pleasurable. The problem is a general one. Theories that explain the presence of genuine moral virtue on the basis of transformation of a recalcitrant human nature have difficulty explaining how the conditions favorable to such a transformation are ever set in place. The temptation is to illicitly presuppose the presence of those conditions.

To fit with Xunzi's story of the origin of morality, there must be attributed to human nature motivational tendencies that satisfy three requirements: they must be consistent

---

32. John Stuart Mill, *Utilitarianism*, chap. 4, in *Utilitarianism, On Liberty, Essay on Bentham* (New York: World, 1962), 290–1. There is a basis in Mill for a less reductive explanation of the pleasures of virtue, even though this is not the explanation he gives in utilitarianism. Mill does not have an egoistic psychology, so he can acknowledge the existence of sympathetic emotions that are not based on any calculations of self-interest. The pleasures of virtue may on this view be derived from the satisfaction of our concerns for others. Later, I shall suggest a similar move for Xunzi.

with Xunzi's claim that human nature is evil; they must not have moral content; and they must provide some motivational efficacy to beliefs about duty when duty is invented/discovered. In fact, I claim that we find such capabilities in those chapters where Xunzi describes the transforming effect of ritual and music. Consider the chapter on rites and in particular the discussion of the rationale for the three-year mourning period for the death of a parent. Why this particular period? Xunzi explains that this is the time when the pain of grief is most intense. But why is grief the emotion felt upon the death of a parent? Xunzi explains that all creatures who possess awareness love their own kind, and "since no creature with blood and breath has more awareness than man, the feeling of a man for his parents is not exhausted even till death."[33] On the subject of sacrificial rites to the dead, Xunzi says that "sacrifice originates in the emotions stirred by remembrance and recollection of the dead and by thinking of and longing for the departed." Rites are needed to give expression to these emotions, which otherwise will be "frustrated and unexpressed." Rites "express the highest loyalty, faithfulness, love, and reverence."[34]

Xunzi here *presupposes* human emotions that are quite different from the ones he cites in arguing for the evilness of human nature. These emotions constitute the raw material in human nature that is amenable to being shaped toward a love of virtue and a delight in ritual. The Confucian virtue of filial piety strengthens, refines, and directs the primitive impulse of love of one's parents and the primitive impulse to reciprocate for the greatest of benefits—one's life and nurturance. The three-year mourning period and sacrificial rites strengthen, refine, and direct the natural feelings of grief and remembrance. It now becomes clear how Xunzi could claim with plausibility that human beings can come to love morality—because it allows full expression of natural and deep human emotion.

So far I have addressed the requirement that capabilities attributed to human nature provide beliefs about right and wrong and some motivational efficacy once these beliefs are acquired. What about the requirement that the capabilities have no original moral content? The natural feelings that rites work upon are not yet moral in content. They are primitive responses not yet refined and regulated by moral thoughts of right and wrong. One mourns for a parent simply, with no thought of its rightness or of the forms it should take. Xunzi now has a picture of human nature that allows him to explain the transformation from self-interest to a love and delight in morality. On this view, we love it because it expresses, channels, and strengthens some of our natural human feelings.

And it is quite plausible that we do have some natural feelings that are congenial to morality even if they aren't moral feelings. For example, we observed in chapter 1 that the feeling of a debt of gratitude for a kindness or a gift is something we all know, and that in Chinese society that feeling is greatly magnified. Such a feeling, as an innate

33. *Xunzi*, trans. Knoblock, bk. 19.18, vol. 2, p. 637.
34. *Xunzi*, trans. Knoblock, bk. 19.20, vol. 2, p. 645.

impulse, need not be interpreted as a moral feeling, but simply a strong impulse to return good for good. It becomes a moral feeling after morality is devised. As suggested in the previous chapter, moral thoughts come to govern and even be embedded in the intentionality of the feeling (feeling that it is one's duty to return good for good). Further, there is good reason to think that morality would require reciprocity as well as defining its acceptable forms. As Xunzi argued, human beings cannot get along without helping each other. And it seems plausible, as observed in section 2.8, that helping behavior would be extinguished if it were systematically unreciprocated.

It also is relevant to note another set of feelings and desires to which morality may answer: those having to do with fear of death and the desire for immortality. If they are innate, they certainly seem to spring from something very basic to the human condition. Confucianism does not have anything interesting to say about an afterlife. Confucius himself seemed agnostic about the question. Then how does the Confucian ethic address the fear of death and desire for immortality? Here is a passage from the Zuo Xhuan (*Tso Chuan*) (Zuo's Commentary on the *Spring and Autumn Annals*, Duke Jiang, twenty-fourth year): "I have heard that the best course is to establish virtue, the next best is to establish achievement, and still the next best is to establish words. When these are not abandoned with time, it may be called immortality."[35]

What about the requirement that capabilities attributed to human nature be consistent with Xunzi's claim that human nature is evil? Even if the feelings of love of parents, grief and remembrance when they die, and the desire for immortality are not yet moral feelings, how could human nature be evil if it contains them? How could it be evil if it contains feelings that are congenial to morality? The answer, I think, lies in construing his claim that human nature is evil to be more sophisticated. Human nature is not evil because it contains nothing but anarchic desire and feeling. It is evil because the most self-concerned desires and feelings are the ones that *dominate* in conditions of insecurity and lack of order. Even the better ones (judgments of better and worse are made, of course, from the retrospective of already having had morality inculcated in us) lead to bad results when unguided and undisciplined by moral thoughts. So interpreted, I find Xunzi's claim about human nature has a great deal of plausibility to it. It also should be noted that love, grief, and the desire for immortality may be expressed in a wide range of ways, only some of which are compatible with morality. These feelings must be moralized in order for them to result in moral behavior.

To conclude this discussion of Xunzi, let me make a case for the idea that I have found a plausible way not only for Xunzi to explain the path to moral transformation but also for me to make the claim that this path suggests an answer to the Freudian challenge to morality. Recall that an answer to that challenge would have to show that there are some needs, some desires, other than the avoidance of fear, and not shallow

35. I use the translation by Wing-tsit Chan, *A Sourcebook of Chinese Philosophy* (Princeton: Princeton University Press, 1963), 13.

ones, that the establishment of the superego satisfies. The basis for an answer that Richard Wollheim derives from Freudian and neo-Freudian theories is a postulated need to control aggression toward a loved person. Wollheim's conclusion parallels the conclusion we have reached about Xunzi. Human nature is for him still evil in a very substantial sense. But it has elements that make it possible for human beings to be fulfilled by morality. And by "fulfilled," I do not mean simply have one's narrow self-interest satisfied. Morality serves to express certain latent emotions such as love and the desire to reciprocate for benefits received. Further, righteousness, ritual, and music not only allow expression of these emotions but channel and shape them so that originally narrow self-interest becomes much broader and more firmly connected to the interests of others. Morality does not eliminate nonmoral sensual desires but limits them and channels their satisfaction in ways that are more compatible with moralized emotions and desires. Morality can provide coherence to our characters that was not there before.

I have spent some time explaining Xunzi's problem of explaining the human capability for moral motivations and behavior because I think he starts with a plausible naturalistic picture of the origin of morality—more plausible than Hobbes's. Perhaps the point where I have brought him in solving the explanatory problem is closer to Hume's conception, but Xunzi's problem and its solution is illuminating precisely because Xunzi starts out being so much more pessimistic about human nature and its hospitality to morality than Hume ever is. If I am right, the solution teaches us that the pessimism must be tempered if the explanatory problem is to be solved. Note a certain parallel between this progression of thought in Xunzi and the one that has appeared in evolutionary theory about human motivation. At first, the individual's drives to self-preservation and reproduction seemed to be the only drives that could emerge from the mechanism of natural selection. The problem is that where the theory seemed to leave us was not where human beings, and the complexity of their motivations, are, and so theorists turned back to the theory to see if it had more resources for explaining that apparent complexity. It now looks as if it does, and what now emerges from the theory is a profound ambivalence in human beings between various forms of narrow self-interest, altruism toward family and strangers, tendencies to reciprocate benefit and to punish noncooperation. This seems to me a much better fit between the place where theory leaves us and the place we seem to be.

So far, we have a case for saying that adequate moralities answer to and satisfy some central natural human propensities, and that they come to penetrate and deeply shape these propensities. This much amounts to a partial support for whatever confidence we have in our moral commitments. However, to assert that some forms of flourishing involve a moral life, don't we have to show not only that a moral life answers to natural propensities but also that these propensities answer to "true" needs, as Wollheim characterizes them? Moreover, it may be objected that talk of "needs" is viciously circular in the context of trying to show that morality does answer to needs. In section 4.2, after all, I suggested that the concept of need was intimately related to the concept of flourishing. In fact, need may ultimately require cashing out in terms of what is required for flourishing. But if the concept of flourishing is a normative one, and if a component of that normativity is a moralized view of what constitutes flourishing, we have traveled in a vicious circle. We are trying to show that morality satisfies morality!

8.5 NEEDS AND FLOURISHING

To satisfactorily address this objection, I need to discuss more closely the concept of need. David Wiggins distinguishes two basic senses of a 'need'. One sense is instrumental, where the claim about what someone needs is relative to some purpose and there are no limits of what the purpose may be. The second is the absolute or categorical sense of the word, where what is needed is required by the avoidance of harm to human beings. Wiggins further observes that our judgments of harm are indexed to the idea of well-being or flourishing. This introduces a further relativization to need: "What constitutes suffering or wretchedness or harm is an essentially contestable matter, and is to some extent relative to a culture, even to some extent relative to people's conceptions of suffering, wretchedness and harm." Wiggins maintains, however, that despite the contestability of many needs claims, other of these claims are not seriously contestable and are more or less decidable.[36] Human beings need to maintain a minimal level of physical integrity and functioning, which seem a prerequisite to any other level of flourishing. As I argued in section 4.7, they need knowledge of social norms, a reasonable balance between different aspects of their identities, and a minimal level of self-respect or self-esteem.

Part of the point of my excursion into Xunzi's problem, moreover, was precisely to identify the ways in which morality could be said to answer to rather powerful needs and feelings. By "powerful," I mean that they often motivate behavior, even in the face of strong counter-motivations, as suggested in section 4.4. They further manifest motivational power across a wide variety of cultures. Their frustration ramifies through individuals' lives and adversely affects their ability to achieve other highly valued ends. Further, a need may not be something that is desired in any ordinary sense (e.g., may not be acknowledged by its possessor) though it is rooted in human nature and has motivational force because of that nature.

I mean what Garrett Thomson identifies as interests (first discussed in sec. 2.6), as opposed to desires in the ordinary sense. Interests underlie desires and constitute the motivational force of desires. Desire can shift from object to object, but something associated with it—Thomson calls it motivational forces—remains constant and explains how the shifts are connected to each other. What seems to motivate a desire is not necessarily congruent with the object of desire. Recall Thomson's example of the man who works hard in order to impress his friends even though he shuns close ties because he fears rejection. We might say that what he really wants is not so much

---

36. David Wiggins, "Claims of Need," in *Needs, Values, Truth: Essays in the Philosophy of Value*, 3rd ed. (Oxford: Oxford University Press, 1998), 11–2.

praise but stable affection, that he has an interest or a want for affection. The interest motivates the desire. Viable conceptions of flourishing center on interests that are deeply rooted in human nature such that they can be identified as what human beings really want, that have powerful motivational force in overriding other interests, and whose satisfaction or frustration widely ramifies throughout a person's character and life. These might be called needs, and "true" ones at that.

As a further response to the objection, the reader is reminded of the more modest aim being pursued here: to show that some forms of flourishing are indeed partly constituted by promoting the flourishing of others. The aim is not to show that all forms of flourishing are so constituted. If there are any viable conceptions of flourishing, all I am assuming is that among such conceptions there will be some that include the satisfaction of the aforementioned needs.

Another possible objection is that even if morality does meet some deep needs, it may still frustrate other needs that may be equally or more important than the ones it meets. We are returning to the territory discussed in sections 6.4 and 6.5, where I argued that the realm of the personal does not have any fixed, universal degree of conflict with that part of morality that comprises impersonal values. Again recall the more modest aim of showing that some forms of flourishing are partly constituted by promoting the flourishing of others. What would lives that fulfilled such forms look like? Are some of the more mundane personal satisfactions simply unimportant to the agents? Or is it, as I suggested in chapter 6, more a matter of mediating a commitment to moral values through a commitment to personal values?

8.6 A FORTUNATE LIFE

In discussing this question, I want to look at a particular life and therefore simultaneously act on Lear's suggestion that we look at some actual cases of flourishing to show some forms of it are compatible with a moral life. Consider John Berger's study of a country doctor, John Sassall, who has chosen to work in a remote and impoverished English community. In describing the intimate doctor-patient relationship that Sassal has with members of the community, Berger describes the patient's psychological need for "recognition." As soon as we are ill we fear that our illness is unique, observes Berger. We feel that the illness, a potential threat to our very being, is unique, and are relieved when the doctor gives it a name, thus separating it from us and depersonalizing it. Sassall, in his resolve to treat his patient as a total personality, must also address the role of unhappiness, emotional or mental disturbance, in illness. Here too, what is wrong is tied to a sense of uniqueness: "All frustration magnifies its own dissimilarity and so nourishes itself."[37] Sassall's task, then, includes recognition of the patient as a

37. John Berger, *A Fortunate Man,* with photographs by Jean Mohr (New York: Pantheon Books, 1967), 74.

person: "If the man can begin to feel recognized—and such recognition may well include aspects of his character which he has not yet recognized himself—the hopeless nature of his unhappiness will have been changed."[38] Such recognition is achieved by the doctor presenting himself as a comparable man, and that demands from the doctor a "true imaginative effort and precise self-knowledge."

> it is the doctor's acceptance of what the patient tells him and the accuracy of his appreciation as he suggests how different parts of his life may fit together, it is this which then persuades the patient that he and the doctor and other men are comparable because whatever he says of himself or his fears or his fantasies seems to be at least as familiar to the doctor as to him. He is no longer an exception. He can be recognized. And this is the prerequisite for cure or adaptation.[39]

Sassall is to be recognized as a good doctor, suggests Berger, not by his cures, but because he meets a deep but unformulated expectation of the sick for a sense of fraternity. What is interesting for our purposes here is Berger's explanation of why Sassall needs to work in this way: "He cures others to cure himself." When Sassall was younger, he strove to realize a sense of mastery through the skill with which he dealt with emergencies. His image of the doctor, back then, was above all of a person in command and composed, whereas everybody else was fussing and agitated. He remained the central character in his own drama of mastery. Now the patient is the central character. He tries to recognize each patient and tries to set an example wherein the patient can recognize her or himself. Berger concludes: "His sense of mastery is fed by the ideal of striving towards the *universal*."[40] The underlying motive for Sassall's attempt to proliferate his self into many selves is a passion for knowledge. He wants to experience all that is possible, and the patient is his material, but for that reason, the patient, in his totality, is sacred. When patients are describing their conditions or worries to Sassall, he says again and again, "I know," "I know." Yet, observes Berger, it is what he says while he is waiting to know more. He already knows what it is like to be this patient in a certain condition, but he does not yet know the full explanation of that condition, or the extent of his own power.

Sassall furthermore serves the community as a whole in such a way that it can recognize itself as a community. Any general culture, writes Berger, acts as a mirror that enables individuals to recognize themselves—or at least to recognize those parts of their selves that are socially permissible. The culturally deprived have far fewer ways of recognizing themselves. Their emotional and introspective experience especially must in great part go unnamed for them. Sassall "belongs" to the community, yet he is

38. Berger, *Fortunate Man*, 75.
39. Berger, *Fortunate Man*, 76.
40. Berger, *Fortunate Man*, 77.

privileged in the sense of possessing the power to comprehend and realize for the community what it feels and incoherently knows. He is the "objective witness" to their lives, the clerk of the community's records.

I have summarized Berger's study of Sassall and his community at some length because it reveals the ways in which "promoting the flourishing" of others may be intimately tied to one form of a flourishing life. Notice how the ways in which his life is flourishing are so different from the standard picture of the moral saint or exemplar: he is in no way acting simply from a desire to aid others. Berger says that Sassall cures others to cure himself, but this in no way implies that he views others as mere means. Each person in his or her totality is sacred as an exemplar of what is possible in the human condition.

Susan Wolf, in her influential study "Moral Saints," describes what she sees to be a radical conflict between the moral point of view and the standpoint of individual perfection.[41] The moral point of view bids us to strive for moral perfection, where this requires that one's life be dominated by a commitment to improving the welfare of others or of society as a whole. But this means, Wolf argues, that persons whose lives are dominated by such a commitment, moral saints, could never be deeply interested in intellectual inquiry, sports, art, or the other activities that enrich human life. After all, if one were to pursue these activities wholeheartedly and for their own sakes, one could not be fully responsive to the needs of others. In short, concludes Wolf, the ideal of moral perfection is incompatible with an ideal of individual perfection, according to which we strive for good, interesting, and worthwhile lives.

In Wolf's terms, Sassall is indeed a fortunate man. Sassall has combined a life of service with a life that addresses his thirst for all possible experience. His life is not at all a self-denying one, yet it is a morally admirable one, perhaps even a noble life. But he just contingently has personally fulfilling interests that align with a moral project. On Wolf's argument, the personal interests he has are not endorsed by moral imperatives unless they happen to serve as means to a moral project, and the problem is that the person who has them can never regard them as good to have only if they serve a moral project. The strength of her argument, however, rests on the assumption that morality is to be identified with the impersonal perspective, and much of the thrust of this book is that moralities are diverse and pluralistic in the kinds of values they contain. In fact, while the impersonal perspective is an extremely important strain in modern Western moralities, it is a mistake to identify it as *the* defining strain. The fact that it is not the single defining strain accounts for the stress and ambivalence we feel about conflicts between special duties associated with the personal perspective and duties owed to all arising from the impersonal perspective. The conflict she sees as lying *between* morality and another perspective that values personal excellence and

41. Susan Wolf, "Moral Saints," *Journal of Philosophy* 79 (1979): 419–39.

fulfillment is a conflict that in this book lies *within* morality. This is not to deny that there will be conflicts between what individuals need to do based on their personal projects and what they need to do as required by morality. Such conflicts can exist, however, because moralities, as argued in sections 2.8 and 2.9, typically aim to produce a balance between self-interest and other-interest that is necessary for producing a stable form of social cooperation. Now it is true that an acceptable balance in moral terms is not necessarily acceptable from the standpoint of what is fully required by an individual's personal projects. But if moralities cannot eliminate such conflicts with extramoral perspectives, they can and must from the standpoint of one of their primary functions attempt to configure a balance between personal and impersonal imperatives. The *kind* of stark conflict Wolf envisions, where the fulfillment of personal interests can only be countenanced as means to the fulfillment of impersonal moral projects, rests on an unduly restricted picture of morality's reach and on a detachment of morality from its place and function in a naturalized conception of human life.

The proper conclusion is that the ideal of moral sainthood as Wolf defines it is insipid and psychologically unrealistic, as Wolf thinks it is, but this ideal cannot be associated with morality per se. It can be associated with a powerful ideal of purity of motive that has been very influential in Western moral traditions since Christianity, but that ideal has never, even with Western moral traditions, existed as the single dominant strain. As we saw in sections 6.5 and 6.6, the ideal of strong equality is not psychologically unrealistic per se, but only appears so when we do not take into account the ways in which a moral commitment to impersonal values can be mediated by a commitment to personal values. We seem to have arrived at the same conclusion here by way of examining one form of a flourishing life that partly consists in promoting the flourishing of others. Sassall derives deeply personal satisfactions from his life of service to that rural community at the very same time that he aids in the flourishing of others. That is what makes him a fortunate man.

It is important to qualify this conclusion with the point that Sassall is subject to disquieting questions in the course of his life of service. As Berger puts it,

> If as a doctor he is concerned with the total personality of his patients and if he realizes, as he must, that a personality is never an entirely fixed entity, then he is bound to take note of what inhibits, deprives or diminishes it. It is the unwritten consequence of his approach.[42]

Sassall is by no means helpless. He can safeguard their health, urge improvements in the village through the Parish Council, and explain parents and children to each other. But the more he thinks of educating them "according to the demands of their

---

42. Berger, *Fortunate Man*, 135.

very own minds and bodies before they have become resigned" he has to ask of himself by what right he does this. So he compromises:

> as the limitations of his energy would anyway force him to do; he helps in an individual problem, he suggests an answer here and an answer there, he tries to remove a fear without destroying the whole edifice of the morality of which it is part, he introduces the possibility of a hitherto unseen pleasure or satisfaction without extrapolating to the idea of a fundamentally different way of life.[43]

The contrast between Sassall's expectations for them and their own expectations for themselves is tied to his deep depressions, which can last from one to three months at a time. He must feel inadequate in the face of the suffering of his patients because he has taken responsibility for their lives.

The sobering part of the lesson from Sassall's life is that those who take a good part of their flourishing from promoting the flourishing of others can be vulnerable to deep depression in the face of limitations that they can only partially overcome. Individuals such as John Sassall cannot provide a complete answer to Thrasymachus, even along Lear's and Williams's more modest conception, as long as the rest of us are neither willing nor able to do enough. Even more sobering, perhaps, is the fact that Sassall's way of life as it stands now would be impossible were it not for these crushing limitations. He would not be the community's clerk of records if it were not for the inarticulateness of its members. Perhaps he could serve some of the same function among highly articulate and educated members of a middle-class community, but that would not present a challenge to the same degree as Sassall finds in his actual circumstances. Our very forms of flourishing can be tied to the existence of injustice. The more optimistic note on which we could end is that a life of promoting the flourishing of others is not by its very nature thus infected.

We may be entitled to have confidence in the *idea* of a moral life, then, but not necessarily in the moral life as our moralities currently define it, not if our moralities simply accept a state of affairs in which individuals are left to do the best they can for a great many people whose possibilities for personal fulfillment have been suppressed from the very beginning. Such suppression need not be the result of the operations of some abstract, dominating power, as in Foucault, nor need they be the result of purposeful manipulation by groups who benefit from the suppression of the interests of others, say, as Horkheimer and Adorno would have it in their *Dialectic of Enlightenment*.[44] The suppression need not be the result of or only the result of the intentional action of human beings to be something that needs to be corrected, any

---

43. Berger, *Fortunate Man*, 141.
44. Max Horkheimer and Theodor W. Adorno, *Dialectic of Enlightenment,* trans. John Cumming (New York: Seabury Press, 1944). According to Horkheimer and Adorno, the beneficiaries of the

more than the human disaster a hurricane or earthquake wreaks is none of our business because human beings did not intentionally cause it. As argued in chapter 6, it is neither realistic nor unrealistic to claim that there can be a more satisfactory balance struck between the personal and impersonal perspectives such that the suppression of opportunities for personal fulfillment is much less widespread than it is now. To that extent and in that way, we are not entitled to have confidence in our moralities.

Horkheimer and Adorno associate these ills not only with a controlling, cohesive capitalist class but also with Enlightenment morality that disenchants nature and sees it as something to be controlled and manipulated and at the same time supposedly celebrates humanity and human individuality. They ask how much individuality the Enlightenment has truly delivered, and again their critique retains some force, despite overblown generalizations and suspect theories about causal connections. One need not think that the need for amusement was some sinister creation of a ruling elite in order to accept Horkheimer's and Adorno's charge that amusement has become a means "not to think about anything" and to forget suffering "even where it is shown," that is a flight, not from a wretched reality, but from "the last remaining thought of resistance."[45] One need not accept their nearly paranoid claim that "everyone is enclosed at an early age in a system of churches, clubs, professional associations, and other such concerns, which constitute the most sensitive instrument of social control" in order to be disturbed by the lack of individuality in a society that is supposed to celebrate and protect it.[46] There is hyperbole, but not enough to comfort us, in their remark that "personality scarcely signifies anything more than shining white teeth and freedom from body odor and emotions."[47]

Arlene Stairs, whose study of the Inuit conception of the self was briefly cited in chapter 4, has some interesting comparative observations about tolerance of individuality. She finds that a proper description of Inuits' attitudes toward individuality takes us beyond the standard individualistic/communal and competitive/cooperative dichotomies: "Inuit show us both communal forms of individualization, in which members fill diverse roles according to family structures and abilities, and selective forms of competition in activities of both physical survival and social bonding." Western forms of competition

---

present distribution of power and property harness the forces that centralize ownership and control and employ economic, political, and cultural means to defend the status quo. Most areas of cultural life become coopted and transformed into modes of controlling individual consciousness. Simultaneously, culture becomes an "industry." The profit motive is transferred on to cultural forms, and more and more artistic products become mere commodities.

45. Horkheimer and Adorno, *Dialectic,* 144.
46. Horkheimer and Adorno, *Dialectic,* 149.
47. Horkheimer and Adorno, *Dialectic,* 167.

paradoxically rest as much on standardization as on individualization of identity. A normality is implied that may be much narrower than in Inuit culture. Deviation and failure in Inuit society must be extreme before a person is rejected from the community, in contrast to the criminal, educational (streaming), and physical or mental health segregations common in Western society.[48]

What makes this point so telling, of course, is that individuality is supposed to be a benefit of Western liberal societies. Yet individuality for most people who have the luxury of choosing (this group might not constitute the majority of the population) seems to come down to the freedom to select from among a limited set of "lifestyles." One defines oneself as an individual by choosing one of these prefabricated forms, defined primarily by such features as one's age, where one lives, whether one goes to a health club, how one chooses to dress, and whether one drinks beer or wine and what kind.

I have a great deal of sympathy for Horkheimer and Adorno's critique of Enlightenment moralities, even if I do not see the problem as ultimately lying in the omnipresent and brutally efficient manipulations of a ruling class. Their critique retains much its force despite their overestimation of the systematic nature of domination, in much the same way that Foucault's critique retains its force despite a similar failure. Even if there is no systematic stunting of individuality, no systematic control of people's perceptions of their own needs, even if most people do not see the order as oppressive and distorting their needs, that does not mean that people are free to be true individuals or in control of their perceptions of their needs. If the insecurities of life under advanced forms of capitalism drives us to prefabricated forms of 'individuality' and to seek numbing forms of entertainment, that is no less a pity and a shame than if someone or something were trying to bring these effects about.

To the extent that a morality that celebrates individuality and the opportunities for personal fulfillment leaves us no real vision for realizing these values, then, we have reason to be less confident of it. But that is an incentive to engage in the kind of exploration of realistic possibility discussed in chapter 6, not an incentive to dismiss the project of *making* our moral commitments ones in which we might justify have confidence.

48. Arlene Stairs, "Self-Image, World Image: Speculations on Identity from Experiences with Inuit," *Ethos* 20 (1992): 124.

9

Coping with Moral Difference

This final chapter returns to practical problems arising from accepting a plurality of true or justified moralities. In chapter 3, I originally brought them up as possible objections to pluralistic relativism. In this chapter, I develop strategies for dealing with them as problems central to our moral lives. These are problems about how to have confidence in one's moral commitments while recognizing that different commitments are equally justified. They are problems about how to act toward others who have those different commitments. They are problems about how we might learn from others. These practical problems, then, can prompt us to look inward at our own commitments, and also outward at others who do not share our commitments, or at least not all of them. Inward focus prompts us to ask what we are to do with our selves. The outward focus prompts us to ask what we are to do about the others. I start with the inward focus.

Among the plurality of ways of life that are equally worthy of being chosen, one hopefully finds one's own way of life, or some appropriate modification of it upon critical reflection. If so, one aims to continue one's commitment to that particular way of life and yet act on the recognition that other ways of life are no less worthy of being chosen. Can one do both at the same time? The next section concerns Richard Rorty's answer.

Some of the material in this chapter is contained in "Dwelling in Humanity or Free and Easy Wandering?" in *Technology and Cultural Values: On the Edge of the Third Millenium*, ed. Peter D. Hershock, Marietta Stepaniants, and Roger T. Ames (Honolulu: University of Hawaii Press, 2003), 400–15, "Fragmentation in Civil Society and the Good," in *Civility*, ed. Leroy Rouner (Notre Dame, Ind.: University of Notre Dame Press, 2000); and "Coping with Moral Conflict and Ambiguity," *Ethics* 102 (1992): 763–84, reprinted with an expanded section on multiculturalism in *Defending Diversity: Contemporary Philosophical Perspectives on Pluralism and Multiculturalism*, ed. Lawrence Foster and Patricia Herzog (Amherst: University of Massachusetts Press, 1994), 13–37.

9.1 Rorty's Ethnocentrism

Richard Rorty approaches the question in the language of "final vocabulary" and "irony." Our final vocabulary of is a set of words employed to justify actions, beliefs, and lives. It is final in the sense that there are no noncircular argumentative means to dispel doubt about the worth of those words. Ironists have radical and continuing doubts about their own final vocabularies because they have been impressed by other vocabularies taken as final by others; they realize that argument phrased in their final vocabulary can neither underwrite nor dissolve these doubts; and they do not think that their vocabulary is closer to reality than others or that it is in touch with a power greater than themselves.[1] The opposite of irony is "commonsense," the watchword of those who un-self-consciously describe everything important in terms of the final vocabulary to which they and those around them are habituated.

To those who worry that irony (which he finds in the works of Hegel, Nietzsche, Derrida, and Foucault) dissolves the "social glue," Rorty asks why we should suppose philosophy ever could serve as such glue. All the social glue we need

> consists in little more than a consensus that the point of social organization is to let everybody have a chance at self-creation to the best of his or her abilities, and that that goal requires, besides peace and wealth, the standard "bourgeois freedoms." This conviction would not be based on a view about universally shared human ends, human rights, the nature of rationality, the Good for Man, not anything else. It would be a conviction based on nothing more profound than the historical facts which suggest that without the protection of something like the institutions of bourgeois liberal society, people will be less able to work out their private salvations, create their private self-images, reweave their webs and belief and desire in the light of whatever new people and books they happen to encounter.[2]

To the objection that this glue is not thick enough, that the "metaphysical" rhetoric of universality and rationality is needed for the stability of free institutions, Rorty replies that (what he takes to be) the decline of religious belief has not weakened but instead strengthened liberal societies. What is essential is social hope—hope that "life will eventually be freer, less cruel, more leisured, richer in goods and experiences, not just for our descendants but for everybody's descendants."[3] Philosophical beliefs do not bind people together but rather "common vocabularies and common hopes." In the ideal liberal society, says Rorty, people would be commonsensically "nominalist

---

1. Richard Rorty, *Contingency, Irony, and Solidarity* (Cambridge: Cambridge University Press, 1989), 73–4.

2. Rorty, *Contingency*, 84–5.

3. Rorty, *Contingency*, 86.

and historicist." That is, they would see themselves as contingent through and through, without feeling any particular doubts about the contingencies they happened to be. They would feel no need to answer the question "Why are you a liberal?" or "Why care about the humiliation of a stranger?" However, the public rhetoric cannot be ironist because we cannot "imagine a culture which socialized its youth in such a way as to make them continually dubious about their own process of socialization." For this reason, "irony seems inherently a private matter."[4]

Rorty addresses a second objection to his view: that irony and liberalism make an incoherent combination. There is, he admits, at least a prima facie tension between the idea that social organization aims at human equality and the idea that human beings are simply incarnated vocabularies. The idea that we all have an overriding obligation to diminish cruelty, to make human beings equal in respect to their liability to suffering, seems to take for granted that there is something within human beings that deserves respect and protection quite independently of the language they speak. People are rightly suspicious of ironists because ironists refuse to take them on their own terms—they want to be "taken seriously just as they are and just as they talk. It is to humiliate people to make the things that seemed most important to them look futile, obsolete, and powerless."[5] Further, ironists are resented because their redescriptions do not promise to make things better. Unlike metaphysicians, they cannot promise that adopting their redescriptions of yourself or your situation makes you "better able to conquer the forces which are marshaled against you."[6] Liberal metaphysicians want our wish to be kind to be bolstered by an argument involving reference to a common human essence that is more than our ability to feel pain. Liberal ironists want our chances of being kind to be expanded by redescription. They think that recognition of a common susceptibility to humiliation is the only social bond that is needed.

Rorty is right to at least question the "metaphysician's" assumption that philosophy can serve as social glue. Those who fear the effects of the widespread acceptance of relativism too often make that assumption unreflectively and implicitly. They need to say what is gained by proving that there is a single true morality. Would people be any more inclined to be more cooperative, less self-serving, when moved to recognize that there is a set of universal moral truths? Given the high level of abstraction at which moral truths would undoubtedly be proven, it is an open question as to whether they would be any more likely than they are now to agree on specific courses of action as the moral action. And would be any more inclined to do what they perceive to be the moral course of action?

However, there seems something false about Rorty's tacit assumption that we can simply follow "the norms of the day" embedded in our final vocabularies. As Thomas

4. Rorty, *Contingency*, 87.
5. Rorty, *Contingency*, 89.
6. Rorty, *Contingency*, 91.

McCarthy has pointed out, social norms "are neither fully spelled out nor algorithmically applicable, and social situations are not predefined but are actively constituted by the participants' own activities."[7] In part, the need for the agent's own activities of constituting social norms is necessitated by the generality and abstractness of the norms. Respect, friendship, and decency can mean a wide range of behaviors, and which meanings they have depends on what is established within a culture as respectful, friendly, and decent behavior. In the children's book *The BFG* by Roald Dahl, Sophie expresses concern about the Big Friendly Giant's favorite beverage, Frobscottle, because its fizzy bubbles go in one end and come out the other with rude sounds. The BFG expresses surprise about her concern, since among Giants those sounds are not rude but signal happiness and warm contentment. This part especially delights American children with its playful reference to what adult culture deems to be rude sounds, but introduces them to a truth about the cultural variability of 'decent' behavior (in general, the culture of adults gets a thorough drubbing in Dahl's books). Individual constitution of social norms is also made necessary by conflicts between central values contained in their moralities. While moralities generally individuate by the kinds of priorities they set in such conflicts, a good deal is still left up to individuals on given occasions to specify what sort of priority will concretely take shape.

For example, Confucian morality and Chinese traditional morality in general place a great deal of value on filial piety, and many would argue that this is the greatest value within these moralities. The text of the classical philosopher Mencius, however, presents stories illustrating both that this value and the way it takes priority over other important values cannot be spelled out formulaically. Consider the question of whether filial piety (*xiao*) means obedience or service to parents. Many would not even think to distinguish between these two dimensions of filial piety. A story in the *Mencius* about the sage-king Shun and his father illustrates the possibility that service and obedience require incompatible actions in some situations. Shun wanted to marry (*Mencius* 4A26) but knew that his father would not grant him permission. Mencius defends Shun's decision to marry without telling his father by arguing that the most serious way of being a bad son is to have no heir. To the morally noble person (the *junzi*), concludes Mencius, this was as good as having told his father. In most situations, of course, it is a grave offense against filial piety not to ask for permission to marry. In this particular situation, telling his father would have resulted in a worse offense against the ideal of service to one's father. This concrete meaning of filial piety as applied to the action in question could not have been deduced from any abstract norm. The concrete, action-guiding meaning of even a single value cannot be read off in any simple and general way. Values such as filial piety are complex and have different dimensions that can come into conflict with each other. How these conflicts are to be resolved depends on

7. Thomas McCarthy, *Ideals and Illusions: On Reconstruction and Deconstruction in Contemporary Critical Theory* (Cambridge, Mass.: MIT Press, 1991), 30.

what is at stake in the particular situation that gives rise to the conflict. In this case, it was a graver offense against filial piety not to provide the father with an heir.

Consider a story about Shun's dealing with a value conflict. When asked what Shun would do if his father killed a man (7A35), Mencius replies that the only thing to do is to apprehend him. Shun could not interfere with the judge, who was acting on the law. However, Mencius continues, after his father was apprehended, Shun would then have cast aside the empire and fled with his father to the seacoast. This Shun story is interesting for the way it strikes a balance between different values in tension with one another, given the context. Shun's refusal to interfere with the judge acknowledges the value of fairly administering the larger social order. Fleeing with his father, on the other hand, honors the value of greater loyalty to family. Shun honors both values at *different moments* in his dealing with the situation. Deduction from principle could not yield such a specific balance.

To say that individuals must interpret moral norms and thereby constitute their concrete meanings is not to say that they make these meanings up from thin air. For one thing, all the Shun stories in one way or another assert the supremacy of filial piety, even as they seek ways to honor other values that come into conflict with it. For another thing, the stories themselves illustrate the sort of guidance that a moral tradition provides to its members, in addition to the statement of general moral norms. It provides paradigms or exemplars of people and events that illustrate who interpreted the norms wisely and well. While there is no way that one could formulaically apply the lessons of these exemplars to one's own situation, one gets a sense of how one could carry on in their spirit. Their actions and thoughts provide resources for thinking about one's own situation.

Rorty was right to recognize that our concrete norms provide the really useful meaning of any general notions we may have, such as the Confucian ideal of the highest realization of human nobility or the Western liberal's ideal of freedom. But he fails to recognize the loose fit between any particular norm and these abstract ideals; he fails to address the need for interpretation of these ideals and the possible conflicts and ambiguities of interpretation that must be sorted out by individuals who are "following the norms of the day." His picture of how we embody our final vocabularies relies too much on our being the passive receptors and bearers of these vocabularies, at least when he is dealing with the problem of how we may be confident of our vocabularies. If we do not have to question "Why this final vocabulary?" we do have to question "Why this or that way of interpreting this or that final word in application to the present situation?" The latter question can pose a question of confidence no less than the former.

Rorty's attempt to compartmentalize irony fails. The contingency of our final vocabularies cannot be confined to the ironist's study. It now constitutes part of public discourse and argumentation. When final vocabularies conflict, we believe their contingency must somehow be taken into account. The abortion debate is an example.

Harry Blackmun, in writing the majority opinion of *Roe v. Wade*, noted the wide cultural and historical variation of opinion on the question of when life begins, and concluded that "when those trained in the respective disciplines of medicine, philosophy, and theology are unable to arrive at any consensus, the judiciary, at this point in the development of man's knowledge, is not in a position to speculate as to the answer."[8] The contingency of our final vocabularies, and the relevance of that contingency to our coping with their conflict in the public sphere, cannot be kept a secret among intellectuals who are common-sense democrats in public. And that is partly because the very meaning and application of Rorty's most central values are at the center of these debates: freedom (in the case of abortion, the woman's) and prevention of cruelty (in the case of abortion, the alleged cruelty of taking a human life).

9.2 Raz's Pessimism about the Tension between Pluralism and Moral Engagement

In diametrical opposition to Rorty, Joseph Raz holds that it is impossible to recognize a plurality of equally justified ways of life and to remain engaged with one's own way. Imagine, he asks us, that the

> Skills and character traits cherished by my way of life are a handicap for those pursuing one or another of its alternatives. I value long contemplation and patient examination: these are the qualities I require in my chosen course. Their life, by contrast, requires impetuosity, swift responses, and decisive action, and they despise the slow contemplative types as indecisive. They almost have to. To succeed in their chosen way, they have to be committed to it and to believe that the virtues it requires should be cultivated. They therefore cannot regard those others as virtues for them. By the same token it is only natural that they will value in others what they choose to emulate themselves.... Of course, pluralists can step back from their personal commitments and appreciate in the abstract the value of other ways of life. But this acknowledgment coexists with, and cannot replace, the feelings of rejection and dismissiveness. Tension is an inevitable concomitant of value pluralism. And it is a tension without stability, without the prospect of reconciliation of the two perspectives, the one recognizing the validity of competing values and the one hostile to them. One is forever moving from one to the other.[9]

---

8. Justice Harry Blackmun, in the majority opinion of the Supreme Court on *Roe v. Wade*, 410 U.S. 113 (1973), available at http://caselaw.lp.findlaw.com/scripts/getcase.pl?navby=CASE&court=US&vol=410&page=113. Rev. August 24, 2005.

9. Joseph Raz, "Multiculturalism: A Liberal Perspective," *Dissent* 41 (1994): 73.

9.3 A Promising Suggestion from the *Zhuangzi*

To point toward a possible solution to Raz's dilemma that does not return us to the ethnocentrism of Rorty, I turn to the classical Chinese text the *Zhuangzi*, traditionally attributed to the Daoist Zhuangzi (Chuang Tzu).[10] The text is well known for the skeptical lampooning of those who think they know the truth, including the moral truth. Yet the text also seems to be recommending a way of life to its audience. David Nivison presents the duality of these two perspectives as a duality between a detached perspective, from which one's own particular way of life is simply one among many, and the engaged perspective, from which one seeks to live one's way of life.[11] The problem of interpreting the *Zhuangzi* is the problem of figuring out how one can be consistent in doing both these things. Interestingly, this problem of interpretation parallels the problem for pluralistic relativism I have just described. Pluralists, as Raz describes them, are continually alternating between a detached perspective, from which, stepping back from their personal commitments, they appreciate in the abstract the value of other ways of life, and the engaged perspective, from which they cannot help but be dismissive of other ways on the other hand. Even though the dualities between detachment and engagement as found in Raz and the *Zhuangzi* are parallel, I believe that the *Zhuangzi* has a better way of combining the two perspectives. To understand how he is able to do this, we must understand better the skepticism that underlies Zhuangzi's detached perspective.

The *Zhuangzi* contains more than one way of arriving at the skeptical view that no one moral perspective is uniquely correct. Chapter 2 contains an argument that is a familiar weapon of skeptics, ancient and modern, East and West: if doubt is cast on the unique validity of one's own perspective, one has no noncircular argumentative recourse to dispelling that doubt; all justifications of any perspective are at best arbitrary in this sense. However, there is another strain of argument to be found in the *Zhuangzi*. Rather than pointing out the arbitrariness of any attempted justification for any given moral perspective, this argument calls our attention to the real value in other perspectives.

Contrary to some interpretations of Zhuangzi's work, he does not dismiss moral values. As mentioned earlier, he appears to accept love of parents and duty to ruler as necessary elements of human existence. In chapter 5, men who have lost feet as punishment for crime are scorned, but not by their Daoist masters, who see what is of *worth* in them. When Confucius refuses an amputee an audience because of his criminal history, Zhuangzi scolds Confucius for failing to act like heaven and earth: "There is

---

10. At this point, the first seven chapters, the so-called inner chapters, are thought to be an actual products of the historical person Zhuangzi, and my interpretation is mainly based on these chapters and on a few others that I judge to be consistent with the themes found in the inner chapters.

11. David Nivison, "Hsün Tzu and Chuang Tzu," in *Chinese Texts and Philosophical Contexts: Essays Dedicated to Angus C. Graham*, ed. Henry Rosemont Jr. (Lasalle, Ill.: Open Court, 1991), 129–42.

nothing that heaven doesn't cover, nothing that earth doesn't bear up."[12] In chapter 1, Zhuangzi chastises his friend Huizi for failing to see beyond the ordinary, humdrum uses of some large gourds. Huizi tried using one of the gourds for a water container, but it was so heavy he couldn't lift it. He then tried to make dippers from them, but they were too large and unwieldy. He deemed the gourds of no use and smashed them to pieces. Zhuangzi asks why he didn't think of making the gourd into a great tub so he could go floating around the rivers and lakes, instead of worrying because it was too big and unwieldy to dip into things. "Obviously you still have a lot of underbrush in your head!" concluded Zhuangzi. Note that Zhuangzi does not deny that the more ordinary uses are genuine uses for the gourds, and clearly, they are. Rather, Zhuangzi's point is to clear the underbrush from our heads and get an *enlarged* view of what is of value.

Zhuangzi undermines the assumption that our own perspectives are uniquely correct not by discrediting them but by undermining their claim to have exhausted what there is to see, and this involves opening our eyes to perspectives other than our own. We are not disabused of the notion that our moral codes embody real values. We are compelled to recognize that others embody real values just as ours do. In this strain of argument I am highlighting, then, Zhuangzi's appreciation for diversity is a *moral* stance at the same time that it constitutes a distancing from one's own original moral commitments.

His appreciation for diversity is a version of the moral ambivalence identified at the beginning of this book. The strongest case for pluralistic relativism includes not only the claim that other moralities are as justified as our own but also the recognition of the genuine values that compose those moralities. Moral values are human inventions that answer to compelling human needs and desires, and are subject to the constraints derived from human nature and the function of facilitating and promoting social co-operation. The classical Confucian Xunzi saw the Confucian version of morality as the uniquely best way to satisfy the function that morality evolved to satisfy. The Zhuangist vision of our moral commitments is as naturalistic as Xunzi's, but posits no uniquely best way to satisfy those needs. Instead, there are plural ways to satisfy those needs, none of them the best because each succeeds in honoring certain basic values at the cost of sacrificing others. Every coherent moral code cuts out something of genuine value. Every coherent code, in defining what is right, also requires what is wrong.

9.4 HOW ZHUANGZI COMBINES THE DETACHED AND ENGAGED PERSPECTIVES

Recall the original problem posed for the viability of our moral commitments by recognizing that there are worthy commitments other than our own. Raz's argument is that the detached perspective from which we recognize the worth of other

---

12. Chuang Tzu, *Chuang Tzu: Basic Writings,* trans. Burton Watson (New York: Columbia University Press, 1963), 67.

commitments undermines the engaged perspective defined by our own commitments. The swift responders and decisive actors "almost have" to despise the long contemplators and patient examiners. They cannot regard qualities of patience as virtues for them. By the same token, says Raz, it is only natural that they will value in others what they choose to emulate themselves. Detachment and engagement cannot coexist at the same time in the same mind, but must alternate in ascendancy.

Zhuangzi's challenge to our narrow perspectives is also a challenge to this picture of the tension between the detached and engaged perspectives. On his argument, the detached perspective from which we recognize a broader array of genuine values is also an engaged perspective from which our original moral commitments become broader and more inclusive. To recognize others' commitments or one's own as partial selections from a universe of value is, after all, to recognize that such commitments concern genuine value, if not all value. Zhuangzi's constructive skeptical argument holds that typical normative perspectives go astray in claiming an exclusive and comprehensive insight into value, and it encourages us to retain our own commitments as commitments to genuine values, but also to expand our view of what other commitments have a similar status.

Consider again Raz's example. The swift responders and decisive actors may not strive to realize the patient qualities in themselves, but recognition of such qualities as virtues may take other forms. It may involve seeing that the long contemplators and patient examiners have their place as well, perhaps even in one's own society. Perhaps the two sets of qualities are complementary to each other within a larger social context, where some are needed to be swift and decisive, but others are needed to give a view from a larger and longer perspective. One may value swiftness and decisiveness in oneself, because, say, one views it as an admirable trait and one has the temperament to do that sort of thing well, but that does not mean that one needs to denigrate those qualities that enable others to give the longer view. Perhaps many do tend to value in others what they value in themselves, but it is a leap to say as Raz does that it is natural, and it is implausible to say that it is inevitable.

Now of course, there will be cases in which what it takes to realize one way of life will exclude what it takes to realize another way of life. One cannot recognize the worth of both those ways of life in the sense of making equal effort to realize both of them. That would be practical incoherence. That is why it is perfectly acceptable to dedicate oneself to the realization of one or a few ways of life among the many ways one might find equally valuable. We can certainly remain committed to our ways of life because we could not possibly strive equally to realize all valuable ways of life. To choose our ways for this reason is not to despise or dismiss the other ways.

However, more needs to be said, because the Zhuangist perspective should amount to more than mere acceptance of other ways of life while one remains set on one's originally narrow course. Recognizing the worth of other ways of life can and often should have a deeper and wider effect on one's original moral commitments. If one genuinely appreciates the use of gourds as tubs to float around in, one is unlikely to remain the sort of person who smashes them when one cannot use them as water dippers. If one opens up one's mind to new sources of value, one should sometimes go beyond acceptance of the new toward incorporating it into one's commitments. One need not try to incorporate an entirely different way of life into one's commitments. Alternatively, one seeks to affirm certain values underlying that other way of life by balancing one's efforts to realize them in relation to values one already affirms. In other words, our moral commitments must remain open-ended and flexible, to a certain degree indeterminate with respect to what values it affirms and what the relationship of priority is among those values in case of conflict. We must remain ready to affirm values and priorities that are not presently encompassed by our current commitments.

9.5 TRANSFORMING MORAL COMMITMENTS

At this point, however, we might renew our worry as to how we can regard with equanimity this readiness to incorporate new values. How can we be ready to do this without destabilizing our commitments? An answer to this worry might begin with the recognition that our familiar moral commitments are never as secure and stable as they are typically cracked up to be. These commitments are never fully determinate, whether or not we remain open to new values. Consider again the moral ambivalence between special duties arising from the personal perspective and duties owed to all arising from the impersonal perspective. As argued in section 1.6, there is no determinate, general ranking that orders these two kinds of duties. Most of us would place less priority on special duties than an ethic such as Confucianism does, but neither do we adhere to a thoroughgoing impersonalism. And yet, it would be very difficult to articulate in general terms exactly what sort of balance we have struck. In life we muddle along, first trying to avoid creating or getting into situations where important values come into conflict. If they come into conflict despite our efforts, we try to strike a reasonable balance between these values, but what seems reasonable is very much tied to the particular circumstances of the conflict as it arises. There is "no constant rule," as chapter 17 of the *Zhuangzi* says.

This is not to deny that the moralities to which we have become committed have certain general features that distinguish them from other moralities. Some distinguishing general features involve a focus on particular sorts of general values rather than others or involve certain general kinds of priorities struck among several general values. However, such priorities are by no means fully determinate within any given morality, if what we mean by a morality is something that we actually employ in our lives and not a purely theoretical construction. A living morality is itself an uneasy, somewhat indeterminate combination of values that are not easily held together. There is, in other words, a kind of open texture to the priorities that distinguish one morality from another. And where there is an open texture, there is the possibility for fluidity: change over time in the balance between two values in tension with one another; and, furthermore, change in the balance according to different circumstances. This is the sense in which our moral commitments are never as determinate as they are cracked up to be.

So now it looks as if the Zhuangist recommendation to open up our minds to new values and the way they might enter in combination with our original moral commitments is not so different from what we have been doing all along. It is not so different from how we have been reasoning about moral problems all along. Our original commitments necessitate the attempt to hold together values that are not easily held together. It is in this sense that the new, more inclusive engagement recommended by Zhuangzi looks more like what we had to be doing all along, except that we must now be ready for additional challenges to balance old values with new ones.

This picture of open-ended and flexible moral commitment requires that we abandon the theorist's ambition of formulating general principles that can be deductively employed to settle conflicts between values. Rather, we start with particular conflicts and negotiate them for the circumstances at hand. I have mentioned that such reasoning is characteristic of the Confucians and Mencius in particular. Mencius affirms the priority of special duties, but that does not mean that the concrete meaning of that priority can be deductively read off from some general principle, the meaning of which is independent of the way that he and others in the Confucian tradition interpreted it in concrete circumstances. And whatever balance we strike between the personal and impersonal perspectives is in great part constituted by many individual interpretations of that balance.

Recent psychological research and theory about judgment formation has emphasized the value of informal kinds of reasoning that rely on global assessments of the situation at hand rather than analytical methods relying on inferential rules or algorithms. Much of the impetus for this recent work has stemmed from recognizing that human reasoning in response to complex situations is subtler than can be captured by formal inferential or standard computational models. Some of this work has been more careful about the phenomenology of judgment formation than philosophers have generally been.

For example, Hammond and his colleagues note that there is common contrast between intuitive versus analytical reasoning and that a common defect of the way this contrast is usually made is that intuitive reasoning is defined as the negation of whatever analytical reasoning is defined to be.[13] Very rarely is there a positive characterization of what the intuitive style is. In response to this defect, they define the intuitive and analytical styles in terms of contrasts along several dimensions such as cognitive control (in intuition it is low and in analysis high), rate of data processing (rapid in intuition, slow in analysis), and conscious awareness of the process (low in intuition and high in analysis). The researchers further hypothesize that there are situation types that are more

---

13. See Kenneth R. Hammond, Robert M. Hamm, Janet Grassia, and Tamra Pearson, "Direct Comparison of the Efficacy of Intuitive and Analytical Cognition in Expert Judgment," in *Research on Judgment and Decision Making*, ed. William M. Goldstein and Robin M. Hogarth (Cambridge: Cambridge University Press, 1997), 144–80.

likely to elicit the intuitive versus the analytical styles. People are more likely to use the intuitive style in response to situations in which there are many, continuously appearing "cues" or salient features that are displayed simultaneously and apprehended perceptually, and in which there is no explicit principle, theory, or method available for organizing the cues into a judgment. The analytical style is responsive to situations, for example, in which quantified data are available, and an explicit principle or algorithm is available for organizing the cues into judgment. The researchers tested the engineers on a range of tasks that were more or less suited to the intuitive or analytical styles. They had independent methods of judging the success of the judgments. The researchers found that even on the more analytically suitable tasks, eleven of twenty engineers were more successful with the intuitive style or with a style that was midway between intuition and analysis (they call this midway style "common sense," which is working with some rough rules seasoned with plenty of intuitive judgment). Even when a problem seems most suitable for the analytical style, many people might lose a "feel" for what plausible solutions should look like and simply accept whatever answer emerges when they "plug in" the input data. If they should make a mistake in applying the algorithm, they are less likely to sense that a solution cannot be right. By contrast, when they apply the intuitive style, they have a "feel" for how various factors vector to produce an overall result, and are less likely to make large mistakes.

One of the interesting implications of this study is that a piece of reasoning may be more or less intuitive or analytical, depending on where it falls along the various dimensions that define the styles. What is also good about the way they define intuition is that it discourages the frequent philosophical presupposition that intuition must be some sort of simple seeing. It rather encourages a picture of an intuitive process that takes in various perceptual cues in an informal manner and organizes them in a judgment. The fact that we are not conscious of how we organize them does not imply that we do not in fact organize them.

"Connectionist" models of the mind are relevant to this theme that we organize information in ways not articulable by reference to principle or algorithm.[14] Such models arose from recognizing the failures of models of the mind as a digital computer with a CPU and a stored program. Human cognitive transitions seemed too subtle and complex to be explained by computation, that is, the manipulation of representations in accordance with programmable rules or algorithms. In connectionist models, there are no general inferential rules, for example, stored in a program. Nor is there anything like applying the rules that exists as a distinct process in such models. Rather, information is stored in patterns of activation between input and output nodes in the neural network. Knowledge need not be explicitly represented or stored as a data structure, but stored in the strengths or weights of activation between nodes—how

---

14. See Terence E. Horgan and John Tienson, *Connectionism and the Philosophy of Psychology* (Cambridge, Massachusetts: MIT Press, 1996).

strongly a signal is relayed between input and output nodes. Connectionist models allow us to see how it might be possible for us to process large amounts of information and have it stored in the patterns of activation of the neural network. Even when activated, there is no necessity that the processing be available to consciousness.

9.6 WHY ACTING IN THE LIGHT OF PLURALISTIC RELATIVISM IS NOT SO DIFFERENT FROM DEALING WITH OTHER MORALLY COMPLEX SITUATIONS

In this light, one's moral commitment to a certain configuration of values and principles is more like a commitment to take certain kinds of reasons into consideration in one's decision-making. One's understanding of what those reasons imply for action and of how they are to be weighed against other reasons may evolve in one's dealings with new situations, including situations in which one has gained a fresh appreciation for other ways of life. An example of such evolving understanding appears in Walter Feinberg's discussion of the work of Takeo Doi, the Japanese psychoanalyst. Doi identifies the quest for dependency on others as characteristic of the Japanese personality. At first Feinberg considered this quest as the denial of Western values such as freedom and equality. But he came to an understanding of this quest as a drive for relationships of care and trust: wanting someone who can be trusted as always acting out of care and concern for one's well-being. He suggests that we have something to learn from the "gentle relationship between Japanese adults and children, along with the sense of mutual caring and responsibility that teachers in Japan develop with some success among young children." He connects the Japanese valuing of dependency with that aspect of Western feminism that stresses an ethic of care and the value of relationship with others. This kind of encounter with another culture, Feinberg concludes, provides a foundation for reconsidering the commitments and goals of the educational process.[15] Such reconsideration, I might add, does not require that we place the same amount of emphasis on the ideal of relations of care and trust as the Japanese do. It does require that we recognize that ideal as something that we ourselves have reason to prize. One can learn from other cultures without copying the choices they have made.

Another example of the way that people in one culture attempt to learn from other cultures is found in Japan itself, where Western influences have met with different strands of the traditional culture and have resulted in interesting permutations. In a study of Japanese, American, and Chinese preschools, preschool teachers and administrators from the three societies viewed and commented on videotapes of activities in

---

15. Walter Feinberg, "A Role for Philosophy of Education in Intercultural Research: A Reexamination of the Relativism-Absolutism Debate," *Teachers College Record* 91 (1989): 161–76.

preschools in the other societies. Virtually all the Japanese teachers who viewed the American tape contrasted what they perceived to be typically American "individualism" with the "groupism" they believe characteristic of their own society and schools. At the same time, they contrasted their sort of groupism with the Chinese version, which some saw as lacking in genuine group feeling and others saw as too authoritarian and rigid.[16]

The Japanese emphasized the view that group activities can be joyful and sponta-neous because they are compatible with natural human feeling, that a child's humanity is most fully realized not in being independent from the group but in becoming more able to cooperate with and fuse with something larger than the self. In contrast to the Chinese activities that were viewed, Japanese group activities seemed loosely structured, with the teachers applying very liberal criteria as to what counted as participating in a group's activities. There also appeared to be a conscious attempt by teachers to refrain from intervening in altercations between children, based on the view that children should be left as much as possible to work out their relations to each other, thus cultivating peer ties rather than the hierarchical ties between teacher and individual child.

The Japanese very self-consciously identify this preschool philosophy as an attempt to steer a course between the loneliness and anomie they associate with American individualism and the rigid authoritarianism they associate with China, or in the case of some teachers and administrators, with their own traditional culture.[17] This kind of phenomenon, of an attempted synthesis between culturally embodied ethical systems, is not unique, though it is usually less self-conscious. Indeed, such transformations have influenced the ethical systems we hold now, and they will continue to do so in the future because cultures and the ethical systems they embody are permeable. One Japanese administrator expressed attraction to and admiration for some features of the American preschool philosophy but found in these features something that was not "quite right or appropriate or feasible for the Japanese," "in a crucial way not really right for Japan."[18] The perception that other communities have something worthwhile, but that to take from them wholesale is not quite right for one's own, is often the more complex basis on which communities can bridge differences and gain greater respect for one another.[19]

16. Thomas Seung has brought to my attention that using the label "groupism" in contrast to "individualism" may be seriously misleading about the philosophy underlying Japanese social practices and institutions. I agree. Such philosophies, as lived in Japan and elsewhere, do not necessarily contrast the group with the individual so as to imply that their interests are typically in conflict. Rather, the idea is that the individual finds her full realization as a human being in the group.

17. Joseph J. Tobin, David Y. H. Wu, and Dana H. Davidson, *Preschool in Three Cultures: Japan, China, and the United States* (New Haven: Yale University Press, 1989), 38–44.

18. Tobin, Wu, and Davidson, *Preschool,* 53.

19. As Amélie Rorty has pointed out to me, people in one culture may have their own distinct interpretation of what is of value in another culture, an interpretation that may not be identical to the

So far, I have addressed the problem of accepting differences between ways of life without contradicting the idea of having moral commitments of one's own. I have argued that one can combine these two things provided that one's path to accepting difference is through crediting the value of other ways of life rather than discrediting the idea of their value. I have argued that a natural consequence of such a recognition is that one seeks to integrate at least some of values one sees in other ways of life into one's own commitments, and that this project of integration is not so different from what we do all along in attempting to reconcile the plurality of values typically present in our moralities.

Still, there is a limit to the extent that we can incorporate the values of other ways of life. Our commitments will likely remain different from the commitments of those who are committed to those other ways of life. When we are interdependent with those others, for example, if we live in the same society with them, it will often be impossible for us and for them to simply live and let live. Furthermore, sometimes we will be unable to see the value or worth in a particular aspect or practice that goes into another way of life. Or we may think that a practice violates universal constraints on adequate moralities. How should we act toward these others with whom we are in such serious disagreement? I turn now to the problems raised by pluralistic relativism for the question of how to act toward others with moral commitments that may be as justifiable as our own.

9.7 ACCEPTING DIFFERENCES FROM OTHERS

In section 2.12, I argued that an adequate morality must contain the value of accommodation between people who are in serious moral disagreement with one another. In this concluding chapter, I elaborate on that argument and develop more fully the necessary conception of accommodation. Some recent attempts to address the question of how to deal with serious moral disagreement have endorsed the idea of accommodation. I shall argue that their conceptions of accommodation are inadequate or incomplete, and that a more adequate conception must discuss the problem of how people in moral conflict are to live with one another. I shall explain how accommodation is a moral value rooted in the fact that serious conflict is a regular feature of our ethical lives, involving people with whom continuing relationships are both necessary and desirable. We already have in practice strategies of accommodation that constitute our practical commitment to this value. What we have lacked is the philosophical commitment to articulating and defending it.

---

one that people in that other culture may place on it. This is not to deny that there can be an overlap between the values of different cultures but to recognize the more complex phenomenon that the nature of the overlap will be subject to different interpretations. This is another kind of ambiguity that plays a role in the bridging of differences.

9.8 RECENT CONCEPTIONS OF ACCOMMODATING
   MORAL DIFFERENCES

Thomas Nagel has argued for restraint in the coercive exercise of political power when one is engaged in a particular kind of intractable moral conflict. This liberal principle of tolerance gains support from the contractualist idea that one should not impose arrangements, institutions, and requirements on grounds that people could reasonably reject, that is, when the disagreement comes down to a "bare confrontation between personal points of view."[20] Such disagreements, for Nagel, include conflicts over religious faith, abortion, and the killing of animals for food. Let us call such disagreements "brute" without implying that Nagel would in any way agree with the terminology.

Nagel contrasts the disagreements I call brute with disagreements between informed, reasonable people that depend on differences in the evidence they possess, in their assessments of the evidence, and ultimately on differences in judgment. Parties to such "reasonable" disagreements, as I shall call them, can think of themselves as appealing to a common, objective method of reasoning that each interprets and applies imperfectly. Disagreements over social justice, for example, between economic liberals and radical libertarians, Nagel thinks, are closer to being reasonable disagreements, and they are properly the subjects of state action. Nagel's argument for state neutrality on brute disagreements does not rest on the skeptical premise that brute disagreements necessarily rest on unjustified belief, but instead on the principle that justifying the use of political power requires a higher standard of objectivity, one that takes us "outside ourselves to a standpoint that is independent of who we are."[21] Restricting the policy of neutrality to brute disagreements prevents political paralysis. The state cannot be limited to acting only in those matters upon which all informed, reasonable people could agree.

One problem with Nagel's distinction is that applying it to disagreements on specific policy matters between internally diverse groups can be a highly uncertain matter. Actual disagreements often involve a variety of argumentation between opposing sides. Some types of argumentation make the disagreement look brute; other types make it look reasonable. Libertarians, for example, sometimes confer on the right to acquire and transfer property such an absolute importance that it seems difficult to avoid brute disagreement between them and others who place any importance on the notion of need in matters of social justice. At other times they argue for the same social policies on the

20. Thomas Nagel, "Moral Conflict and Political Legitimacy," *Philosophy and Public Affairs* 16 (1987): 232. An important statement of the contractualist idea is in Thomas Scanlon, "Contractualism and Utilitarianism," in *Utilitarianism and Beyond*, ed. Amartya Sen and Bernard Williams (Cambridge: Cambridge University Press, 1982), 103–28.

21. Nagel, "Moral Conflict," 229. He does note, however that some disagreements may be brute yet unavoidably be subjects for state action, such as those over the morality of nuclear deterrence and the death penalty.

244 Having Confidence in Our Moral Commitments

basis of claims that look to be the subject of reasonable disagreement: on the ineffectiveness and undesirable side-effects of state attempts at redistribution of wealth and
income, for example. They often alternate between the two justifications in such a way
that it seems indeterminate which justification is primary. Perhaps some individuals
within the group of libertarians hold determinate positions, but they may hold different
determinate positions. We furthermore could wonder if we have a sufficient grasp of the
distinction in theory. The distinction between brute and reasonable is too uncertain in
application to ground the policy of state neutrality as an accommodation to serious
moral conflicts.

Another plausible criticism, given by Amy Gutman and Dennis Thompson, is that
the distinction throws too much into the brute category, including disagreements over
the liberal's belief in human equality, a belief "which underlies those coercive state
policies that Nagel rightly wants to defend."[22] They also argue that Nagel's implicit
identification of state inaction with state neutrality is misguided: "the failure of the
state to act can subject citizens to as much coercion and violation of their rights as a
decision to act."[23] The strategy of inaction offers "a false impartiality in place of social
recognition of the persistence of fundamental conflicts of value in our society."[24]
Gutman and Thompson accordingly propose to shift the focus to principles governing
the process of collective deliberation over these fundamental conflicts. Such principles
express the democratic virtue of mutual respect between citizens, and, for example,
require that citizens acknowledge the positions they oppose as based on moral principles about which reasonable people may disagree. Those who are prochoice and
prolife, for example, should be prepared to recognize that their opponents base their
views on sincerely held moral principles. Another principle is that one must be prepared to change one's views in the face of evidence one cannot refute upon reflection.

Nagel's demanding standard of objectivity for the exercise of political power does
seem to require neutrality on too many issues of the greatest moral import.[25] If confronted with the choice, many people would and in fact do reject or override the
standard of higher objectivity in favor of pressing their moral positions in the public
domain. It is not clear, for example, that prolife advocates on the issue of abortion are
rationally compelled to accept the argument for state neutrality on abortion, even if
they accept the bruteness of their disagreement with prochoice advocates as a reason for

22. Amy Gutman and Dennis Thompson, "Moral Conflict and Political Consensus," Ethics 101
(1990): 67.
23. Gutmann and Thompson, "Moral Conflict," 68.
24. Gutmann and Thompson, "Moral Conflict," 75.
25. A point I myself had not sufficiently considered in an earlier discussion of the issues in Moral
Relativity (Berkeley: University of California Press, 1984). In chap. 12, I presented an argument for
nonintervention by the state in the sort of moral disagreements I have labeled brute here. I did
concede, even at that time, that the moral reasons for nonintervention could be overridden by other
moral reasons.

tolerance. It also is understandable why they would regard *Roe v. Wade* as far from a position of state neutrality on the morality of abortion, but in practice an endorsement of moral permission. Prochoice advocates, on the other side, could reasonably object that prohibition of state funding of abortion, though justifiable on neutralist grounds, leads to a de facto violation of poor women's rights.

Even if the distinction between brute and reasonable were clearer in practice, Gutman and Thompson give a compelling case for the necessity of admitting some brute disagreements on the agenda for state action. Their principles for democratic discussion constitute a constructive and necessary part of what it would mean to take accommodation seriously as a moral value. Conducting fair discussions with those with whom one is in serious disagreement is, after all, one way of accommodating them. However, their principles are largely procedural in nature and are presented as ways to protect and to facilitate the search for moral truth. When the subject of public discussion is a disagreement that could be called brute, however, the principles have uncertain value for facilitating discovery of the truth. And even if a public discussion governed by these principles eventually yields significantly greater convergence of views on an issue, what is left unaddressed is the matter of how people on opposing sides are to get along with one another in the meantime. And by "get along," I do not mean "discuss with one another their differences." If disagreements concern matters of the highest moral importance for people, they will and must do more than discuss them in democratic fashion.

Stuart Hampshire's conception of "bare" or "procedural" justice provides some clues as to how we might go further than the idea of accommodation as fair discussion. According to Hampshire, there is a universal core concept of justice that underlies the variety of culturally specific and "thickened" conceptions of justice and the good. Varied social roles and functions, each with its typical virtues and its obligations, and premised upon some conception of the good, "have been the normal situation in most societies throughout history."[26] The core concept does not yield a way of making these roles cohere within an accepted and overarching whole but enables them to coexist in civil society and, as far as possible, without any substantial reconciliation between them and without a search for any further common ground than procedural justice itself. The core concept requires equal and fair dealing between proponents of rival conceptions of the good, for example, fair compromise in balancing concession against concession.

Hampshire's core concept of justice is, unlike Nagel's liberal tolerance and Gutman and Thompson's ideal of fair and democratic discussion, a substantive conception that addresses how people in serious moral conflict with each other are to live together in one society.[27] He argues for the core concept from a view of human nature and its

---

26. Stuart Hampshire, *Innocence and Experience* (Cambridge, Mass.: Harvard University Press, 1989), 108.

27. Sometimes he presents the core concept, however, as if it were a purely procedural one. This is when he talks of the conception as an extension of the canons of practical rationality: just as promoting

relation to the diverse range of goods prized by human beings. He holds, on the one hand, that human nature contains common needs and potentialities that give rise to obligations of love, of friendship, of families and of kinships, and to duties of benevolence or at least restraints against harm and destruction of life. The common needs of human nature make the core concept of justice possible. Hampshire holds, on the other hand, that human nature contains a drive to develop "separate and conflicting identities defined by language, religion, exclusive customs and prohibitions, and the histories of groups." This drive to diversity makes the core concept a stabilizing necessity.[28]

Hampshire has specified a substantive kind of ethical accommodation—peaceful coexistence between adherents of rival moral conceptions—and he has argued for the necessity of accommodation based on the plausible claim that diversity of value is the normal situation in most societies throughout history. My own conception of accommodation lies in the directions in which Hampshire has pointed. Martin Benjamin has also pointed in these directions in arguing for the need to respect ways of life and on the need for people working together to compromise on their moral differences for the sake of pursuing their common ends.[29] I shall elaborate on my own conception next, connecting it with some of the main themes comprising pluralistic relativism.

9.9 THE NATURE OF SERIOUS MORAL CONFLICT

Let us return to Nagel's conception of moral conflicts that elude our attempts to resolve them through the use of a common reason, but this time let us forgo the distinction between brute and reasonable disagreements and use the category of "serious disagreement" to embrace either kind, as well as those indeterminately falling in between these categories. The reason for doing this is not only because the distinction between

---

and accepting arguments for and against a proposal are the essence of practical rationality, so rival conceptions of the good must be given their day in court. But if this were all there were to the bare conception of justice, it would not promote the coexistence of rival conceptions. A fair hearing is one thing. Being protected, as far as possible, against the coercive encroachments of rival conceptions of the good is quite a more substantive thing, and it is clear that Hampshire has this in mind.

28. Hampshire's conception of this drive is really of a cluster of distinguishable ones. He thinks the drive to separate identities is a universal tendency not only of groups but of individuals (the drive to "individuality"), and he tends to associate the drive to diversity with a drive to divisiveness, to opposition toward others who are different (*Innocence and Experience*, 33–4). The strength of the case for attributing these different drives to human nature varies. The case for attributing the drive to distinct communal identities is strong. The case for attributing a drive to "individuality" seems rather culturally specific, and the drive to divisiveness seems common but not at all universal. Significant diversity of value across communities seems sufficient, however, to motivate Hampshire's conception of bare justice.

29. Martin Benjamin, *Splitting the Difference: Compromise and Integrity in Ethics and Politics* (Lawrence: University of Kansas Press, 1990).

brute and reasonable is indeterminate for important kinds of moral disagreement but also because the practical significance of the distinction becomes less important if we do not use it as a basis for precluding certain moral conflicts from the political agenda.[30]

Compare two pictures of serious disagreement. According to one picture, there are huge interpersonal differences among ultimate moral principles. Perhaps universally held principles exist, but these lack any real normative bite. For example, no one who holds moral concepts can deny that it is wrong to torture someone on a whim, but such principles determine very little of the ethical life.[31] The other picture of disagreement recognizes that even in large, heterogeneous societies such as the United States, there are widely held substantive moral principles. It is held to be wrong not only to torture people on whim but also to torture or even imprison them for criticizing political leaders. Even in one of the most divisive moral debates taking place in the United States, that concerning the moral permissibility of abortion, the source of disagreement seems not so much to be a difference in the ultimate moral principles held by the opposing sides, as partly a difference over the applicability of a commonly held principle requiring the protection of human life and partly a difference over the relative weight to be given in the circumstances to another widely held principle requiring the protection of individual autonomy.

The two sources of serious disagreement, in fact, are often intertwined. A disagreement over the way that boundaries of one principle should be drawn is often connected to disagreement over when that principle comes into conflict with another principle. Prochoice people sometimes argue that the fetus, at least in the earlier stages of development, does not fall under the principle requiring the protection of human life. The principle protecting a woman's autonomy therefore does not conflict with that principle in the case of abortion in the early stages. Prolife people draw the boundaries of the former principle so that it does come into conflict with a woman's autonomy or so that it provides a limit to the extent of her autonomy.

My main point here is to repeat a theme first developed in chapter 1: that the values accounting for each side's position are not drawn from moral universes that are alien to the other. This is not to deny that people can hold different sets of ultimate moral principles, but it is seriously misleading to characterize serious moral disagreement as typically involving a difference in the ultimate principles held. Sometimes the principles entering into a disagreement are held in common by opposing sides, and it is the boundary of application that is at issue, or the relative priority to be given to conflicting principles in the circumstances. Serious disagreement need not result from radical difference, but may in fact exist within groups that may reasonably be called

---

30. I am indebted to Mitchell Silver for bringing this point to my attention.

31. See Stephen Schiffer, "Meaning and Value," *Journal of Philosophy* 87 (1990): 602–14, for such a picture. R. M. Hare seems to suggest such a picture in his earlier work, such as *The Language of Morals* (London: Oxford University Press, 1964).

communities of moral belief, that is, communities that are more or less cohesive in accepting the same principles, at least in comparison with certain other groups.

Whether a given group is a community of belief is itself a relative matter and a matter of degree. Compared to medieval Japan, the moral differences among North Americans on most moral issues seem relatively minor. But a comparison of groups within the United States, differentiated by class and level of education, will yield important, even fundamental moral differences. The type of moral issue sometimes makes a difference. On matters of the right to criticize political leaders, a group may form a relatively uniform community of belief, but not on matters of distributive justice concerning wealth and income. Some types of duties are recognized across deeply different cultures, as Hampshire notes, and I agree with him that this is partly to be explained by reference to a common human nature.[32]

The picture of moral differences as intertwined with commonalities corresponds to the thought first articulated in the first chapter: that other people and other cultures are confronted with choices familiar to us, even if we do not give the same answer as they do. But even if we do not give the same answers, we may see why others may have chosen their answers to the following questions: which values to prize the most; whether to promote the ideal of balance between human virtues in tension with one another or more of a single-mindedness in the pursuit of one set of virtues that are relatively compatible with each other; whether to emphasize prohibitions of the ex-ploitation and use of persons for the sake of larger, desirable ends or to allow suffi-ciently desirable ends to override the wrongness of exploitation; whether to prize most the goods of community and interdependence or the goods of promoting individuality and autonomy; whether to give priority to excellences that probably can be achieved only by a few or to ensuring the conditions that make possible a decent and satisfying life for all.

Acceptance of irreducible plurality in fundamental moral belief is heightened by the ability to see the values and moral themes accepted by other individuals and cultures as developments of choices that one (or one's people, one's culture) might have made in different circumstances. Having this ability is not to automatically approve of the choices others have made. To understand does not necessarily mean that one would make one's own choices any differently. But understanding may appropriately en-courage a healthy caution before leaping to the conclusion that there is a set of choices of values and priorities that would be uniquely determined through use of a "common reason."[33] Most important, understanding leads us to expect serious moral conflict to

---

32. See my "On Flourishing and Finding One's Identity in Community," *Midwest Studies in Philosophy* 13 (1988), special issue, *Ethical Theory: Character and Virtue*, ed. Peter A. French, Theodore E. Uehling Jr., and Howard K. Wettstein: 324–41.

33. Understanding why others have made different choices could have different possible conse-quences. One could understand others' choices but believe that they were mistaken, being prepared to

be a regular part of our moral lives. It is unrealistic to expect that even groups united by language, religion, customs, and histories could produce uniformity of belief about the right set of choices to be made. We must expect to deal as a regular matter with those who have made different choices, even when we cannot be very sympathetic to their choices.

This picture of moral conflict contains further complications. If conflict arises from common choices between values, one would expect that in large and diverse cultures such as that of the United States, significant numbers of people occupy the space between those who take hard-and-fast opposing positions. For example, take those who find themselves with uncertain and indeterminate positions on the morality of abortion.[34] There may be indeterminacy of position with respect to the breadth of application of the right to life, or with respect to the relative priority of autonomy versus the protection of at least potential persons. Even those who take somewhat firm positions on the issue could enter a greater state of uncertainty if they were persuaded that there are no commonly held principles that justify their positions.

Furthermore, the second picture of moral conflict leads us to expect significant conflict and even incoherence in the belief systems of many individuals in matters where important values regularly come into conflict. Beliefs about such matters might be inchoate or incoherent to such a degree that they resist any ordering through imposition of a consistent set of principles. This is true, I believe, for many individuals with respect to disagreements over distributive justice in the United States. It is arguable, for example, that there is no fact of the matter as to whether many people hold beliefs about distributive justice that are consistent with something like Rawls's difference principle or a rather minimal liberal welfarism.

Arguments about distributive justice often mask a significant degree of indeterminacy in belief about general principles governing the distribution of wealth and income. Some conservative arguments against significant redistribution by the state depend on claims about the ineffectiveness, waste, inefficiency, and corruption of such attempted redistributions. Or they may depend on claims about the undermining effects on incentives to productivity. Many of these arguments are in fact consistent with liberal and egalitarian principles because such principles are stated at such a high level of abstraction from empirical considerations. Consider Rawls's second principle

---

explain how they were mistaken. One could understand them, and believe them mistaken, yet presently be unable to provide an explanation of how they were mistaken. One could understand them, and be unable to deem them mistaken, but also be unable to deem them acceptable either. And finally, one could come to accept what one initially rejected. Serious disagreement exists between the first and last possibilities.

34. In writing about indeterminacy of moral positions and of belief, I am assuming that belief is a propositional attitude we attribute to people on the basis of verbal and behavioral patterns. Sometimes the character of specific patterns that people display is evidence for indeterminacy in the propositional object of belief.

of justice in this regard. The point is not that conservative arguments against state redistribution actually presuppose such principles, but that they are consistent with a number of conflicting general principles of distributive justice. Much of the point of these arguments, in fact, is to produce agreement on relatively concrete policy matters while avoiding explicit commitment to general principles that one's audience may reject. One characteristic form of such arguments ("Whether one holds general principles A, B, or C, no good aim is served by policy X") is a useful rhetorical strategy when dealing with an audience whose fundamental beliefs may be indeterminate, incoherent, or irreducibly diverse.

But remember that such diversity, indeterminacy, and ambiguity is compatible with significant areas of agreement within the moral tradition of large, heterogeneous societies such as the United States. People in the United States are overwhelmingly committed, at least de facto, to the justness of providing some form of minimal welfare for all members of society. Such agreement is even more salient on questions of the civil liberties than on many matters of the distribution of wealth and income. Or consider the way that some former advocates of the death penalty have come to suspend their advocacy given evidence that class and race make it much more likely that one is likely to be sentenced to death for a given type of serious crime, or recent DNA evidence that significant numbers of people have been in fact innocent of the crimes for which they have been sentenced to death.[35] Even though these former advocates adopt principled positions that favor death as a proportionate penalty for the most serious of crimes, or that favor death as an acceptable deterrent against such crimes, they share with opponents of the death penalty the values of fairness in administering criminal punishment and protection of the innocent. That point of agreement in principle may be sufficient to produce agreement in practice despite other disagreements in principle.

Disagreement within a society appears to be more or less pervasive as one varies the set of moral issues at hand. This can hold true with respect to single principles that are very general in nature and cover a diverse range of policy issues. There may be no answer to the question of whether people hold the same principle, but only one relativized to certain types of application. A given group of individuals may form a relatively harmonious community of belief on one principle or one set of its applications, but then form a fractious community or even belong to different and opposed communities on another principle or another set of applications.

The portrait of moral diversity advanced in this book points to the ubiquity of serious disagreement and therefore to the constant necessity for accommodation. The

---

35. In March 2000, the Illinois governor and death penalty supporter George Ryan declared a moratorium on executions in his state after thirteen men on death row were exonerated by new evidence. In May 2000, the generally conservative New Hampshire legislature voted to abolish the death penalty, based on concerns about the fairness and accuracy with which the death penalty is meted out.

ideal of peaceful coexistence with the morally other is sometimes applied primarily to separate moral communities with more or less cohesive internal identities and whose main problem is to coexist with other moral communities (we often get such a picture from Hampshire's writings). If the picture of moral diversity advanced here is correct, then accommodation is needed *within* relatively cohesive moral communities also, and not just for peaceful coexistence but also for the day-to-day constructive relationships that make striving toward shared ends possible. The picture of moral diversity advanced here also supports the *possibility* of accommodation, insofar as it points to the likelihood of shared values as well as the ubiquity of serious disagreement. The shared values provide some leverage for possible resolutions of the disagreements and also constitute part of a shared background that contributes to the perception of affinity between the contending parties.

9.10 THE CONTENT OF ACCOMMODATION AS A MORAL VALUE

I argued in chapter 2 that any adequate morality must have in some degree the value of accommodation on the grounds of the inevitability of serious disagreement. Apart from this argument, there are at least two other bases for recognizing the value of creating or sustaining noncoercive relations with others who are in fundamental moral conflict with us, but I am not claiming that these grounds need to be seen as equally compelling by the practitioners of all justifiable moral traditions. First, we may simply value such relationships as ends in themselves. It can be of intrinsic moral value to live in communities based not only on some degree of agreement in moral belief but also on ties of affection or loyalty, or on a limited set of common goals that may be educational, artistic, political, or economic in nature. As a matter of fact, we do typically live in communities with genuine bases other than identity of moral belief, communities that are often absolutely essential to the shape and meaning of our lives. Second, the project of cooperating with others to promote common moral ends often requires accommodation to one's moral differences with them. This necessity is especially salient in communities of moral belief with blurred boundaries that shift with the issue and the relevant principles applied. One's ally in promoting a moral position on one issue becomes a potential adversary on another issue. The moral worth of accommodation is both intrinsic and derives from the worth of other moral ends that are shared.

Note that on both the first and second ways of grounding the value of accommodation, the rationale is not that accommodation is a *modus vivendi*, acceptable only because the alternatives are in nonmoral terms worse.[36] Living with others in productive ways, despite our moral differences with them, can itself be morally valuable. It

---

36. Thanks to Peter Railton for helping me to clarify this point. Benjamin, in *Splitting the Difference*, argues for the necessity of compromise between serious moral differences on the grounds of the

can be a particularly strong form of respect for persons, and being able to show this kind of respect is a sign of moral maturity. The willingness to live with others despite moral differences promotes cooperation on the moral ends that are shared. In fact, we already do recognize the moral value of accommodation in practice, if not in theory. We find that people do reason from this value.

Consider Carol Gilligan's well-known discussion of children's reactions to Heinz's dilemma, in which Heinz considers whether or not to steal a drug that he cannot afford to buy in order to save the life of his wife. After it is stated that the druggist refuses to lower the price, the question is asked, "Should Heinz steal the drug?" Jake, an eleven-year-old boy, constructs the dilemma as a conflict between the values of property and life, and places priority on life. Amy, an eleven-year-old girl, considers "neither property nor law" but rather the effect that the theft could have on the relationship between Heinz and his wife. If Heinz is caught, Amy reasons, the situation for his wife could be worse in the long run. They should really just talk it out and find another way to make the money. Amy conceives the solution as making the wife's condition more salient to the druggist, or failing that, as appealing to others who are in a position to help. Gilligan concludes, "these two children see two very different moral problems—Jake a conflict between life and property that can be resolved by logical deduction. Amy a fracture of human relationship that must be mended with its own thread."[37]

The sort of moral reasoning Gilligan takes to be exemplified by Amy's reaction is a complex phenomenon. Relevant to my purpose here is Amy's move of replacing the question "Would Heinz be right to steal the drug or not?" with "How can these relationships—that between Heinz and his wife, and between Heinz and the druggist, be sustained or mended?" I will not address the hypothesis that this sort of move in reasoning is more characteristic of women than of men. It does seem a common move that both men and women can make in everyday moral life. And a frequent occasion on which we do change the question is when the resolution of a conflict through determination of which side is in the right ends in a standoff, and when resolution in some manner is still what we seek. Amy's change of questions reflects the moral value she places on accommodation.

Moral conflict is not exhausted by conflict between beliefs about what is good or right. There is a conflict in what each party wants to happen next in the world. That conflict is often set in the context of a broader relationship between the parties, which

---

desirability of preserving cooperative relationships. I am unclear, however, as to whether he attaches a distinctly moral value to such relationships, as I do. At one point, he talks about moral compromise between members of a medical team as being highly desirable "from the standpoint of overall team effectiveness" (30–1), and I am unsure as to how he thinks of the desirability of "team effectiveness."

37. Carol Gilligan, *In a Different Voice* (Cambridge, Mass.: Harvard University Press, 1982), 25–31.

each party may have reason to sustain, both for the moral reasons identified earlier and perhaps for nonmoral reasons as well. The question of how to resolve the conflict in what each wants, or in any case how to muddle through it, need not require a determinate answer to the moral rights and wrongs of the issue. It may receive an answer in terms of what will sustain the broader relationship in ways consistent with the reasons for sustaining that relationship.

Whether we give philosophical legitimacy to this kind of reasoning, we employ it all the time in our everyday lives. Consider a philosophy department highly unusual in its diversity. Its members represent very different approaches and conceptions of philosophy: analytic, Anglo-American philosophy, continental European approaches, feminist philosophy, and Asian philosophy, let us say. The department is trying to decide among several candidates for a position. Groups within the department have different favorite candidates, and each believes that its choice is the best for the whole department. Yet in the interests of harmony within the department, some groups will agree upon someone who is the second or third best candidate for them. These groups may even believe that they could win a plurality for their first choice if it came to a vote but may also believe that the enmity and hostility created by such a victory would have unacceptable costs for the climate of trust and cooperation within the department, a climate to which they attach moral, as well as prudential, value. They may also expect that the other groups benefiting from this decision will take this into account the next time there is a similar conflict.

If Gilligan is correct in claiming that this sort of moral reasoning is more characteristic of women than of men, there is a kind of division of moral labor in this society. It is possible, however, that other moral traditions recognize no such comparable gendered division of labor. Consider Antonio Cua's interpretation of the Confucian virtue of *ren*. This virtue, he says, involves an attitude toward human conflicts as subjects of "arbitration" rather than "adjudication." Arbitration is an attempted resolution of disputes oriented toward the reconciliation of the contending parties.[38] The arbitrator is "concerned with repairing the rupture of human relationship rather than with deciding the rights or wrongs of the parties" and, accordingly, attempts to shape "the expectations of the contending parties along the line of mutual concern, to get them to appreciate one another as interacting members in a community."[39] Under Confucianism, says Cua, an appeal to objective principles that specify "rights and wrongs" is likely to alienate people from one another instead of encouraging them to

38. It was pointed out to me by Thomas Seung that the word 'arbitration' may be a misleading label for the sort of process Cua has in mind, since it usually implies the intervention of a third party. Perhaps 'conciliation' is a better term that allows for a resolution that can be effected by the contending parties themselves.

39. Antonio Cua, "The Status of Principles in Confucian Ethics," *Journal of Chinese Philosophy* 16 (1989): 281.

maintain or develop relationships. And finally, Cua strikingly suggests the need for Confucianism to develop such principles to be applied when arbitration fails.

A natural reaction to this proposal might be that Cua has got it the wrong way around. Certainly one should try to determine the rights and wrongs first, and in case that ends in serious disagreement, then one should seek arbitration. This would be treating arbitration as a second-order value, a value to be applied when the first-order value of resolution via adjudication fails. Cua treats adjudication as the second-order value, waiting in the wings in case the first-order value of arbitration fails. But he has not got it the wrong way around. His proposal reflects the centrality accorded to harmony and reconciliation as first-order values within the Confucian tradition. Living well with others, despite one's moral differences with them, is itself a primary moral value. The concern that applying objective principles would be a threat to harmony is an indication of the importance of this first-order value. By contrast, proposing arbitration as a second-order value would be natural in the Anglo-American tradition of moral philosophy, given that adjudication has become the paradigm in this tradition for resolving disputes through moral reasoning.

If there is a difference between the Anglo-American and ancient Confucian traditions, however, it is primarily one of emphasis placed on arbitration and adjudication as first-order values. The Confucian tradition is not entirely lacking in principles that help to specify the rights and wrongs between contending parties.[40] In both traditions, reconciliation can function either as a first- or a second-order value. It is difficult to see how reconciliation could not be a factor at least sometimes in our deliberations about what it is right to do, especially given the assumption that morality is in some significant degree about the regulation and mediation of interpersonal conflict of interest. However, it can also serve as a second-order value, guiding one's attempts to deal with failures in adjudication.

9.11 WHAT WOULD IT MEAN TO ACT
ON THE VALUE OF ACCOMMODATION?

What would it mean to go beyond the policies of fair discussion and peaceful coexistence when acting on the moral value of accommodation? One meaning of accommodation that goes beyond these ideas is to act on one's moral position in a way that minimizes potential damage to one's broader relationship to others who have opposed positions. This may be desirable not just because one desires peaceful coexistence with them, and not just because one may find it necessary to join forces with them on other issues, given that the boundaries of moral communities are blurred, fluid, and relative

---

40. Consider the virtue of *shu*, sometimes translated as sympathetic understanding, which has been called the Confucian equivalent of the Golden Rule; see *Analects*, trans. D. C. Lau (London: Penguin, 1979), 6.28.

to the principle or set of applications at hand. These are valid enough reasons, but another reason is that minimizing damage to the broader relationship makes it likelier that opposed sides will be able to regard each other as people to whom it is possible to stand in some positive moral relationship of respect and nonmanipulation rather than simply opponents in a contest to see whose position becomes enforced by our common institutions.

Maintaining the possibility for such a moral relationship is not just necessary for sustaining whatever broader relationship exists between moral opponents but also promotes the possibility of compromise on the very issues that divide them. I was once surprised to hear an activist on the prochoice side of the abortion issue express regret that *Roe v. Wade* came down at the time it did. In this person's opinion, the ruling had the unfortunate effect of making prolifers feel that they had lost a political battle and that the issue then became for them who would win the war. An opportunity for further dialogue and eventual compromise had been lost.[41] His calculation was based on a personal reading of the psychological and political climate at the time, and is debatable, but it is the sort of thing that must be considered when asking what accommodation might mean in disputes such as that over abortion. Even from the prochoice point of view, there is room in hindsight for the troubling thought that the highest court's decision had the effect of turning public discussion of the issue into a pure contest of political wills.

Another principle of accommodation arises from the recognition that any substantive ethical system will create a range of options as to when and in what manner one attempts to realize its values. One must choose where to direct one's energies when there are many large gaps between the way things ought to be and the way things are. Taking the value of accommodation seriously requires that, other things being equal, one select foci for attention that minimize the opportunity for serious disagreement. The task of selection will often involve the question of the degree of generality that one's moral positions should have, as one carries these positions into the forum of public debate and discussion. The most general principles of an ethical system, even when commonly accepted, are liable to give rise to serious conflict over the extent of their application and their priority relative to other principles in cases of conflict. It is sometimes easier for people to come to an agreement on more specific instances covered by these principles than it is to come to an agreement on the more abstract and general levels.

41. In *Ideals, Beliefs, Attitudes, and the Law* (Syracuse, N.Y.: Syracuse University Press, 1985), 96–7, Guido Calabresi observes that before *Roe v. Wade* a number of state legislatures moved toward permitting abortion, some going as far as the Supreme Court decision. After the decision, there was a new sense of "desperate embattlement," where there was "almost fanatical pressure to forbid abortion." Calabresi criticizes *Roe v. Wade* for categorically excluding the metaphysics of the prolife side as irrelevant to the constitutional question of whether the fetus should be treated as a person. He argues that this exclusion was deeply offending.

For example, consider the earlier suggestion that few people in the United States have a coherent and stable set of beliefs that correspond to the very general and abstract philosophical theories of justice. Perhaps this is a defect in our moral knowledge, but the situation has its advantages in comparison to certain other possible situations of pervasive ideological warfare, with most people falling into one clearly defined camp or another. Despite our inability to agree on the question of how egalitarian the distribution of wealth and income ought to be, the overwhelming majority agrees that the minimal state is simply not enough, that there ought to be some redistribution for the sake of addressing need. How far this principle ought to be applied, of course, is a matter of endless disagreement, and that is because many different theories of justice are compatible with it and incompatible with each other in specifying the extent and nature of its application. But there are some instances on which a reasonably widespread if not unanimous consensus can be reached. From the perspective that takes accommodation seriously, there is reason to concentrate on the less general issues of distributive justice.

Disagreement with others on the level of the most general and comprehensive principles may be radical, while on the more concrete levels where we consider what can be done now, given the present circumstances, and given what has already happened, disagreement may be less severe because everyone's options have been narrowed. Those on the robustly egalitarian end of the spectrum on matters of distributive justice, for instance, must take into account the present and foreseeable prospects for realizing anything remotely resembling their ideals. Libertarians should come to a similar recognition, despite the fact that much of the current political rhetoric leans vaguely in their direction. In both cases, emphasizing one's disagreements with others on the most general and comprehensive principles of distributive justice may not be the most prudent strategy. It may be better to emphasize agreement with others on more limited and concrete matters of distributive justice, at least for now.

Another principle of accommodation arises from the understanding of some serious disagreements that was described in the previous section. The understanding is that these disagreements are the result of different choices peoples have made about the relative emphases and priorities to be given to things that are commonly acknowledged to have value for human beings. Though the relative emphases and priorities held by the others are not ones that are adopted in one's own ethic, one understands how these others arrived at the choices made and to some extent the satisfactions of the way of life that is so structured. Such an understanding, under an ethic that takes accommodation seriously, leads to openness to influence by others, and by their conceptions of the good and thick conceptions of the right.

The accommodating impulse here takes the form of willingness to bridge differences. Sometimes this results in a willingness to trade concessions. As suggested earlier, those who take hard-and-fast liberal and conservative positions on the morality of abortion may have to recognize not only the seriousness of their disagreement with each other but also that there are many people who display considerable indeterminacy of belief about the matter. In such cases, those inclined to take determinate positions may show an openness to the influence of others by being willing to compromise on the legal issues, for example, recognizing a legal right to abortion but qualifying or restricting that right in certain ways, where the content and extent of these restrictions would be subject to negotiation.[42]

An openness to be influenced by others, to bridge differences, may also take the form of a preparedness to expand one's conception of the good and the right upon further understanding and appreciation of other ways of life, as I argued at the beginning of this chapter. This sort of preparedness goes beyond what could be required by the ideal of fair and democratic discussion—beyond, for example, the passive virtue of being prepared to change one's views in the face of undermining evidence. Learning from others often requires instead an active willingness to gain a more vivid and detailed appreciation of what it is like to live their ways of life, an appreciation that can only be achieved through significant interaction with them.

Let me stress that even if one is committed strongly to the moral value of accommodation, it cannot always take precedence over one's other moral values. In particular, it cannot always take precedence over the values that constitute the source of serious disagreement with others. One may simply judge in the end that these values are too important to compromise on, at least on a given occasion. A conservative on abortion may accept legal permission of abortion in the early stages of fetal development as an accommodation, but be unwilling to accept any sort of compromise on infanticide as it is practiced in some countries. And she may be unwilling to accept compromise even if she sees her disagreement with those who practice infanticide as irresolvable through the use of a common reason.[43]

How do we distinguish between disagreements in which accommodation is more important and disagreements in which it is more important to stand fast? I believe that ultimately it is a matter of judgment in the concrete situation, and that it is impossible to formulate anything very useful in the way of general guidelines. But if this is a difficulty, it is not because the value of accommodation is involved. We could make the same conclusion about the necessity of contextualized judgment in conflicts that do not involve accommodation, such as conflicts involving the prohibition of the use of persons for the sake of larger, desirable ends. Whether some end is sufficiently compelling to justify overriding the prohibition is ultimately a matter of judgment. Con-

42. It would be essential that the idea of qualifying or restricting rights be presented sincerely in the spirit of compromise, and not simply as a covert way of gaining ground in the battle to repeal abortion rights altogether. See Benjamin, chapter 6 of *Splitting the Difference*, for an interesting discussion on the possibilities of compromise on abortion.

43. Leonard Harris impressed upon me the need to take into account what other values are at stake in deciding whether to accommodate.

textualized judgment will always be a necessity for someone who believes that the sources of moral value and duty are irreducibly plural.

Nevertheless, it is possible to identify certain factors that should influence judgment on the desirability of accommodation, even if these factors do not determine judgment by way of general principles. For example, one's willingness to accommodate others should depend on one's assessment of their willingness to reciprocate. Seeing that others are merely pressing their positions to gain concessions is a reason not to accommodate.[44] More constructively, that may be a reason to remind these others that the process of attempted accommodation takes place within the context of an ongoing relationship that may be severely damaged by an unwillingness to accommodate. One also has less reason to accommodate if the other side justifies its stand in terms of values to which it does not adhere in other contexts. This kind of inconsistency can reflect a lack of commitment to the professed values or even insincerity. On the other hand, one must be on guard against the possibility that charging the other side with insincerity can be a convenient way to avoid confronting an opposing position as a genuine moral position. Charging insincerity sometimes substitutes for a willingness to admit that an opponent's moral positions are complex (indeed, as complex as one's own) rather than inconsistent.

Further, the question of whether one should accommodate others is often bound up with one's relation of power to them. A group may feel subordinated and marginalized to the extent that others do not take its views seriously. It therefore may deem unacceptable any proposal that it accommodate to others. A reason why the abortion conflict has been so intractable is that significant numbers of people belonging to both sides feel themselves to have been disempowered, not given sufficiently serious attention by those who do have power in this context. Recognizing the moral value of accommodation is not always a way to resolve deadlocked conflicts. It does help, however, to note that accommodation need not always serve as a simple substitute for pressing one's position against others. Sometimes it is appropriate only *after* a process of conflict and each side's pressing its own position against the other. Compromise on the abortion conflict may emerge as a real possibility when enough people on opposing sides have succeeded in being taken seriously and in exercising leverage on those who do have power.[45]

Thinking about how to realize the value of accommodation requires thinking not only about strategies of accommodation and the conditions under which it is acceptable but also about virtues that enable people to devise and effectively act on strategies. The virtues of resourcefulness and creativity are necessary for the ability to act on one's own moral position while minimizing damage to one's relationship with

---

44. Lawrence Becker and Thomas Hill Jr. pointed out this sort of problem to me.

45. Comments from Patricia Mann, Jane Martin, and Nancy (Ann) Davis helped me to think further about the complexities of the abortion issue, even if I was not able to satisfy their worries. There

those in opposition, for the ability to find concessions acceptable to oneself and others, and for the ability to incorporate elements from ethical systems conflicting with one's own. And of course, we need the virtue of being able to cope with ambiguity, where coping involves the willingness to deal with considerable indeterminacy of belief, and where it involves the impulse to avoid commitment to general and abstract principles about which there is radical disagreement in favor of focusing on more specific issues on which moral opponents could converge.

We need to investigate the reasoning, the intentional structures and psychological prerequisites of virtues that make accommodation possible, as we have done for the more commonly treated virtues such as courage. Indeed, it is remarkable that moral philosophy has paid comparatively little attention to the relevance of creativity, re-sourcefulness, and the ability to cope with ambiguity to our abilities to deliberate and act well, and perhaps this is an indication of the dominance of the adjudication model, together with the top-down model of moral reasoning from the abstract and general to the less so.

These points have implications for those of us who are educators. It is now a commonplace to espouse the values of critical thinking, dissent, and independence of thought. But alongside these virtues, students equipped to be citizens in a diverse society must also be given ways of expressing and of symbolizing how there can be community with those who are in deep disagreement with them. For example, we must think about what it might concretely mean for students to truly listen not only to their teachers but also to each other in discussion. We need to examine our deeply rooted habits concerning whom we praise and for what reasons. These habits generate habits in our students. Do we tend to reserve our highest praise for virtuoso performances in which students are able to defend their own positions against all criticisms and to effectively criticize the positions of others? Or do we praise as highly a student's openness to the possibility that others have a significant basis for their beliefs, a willingness to revise one's own positions in the light of a deeper understanding of how others think? Changes in these habits of listening and of responding to others may cut more deeply than changes in content of curriculum. They are at the very center of an ongoing community capable of accommodating differences.

---

is, I think, some illumination to be gained from comparative study of how different countries have treated the abortion controversy. Many in the United States were surprised that a "morning after" pill was approved by the French government, one version of which is included in the standard kit for school nurses. To a greater degree in France than in the United States, there is a tradition of comity in the political process in which contending groups—in this case, nurses' unions, students' unions, cardinals, parents, doctors, women's groups, the ruling Socialist Party, and the ministry of education— have a voice in reaching a workable compromise. All had the common goal of reducing the number of abortions, and indeed, France has a much lower rate of abortion than the United States. See Diane Johnson, "Abortion: The French Solution," *New York Times*, February 22, 2000, available at www.nytimes.com/books/00/04/16/specials/johnson-franceed.html. Rev. August 24, 2005.

Adjudication and independent and critical thinking are of course important, but focusing on them as exclusively as we have has led to a neglect of the genuinely practical questions confronting relativists and universalists alike, which have to do with dealing with those others with whom we are currently in serious disagreement. Fortunately, we are practical beings as well as philosophical ones and have had to deal with such disagreements in our practical lives. We can draw from that fund of experience to articulate the philosophical account we need.

9.12 Living in a Multicultural Society

The picture I have drawn here of moral diversity and our need and ability to cope with it bears on the recent trends of multiculturalism and the growing recognition of a need to appreciate cultural diversity. Let me address two worries about that trend: that it promotes a corrosive skepticism about the values that must be shared in a democratic society, and that it promotes instability and conflict among different ethnic and cultural groups.

The first worry is that in teaching the worth of other cultures we undermine belief in the objective rightness of our own democratic values.[46] This worry underlies, I suspect, the objections that many have lodged against multicultural education, particularly against the introduction alongside the accepted "Great Works" of Western culture of texts by women and people of cultures other than the dominant ones. One answer to this worry is that there are reasons to appreciate cultural diversity and to learn about other cultures that are entirely consistent with a belief that values can be objectively right, even in the very strong sense that there is a single true morality. After all, one can think that one can learn from other cultures as long as one retains a reasonable degree of humility about what one knows. The case for trying to learn from other cultures gains support from the picture of cultural diversity I have been drawing throughout this book: that other cultures are not alien configurations of strange values but recognizable attempts to deal with certain universal patterns of conflicts between familiar values. The fact that other cultures may have taken different paths in response to these conflicts and may have emphasized to a greater degree than we do certain familiar values means that we may very well have something to learn from them even if we do not desire to copy the paths they have taken.

Respect for other cultures can rest on the recognition that these cultures prize things that we ourselves prize, even if not in the same way or to the same degree. We recognize that other cultures embody different choices in the selection of which values

---

46. Something like this worry is expressed by William Galston, *Liberal Purposes: Goods, Virtues, and Diversity in the Liberal State* (Cambridge: Cambridge University Press, 1991), 251–5. See also Michael Sandel, "Morality and the Liberal Ideal," *New Republic*, May 7, 1984, 15–7.

to emphasize most fully, but we recognize that this is a world in which we cannot emphasize all important values equally. This is not to lapse into a mindless skepticism about values. Indeed, as I have argued in presenting a certain picture of cultural diversity, we can presuppose that a certain range of values is appropriate for human beings. If we recognize that no culture could maximize all things human beings prize, if we recognize that we may learn from other cultures because of the values they emphasize, we will be glad that there are other cultures. We will see cultural diversity as a good rather than as a problem.

To some extent, the multicultural movement has encouraged the first worry about skepticism by adopting the picture of other cultures as totally alien configurations of strange values. This is not only untrue of many of the crosscultural comparisons I have drawn throughout this book but also fails utterly in presenting a positive case for the appreciation of other cultures. This picture may prevent us from judging our own culture to be superior to others, but it may equally cause us to withhold any judgment, including the judgment that the others have value. After all, if other cultures are so foreign to our sensibilities, why should we think ourselves qualified to judge them at all? Of course, those who present the first picture may intend that we withhold judgment. They sometimes talk as if respecting cultures *means* withholding judgment about their values. But this way of supporting multiculturalism is ultimately stultifying. It provides no basis for saying what we can *learn* from other cultures, and multiculturalism in its most appealing forms does mean such appreciation. What justification, after all, could teachers have for assigning texts from other cultures if we do not understand the worth in them?

Now, of course, I have been arguing throughout this book that many of our values may not be objectively right in the strongest sense, of being the only true ones people should adopt. My own position, then, may be taken to imply a "corrosive skepticism," even if multiculturalism in general need not. If skepticism means that we cannot take our own way of doing things as somehow writ into the fabric of nature, and that others may be equally if not more justified in adopting other ways, then I am skeptical. But I see no good way of avoiding this kind of skepticism, and have argued that our moral commitments need not necessarily be undermined. It is their basis that must be reconceived. It also is true that reconceiving the basis of our commitment to our values must affect the way we act toward others with whom we are in serious moral disagreement, but as I have argued in this chapter, we do have our ways of dealing with such disagreement.

Let me turn to the second worry about multiculturalism. The worry is that in teaching the worth of different cultures, we are promoting a "balkanization" of multicultural societies. The worry, in other words, is that valuing cultural differences will encourage culturally distinct groups to always press their interests over the common interests of the multicultural society. What could motivate cooperation between groups with ethical traditions that conflict? To value differences is to value the source of conflict, isn't it?[47] To address this worry, we need to recognize a fact I have emphasized in this chapter: that serious disagreement about values and their proper application is to be found within cultures as well as across cultures. Even communities founded on single cultural traditions must deal with serious disagreement within their ranks. If strict uniformity in ethical belief were a necessary condition of having a real community, then we would have very few, if any, communities. But, I have argued, we do have ways of holding a community together in the face of serious internal disagreement, and these ways are applicable to a multicultural society that does not attempt to suppress difference or to assimilate all into a single dominant culture.

Recognizing that a value of accommodation is crucial for the stability and integrity of societies and their ethical traditions, then, goes some way to addressing the balkanization worry. Of course, communities that are relatively diverse can come under greater stress. And we must recognize that acting on the value of accommodation does not always succeed in managing conflict. Consider, for example, the defeat of the constitutional proposals in Canada that were an attempt to accommodate longstanding grievances of Quebecois that have led some to press for separation. Even if accommodation is held as a value by both sides of a conflict, it will not always take precedence over the other values that constitute the source of the conflict. These other values may simply be held to be more important than accommodation.

Sometimes the disagreement may come in assessing whether accommodation is more or less important than other values at issue. Consider an example of a controversial case involving multiculturalism and gender equality and rights issues. When a Seattle, Washington, hospital asked Somali immigrant mothers whether they wanted their boys circumcised, these mothers requested to have their boys *and* girls circumcised.[48] The type of 'circumcision' they requested for girls is also called "female genital mutilation" by many of its opponents, and "female genital cutting" by those who wish a more neutral name for the practice. One additional reason for the term "cutting" rather than "circumcision" or "mutilation" is that forms of this practice vary significantly across parts of Asia and Africa, from a pricking of the genitalia to draw a drop of blood, to removal of the hood of the clitoris, to removal of the entire clitoris, to removal of all external genitalia with stitching together of the resulting wound. The women on whom it is practiced range from infants to adult women who consent to it.

Just as the practice has a variety of forms, it has a variety of rationales. The one that has made the practice notorious is that it helps to prevent promiscuity and to ensure chastity for future husbands. Sometimes a religious rationale is given. Muslims who

47. Something like this worry is expressed by Stephen Rockefeller in his comment on Charles Taylor's essay, in Taylor, *Multiculturalism and the Politics of Recognition: An Essay*, ed. Amy Gutmann (Princeton: Princeton University Press, 1993), 87–98.

48. See Doriane Lambelet Coleman, "The Seattle Compromise: Multicultural Sensitivity and Americanization," *Duke Law Journal* 47 (1998): 717–80.

engage in the practice often believe that the prophet Mohammed sanctioned it, though this is seriously contested within the religion. However, in some communities the practice is regarded as rendering the body fertile, as a rite of passage, and a test of courage and endurance to pain that binds together the community of women who practice it.[49] Fuami Ahmadu, a young African scholar born in Sierra Leone but raised in the United States, returned to her country of birth to undergo the cutting that is traditional in her Kono tribe.[50] She disputes a claim often made in criticism of the practice—that it diminishes sexual pleasure for women, arguing that the criticism presupposes an excessively mechanical picture of sexuality, omitting the role of the most important sexual organ—the mind. One of the other counterarguments given is that critics of the practice assume a controversial conception of the human body as complete and given at birth. Others point out that Western critics conveniently forget this when the time comes for plastic surgery or other forms of bodily enhancement. In light of such variety in form and rationale, some have cautioned against one-dimensional or superficial evaluations of the ritual practice.[51] They have also cautioned against the automatic assumption that patriarchal control must always be the underlying function of the practice, noting the diversity of meanings and circumstances of the practice and the fact that women are among the defenders of the practice.

All this forms the background for the problem that confronted the Seattle hospital. It serves a large immigrant community and makes it a priority to be sensitive to the distinct cultural practices of the people it serves. On the other hand, the medical staff could not contemplate performing anything like a traditional cut on girls. Some of the immigrant parents themselves suggested the compromise solution of performing a symbolic pricking of the clitoris to produce a drop of blood. The hospital agreed, partly on the grounds that the parents expressed their intentions to send their daughters elsewhere to have the procedure done if not in the hospital, and hospital staff believed that if done elsewhere the procedure would likely be far more radical and dangerous. However, the hospital was forced to withdraw its compromise policy in the face of a firestorm of protest against anything that could be remotely construed as a concession to the traditional practice. This last event constituted a missed opportunity for a successful negotiation between important values. On the one hand, there is the value of respect for cultural and religious beliefs and practices, the meaning and true rationale of which can be

---

49. For an informative survey of the rationales and meanings of the practice, see Ellen Gruenbaum, *The Female Circumcision Controversy: An Anthropological Perspective* (Philadelphia: University of Pennsylvania Press, 2001).

50. Fuambi Ahmadu, "Rites and Wrongs: An Insider/Outsider Reflects on Power and Excision," in *Female "Circumcision" in Africa: Culture, Controversy, and Change*, ed. Bettina Shell-Duncan and Yiva Herlund (Boulder, Colo.: Lynne Rienner, 2001), 283–312.

51. See L. Amede Obiora, "Bridges and Barricades: Rethinking Polemics and Intransigence in the Campaign against Female Circumcision," *Case Western Reserve Law Review* 47 (1997): 275–378.

multifarious and/or extremely elusive. This is no less true of the dominant cultural and religious practices in the United States. On the other hand, there is an imperative to assert the unacceptability of at least the extreme forms of the practice that can be reasonably construed as serving patriarchal control and in any case as posing the threat of severe medical harm. The Seattle's hospital's proposal seems a reasonable way of negotiating between these values, but it was ultimately defeated by those who took uncompromising opposition to anything like female circumcision, and though I do not share that position, I can certainly respect the concern for gender equality that underlies it.

The anthropologist Richard Shweder has proposed that liberal, pluralistic societies should try to accommodate groups that desire to engage in the practice in case two conditions are met: first, that only minor procedures such as those proposed by the Somali parents and the Seattle hospital should be performed on those below the age of consent (no major irreversible alterations of the body); and second, that those who have reached the age of consent should have the right to alter their bodies in substantial ways.[52] I think this is an appropriate form of compromise that expresses both respect for a group's cultural practices and the value of autonomy, applied not just to the group but also to individuals who choose to have the practice performed.

There will be hope for sustaining a diverse community when the value of accommodation is reinforced by other considerations. Earlier, I suggested that understanding how other cultures differ from one's own can involve understanding how the others affirm values familiar to us. It is important to affirm commonality as well as difference, and to seek common purpose in promoting shared values. A multicultural education can be a civic education if it affirms commonality and the possibility of shared purposes as well as difference. Remember Feinberg's attempt to understand the Japanese drive for dependency not so much as the denial of Western values of freedom and independence but as the affirmation of the human need for relationships of unconditional trust and care. Recognition of such commonality and the will to form common purpose based on commonality helps to mitigate the divisive effects of difference. Furthermore, the value of diversity itself helps to hold a diverse society together. If we recognize that no culture could maximize all the things human beings prize, if we recognize that we may learn from other cultures because of the values they emphasize, we will see a diverse society not as a necessary evil but as a good thing, and have that much more reason to hold it together.

We must be careful, moreover, not to accept the implicit assumption underlying many versions of the balkanization worry: that it is cultural and ethical differences that cause conflict and partiality for one's own group. This assumption is too simple an analysis of the causes of conflict. Consider one of the most highly charged conflicts between groups in our society: that between whites and African Americans. There are

52. Richard Shweder, *Why Do Men Barbecue? Recipes for Cultural Psychology* (Cambridge, Mass.: Harvard University Press, 2003), 206.

some on both sides of this conflict who see this as a cultural conflict, but even they will admit that it is more than that. We should look not merely to cultural difference but to the causes of inequality among groups. And once we do, we may conclude that the proper emphasis should be the correction of inequality, not the elimination of cultural difference. We lack very clear measures for determining what cultural differences are "big," but the cultural gap between white Americans as a group and African Americans who have been in the United States for more than two generations is not among the largest gaps even within the United States. If there is particularly intense conflict between these two groups, it cannot be put down to culture.

For one thing, the group of African Americans is becoming increasingly diverse (in education and socioeconomic status) in ways that reflect the population of the larger society. Even the so-called culture of the urban "underclass" in the United States could be said to be an extension of larger cultural trends. Many of the signs of social breakdown in this class are reflected throughout the larger society, regardless of race and class. As Jennifer Hochschild has observed, "fewer Americans of all races and classes are holding jobs, getting or staying married when they have children, abstaining from illegal drugs."[53] I noted earlier that imbalance in the power relations between two groups may present barriers to accommodation between them. My point here is that power imbalance, along with the perception of injustice, may be the primary cause of conflict and not cultural difference.

We must take into account the role of inequality when addressing the tensions between racial and ethnic groups in schools, colleges, and universities. For an example of such tensions, consider a study of white and African American students' attitudes toward diversity in the University of California at Berkeley.[54] Many of the white students who were interviewed expressed a desire for interaction with students of other racial and ethnic groups. They felt frustrated by a climate of heightened racial consciousness, and by proliferation of organizations along racial-ethnic lines. On the other hand, African American students indicated a preference for same-group friendships, social activities, and organizations. They appreciated the opportunity to discover and explore their racial identity with other African Americans.[55]

This experience at Berkeley may be interpreted as indicating the tensions between the ideals of diversity and interracial community. But we must consider the reasons why social interaction along racial and ethnic lines is so emotionally charged. It is charged, for one thing, by the perception of many African American students that progress toward racial equality has stalled and that white society has permitted them

---

53. Jennifer Hochschild, "The Politics of the Estranged Poor," *Ethics* 101 (1991): 568.

54. The entering class of 1991 at Berkeley was 32 percent Asian American, 30 percent white, 20 percent Chicano/Latino, and 7.5 percent African American. See Institute for the Study of Social Change, *Diversity Project: Final Report* (Berkeley, Calif.: Institute for the Study of Social Change, 1991), iii.

55. Institute for the Study of Social Change, *Diversity Project*, 14, 28, 37.

to achieve as much equality as it is willing to tolerate. It is charged, for another thing, because African American identity includes a common experience of oppression.[56]

The apparent tension between diversity and interracial community cannot be understood without the context of enduring inequality and injustice. Furthermore, the preferences of African American and white students can be described in other ways that make the conflict something more complicated than one between diversity and interracial community. While African American students preferred same-group affiliation on the level of individual day-to-day interaction, they favored programs that promoted interracial understanding. The conflict between the preferences of white and black students, then, may be described as one between two different conceptions of community, in which diversity and commonality of experience and outlook are both valued in different ways and given different emphases. To mitigate the conflict, it is necessary to provide opportunities for individual interracial interaction for those who desire it. But at this point it is difficult to fault those who seek through intragroup interaction to affirm their racial and ethnic identities when they have for so long been subjected to domination and shaming. The ideal of individual and interpersonal interracial community may have to wait until more justice is achieved.

As far as the newer immigrant groups are concerned, it is ironic that such a furor has arisen over the question of whether their cultures should be accepted and celebrated as part of the American mosaic. It is ironic because the most salient cultural differences have to do with the value the new immigrants place on family and on mutual support within the family and ethnic neighborhood. As one person has put it in an internet newsgroup on issues of concern to Asian Americans, Asian Americans are placed on the defensive for such values: as he sardonically puts the situation, "We apologize for respecting our parents' decisions! We're sorry we believe our family is more important than ourselves."[57] Such values remind us of the American past, rather than some strange and threatening foreign culture. If such values seem strange to us, it is an indication of how far we have strayed from past tradition.

9.13 DEMOCRATIC RITUAL AND ITS POSSIBLE ROLE IN BRIDGING DIFFERENCE

In his study of morality, politics, and power in a Chinese village during the 1970s, Richard Madsen utilizes a conception of ritual in which the

> participants pour a rich variety of emotions into the performance of a series of stylized actions that are held to represent some phase of the fundamental meaning of their life together. The main symbols making up the rituals are

56. A point made to me in correspondence by Laurence Thomas.
57. On the internet newsgroup, available at soc.culture.asian.american. Rev. March 24, 1998.

actions rather than words. In some cases these emotionally resonant symbols express a richer meaning than can be put into any discursive verbal argument. The emotional resonance and fertile noetic ambiguity is what gives rituals everywhere their integrative power. The participants in a ritual become a community of feeling and sharers in a common experience that is drenched with meaning but cannot be expressed by any single set of discursive ideas. They often experience the ritual as expressing a common primordial understanding that is the font of subsequent discursive understandings. This does not mean that one can discursively interpret a ritual in any way one wishes. There is usually a range of orthodox interpretations of a ritual and some clear ideas about which interpretations would be unorthodox. But often the range of orthodox interpretations is fairly wide, so that a ritual can unite a broad group of people with different approaches toward life. Thus regular participants in certain rituals can within limits argue about their common moral responsibilities to their community and yet recognize that they are united by a shared moral understanding that transcends their words.[58]

What is especially morally valuable in this species of ritual, as Madsen describes it, is the openness and ambiguity of meaning corresponding to the shared understanding that transcends words. It allows harmony to be something different from agreement on a set of doctrines that are articulated at such a level of specificity such as to exclude many of the possible participants.

The obvious should be noted here: not all rituals function in this way. Rituals can be fashioned with the intent of cultivating and enforcing ideological conformity. Madsen uses the phrase "rituals of struggle" for practices that center on the stylized recitation of sacred doctrine, such as the cult-like performances that revolved around Mao's sayings. Rituals of struggle ought not to be confused with rituals that can foster a sense of commonality without insistence on belief on a specific set of doctrines. It might be objected, however, that there is no conceptual room for rituals that balance difference and commonality. In the absence of agreement on values and doctrines, it might be claimed, ritual delivers no real substance that grounds agreement but only some vague emotional connection between the participants. Even if ritual succeeded in creating emotional ties, how could it provide a stable balance between difference and commonality?

But as Madsen points out, there is a bounded range of orthodox interpretations for a ritual, even if the width of that range is significant. A wedding, the burial and mourning of deceased parents, and a village feast are rituals that embody and foster certain

58. Richard Madsen, *Morality and Power in a Chinese Village* (Berkeley: University of California Press, 1984), 21–2. Madsen acknowledges his debt in conceptualizing this type of ritual to Victor Turner, *The Forest of Symbols: Aspects of Ndembu Ritual* (Ithaca: Cornell University Press, 1967), 19–20.

notions of proper human relationships. To advance the aim of affirming commonality, participants must have some significant degree of agreement on what it is these rituals embody and foster. Yet the degree of agreement needed remains open and ambiguous, partly because, as Madsen puts it so well, much of the meaning of ritual is carried by actions. Even when the meaning is carried by words, reconciliation can be achieved by regulating the degree of specificity of meaning. The effectiveness of ritual in reconciling commonality and difference gives fresh meaning to the homily that what is *not* said is every bit as important as what *is* said. As D. C. Lau remarks, one Confucian rationale for study of the *Book of Odes* is that it provides one with a store of quotations for delicate situations such as diplomatic exchanges and within which one can couch one's meanings in a sufficiently indirect and somewhat ambiguous way.[59]

Rituals that bring together participants despite serious disagreements in value, then, do so through emphasizing the values the participants really do share while leaving ambiguous and indeterminate the areas of disagreement. One can grasp the value of such rituals from opposing metaphysical and epistemological perspectives on moral truth. If there is a final and single truth as to how the relevant disagreements should be resolved, it is not at all obvious to all reasonable and informed people of good will what that truth is. From the perspective of assuming the truth of such a possibility, there is a strong case that a tradition must remain open to continued attempts to deepen understanding of whatever the truth is. From the perspective that there simply is no final and single truth as to how at least some of these conflicts should be resolved, either in general or in certain contexts (i.e., that resolutions of some conflicts are a matter of collective choice and invention rather than discovery of a preexisting truth), a tradition acknowledges this state of affairs by leaving it open as to how such conflicts are to be resolved.

Chinese Confucians have always had a keen appreciation for the value of ritual. Western democratic traditions, I believe, can learn from this appreciation. It is a necessary condition for a viable democracy that there be widely shared values, but that is hardly a sufficient condition. Freud used the memorable phrase "the narcissism of minor differences" to indicate that groups predisposed to contend with each other will magnify apparently small points of disagreement into contests between Good and Evil.[60] On the other hand, a viable democracy is consistent with robust disagreement over how widely shared values are to be interpreted and ordered, as long as the areas of agreement seem more important than the areas of disagreement. Rituals can help in the task of making these areas of agreement more important. The sort of common democratic culture that is necessary partly rests on sufficient agreement on values, but it cannot rest solely on such agreement. It is as much an achievement as a discovery of

59. D. C. Lau, introduction to Confucius, *The Analects*, 42.

60. Sigmund Freud, *Civilization and Its Discontents*, trans. James Strachey (New York: Norton, 1961), essay 5, 61.

agreement. It is an achievement in which members of a common culture actively seek to understand one another well enough so that they do indeed discover the points of agreement. It is also an achievement in the sense that they must cultivate the dispositions to act on the points of agreement and attitudes of mutual respect for one another, at the same time that they contend with one another over their differences.

Let me conclude with some suggestions as what sort of moral and political rituals might be in accord with both the aim of combining respect for difference with commonality that supports respect for difference. *Voting* in an election is the quintessential democratic institution, and I think that something is learnt about its importance and role in a democracy by viewing it as ritual. Why should we vote? Most of us have probably heard urgings to vote because "you never know when it might be your vote that makes the difference." From the standpoint of the individual deliberating as to whether there is sufficient reason for her to go to the polls, the proffered justification will in most cases be unpersuasive. One knows that, in all likelihood, one's vote will *not* make any difference to the outcome. Another kind of justification for voting that is not as consequentialist in nature is that failing to vote is a morally objectionable form of free-riding. A democracy works only if enough people vote, and therefore the ones who yield to convenience or apathy and fail to vote are benefiting from the acts of those who do not so yield. This argument certainly has more force than the first, but can be circumvented by the argument that if something is owed to those who vote, then the payment need not take the form of someone else voting. Why not just issue voters a payment voucher? Given the desperately low participation in elections in the United States, it is difficult to reject that suggestion out of hand, but the reasoning behind it fails to explain why it is important for each individual citizen to vote. It is not just that those who choose not to vote would be free-riding on those who do vote. Even if those who voted were literally repaid precisely by the people who chose not to vote, it would still be a bad thing that those people chose not to vote. But why would it be a bad thing?

My suggestion is that voting needs to be renewed as the central political *ritual* it is. It is not because one's vote might possibly decide an election, though there will be unusual occasions where they might indeed do that. It is not because one should avoid being a free-rider (even though one should avoid that), because there are ways to avoid free-riding that do not capture the importance of voting. It is because voting is a ritual that can foster and promote the reconciliation between difference and commonality that one has a civic duty to participate. The way that voting represents difference, of course, should be familiar. Consider, however, familiar actions that are part of the voting ritual: going to a common place to cast one's vote alongside others; and the act of walking past campaign workers who must assume in their actions that one is still open to their candidate or cause. Moreover, there is the ritual act of courteous response to their actions, to take the literature, to stop and listen for a short time, or simply to nod and smile, even if one has absolutely no intention of voting according to their wishes. Consider the related ritual acts of the candidates on election night: the speech of the victor verbally extending a hand in reconciliation; the loser extending congratulations to the victor and, yes, calling for unity. Of course, there are mechanical and insincere performances of these ritual acts, but the more hopeful lesson is that we should insist on candidates with the character and perspective on their place in the scheme of things that would enable them to perform these rituals in genuine fashion.

John Stuart Mill at one time advocated the idea of the open ballot. The rationale was to promote a conception of voting as the deliverance of one's considered judgment on what would best promote the general welfare.[61] By making one's judgment public, and therefore having to be prepared to defend it, one is prompted to enact a certain conception of citizenship. The rituals of declaring and defending one's position would be important not just because of what they might contribute to a useful debate on the issues but also because one is acting as if one's vote is based on a judgment that needs to be defensible to other citizens. And acting in this way is a way of strengthening the general disposition to do so. I agree with the aim of Mill's proposal, but I am reluctant to sacrifice the protections afforded by the secret ballot against various forms of coercive attempts to force a harmony among individuals that does not exist. Of course, there are contexts in which coercion is less of a factor: tenured professors voting on university policy might reasonably be required to publicize and defend their votes. In such contexts, the open ballot is a reasonable option.

Where coercion is a reasonable danger, however, an alternative practice that also expresses a renewed commitment to voting as central democratic ritual is to make it compulsory. A country such as Australia has achieved very high turnout rates with relatively modest fines for failure to vote. Requiring people to vote combats the idea that it is no one's business but one's own whether one votes or not. One may keep one's vote and one's views secret, but one must contribute to the process of collective decision. The ritual of voting, the way it brings citizens together for a decision, matters too much to make it purely optional. If voting is made compulsory, then a necessary second step in reform is to allow voters to express a sentiment they currently express by declining to vote: the opportunity to check a box labeled "none of the above." Disillusionment and alienation from dominant political agents, forces, and institutions should have a channel of expression in the most central of democratic political rituals.[62]

To avoid misunderstanding of the proposal put forward here, let be noted that there is no intention to reduce voting to pure ceremony. Voting, of course, has a perfectly practical function outside of expressing a desired reconciliation between commonality and difference. The proposal rather draws attention to the ceremonial

61. I owe my awareness of this fact to a former colleague at Brandeis, Andreas Teuber. See John Stuart Mill, "Thoughts on Parliamentary Reform," in *J. S. Mill: Collected Works*, ed. J. M. Robson (Toronto: University of Toronto Press, 1977), 19:331–8; and "Considerations on Representative Government," 19:488–95.

62. Some have objected that my proposal is far too utopian to stand a chance of being adopted. Some have argued more specifically that it runs against the trend of adapting electronic technology to make actions such as voting far more convenient and therefore more widespread. Part of my reply is

dimensions of the activity without denying its other dimensions. Marriage and burial rites, two paradigms of ceremonial rituals, also have very practical functions. The Confucian perspective on ritual in fact notes the difference between these different expressive and practical dimensions. Xunzi (chapter 19) holds that the various different dimensions of ritual must be kept in balance. When the dimensions of form and meaning are emphasized to the point of slighting their emotion and practical use, rituals become florid. When their emotion and practical use is emphasized to the point of slighting their form and meaning, rituals become lean. The mean between these extremes is the thing to aim for.

Practices that simultaneously have ceremonial, emotionally expressive, and practical functions, such as voting, can be especially potent in moral and civic education. Pure ceremonies, unconstrained by practical purpose and unexpressive of civic feelings, may become stultifying and meaningless or insufferably pedantic. Ceremonies expressive of civic feelings but devoid of practical purpose may become merely entertaining displays. Purely practical activities, on the other hand, lack the recurrent dramatic structure of ceremonial rituals that enables them to evoke and express value and feeling. They therefore can have far less of a role in the evocation, training, shaping, and strengthening of attitudes and dispositions of character. When the ceremonial, expressive, and practical functions are all present and have intrinsic connections to one another, as they can in the case of voting, they may be the most potent instruments of moral and civic education.

There are other examples of such practices that weave together the ceremonial, expressive, and practical. The *Mencius* puts forward a proposal for the *jing(ching)*-field system, commonly translated as the "well-field" system. A *jing* is a piece of land divided into nine parts.

> If those who own land within each *jing* befriend one another both at home and abroad, help each other to keep watch, and succour each other in illness, they will live in love and harmony. A *jing* is a piece of land measuring one *li* square, and each *ching* consists of 900 *mu*. Of these the central plot of 100 *mu* belongs to the state, while the other eight plots of 100 *mu* each are held by eight families

---

that advance in technology is not in itself the engine of history. Nontechnological interests shape our decisions as to which technologies we use and when we use them. Consider that we have long had the capabilities of making registration for voting far more convenient and widespread among citizens (such registration can be conducted along with motor vehicle registration, for example). We have yet to seize upon this opportunity, and part of the explanation may be that some of our political leaders think they will be put at electoral disadvantage if greater proportions of the citizenry *are* registered to vote. Another objection in the spirit of "It's too utopian" is based on the observation that proposals such as mine have been made in the past and have never been taken up. I find this argument from induction unpersuasive, especially with reference to a relatively young nation such as the United States. In any case, there is not much warrant in proceeding as if arguments for the moral and political value of a possible practice, no matter how strong, can have no effect on the likelihood of its being adopted.

who share the duty of caring for the plot owned by the state. Only when they have done this duty dare they turn to their own affairs.[63]

The proposed practice has a very practical point, of course. But it also expresses the reconciliation of harmony and fragmentation. The shared labor on the state-owned land represents harmony. The family-owned plots represent a kind of fragmentation. The *jing*-field system can be taken to represent their reconciliation. The practice of first sharing labor and of then turning to one's family affairs can become a ceremony for the participants. It can tell a story in words and actions that carries the meaning of that reconciliation in symbolic and expressive ways. The meaning goes beyond the concrete practical function of fairly dividing the burdens of taxation, but note that that concrete practical function does instantiate the broader meaning.

In a modern democracy, an analogy to Mencius's proposal might be some form of community or national service: not just the purely optional and underfunded gestures recently implemented, but at the least a serious call to service to a wide range of citizens that can only be set aside by an individual for good reasons, as in the American jury system. In fact, one of the possible ideas for service is calling on citizens to serve on juries or panels charged with making recommendations on initiatives, referendums, or policy issues. Experiments along these lines have shown that citizens called upon to serve on such a jury panel have taken their responsibilities seriously and have striven to formulate recommendations that transcend partisan interests.[64] As in the case of voting, one of the important functions of such service may lie in its ceremonial and expressive dimensions, and not just the practical recommendations that may result from the process. Participation on such panels might be a one-time event for individuals, but public knowledge of the general practice of drafting citizens can have a broader educative effect. Another idea along these lines is a component of service learning in our schools, with the added advantage of catching future or young citizens at developing stages.

I certainly do not offer the notion of democratic ritual as a comprehensive solution. I believe there is enough promise in these suggestions to recommend the work of discovering how much we share with one another to all of us who are hopeful for democracy. Indeed, I believe hopefulness to be a central democratic virtue, and one that must be cultivated through our rituals.

63. *Mencius* 3A3. Translation adapted from D. C. Lau, *Mencius* (London: Penguin, 1970), 99–100. A li is about 500 meters.

64. I first encountered this idea in Robert Kane, *Through the Moral Maze: Searching for Absolute Values in a Pluralistic World* (New York: Paragon House, 1994).

Bibliography

Ahmadu, Fuambi. "Rites and Wrongs: An Insider/Outsider Reflects on Power and Excision." In *Female "Circumcision" in Africa: Culture, Controversy, and Change*, ed. Bettina Shell-Duncan and Yiva Herlund, 283–312. Boulder, Colo.: Rienner, 2001.

Ainsworth, Mary D. *Infancy in Uganda: Infant Care and the Growth of Love.* Baltimore: Johns Hopkins Press, 1967.

Axelrod, Robert, and William D. Hamilton. "The Evolution of Cooperation." *Science* 211 (1981): 1390–6.

Bachnik, Jane M. "The Two 'Faces' of Self and Society in Japan." *Ethos* 20 (1992): 3–32.

Baier, Annette. "What Do Women Want in a Moral Theory?" *Noûs* 19 (1985): 53–63.

Batson, C. Daniel. *The Altruism Question: Toward a Social-Psychological Answer.* Hillsdale, N.J.: Erlbaum, 1991.

Beattie, J. M. *Other Cultures.* New York: Free Press of Glencoe, 1964.

Becker, Lawrence. *Reciprocity.* London: Routledge and Kegan Paul, 1986.

Bellah, Robert N., Richard Madsen, William M. Sullivan, Ann Swidler, and Steven M. Tipton. *Habits of the Heart.* Berkeley: University of California Press, 1985.

Benedict, Ruth. *Patterns of Culture.* New York: Penguin, 1934.

Benjamin, Martin. *Splitting the Difference: Compromise and Integrity in Ethics and Politics.* Lawrence: University of Kansas Press, 1990.

Berger, John. *A Fortunate Man.* New York: Pantheon Books, 1967.

Berlin, Isaiah. *The Crooked Timber of Humanity,* ed. Henry Hardy. Princeton: Princeton University Press, 1990.

———. "Two Concepts of Liberty." In *Liberty: Incorporating Four Essays on Liberty,* ed. Henry Hardy, 1662–17. Oxford: Oxford University Press, 2002.

Billig, M., and H. Tajfel. "Social Categorization and Similarity in Intergroup Behavior." *European Journal of Social Psychology* 3 (1973): 27–52.

Blackburn, Simon. *Essays in Quasi-Realism.* New York: Oxford University Press, 1993.

———. "Meet the Flintstones," *New Republic,* November 25, 2002, 28–33.

Blackmun, Harry. Majority Opinion of the Supreme Court on *Roe v. Wade.* 410 U.S. 113 (1973). Available at http://caselaw.lp.findlaw.com/scripts/getcase.pl?navby=CASE&court=US&vol=410&page=113. Rev. August 24, 2005.

Blum, Lawrence. "Gilligan and Kohlberg: Implications for Moral Theory." *Ethics* 98 (1988): 472–91.

——. "Opportunity and Equality of Opportunity." *Public Affairs Quarterly* 2 (1988): 1–18.

Boehm, Christopher. "The Evolutionary Development of Morality as an Effect of Dominance Behavior and Conflict Interference." *Journal of Social and Biological Sciences* 5 (1982): 413–22.

Bond, E. J. *Reason and Value.* Cambridge: Cambridge University Press, 1983.

Bouchard, Thomas J., Jr., David T. Lykken, Matthew McGue, Nancy L. Segal, and Auke Tellegen. "Sources of Human Psychological Differences: The Minnesota Study of Twins Reared Apart." *Science* 250 (1990): 22–39.

Bowen, Murray. *Family Therapy in Clinical Practice.* New York: Jason Aronson, 1978.

Bowlby, John. "The Nature of the Child's Tie to His Mother." *International Journal of Psycho-Analysis* 39 (1958): 350–73.

Bowles Samuel, and Herbert Gintis. *Schooling in Capitalist America.* Boulder, Colo.: Perseus Books, 1977.

Boyd, Richard. "How to Be a Moral Realist." In *Essays on Moral Realism*, ed. Geoffrey Sayre-McCord, 181–82. Ithaca: Cornell University Press, 1988.

Boyd, Robert, and Peter J. Richerson. *Culture and the Evolutionary Process.* Chicago: University of Chicago Press, 1985.

——. "The Evolution of Reciprocity in Sizable Groups." *Journal of Theoretical Biology* 132 (1988): 337–56.

——. *Not by Genes Alone: How Culture Transformed Human Evolution.* Chicago: University of Chicago Press, 2005.

Brandt, E. M., and G. Mitchell. "Pairing Pre-Adolescents with Infants (Macaca Mulatta)." *Developmental Psychology* 8 (1973): 222–28.

Brandt, Richard. *Ethical Theory.* Englewood Cliffs, N.J.: Prentice-Hall, 1959.

Bruch, Hilda. *Conversations with Anorexics*, ed. D. Czyzewski and M. A. Suhr. New York: Basic Books, 1988.

Buchanan, Allen E. "Assessing the Communitarian Critique of Liberalism." *Ethics* 99 (1989): 852–82.

Buller, David J. *Adapting Minds: Evolutionary Psychology and the Persistent Quest for Human Nature.* Cambridge, Mass.: MIT Press, 2005.

Buss, David. "Sex Differences in Human Mate Selection: Evolutionary Hypotheses Tested in Thirty-seven Cultures." *Behavioral and Brain Sciences* 12 (1989): 1–49.

——. *The Evolution of Desire: Strategies of Human Mating.* New York: Basic Books, 1995.

Calabresi, Guido. *Ideals, Beliefs, Attitudes, and the Law.* Syracuse, N.Y.: Syracuse University Press, 1985.

Card, Claudia. "Gender and Moral Luck." In *Identity, Character, and Morality: Essays in Moral Psychology*, ed. Owen Flanagan and Amélie Rorty, 199–218. Cambridge, Mass.: MIT Press, 1990.

Caspi, A., McClay, J., Moffitt, T. E., Mill, J., Martin, J., Craig, I. W., Taylor, A., and Poulton, R. "Role of Genotype in the Cycle of Violence in Maltreated Children." *Science* 297 (2002): 851–4.

Chan, Sin Yee. "Gender and Relationship Roles in the *Analects* and the *Mencius*." *Asian Philosophy* 10 (2000): 115–31.

Chan, Wing-Tsit. *A Sourcebook in Chinese Philosophy.* Princeton: Princeton University Press, 1963.

Chodorow, Nancy. *The Reproduction of Mothering: Psychoanalysis and the Sociology of Gender.* Berkeley: University of California Press, 1978.

Chuang, Tzu. *Chuang Tzu: Basic Writings.* Translated by Burton Watson. New York: Columbia University Press, 1963.

Clark, Andy. "Connectionism, Moral Cognition, and Collaborative Problem Solving." In *Mind and Morals: Essays on Ethics and Cognitive Science,* ed. Larry May, Marilyn Friedman, and Andy Clark, 109–28. Cambridge, Mass.: Bradford Books, 1998.

Coleman, Doriane Lambelet. "The Seattle Compromise: Multicultural Sensitivity and Americanization." *Duke Law Journal* 47 (1998): 717–80.

Coles, Robert. *The Moral Life of Children.* Boston: Atlantic Monthly, 1986.

Confucius. *Confucius: The Analects.* Translated by D. C. Lau. London: Penguin, 1979.

Cooley, Charles, Robert C. Angell, and Lowell J. Carr. *Introductory Sociology.* New York: Scribner's, 1933.

Cooper, David E. "Moral Relativism." *Midwest Studies in Philosophy* 3 (1978): 97–108.

Cua, Antonio S. "The Status of Principles in Confucian Ethics." *Journal of Chinese Philosophy* 16 (1989): 273–96.

———. "The Ethical and Religious Dimensions of *Li.*" *Review of Metaphysics* 55 (2002): 471–519.

Cullen, Kevin. "Haunted by Death in Somalia." *Boston Globe,* July 15, 1993, 19.

Daniels, Norman. "Reflective Equilibrium." In *The Stanford Encyclopedia of Philosophy.* Rev. April 28, 2003. Available at http://plato.stanford.edu/archives/sum2003/entries/reflective-equilibrium/.

Damasio, Antonio. *Descartes' Error.* New York: Avon Books, 1994.

Darwall, Stephen. *Impartial Reason.* Ithaca: Cornell University Press, 1983.

Davidson, Donald. Introduction to *Inquiries into Truth and Interpretation.* 2nd ed. Oxford: Clarendon Press, 2001.

———. "On the Very Idea of a Conceptual Scheme." In *Inquiries into Truth and Interpretation,* 2nd ed., 183–98. Oxford: Clarendon Press, 2001. Originally published in *Proceedings and Addresses of the American Philosophical Association* 47 (1974).

———. "Radical Interpretation." In *Inquiries into Truth and Interpretation,* 2nd ed., 125–40. Oxford: Clarendon Press, 2001. Originally published in *Dialectica* 27 (1973): 313–28.

———. "Thought and Talk." In *Inquiries into Truth and Interpretation,* 2nd ed., 155–70. Oxford: Clarendon Press, 2001. Originally published in *Mind and Language,* ed. Samuel Guttenplan. Oxford: Oxford University Press, 1975.

De Tocqueville, Alexis. *Democracy in America.* Translated by George Lawrence. Edited by J. Mayer. New York: Doubleday, 1969.

De Waal, Frans B. M. *Peacemaking among the Primates.* Cambridge, Mass.: Harvard University Press, 1989.

DeCew, Judith Wagner. "Moral Conflicts and Ethical Relativism." *Ethics* 101 (1990): 27–41.

DeSousa, Ronald. *The Rationality of Emotion.* Cambridge, Mass.: MIT Press, 1987.

DeVos, George. *Socialization for Achievement.* Berkeley: University of California Press, 1973.

———. "Dimensions of the Self in Japanese Culture." In *Culture and Self: Asian and Western Perspective,* ed. A. J. Marsella, G. DeVos, and F.L.K. Hsu, 141–84. London: Tavistock, 1985.

Doniger, Wendy. "What Did They Name the Dog?" Review of *Twins: Genes, Environment and the Mystery of Identity,* by Lawrence Wright. *London Review of Books,* March 19, 1998.

Donnelly, Jack. *Universal Human Rights in Theory and Practice.* Ithaca: Cornell University Press, 1989.

Doris, John. *Lack of Character: Personality and Moral Behavior.* Cambridge: Cambridge University Press, 2002.

Dretske, Fred. *Knowledge and the Flow of Information.* Cambridge, Mass.: Bradford Books, 1981.

Dubisch, Jill. "The Domestic Power of Women in a Greek Island Village." *Studies in European Society* 1 (1974): 23–33.

Emmerson, Donald K. "Singapore and the 'Asian Values' Debate.'" *Journal of Democracy* 6 (1995): 101–2.

Fagot, B. "Attachment, Parenting, and Peer Interactions of Toddler Children." *Developmental Psychology* 33 (1997): 489–500.

Falk, David. "'Ought' and Motivation." *Proceedings of the Aristotelian Society* 48 (1947–48): 111–38.

Fehr, Ernst, and Urs Fischbacher. "The Nature of Human Altruism. *Nature* 425 (2003): 785–91.

Feinberg, Walter. "A Role for Philosophy of Education in Intercultural Research: A Reexamination of the Relativism-Absolutism Debate." *Teachers College Record* 91 (1989): 161–76.

Fendrich, M., M. Huss, T. Jacobsen, M. Kruesi, and U. Ziegenhain. "Children's Ability to Delay Gratification: Longitudinal Relations to Mother-Child Attachment." *Journal of Genetic Psychology* 158 (1997): 411–27.

Festinger, Leon. *Theory of Cognitive Dissonance.* Stanford: Stanford University Press, 1965.

Flanagan, Owen. *Varieties of Moral Personality: Ethics and Psychological Realism.* Cambridge, Mass.: Harvard University Press, 1991.

———. "Ethical Expressions: Why Moralists Scowl, Frown, and Smile." In *The Cambridge Companion to Darwin,* ed. Jonathan Hodge and Gregory Radick, 377–98. Cambridge: Cambridge University Press, 2003.

Fleischacker, Samuel. *Integrity and Moral Relativism.* Leiden: Brill, 1992.

Foot, Philippa. "Moral Beliefs." In *Theories of Ethics,* ed. Philippa Foot, 83–100. London: Oxford University Press, 1967.

———. "Morality and Art." *Proceedings of the British Academy* 56 (1970): 131–44.

———. "Morality as a System of Hypothetical Imperatives." *Philosophical Review* 81 (1972): 305–16.

———. "Reasons for Action and Desires." *Proceedings of the Aristotelian Society,* supp. vol. 46 (1972): 202–10.

———. "Does Moral Subjectivism Rest on a Mistake?" *Oxford Journal of Legal Studies* 15 (1995): 1–14.

Foucault, Michel. *The Foucault Reader.* Edited by Paul Rabinow. New York: Pantheon, 1984.

———. *The History of Sexuality: The Use of Pleasure.* New York: Vintage, 1990.

Frazer, Sir James. *The Golden Bough.* 3rd ed. London: MacMillan, 1936.

Freud, Sigmund. *Civilization and Its Discontents.* Translated by James Strachey. New York: Norton, 1961.

Friedman, Marilyn. "Beyond Caring: The De-Moralization of Gender." *Canadian Journal of Philosophy,* supp. vol. 13 (1987): 87–110.

Friedman, Michael. "Philosophical Naturalism." *Proceedings and Addresses of the American Philosophical Association* 71 (1997): 7–21.

Frye, Marilyn. *The Politics of Reality.* Trumansburg, N.Y.: Crossing Press, 1983.

Fung, Yu-Lan. *A History of Chinese Philosophy.* Translated by Derk Bodde. Princeton: Princeton University Press, 1952.

Galston, William. *Liberal Purposes: Goods, Virtues, and Diversity in the Liberal State.* Cambridge: Cambridge University Press, 1991.

Gauthier, David. *Morals by Agreement.* Oxford: Clarendon Press, 1986.

Geertz, Clifford. *The Interpretation of Cultures.* New York: Basic Books, 1973.

———. "From the Native's Point of View: On the Nature of Anthropological Understanding." In *Culture Theory: Essays in Mind, Self, and Emotion,* ed. Richard Shweder and Robert Levine, 123–36. Cambridge: Cambridge University Press, 1984.

Gewirth, Alan. *Reason and Morality.* Chicago: University of Chicago Press, 1978.

Gibbard, Allan. *Wise Choices, Apt Feelings: A Theory of Normative Judgment.* Cambridge, Mass.: Harvard University Press, 1992.

———. *Thinking How to Live.* Cambridge, Mass.: Harvard University Press, 2003.

Gilligan, Carol. *In a Different Voice: Psychological Theory and Women's Development.* Cambridge, Mass.: Harvard University Press, 1982.

Gilligan, Carol, Nona Lyons, and Trudy Hanmer, eds. *Making Connections: The Relational World of Adolescent Girls at Emma Willard School.* Cambridge, Mass.: Harvard University Press, 1990.

Gilligan, Carol, Janie Victoria Ward, and Jill McLean Taylor, eds. *Mapping the Moral Domain: A Contribution of Women's Thinking to Psychological Theory and Education.* Cambridge, Mass.: Center for the Study of Gender, Education, and Human Development, Harvard University Graduate School of Education. Distributed by Harvard University Press, 1988.

Gintis, Herbert. *Game Theory Evolving.* Princeton: Princeton University Press, 2000.

Goldman, Alvin. *Epistemology and Cognition.* Cambridge, Mass.: Harvard University Press, 1986.

———. "Empathy, Mind, and Morals." *Proceedings and Addresses of the American Philosophical Association* 66 (1992): 17–42.

Graham, A. C. *Disputers of the Tao: Philosophical Argumentation in Ancient China.* La Salle, Ill.: Open Court, 1989.

Gray, John. *Berlin.* London: Fontana, 1995.

Gruenbaum, Ellen. *The Female Circumcision Controversy: An Anthropological Perspective.* Philadelphia: University of Pennsylvania Press, 2001.

Gutman, Amy, and Dennis Thompson. "Moral Conflict and Political Consensus." *Ethics* 101 (1990): 64–88.

Haakonssen, Knud. *The Science of a Legislator: The Natural Jurisprudence of David Hume and Adam Smith.* Cambridge: Cambridge University Press, 1981.

Haley, John Owen. "Confession, Repentance, and Absolution." In *Mediation and Criminal Justice: Victims, Offenders, and Community,* ed. Martin Wright and Burt Galaway. London: Sage, 1989.

Hall, David L., and Roger T. Ames. *Thinking through Confucius.* Albany: State University of New York Press, 1987.

———. "Chinese Philosophy." In *Routledge Encyclopedia of Philosophy,* ed. E. Craig. Rev. 2003. Available at www.rep.routledge.com/article/G001SECT4.

Hamilton, W. D. "The Genetical Evolution of Social Behavior." *Journal of Theoretical Biology* 7 (1964): 1–52.

Hammond, Kenneth R., Robert M. Hamm, Janet Grassia, and Tamra Pearson. "Direct Comparison of the Efficacy of Intuitive and Analytical Cognition in Expert Judgment." In *Research on Judgment and Decision Making,* ed. William M. Goldstein and Robin M. Hogarth, 144–80. Cambridge: Cambridge University Press, 1997.

Hampshire, Stuart. *Innocence and Experience.* Cambridge, Mass.: Harvard University Press, 1989.

Hampton, Jean. *The Authority of Reason.* Ed. Richard Healey. Cambridge: Cambridge University Press, 1998.

Hare, Richard M. *The Language of Morals.* Oxford: Clarendon Press, 1952.

Harlow, H. F., and R. R. Zimmermann. "Affectional Responses in the Infant Monkey." In *Foundations of Animal Behavior: Classic Papers with Commentaries*, ed. L. D. Houck, and L. C. Drickamer, 376–87. Chicago: University of Chicago Press, 1996.

Harman, Gilbert. "Moral Relativism Defended." *Philosophical Review* 84 (1975): 3–22.

———. "Is There a Single True Morality?" In *Morality, Reason and Truth*, ed. David Copp and David Zimmerman, 27–48. Totowa, N.J.: Rowman and Littlefield, 1985. Reprinted in Harman, *Explaining Value and Other Essays in Moral Philosophy*, 771–02. Oxford: Clarendon Press, 2000.

———. "Moral Philosophy Meets Social Psychology: Virtue Ethics and the Fundamental Attribution Error." *Proceedings of the Aristotelian Society* 99 (1998–99): 315–31.

———. "The Nonexistence of Character Traits." *Proceedings of the Aristotelian Society* 100 (1999–2000): 22–36.

Harman, Gilbert, and Judith Jarvis Thomson. *Moral Relativism and Moral Objectivity.* Malden, Mass.: Blackwell, 1996.

Higley, J. D. "Use of Nonhuman Primates in Alcohol Research." *Alcohol, Health and Research World* 19 (1996): 213–6.

Higley, J. D., P. T. Mehlman, R. E. Poland, I. Faucher, D. T. Taub, J. Vickers, S. J. Suomi, and M. Linnoila. "A Nonhuman Primate Model of Violence and Assertiveness: CSF 5-HIAA and CSF Testosterone Correlate with Different Types of Aggressive Behaviors." *Biological Psychiatry* 40 (1996): 1067–82.

Higley, J. D., P. T. Mehlman, R. E. Poland, D. T. Taub, S. J. Suomi, and M. Linnoila. "Aggression, Social Dominance, Serotonin, and Causal Relationships." *Biological Psychiatry* 42 (1997): 306–7.

Higley, J. D., P. T. Mehlman, D. T. Taub, S. B. Higley, B. Fernald, J. Vickers, S. J. Suomi, and M. Linnoila. "Excessive Mortality in Young Male Nonhuman Primates with Low CSF 5-HIAA Concentrations." *Archives of General Psychiatry* 53 (1996): 537–43.

Higley, J. D., and S. J. Suomi. "Effect of Reactivity and Social Competence on Individual Responses to Severe Stress in Children: Investigations Using Nonhuman Primates." In *Intense Stress and Mental Disturbance in Children*, ed. C. R. Pfeffer, 35–7. New York: American Psychiatric Press, 1996.

Higley, J. D., S. J. Suomi, and M. Linnoila. "A Nonhuman Primate Model of Type II Alcoholism? Part 2: Diminished Social Competence and Excessive Aggression Correlates with Low Cerebrospinal Fluid 5-hydroxyindoleacetic Acid Concentrations." *Alcoholism: Clinical and Experimental Research* 20 (1996): 643–50.

———. "Excessive Alcohol Consumption, Inappropriate Aggression, and Serotonin: A Nonhuman Primate Model of Alcohol Abuse." *Recent Developments in Alcoholism* 13 (1997): 1912–19.

Hitchcock, David. *Asian Values and the United States: How Much Conflict?* Washington, D.C.: Center for Strategic and International Studies, 1994.

Hobbes, Thomas. *Leviathan.* Ed. C. B. MacPherson. New York: Penguin, 1982.

Hochschild, Jennifer. "The Politics of the Estranged Poor." *Ethics* 101 (1991): 560–78.

Honneth, Axel. "McDowell and the Challenge of Moral Realism." In *Reading McDowell: On Mind and World*, ed. Nicholas H. Smith, 246–66. London: Routledge, 2002.

Hooker, C. A. *Reason, Regulation, and Realism: Toward a Regulatory Systems Theory of Reason and Evolutionary Epistemology.* Albany: State University of New York Press, 1995.

Horgan, Terence E., and John Tienson. *Connectionism and the Philosophy of Psychology* Cambridge, Mass.: MIT Press, 1996.

Horkheimer, Max. *Critical Theory.* Trans. M. J. O'Connell. New York: Herder and Herder, 1972.

Horkheimer, Max, and Theodor W. Adorno. *Dialectic of Enlightenment.* Translated by John Cumming. New York: Seabury Press, 1944.

Hume, David. *A Treatise of Human Nature.* Ed. L. A. Selby-Bigge. Oxford: Oxford University Press, 1888; 2nd rev. ed. edited by P. H. Nidditch, 1978.

Institute for the Study of Social Change. *Diversity Project: Final Report.* Berkeley, Calif.: Institute for the Study of Social Change, 1991.

Isaac, R. Mark, Kenneth McCue, and Charles Plott. "Public Goods Provision in an Experimental Environment." *Journal of Public Economics* 26 (1985): 51–74.

Isaac, R. Mark, and J. M. Walker. "Group-Size Effects in Public-Goods Provision: The Voluntary Contributions Mechanism." *Quarterly Journal of Economics* 103 (1988): 179–99.

Isen, A. M., and P. F. Levin. "Effect of Feeling Good on Helping: Cookies and Kindness." *Journal of Personality and Social Psychology* 21 (1972): 384–8.

Johnson, Diane. "Abortion: The French Solution." *New York Times,* February 22, 2000. Available at www.nytimes.com/books/00/04/16/specials/johnson-franceed.html.

Kahn, Joel. "Malaysian Modern or Anti-anti Asian values." *Thesis Eleven* 50 (1997): 29–30.

Kant, Immanuel. Preface to the *Groundwork of the Metaphysics of Morals.* Edited by Thomas E. Hill Jr. Translated by Arnulf Zweig. New York: Oxford University Press, 2003.

Kane, Robert. *Through the Moral Maze: Searching for Absolute Values in a Pluralistic World.* New York: Paragon House, 1994.

Katz, Leonard, ed. *Evolutionary Origins of Morality.* Bowling Green, Ohio: Imprint Academic, 2000.

Kingston, Maxine Hong. *The Woman Warrior: Memoirs of a Girlhood Among Ghosts.* New York: Knopf, 1976.

Kitcher, Philip. "The Naturalists Return." *Philosophical Review* 101 (1992): 53–114.

Kohut, Heinz, and Ernest Wolf. "Disorders of the Self and Their Treatment: An Outline." *International Journal of Psycho-Analysis* 59 (1978): 403–25.

Kozol, Jonathan. *Savage Inequalities.* New York: Crown, 1991.

Kumagai, Hisa A., and Arno K. Kumagai. "The Hidden 'I' in Amae: 'Passive Love' and Japanese Social Perception." *Ethos* 14 (1986): 305–20.

Kunda, Ziva. *Social Cognition: Making Sense of People.* Cambridge, Mass.: MIT Press, 1999.

LaFollette, Hugh. "Personal Relationships." In *A Companion to Ethics,* ed. Peter Singer, 327–32. Oxford: Blackwell, 1991.

Lear, Jonathan. "Moral Objectivity." In *Objectivity and Cultural Divergence,* ed. S. C. Brown, 135–70. Cambridge: Cambridge University Press, 1984.

Leinberger, Paul, and Bruce Tucker. *The New Individualists: The Generation after the Organization Man.* New York: HarperCollins, 1991.

MacIntyre, Alasdair. *After Virtue.* Notre Dame, Ind.: University of Notre Dame Press, 1982.
———. "Is Patriotism a Virtue?" Lindley Lecture. Lawrence: University of Kansas, 1984.
———. *Whose Justice? Which Rationality?* Notre Dame, Ind.: University of Notre Dame Press, 1988.
———. *Dependent Rational Animals: Why Human Beings Need the Virtues.* Peru, Ill.: Open Court, 1999.

Mackie, J. L. *Ethics: Inventing Right and Wrong.* London: Penguin, 1977.

Maccoby, E. E. *Social Development: Psychological Growth and the Parent-Child Relationship*. New York: Harcourt Brace Jovanovich, 1980.

Madsen, Richard. *Morality and Power in a Chinese Village*. Berkeley: University of California Press, 1984.

Mansbridge, Jane. *Beyond Self-Interest*. Chicago: University of Chicago Press, 1990.

McCarthy, Thomas. *Ideals and Illusions: On Reconstruction and Deconstruction in Contemporary Critical Theory*. Cambridge, Mass.: MIT Press, 1991.

McDowell, John. "Virtue and Reason." *Monist* 62 (1979): 331–50.

———. "Values and Secondary Qualities." In *Essays on Moral Realism*, ed. Geoffrey Sayre-McCord, 166–80. Ithaca: Cornell University Press, 1988.

———. *Mind and World*. Cambridge, Mass.: Harvard University Press, 1996.

———. "Are Moral Requirements Hypothetical Imperatives?" in *Mind, Value, and Reality*, 77–94. Cambridge, Mass.: Harvard University Press, 1998.

———. "Might There Be External Reasons?" In *Mind, Value, and Reality*, 95–111. Cambridge, Mass.: Harvard University Press, 1998.

———. "Responses." In *Reading McDowell: On Mind and World*, ed. Nicholas H. Smith, 269–305. London: Routledge, 2002.

McNaughton, David. *Moral Vision: An Introduction to Ethics*. Oxford: Blackwell, 1988.

Mencius. *Mencius*. Ed. D. C. Lau. London: Penguin Books, 1970.

Meyers, Robert G. "Naturalizing Epistemic Terms." In *Naturalism and Rationality*, ed. Newton Garver and Peter H. Hare, 141–54. Buffalo: Prometheus Books, 1986.

Mill, John Stuart. *Utilitarianism*. 4th (University of Toronto) ed. London: Longmans, Green, Reader, and Dyer, 1871.

———. *Utilitarianism, On Liberty, Essay on Bentham*. New York: World, 1962.

———. *J. S. Mill: Collected Works*. Edited by J. M. Robson. Toronto: University of Toronto Press, 1977.

Miller, Geoffrey. *The Mating Mind*. New York: Anchor Books, 2000.

Minoura, Yasuko. "A Sensitive Period for the Incorporation of Cultural Meaning System: A Study of Japanese Children Growing Up in the United States." *Ethos* 20 (1992): 304–39.

Moody-Adams, Michele M. *Fieldwork in Familiar Places: Morality, Culture, and Philosophy*. Cambridge, Mass.: Harvard University Press, 1997.

———. "The Idea of Moral Progress." *Metaphilosophy* 30 (1999): 168–85.

Moore, Barrington, Jr. *Injustice: The Social Bases of Obedience and Revolt*. White Plains, N.Y.: Sharpe, 1978.

Mumme, Donna L., and Anne Fernald. "The Infant as Onlooker: Learning from Emotional Reactions Observed in a Television Scenario." *Child Development* 74 (2003): 221–37.

Nagel, Thomas. *The Possibility of Altruism*. Oxford: Clarendon Press, 1970.

———. "The Fragmentation of Value." In *Mortal Questions*, 128–41. Cambridge: Cambridge University Press, 1979.

———. "What Is It Like to Be a Bat?" In *Mortal Questions*, 165–80. Cambridge: Cambridge University Press, 1979.

———. "Moral Conflict and Political Legitimacy." *Philosophy and Public Affairs*16 (1987): 215–40.

———. *The View from Nowhere*. New York: Oxford University Press, 1987.

———. *Equality and Partiality*. New York: Oxford University Press, 1991.

———. "Pluralism and Coherence." In *The Legacy of Isaiah Berlin*, ed. Ronald Dworkin, Mark Lilla, and Robert B. Silvers, 105–12. New York: New York Review of Books, 2001.

Nathan, Andrew J. *Chinese Democracy*. Berkeley: University of California Press, 1985.

Nivison, David. Review of *The World of Thought in Ancient China*, by Benjamin Schwartz. *Philosophy East and West* 38 (1988): 411–20.

———. "Hsün Tzu and Chuang Tzu." In *Chinese Texts and Philosophical Contexts: Essays Dedicated to Angus C. Graham*, ed. Henry Rosemont Jr., 129–42. Lasalle, Ill.: Open Court, 1991.

———. "'Virtue' in Bone and Bronze." In *The Ways of Confucianism*, ed. Bryan W. Van Norden, 17–30. Chicago: Open Court, 1996.

———. "Xunzi on Human Nature." In *The Ways of Confucianism: Investigations in Chinese Philosophy*, ed. Bryan Van Norden, 203–13. Chicago: Open Court, 1996.

Nowak, M. A., and K. Sigmund. "Tit-for-Tat in Heterogeneous Populations." *Nature* 355 (1992): 250–2.

———. "Strategy of Win-Stay, Loose-Shift that Outperforms Tit-for-Tat in the Prisoner's Dilemma Game." *Nature* 364 (1993): 56–8.

Nussbaum, Martha. *The Fragility of Goodness: Luck and Ethics in Greek Tragedy and Philosophy*. Cambridge: Cambridge University Press, 1986.

———. "Human Capabilities, Female Human Beings." In *Women, Culture, and Development: A Study of Human Capabilities*, ed. Martha Nussbaum and Jonathan Glover, 61–104. Oxford: Oxford University Press, 1995.

Obiora, L. Amede. "Bridges and Barricades: Rethinking Polemics and Intransigence in the Campaign against Female Circumcision." *Case Western Reserve Law Review* 47 (1997): 2753–78.

O'Flaherty, Wendy Doniger. "The Clash between Relative and Absolute Duty: The Dharma of Demons." In *The Concept of Duty in South Asia*, ed. Wendy D. O'Flaherty and J. Duncan M. Derrett, 96–106. New Delhi: Vikas, 1978.

Okin, Susan. *Justice, Gender, and the Family*. New York: Basic Books, 1989.

Orbell, John M., Alphons van de Kragt, and Robyn M. Dawes. "Explaining Discussion-Induced Cooperation." *Journal of Personality and Social Psychology* 54 (1988): 811–19.

Ostrom, Elinor, and James Walker. "Neither Markets nor States: Linking Transformation Processes in Collective Action Arenas." In *Perspectives on Public Choice: A Handbook*, ed. Dennis C. Mueller, 35–72. Cambridge: Cambridge University Press, 1997.

Pincoffs, Edmund. *Quandaries and Virtues: Against Reductivism in Ethics*. Lawrence: University Press of Kansas, 1986.

Platts, Mark. *Ways of Meaning*. London: Routledge and Kegan Paul, 1979.

———. "Moral Reality and the End of Desire." In *Reference, Truth and Reality*, ed. Mark Platts, 69–82. London: Routledge and Kegan Paul, 1980.

Pole, J. R. *The Pursuit of Equality in American History*. Berkeley: University of California Press, 1978.

Poster, Mark. *Critical Theory and Poststructuralism: In Search of a Context*. Ithaca: Cornell University Press, 1990.

Prinz, Jesse. *Furnishing the Mind*. Cambridge, Mass.: Bradford Books, 2003.

Putnam, Robert. *Bowling Alone: The Collapse and Revival of American Community*. New York: Simon and Schuster, 2000.

Qutb, Seyyid. *Milestones*. Damascus, Syria: Kazi, 1993.

Railton, Peter. "Alienation, Consequentialism and Morality." *Philosophy and Public Affairs* 13 (1984): 134–71.

———. "Moral Realism." *Philosophical Review* 95 (1986): 163–207.

———. "Naturalism and Prescriptivity." *Social Philosophy and Policy* 7 (1989): 153–74.

Rawls, John. *A Theory of Justice*. Cambridge, Mass.: Harvard University Press, 1971.

————. *Justice as Fairness: A Restatement*. Cambridge, Mass.: Belknap Press, 2001.

Raz, Joseph. "Multiculturalism: A Liberal Perspective," *Dissent* 41 (1994): 67–79.

Read, K. E. "Morality and the Concept of the Person among the Gahuku-Gama." *Oceana* 25 (1955): 233–82.

Richardson, Henry S. *Practical Reasoning about Final Ends*. Cambridge: Cambridge University Press, 1997.

Rilling, James K., David A. Gutman, Thorsten R. Zeh, Guiseppe Pagnoni, Gregory S. Berns, and Clinton D. Kilts. "A Neural Basis for Social Cooperation." *Neuron* 35 (2002): 395–405.

Rocco, Elena, and Massimo Warglien. "Computer Mediated Communication and the Emergence of 'Electronic Opportunism." Rev. October 24, 1997. Available at www-ceel .economia.unitniit/publications/.

Roetz, Heiner. *Confucian Ethics of the Axial Age: A Reconstruction under the Aspect of the Breakthrough toward Postconventional Thinking*. Albany: State University of New York Press, 1993.

Roland, Alan. *In Search of Self in India and Japan: Toward a Cross-Cultural Psychology*. Princeton: Princeton University Press, 1988.

Rorty, Amélie. "Virtue and Its Vicissitudes." *Midwest Studies in Philosophy* 13 (1988), special issue, *Ethical Theory: Character and Virtue*, ed. Peter A. French, Theodore E. Uehling Jr., and Howard K. Wettstein: 314–24.

Rorty, Amélie, and David B. Wong. "Aspects of Identity and Agency." In *Identity, Character and Morality: Essays in Moral Psychology*, ed. Amélie Rorty and Owen Flanagan, 19–36. Cambridge: MIT Press, 1990.

Rorty, Richard. *Contingency, Irony, and Solidarity*. Cambridge: Cambridge University Press, 1989.

Rosemont, Henry, Jr. *A Chinese Mirror: Moral Reflections on Political Economy and Society*. LaSalle, Ill.: Open Court, 1991.

Rosenberger, Nancy R. "Dialectic Balance in the Polar Model of the Self: The Japan Case." *Ethos* 17 (1989): 88–113.

Ruddick, Sara. *Maternal Thinking*. Boston: Beacon Press, 1989.

————. "Justice within Families." In *In the Company of Others: Perspectives on Family, Community, and Culture*, ed. Nancy Snow, 65–90. New York: Rowman and Littlefield, 1996.

Ryle, Gilbert. *The Concept of Mind*. Chicago: University of Chicago Press, 1984.

Salamone, Stephen D. "Tradition and Gender: The Nikokyrio: The Economics of Sex Role Complementarity in Rural Greece," *Ethos* 15 (1987): 203–25.

Sally, David. "Conversation and Cooperation in Social Dilemmas: A Meta-Analysis of Experiments from 1958 to 1992." *Rationality and Society* 7 (1995): 58–92.

Sandel, Michael. *Liberalism and the Limits of Justice*. Cambridge: Cambridge University Press, 1982.

————. "Morality and the Liberal Ideal." *New Republic*, May 7, 1984, 15–7.

————, ed. *Liberalism and Its Critics* Oxford: Blackwell, 1984.

Sayre-McCord, Geoffrey. "Hume and the Bauhaus Theory of Ethics." *Midwest Studies in Philosophy* 20 (1995): 280–98.

Scanlon, Thomas M. "Contractualism and Utilitarianism." In *Utilitarianism and Beyond*, ed. Amartya Sen and Bernard Williams, 103–28. Cambridge: Cambridge University Press, 1982.

————. *What We Owe to Each Other*. Cambridge, Mass.: Harvard University Press, 1998.

Scheffler, Samuel. *Human Morality*. New York: Oxford University Press, 1992.

————. *Boundaries and Allegiances: Problems of Justice and Responsibility in Liberal Thought*. Oxford: Oxford University Press, 2001.

Schiffer, Stephen. "Meaning and Value." *Journal of Philosophy* 87 (1990), 602–14.

Schotter, A. "Decision Making with Naïve Advice." *American Economic Review* 93 (2003): 196–201.

Sellars, Wilfred. "Empiricism and the Philosophy of Mind." In *The Foundations of Science and the Concepts of Psychoanalysis, Minnesota Studies in the Philosophy of Science*, vol. 1, ed. H. Feigl and M. Scriven, 127–96. Minneapolis: University of Minnesota Press: 1956.

Selznick, Philip. "The Idea of a Communitarian Morality." *California Law Review* 75 (1987): 445–63.

Shils, Edward. "The Study of the Primary Group." In *The Policy Sciences: Recent Developments in Scope and Method*, ed. Daniel Lerner and Harold D. Lasswell, 44–69. Stanford: Stanford University Press, 1951.

Shore, Brad. "Human Ambivalence and the Structuring of Moral Values." *Ethos* 18 (1990): 165–79.

Shun, Kwong-loi. "Moral Reasons in Confucian Ethics." *The Journal of Chinese Philosophy* 16 (1989): 317–44.

Shweder, Richard. *Why Do Men Barbecue? Recipes for Cultural Psychology*. Cambridge, Mass.: Harvard University Press, 2003.

Shweder, Richard, and Edward Bourne. "Does the Concept of the Person Vary?" In *Culture Theory: Essays in Mind, Self, and Emotion*, ed. Richard Shweder and Robert Levine, 158–99. Cambridge: Cambridge University Press, 1984.

Silberbauer, George. "Ethics in Small-Scale Societies." In *A Companion to Ethics*, ed. Peter Singer, 14–28. Oxford: Blackwell, 1991.

Simner, M. L. "Newborn's Response to the Cry of Another Infant." *Developmental Psychology* 5 (1971): 136–50.

Singer, Peter. "Famine, Affluence, and Morality." *Philosophy and Public Affairs* 1 (1972): 229–43.

Skuse, David. "Extreme Deprivation in Childhood: Theoretical Issues and a Comparative Review." *Journal of Child Psychology and Psychiatry* 25 (1984): 543–72.

Skyrms, Bryan. *Evolution of the Social Contract*. Cambridge: Cambridge University Press, 1996.

Smith, Michael. "The Humean Theory of Motivation." *Mind* 96 (1987): 36–61.

————. *The Moral Problem*. Oxford: Blackwell, 1994.

Sober, Elliott, and David Sloan Wilson. *Unto Others: The Evolution and Psychology of Unselfish Behavior*. Cambridge, Mass.: Harvard University Press, 1998.

Stevenson, Charles L. *Ethics and Language*. New Haven: Yale University Press, 1944.

Stairs, Arlene. "Self-Image, World Image: Speculations on Identity from Experience with Inuit." *Ethos* 20 (1992): 116–26.

Strom, Stephanie. "A Shift in Japanese Culture Aids Some Workers Who Want to Go It Alone." *New York Times*, November 16, 2000.

Stroud, Barry. "The Charm of Naturalism." *Proceedings and Addresses of the American Philosophical Association* 70 (1995–6): 43–55.

Sturgeon, Nicholas. "Moral Disagreement and Moral Relativism." In *Cultural Pluralism and Moral Knowledge*, ed. Ellen Frankel Paul, Fred D. Miller Jr., and Jeffrey Paul, 801–15. Cambridge: Cambridge University Press, 1994.

Sugden, R. *The Economics of Rights, Co-operation and Welfare*. Oxford: Blackwell, 1986.

Suomi, Stephen J. "Gene-Environment Interactions and the Neurobiology of Social Conflict." *Annals of the New York Academy of Science* 1008 (2003): 132–9.

Tajfel, H. "Experiments in Intergroup Discrimination." *Scientific American* 223 (1970): 96–102.

Taylor, Charles. *Hegel.* Cambridge: Cambridge University Press, 1975.

———. "Rationality." In *Rationality and Relativism*, ed. Martin Hollis and Steven Lukes, 87–105. Cambridge: MIT Press, 1982.

———. "Foucault on Freedom and Truth." In *Philosophy and the Human Sciences: Philosophical Papers*, 2:152–84. Cambridge: Cambridge University Press, 1985.

———. The Nature and Scope of Distributive Justice." In *Justice and Equality Here and Now*, ed. Frank S. Lucash, 34–67. Ithaca: Cornell University Press, 1986.

———. *The Ethics of Authenticity.* Cambridge, Mass.: Harvard University Press, 1992.

———. *Multiculturalism and the Politics of Recognition: An Essay.* Edited by Amy Gutmann. Princeton: Princeton University Press, 1993.

Thomas, Laurence. *Living Morally: A Psychology of Moral Character.* Philadelphia: Temple University Press, 1989.

Tobin, Joseph J., David Y. H. Wu, and Dana H. Davidson. *Preschool in Three Cultures: Japan, China, and the United States.* New Haven: Yale University Press, 1989.

Tocqueville, Alexis de. *Democracy in America.* Translated by George Lawrence. Edited by J. Mayer. New York: Doubleday, 1969.

Tooby, John, and Leda Cosmides. "The Psychological Foundations of Culture." In *The Adapted Mind: Evolutionary Psychology and the Generation of Culture*, ed. Jerome H. Barkow, Leda Cosmides, and John Tooby, 19–136. New York: Oxford University Press, 1992.

Trivers, Robert. "The Evolution of Reciprocal Altruism." *Quarterly Review of Biology* 46 (1971): 35–56.

Turnbull, Colin. *The Human Cycle.* New York: Simon and Schuster, 1983.

Turner, Victor. *The Forest of Symbols: Aspects of Ndembu Ritual.* Ithaca: Cornell University Press, 1967.

———. *Dramas, Fields, and Metaphors: Symbolic Action in Human Society.* Ithaca: Cornell University Press, 1974.

Van Norden, Bryan. "Mengzi and Xunzi: Two Views of Human Agency." *International Philosophical Quarterly* 32 (1992): 161–84.

Verba, Sidney, Steven Kelman, Gary R. Orren, Ichiro Miyake, Ikuo Kabashima, Joji Watanuki, and G. Donald Ferree Jr. *Elites and the Idea of Equality: A Comparison of Japan, Sweden, and the United States.* Cambridge, Mass.: Harvard University Press, 1987.

Walzer, Michael. *Interpretation and Social Criticism.* Cambridge: Mass.: Harvard University Press, 1987.

Wang, Xiangian. Xunzi jijie. In *Zhuzi jicheng*, 2. Hong Kong: Zhonghua, 1978.

Warnock, G. J. *The Object of Morality.* London: Methuen, 1971.

Wartenberg, Thomas. *The Forms of Power: From Domination to Transformation.* Philadelphia: Temple University Press, 1990.

Whiting, Beatrice Blythe, and Carolyn Hope Edwards. *Children of Different Worlds: The Formation of Social Behavior.* Cambridge, Mass.: Harvard University Press, 1988.

Whyte, William H., Jr. *The Organization Man.* New York: Simon and Schuster, 1956.

Wildman, Jonathan C., Jr. "Elements of Infant-Mother Attachmen." *New Perspectives: A Social Sciences Journal* (1999–2000). Available at www.ycp.edu/besc/journal2000/article1 .html. April 10, 2004.

Wiggins, David. "Claims of Need." In *Needs, Values, Truth: Essays in the Philosophy of Value*, 3rd ed., 1–58. Oxford: Oxford University Press, 1998.

Williams, Bernard. "Internal and External Reasons." In *Moral Luck*, 101–13. Cambridge: Cambridge University Press, 1981.

———. "Persons, Character, and Morality." In *Moral Luck*, 1–19. Cambridge: Cambridge University Press, 1981.

———. *Ethics and the Limits of Philosophy*. Cambridge, Mass.: Harvard University Press, 1985.

Winch, Peter. "Understanding a Primitive Society." In *Rationality*, ed. Bryan Wilson, 78–111. New York: Harper, 1970.

Winnicot, D. W. *The Family and Individual Development*. London: Routledge, 1989.

Winston, Kenneth. "On the Ethics of Exporting Ethics: The Right to Silence in Japan and the U.S." *Criminal Justice Ethics* 22 (2003): 3–20.

Wolf, Susan. "Moral Saints." *Journal of Philosophy* 79 (1979): 419–39.

Wollheim, Richard. *The Thread of Life*. Cambridge, Mass.: Harvard University Press, 1984.

———. "The Good Self and the Bad Self." In *Rationalism, Empiricism, and Idealism*, ed. Anthony Kenny, 151–76. Oxford: Clarendon Press, 1986.

Wong, David B. *Moral Relativity*. Berkeley: University of California Press, 1984.

———. "On Moral Realism without Foundations." *Southern Journal of Philosophy*, supp. vol. 24 (1986): 95–114.

———. "On Flourishing and Finding One's Identity in Community." *Midwest Studies in Philosophy* 13 (1988), special issue, *Ethical Theory: Character and Virtue*, ed. Peter A. French, Theodore E. Uehling Jr., and Howard K. Wettstein: 324–41.

———. "Three Kinds of Incommensurability." In *Relativism: Interpretation and Confrontation*, ed. Michael Krausz, 140–58. Notre Dame, Ind.: University of Notre Dame Press, 1989.

———. "Universalism versus Love with Distinctions: An Ancient Debate Revived," *Journal of Chinese Philosophy* 16 (1989): 252–72.

———. "Is There a Distinction between Reason and Emotion in Mencius?" *Philosophy East and West* 41 (1991): 31–44.

———. "Coping with Moral Conflict and Ambiguity." *Ethics* 102 (1992): 763–84.

———. "Coping with Moral Conflict and Ambiguity." Rev. In *Defending Diversity: Contemporary Philosophical Perspectives on Pluralism and Multiculturalism*, ed. Lawrence Foster and Patricia Herzog, 13–37. Amherst: University of Massachusetts Press, 1994.

———. "Psychological Realism and Moral Theory." *Nomos* 37 (1995), special issue *Theory and Practice*, ed. Ian Shapiro and Judith Wagner DeCew, 108–37. New York: New York University Press, 1995.

———. "On Care and Justice in the Family." In *In the Company of Others: Perspectives on Community, Family, and Culture*, ed. Nancy Snow, 91–101. New York: Rowman and Littlefield, 1996.

———. "Pluralistic Relativism." *Midwest Studies in Philosophy* 20 (1996): 378–400.

———. "Xunzi on Moral Motivation." In *Chinese Language, Thought, and Culture: Nivison and His Critics*, ed. Philip J. Ivanhoe, 202–23. Chicago: Open Court, 1996; reprinted in *Virtue, Nature and Moral Agency in the Xunzi*, ed. Jack Kline and Philip. J. Ivanhoe, 135–54. Indianapolis: Hackett, 2000.

———. "Fragmentation in Civil Society and the Good." In *Civility*, ed. Leroy Rouner, 200–21. South Bend, Ind.: University of Notre Dame Press, 2000.

———. "Crossing Cultures in Moral Psychology." *Philosophy Today* 3 (2002): 7–10.

———. "Reasons and Analogical Reasoning in Mengzi." *Essays on the Moral Philosophy of Mengzi*, ed. Xiusheng Liu and Philip J. Ivanhoe, 187–220. Indianapolis: Hackett, 2002.

———. "Dwelling in Humanity or Free and Easy Wandering?" In *Technology and Cultural Values: On the Edge of the Third Millenium*, ed. Peter D. Hershock, Marietta Stepaniants, and Roger T. Ames, 400–15. Honolulu: University of Hawaii Press, 2003.

———. "Relational and Autonomous Selves," *Journal of Chinese Philosophy* 31 (2004): 419–32.

———. "Comparative Philosophy: Chinese and Western." In *Stanford Encyclopedia of Philosophy*. Rev. Aug. 25, 2005. Available at http://plato.stanford.edu/entries/comparphil-chiwes/.

———. "Where Charity Begins." In *Davidson's Philosophy and Chinese Philosophy: Constructive Engagement*, ed. Bo Mou. Leiden: Brill Academic, forthcoming.

———. "Moral Reasons: Internal and External." Philosophy and Phenomenological Research. Forthcoming May 2006.

Woods, Michael. "Reasons for Action and Desires." *Proceedings of the Aristotelian Society*, supp. vol. 46 (1972): 189–201.

Xunzi. *Xunzi*. Edited and translated by John Knoblock. Vol. 2. Changsha, Hunan: Hunan's People's, 1999.

Zhuangzi [see "Chuang Tzu"]. New York: Columbia University Press, 1963.

Index

Frye, Marilyn, 152
Fung, Yu-lan, 215 n. 31

Galston, William, 260 n. 46
Garrett, Aaron, 29
Gauthier, David, 212
Geertz, Clifford, 40, 125, 190, 197
Gewirth, Alan, 110 n. 50
Gibbard, Allan, 73 n. 83
Gilligan, Carol, 151–2, 252–3
Gintis, Herbert, 56–7, 58
Graham, A. C., 215 n. 30
Gray, John, 97 n. 33
Griswold, Jr., Charles, 29
Gruenbaum, Ellen, 263 n. 49
Gutman, Amy, and Dennis Thompson, 244–5

Haakonssen, Knud, 29, 42
Haley, John, 23
Hall, David, and Roger Ames, 18, 86
Hamilton, William, 49–50, 52 n. 53
Hammond, Robert, 238
Hampshire, Stuart, 98, 245–6, 248, 251
Hampton, Jean, 30
Hare, Richard M., 72–3, 247 n. 31
Harlow, Harry, and R. R. Zimmermann,
     130, 139
Harman, Gilbert, xv, 35, 74, 140 n. 47
harmony, value of, 18–19, 21–2, 67, 254,
     267, 272
Harris, Leonard, 257 n. 43
Hatfield, Elaine, and Richard Rapson, 91 n. 20
Hegel, Georg Wilhelm Friedrich, 116, 229
Higley, J. D., 130 n. 26
Hill, Jr., Thomas, 258 n. 44
Hitchcock, David, 67 n. 74
Hobbes, Thomas, 38, 40–1, 47, 51, 211–4, 219
Hochschild, Jennifer, 265
Honneth, Axel, 34–5
Hooker, C. A., 31–2
Horgan, Terence E., and John Tienson,
     239 n. 14
Horkheimer, Max, 100–1
  and Theodor Adorno, 225–7
human nature
  as contributing to the necessity to balance
     self- and other-concern, 51–9
  as contributing to the necessity of
     community within the family, 149–51

as contributing to the constraint of
     justifiability to the governed, 59–62
as contributing to the necessity of special
     duties, 143–5
dangerous uses of conceptions of human
     nature, 102–4
and flourishing 203–5, 207, 219–27
and motivation, 184, 188–90
objections to the idea of a fixed nature,
     100–2
place in a naturalistic conception of
     morality, xv–vi, 18, 43–7, 68, 71, 246,
     248
and psychological realism, xvi, 44 n. 37,
     159–60, 163–70, 176
role in generating reciprocity norm, 47–51
as social, 115–9, 127–43
see also Xunzi on human nature
Hume, David, 41–2, 105, 181, 183, 219
Humean theories
  of the motivational inertness of practical
     reason, 182–3, 185–6, 192–3
  of reasons as desire-based, 181–3, 191–2

impersonal values, 21, 24–7, 59, 63, 65, 147, 150,
     221, 223–4, 237–8
  and compatibility with personal motives,
     159–76, 226
  and equality, 163–76, 237–8
  see also human nature and psychological
     realism
interests
  concept of, 45
  and needs, 220–1
Isaac, R. M.
  and J. M. Walker, 58 n. 65
  and K. McCue and Charles Plott, 48 n. 42

Johnson, Diane, 259 n. 45
justice
  communitarian and liberal conceptions as
     applied to the family, 151–8
  core concept, 245–6
  see also care ethic, relation to justice; liberal
     ethical theory

Kahn, Joel, 67 n. 75
Kane, Robert, 272 n. 64
Kant, Immanuel, 27, 104, 200